Introduction to Professional Recording Techniques

Introduction to Professional Recording Techniques

Bruce Bartlett

**An Audio Selection from the
Video Bookshelf**

**Knowledge Industry Publications, Inc.
White Plains, NY and London**

© 1987 by Bruce Bartlett. First published by Howard W. Sams & Company/John Woram Audio Series.

This edition published by Knowledge Industry Publications, Inc., 701 Westchester Avenue, White Plains, NY 10604.

International Standard Book Number: 0-86729-254-7
Library of Congress Catalog Card Number: 86-63510

Printed in the United States of America

Trademark Acknowledgements
All terms mentioned in this book that are known to be trademarks or service marks are listed below. In addition, terms suspected of being trademarks or service marks have been appropriately capitalized. Howard W. Sams & Co. cannot attest to the accuracy of this information. Use of a term in this book should not be regarded as affecting the validity of any trademark or service mark.

Aphex Aural Exciter is a registered trademark of Aphex Systems, Ltd.
Auratone is a trademark of Auratone Corp.
dbx is a registered trademark of dbx, Newton, MA, USA, Division of BSR North America, Ltd.
Dolby, Dolby A, Dolby B, Dolby C, Dolby SR, and Dolby Tone are registered trademarks of Dolby Laboratories Licensing Corporation.
GLM is a trademark of Crown International.
Mylar is a registered trademark of E. I. duPont de Nemours and Co., Inc.
Pressure Zone Microphone and PZM are registered trademarks of Crown International.
Variable-D is a registered trademark of Electro-Voice Inc.
Variac is a trade name of General Radio Company.
Yamaha is a registered trademark of Yamaha Electronic Corporation USA.

10 9 8 7 6 5 4 3 2 1

CONTENTS

Foreword   *ix*

John Woram Audio Series   *xi*

Preface   *xiii*

Acknowledgements   *xv*

1 The Recording and Reproduction Chain   *1*
The Parts of the Chain—Summary of Changes—Every Link Is
Important

2 Equipping Your Home Studio   *9*
The Personal Studio—The Recorder/Mixer Demo Studio—The 8-Track
Studio—Optional Extras—Acoustic Treatment—Conclusion

3 Studio Acoutics   *27*
Sound-Wave Basics—Behavior of Sound in a Room—Noise—Choosing
a Recording Room

4 Monitoring   *45*
Room Acoustics—Speakers and Crossovers—Speaker Placement—
Polarity and Stereo Balance—Power Requirements—Room
Equalization—Using the Monitors—Headphones—The Cue System—
Conclusion

5 Hum Prevention *65*
AC Power Wiring—Grounding Procedures—Audio Cables—Shield Connections—Connections to Guitar Amps—Interconnecting Multiple Sound Systems—Other Hum Reduction Techniques—Reducing Radio-Frequency Interference (RFI)—Summary

6 Microphones *81*
Transducer Types—Microphone Characteristics—Special Microphones—Selection Chart—Microphone Accessories—Summary

7 Microphone-Technique Basics *99*
Microphone Selection—Quantity of Microphones—Miking Distance—Using Microphone Placement for Tone Control—On-Surface Techniques—The 3:1 Rule—Minimizing Off-Axis Coloration—Summary of Mic Techniques—Stereo Microphone Techniques

8 Microphone Techniques *119*
Electric Guitar—Electric Bass—Leslie Organ Speaker—Electric Keyboards—The Drums—Percussion—Acoustic Guitar—The Banjo—Mandolin, Dobro, and Fiddle—The Grand Piano—The Upright Piano—The Strings—The Brass—The Woodwinds—The Saxophone—The Flute—The Harmonica—Vocals—Summary

9 Tape Recording *155*
The Analog Tape Recorder—Noise Reduction—Tape Handling and Storage—Editing—The Digital Recorder

10 Signal Processors *177*
The Equalizer—The Compressor—The Limiter—The Noise Gate—The Delay Unit—Doubling—Chorus—Flanging—The Reverberation Unit—The Pitch Shifter—The Psychoacoustic Processor—Summary of Signal-Processor Effects—Sound-Quality Descriptions

11 Mixers and Mixing Consoles *205*
Mixers—Inputs and Outputs—Signal Flow—Mixing Console Sections—Conclusion

12 **Session Procedures**   *223*
Pre-production—Setting Up the Studio—Setting Up the Control
Room—Session Overview—Recording—Breaking Down—Overdubbing—
Mixdown—Summary of the Console Operating Procedures—
Assembling the Master Reels

13 **Creative Sonic Effects**   *247*
Modifying Room Acoustics and Instruments—Microphone Techniques—
Playing with Reverberation and Echo—Console Tricks—Recorder
Tricks—Outboard Equipment—Conclusion

14 **Recording the Spoken Word**   *259*
Consistency—Microphones—Microphone Placement—Controlling the
Announcer's Position and Voice—Reducing Sibilance—Reducing Print-
Through—Recording-Session Techniques—Editing—Proof Cassettes and
Inserts—Sound Effects and Music—Summary

15 **Sampling, Sequencing, and MIDI**   *269*
Sampling—Sequencing—Summary of Sampling and Sequencing—
Memory Multitracking—Synchronizing Synthesizers with MIDI—
Summary

16 **On-Location Recording of Popular Music**   *281*
Monitoring—Recording with Two Microphones—Recording from the
Sound-Reinforcement Mixer—Splitting the Microphones—Ambience
Microphones—Recording Live to 2-Track—Multitrack Recording—24-
Track Recording in a Van Studio—Summary of Techniques—Power
Connections—Interfacing with Telephone Lines—Cables and
Connectors—Pre-production Meeting—Site Survey—Setting Up the
Monitors—Setting Up the Mixing Console for Live Recording—Doing
the Mix—Miscellaneous Tips

17 **On-Location Recording of Classical Music**   *301*
Equipment—Stereo Microphone Techniques—Preparing for the
Session—Session Setup—Microphone Placement—Recording—Editing

18 **Judging Sound Quality** *311*
Classical vs. Popular Recording—Good Sound in a Pop Music
Recording—Good Sound in a Classical Music Recording—Training
Your Hearing—Troubleshooting Bad Sound—Conclusion

19 **Why Do We Record?** *333*
Increasing Your Involvement in Music—Different Ways of Listening—
Different Ways of Monitoring—Why We Record

Glossary *339*

Appendices

A **dB or Not dB** *363*
Definitions—Sound-Pressure Level—Signal Level—Change in Signal
Level—The VU Meter, 0 VU, and Peak Indicators—Balanced vs.
Unbalanced Equipment Levels—Interfacing Balanced and Unbalanced
Equipment—Microphone Sensitivity

B **Introduction to SMPTE Time Code** *373*
How the Time Code Works—Time-Code Signal Details—How To Use
the SMPTE Time Code—Re-striping Defective Code—Synching to
Video—Other Time-Code Applications

C **Further Education** *381*
Books and Magazines—Guides, Brochures, and Other Literature—
Recording Schools

Index *387*

FOREWORD

Some years ago, the editors of *Modern Recording & Music* magazine were approached by a young audio engineer and would-be author. It seems the engineer thought there might be some interest in a short series of feature articles called "Recording Techniques." The editors thought so too, since their magazine appealed to a broad spectrum of musicians and recordists eager to learn more about how to make good recordings. The engineer had just the sort of information the magazine wanted to give its readers and, in February 1982, Part 1 of Bruce Bartlett's "Recording Techniques" appeared in print. Both the author and his editors thought the series might possibly run for almost a full year.

They seem to have underestimated things. As this foreword goes to the typesetter, it is early 1987. Bruce has just finished the latest but certainly not the last installment of "Recording Techniques," which now appears in *db—The Sound Engineering Magazine*.

A few years ago I had the opportunity to work on "Recording Techniques" as one of those editors. It didn't take long to discover that Bruce's articles were reaching a very enthusiastic audience. So when it came time to find authors for a series of audio-related books, Bruce's name was placed high on the list. Obviously there was room in the series for a book that would present the latest recording-studio technology in an easy-to-understand manner. Just as obviously, Bruce was the man to write it.

To find out a little something about Bruce's credentials, just read his biography on the back cover. And then, to find out a little something about how to apply the latest recording-studio technology to your own applications, just read his book.

John Woram

JOHN WORAM AUDIO SERIES

Way back in the dark ages of sound recording, in the year 1959 B.S. (Before Stereo), I got my first job in the recording industry. Like many of my just-getting-started colleagues, I had lots of enthusiasm and little else to get by on. But it almost didn't matter back then. In that monophonic world, recording was pretty much a matter of hoping that the musicians would get it right, which they usually did.

Back then, the first edition (1959) of Howard M. Tremaine's *Audio Cyclopedia* was about all that was available to the reader in search of high-tech information in print. And it was about all that was needed: stereophonic sound had not yet become a marketplace reality, and multi-track recording was still off in the future. There wasn't much need for another book.

But, eventually, stereo did make it out of the lab and into the recording studio. It was followed almost immediately by a new theory of recording. The theory went something like this:

> If two tracks are better than one, then it
> follows that four tracks are better than two.

This was quickly simplified to:

> If T is good, then 2T is better.

As most industry-watchers know, T represents whatever number of tracks are currently available. As the value of T expanded, a parallel expansion affected audio technology in general. This, I am delighted to report, produced yet another parallel—a need for more books on the subject.

The Howard W. Sams/John Woram Audio Series is intended to help meet that demand. It's a wide-ranging series of books at all levels. The common thread is audio technology, but, in each book, the thread follows a different weave. Some books are introductory, some advanced; some are general, others more specific. In short, the series offers a little something for everyone, from the beginner looking for the broad overview to the more advanced reader who is in search of in-depth coverage on a specific audio-related topic.

My first-edition copy of the *Audio Cyclopedia* still sits on the shelf, next to its second-edition update. This year, it was joined by the all-new *Handbook for Sound Engineers: The New Audio Cyclopedia*. These days, it seems there's always room for another good book on audio. And so, here's one more for my audio bookshelf and, I hope, for yours as well.

JOHN WORAM

John Woram, *a respected audio engineering author, is the President of Woram Associates, a consulting firm specializing in professional audio and computer projects. His extensive background in the audio field includes 12 years at RCA Records, where he worked in quality control, tape duplication, tape-to-disc transfer, and recording studio engineering. He was Chief Engineer at Vanguard Records before starting his own company.*

A Fellow of the Audio Engineering Society, Mr. Woram has served as faculty for audio seminars, classes, and lectures; as Director of Special Projects at the Institute of Audio Research; and as Program Director of Music Engineering at the University of Miami. He has written several books on audio and computer topics and is currently senior editor for Mix Magazine.

PREFACE

Recording is a highly skilled craft that combines art and science. It requires technical knowledge as well as musical understanding and a critical listening ability. By learning these skills, you can capture a musical performance and reproduce it with quality sound for the enjoyment and inspiration of others. Your recordings will become carefully tailored creations of which you can be proud. They will be a legacy that can bring pleasure to many people for years to come.

This book is intended for beginning and intermediate recording engineers, producers, and musicians—anyone who wants to make better recordings by understanding recording equipment and techniques. I hope to prepare the reader for work in a home studio, a small professional studio, or an on-location recording session. A high-school background in electronics and sound is helpful.

The book first overviews the recording-and-reproduction chain to instill a system concept. Next, advice is given on equipping a home studio. Then, the following sections are arranged chronologically: studio setup, microphones and microphone techniques, equipment, and control-room techniques. A section on remote recording covers techniques for both popular and classical music.

A special chapter explains how to judge recordings and how to improve them. The engineer must know not only how to use the equipment, but also how to tell good sound from bad. The last chapter answers the question, "Why do we record?"

Finally, an appendix explains the decibel unit, introduces SMPTE time code, and suggests further educational texts.

The book covers many topics not found in similar texts, such as budget recording (including cassette recorder/mixers), hum prevention, the latest monitoring methods, tonal effects of microphone placement, console operation, creative sonic effects, and on-location recording. Also included are many unique charts and guides, such as a microphone selection guide, a microphone classification chart, and guidelines for recognizing good sound and troubleshooting bad sound.

BRUCE BARTLETT

To family, friends, and music.

ACKNOWLEDGEMENTS

Thanks to John Woram for skillfully editing the book and finding a great publisher. Thank you to Larry and Elaine Zide of *Modern Recording & Music* and *db* magazine for giving me permission to draw from my "Recording Techniques" series.

For my education, thank you to The College of Wooster, Crown International, Shure Brothers Inc., Astatic Corporation, and all the studios I've worked for.

A note of appreciation goes to the Pat Metheny Group and Samuel "Adagio for Strings" Barber, among many others, whose music inspired the chapter, "Why Do We Record?"

Finally, to the musicians I've recorded and played with, a special thanks for teaching me indirectly about recording.

1 THE RECORDING AND REPRODUCTION CHAIN

Not long ago, the process of recording a demo tape was involved and expensive. Demo recording required a studio full of fancy equipment, a skilled recording engineer, and many long hours of learning the technology. Nowadays, home-type recording equipment lets you put your musical ideas on tape quickly, easily, and with little expense. With these creative new tools, you can record your musical ideas and can mix them into a finished product. You might even record demos of yourself or your band to send to record companies, or you can practice your recording techniques before going into a professional studio, thus saving the expense of learning the technology on studio time. Once your skills are perfected, you may even earn money recording other musicians.

There are other benefits of recording at home. If you've written a song for your band, you can perform and record all the parts yourself: rhythm guitar, bass, drums, and vocals. Then you can play this complete recording to your band to show them how you envision your song.

When you perform a song, you tend to concentrate on your own instrument. But, when you hear a tape playback of that song, you can listen to the song as a whole. You can better hear what works musically and what doesn't. It's less expensive to do this experimenting at home than in the studio.

These days, making a good recording involves more than just plugging a microphone into a tape deck and hitting the record button. Let's face it: modern recording equipment and techniques are complicated! Before you can achieve a quality recording, there are many functions and procedures to learn and much equipment and terminology to understand.

This book separates the multitude of equipment and procedures into easily understandable parts. It lists the equipment you need, tells what the equipment does, and suggests how to use the equipment effectively.

After studying this book and practicing with actual recording equipment, you'll be making great-sounding tapes that you can be proud of.

The Parts of the Chain

To begin, let's take a quick look at the entire process. Musical sound starts with musicians and their instruments, goes through a series of changes and manipulations, and ends with a musical experience in the ears and mind of the listener. The series of events and the equipment that is involved in sound recording and playback is called the *recording and reproduction chain*. This chapter takes a broad view of the parts of the chain; later chapters will describe each part in detail.

Fig. 1-1 is a block diagram of the recording and reproduction chain, and Fig. 1-2 shows a typical physical layout of the equipment in the chain.

The remainder of this chapter briefly summarizes each link in the recording chain as seen in Fig. 1-1.

Musicians and Instruments

From the recording engineer's viewpoint, a musical instrument is a source of sound to be captured on tape. The musician sees the same instrument as a tool to convert musical ideas and feelings into sound waves (vibrations of air molecules). Both playing technique and instrument quality affect the sound the instrument produces as sound waves travel in all directions from the instrument, and a different frequency balance radiates in every direction.

The loudness of the sound depends on the sound-pressure level, which is measured in *decibels* (dB). The decibel is explained later in Appendix A, but, for now, just think of 1 dB as the smallest change in loudness that we can hear.

Studio Acoustics

After the sound waves leave the instrument, they travel through the air and bounce (or reflect) off the walls, ceiling, and floor of the recording room (studio). Each room surface affects the character of the reflected sound, which, in turn, contributes to the instrument's *timbre* (tone quality) and adds a sense of *ambience* or space.

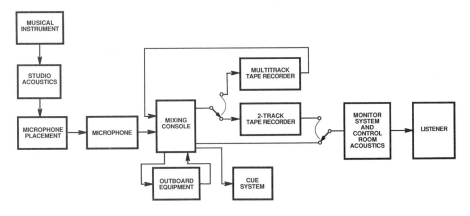

Fig. 1-1. The recording and reproduction chain.

(A) Block diagram.

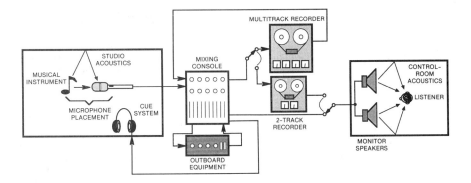

(B) Pictorial diagram.

In your home, the studio can be a large quiet room, such as a basement, garage, or living room, with a separate room used for a control room.

Acoustic treatment is the application of material that absorbs sound reflections, giving you better control of the recorded sound. Two examples are the use of muslin-covered, thick, fiberglass insulation, or thick blankets spaced out from the walls and ceiling.

Microphones

Microphones convert sound waves into corresponding electrical signals. This conversion is necessary because electrical signals are easy to control, modify, and record, and by controlling the electrical signal, you can con-

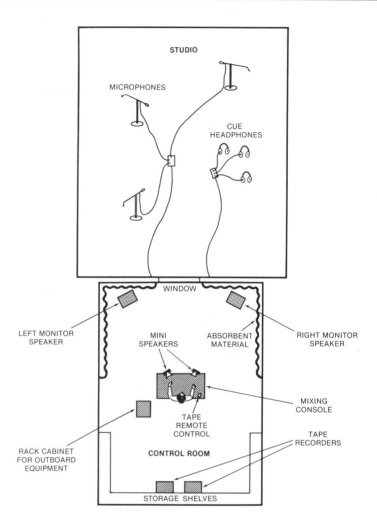

Fig. 1-2. Typical layout of a small recording studio.

trol the sound of the reproduced music. At various stages in the chain, the strength or level of the signal is measured (in dB).

Microphone Technique

Microphone technique is the selection and placement of microphones to pick up sound sources. The type of microphones used and their placement, relative to the instruments, affect the recorded tone quality and the amount of room ambience that is picked up. Often, many microphones are used—one or more per instrument.

The Mixing Console

The electrical signals from all the microphones are conducted via cables to a *mixer* or *mixing console*. A mixer

- Amplifies the signal from each microphone,
- Controls the relative sound levels of the microphones,
- Blends all signals into one or more composite signals,
- Sends the composite signal(s) to tape recorders, amplifiers, and speakers.

A mixing console also

- Adjusts the tone quality of the instruments,
- Sets the stereo position of the instruments,
- Controls special sonic effects,
- Sets up the "mixes" heard in the monitor speakers and the musicians' headphones.

Outboard Equipment

Located external to the mixing console, these peripheral devices (called *signal processors*) produce special effects to further influence the sound quality and, ideally, to enhance the music. Some examples are reverberation, echo, flanging, and compression.

Tape Recorders

Tape recorders convert electrical signals from the mixing console into magnetic signals which are then stored on magnetic tape. A tape recorder acts like a time machine, storing the music in magnetic form, for playback at a later date. Then during playback, the magnetic signals on the tape are converted back into electrical signals, for amplification and transmission.

Noise reduction devices, such as Dolby® or dbx®, often are connected at the input and output of the recorder to reduce tape hiss.

Tracks

Audio signals are stored on tape in the form of magnetic tracks. A *track* is a path on tape which contains a single channel of audio. One or more tracks can be recorded on a single tape. For example, a 2-track tape machine can record two tracks on tape—two independent channels of audio. A multitrack tape machine can record multiple tracks on the tape—4 to 32 independent channels. It's like having many 2-track recorders, all synchronized.

2-Track Recorders

Note in Fig. 1-1 that the signal from the console can go either to a 2-track recorder or to a multitrack tape recorder. If you mix the music as it is performed, you send the mixed signal from the console to a 2-track tape recorder. The tape made on that machine is the final product.

Multitrack Recorders

As an alternative to a 2-track recorder, you can send the signal from each instrument (or from a group of instruments) being recorded to a separate track on a multitrack tape recorder. That is, you can record a different instrument on each track. Then, after the recording session, you play all the tracks through the console to mix or combine them into a pleasing balance. The recorded signals from the tape tracks, rather than the live signals from the microphones, are mixed, using the console.

You can play back the multitrack tape of the recorded performance several times until the mix is perfected. Your final mix is then recorded on a 2-track machine, and the resulting 2-track tape is the final product.

The Cue System

This system enables the musicians to hear each other, and previously recorded material, through headphones. It includes a *cue mixer* that is built into the mixing console, a *power amplifier*, and *headphones*.

The Monitor System

This system includes a *monitor mixer* in the console, a *stereo power amplifier*, *loudspeakers*, and the *control-room acoustics*. It lets you hear the recorded sound of the instruments, either one at a time or blended as the final listener will hear it. The sound from the monitor speakers indicates how well your recording techniques are working.

The monitor system performs as follows: The electrical signal from the mixing console or tape machine is amplified and sent to a pair of loudspeakers or headphones, which convert the electrical signal back into sound waves. Ideally, these sound waves resemble those produced by the original instruments. However, the acoustics of the control room will affect the sound reaching the ears of the engineer. We have arrived at the end of the chain.

Summary of Changes

Let's review all the changes that the music goes through from the start of the chain to the end:

1. The musical instrument converts mechanical energy (motion) into acoustical energy (sound waves).

2. The resulting sound waves are modified by room reflections (studio acoustics).

3. At the microphone, the modified sound waves are converted into electricity (the signal).

4. The signal from the microphone is affected by microphone selection and placement (microphone techniques).

5. All the microphone signals are sent to the mixing console where they are controlled and modified by the console and the signal processors.

6. The modified electrical signal is then recorded—changed into a magnetic signal for storage on magnetic tape.

7. Next, the magnetic tape is played back and the magnetic signal is changed into an electrical signal.

8. The electrical signal is then amplified and changed into sound waves by the monitor amplifier and speaker(s).

9. The loudspeaker sound is next modified by room reflections (control-room acoustics).

10. Finally, the sound strikes the listener's ears and is heard as music (a change from an acoustical phenomenon to a psychoacoustical phenomemon).

While all this is going on, the musicians are listening to each other and to the tape through headphones (using the cue system). And, of course, the monitored sound influences all your recording techniques.

The end product of the recording end of the chain is the master tape. Additional links in the chain include tape copies, record cutting and stamping, and the listener's playback system.

Every Link Is Important

Each link of the recording/reproduction chain contributes to the sound quality of the finished recording. A bad-sounding master tape can be caused by a deficiency in any part of the chain. Conversely, a good-sounding tape is the end result of optimizing every part of the chain. This book suggests some effective methods to reach that goal.

2 EQUIPPING YOUR HOME STUDIO

It's every musician's dream. You want to set up a home recording studio—one with good-quality sound, yet affordable. With today's equipment, you can do just that. A quality 8-track outfit can be assembled for under $6000, a 4-track demo studio for about $2200, and a simple personal studio for around $800. Optional equipment will add $400 or more.

This chapter covers the equipment commonly used in each type of studio just mentioned.

The Personal Studio

A personal studio is one used for your own amusement and practice. You can use this setup as a "notebook" for your musical ideas by recording and mixing the various instruments you use. A personal studio might include the following equipment:

4-track recorder/mixer	$495.00
2 microphones ($100 each)	200.00
2 microphone stands and booms	55.00
Direct box	50.00
Total	$800.00

Recorder/Mixer

A *recorder/mixer* is a small, portable unit combining a mixer with a multitrack recorder. In a personal studio, the recorder/mixer is usually a 4-track cassette recorder with a built-in, two-output mixer. You can record up to two tracks at a time, building up to four tracks for later mixing down to 2-track stereo. For example, you might first record a keyboard part on one track, and then add bass, drums, and vocals on the remaining tracks. With a personal recorder/mixer, the features and sound quality are limited, but are adequate for the purpose. Recorder and mixer features are described later in this chapter.

Blank cassette tape is needed for the recorder/mixer. Metal or chromium tape is recommended for best sound quality.

Microphones

A microphone picks up the sound of an instrument and produces a corresponding electrical signal. Two microphones, each costing at least $100, are recommended. Although $100 may seem like a lot of money to spend for a microphone, you can't skimp here and expect to get quality sound. Any distortion or coloration caused by the microphone may be difficult or impossible to remove later on.

It would be better to have more than two mics, but if you're limited to just two, a cardioid condenser and a cardioid dynamic microphone are recommended. The cardioid pattern helps reject room acoustics for a tighter sound. The condenser type is commonly used on cymbals, acoustic instruments, and studio vocals; dynamics are typically used on drums and electric amps. For more information on microphones, see Chapter 6.

If you plan to record solo instruments or musical ensembles in stereo, with two mics out front, you need to get two cardioid condenser microphones of the same model number.

Microphone stands and booms are also needed. They are used to position the microphones.

Direct Box

This device is a transformer (or circuit) that adapts the output of an electrical instrument to the input of a mixer. A direct box allows you to plug an electric guitar, electric bass, electric piano, or synthesizer directly into the mixer—for a cleaner sound. All these instruments produce an electrical signal that can be fed to a mixer directly. *Note*: Some low-cost mixers have phone jacks for mic inputs. Provided that you use a short cable, you can plug an electrical instrument directly into such an input without using a direct box.

A direct box can be had for as little as $50.00. Or you can build one for about $15.00 using a phone-plug Y-adapter and a microphone impedance-matching transformer (available from your local electronics distributor). However, there's a low-cost alternative to a direct box. You can solder together some direct-connection cables as shown in Fig. 2-1. These cables reduce the amplifier's output signal to a lower voltage that is suitable for a mixer mic input.

Compared to a microphone, the direct-connection cable:

- Costs very little,
- Provides full-range frequency response,
- Doesn't pick up sounds from other instruments,
- Doesn't pick up room acoustics.

To use the cable, simply plug the appropriate end into the amplifier external-speaker jack, and plug the other end into a mixer mic input. Flip

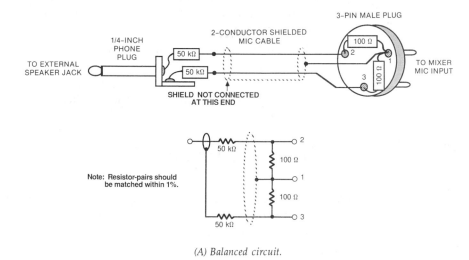

Fig. 2-1. Method for direct connection to an external speaker jack *(Courtesy of Steve Julstrom).*

(A) Balanced circuit.

(B) Unbalanced circuit.

the guitar-amp ground switch to the position where you hear the least hum. You'll probably need to turn down the treble (high-frequency equalization) on your mixer for instruments recorded this way.

Other Items

The following necessary items are not included on the list because you probably already have them:

1. **A studio**. A large quiet room to record in, such as a basement, garage, or living room. A separate room can be used for a control room. If a separate room is not available, you can monitor the recording with closed-cup headphones.

2. **A 2-track cassette deck**. You use this to record your stereo mix of the four tape tracks. With a recorder/mixer, you must set up a stereo mix every time you want to hear the finished product. Rather than doing that each time, you can record the mix onto an external stereo cassette deck.

3. **A monitor system**. This system includes a stereo power amplifier and some accurate loudspeakers; these let you hear what you're recording and mixing. A good home-stereo system or headphones are adequate for monitoring in personal studios.

The Recorder/Mixer Demo Studio

This system uses a full-function mixer with a built-in high-quality 4-track cassette recorder. Three examples are shown in Figs. 2-2, 2-3, and 2-4. They can record up to four tracks at a time and can control special effects, such as artificial reverberation.

A system using such a recorder/mixer is good enough to make demo recordings of yourself or other musicians. Typical equipment includes:

4-track recorder/mixer	$1300
4 microphones ($150 each)	600
4 microphone stands and booms	110
4 cue headphones	160
Total	$2170

Cue Headphones

With these headphones, musicians can listen to previously recorded tracks and can record a new part along with those recorded tracks. The cue

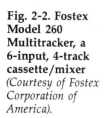

Fig. 2-2. Fostex Model 260 Multitracker, a 6-input, 4-track cassette/mixer *(Courtesy of Fostex Corporation of America).*

headphones plug into a junction box containing several headphone jacks wired in parallel.

Recorder/Mixer (Mixer Section)

Fig. 2-5 is a block diagram showing the signal flow from input to output through a typical mixer. We'll cover each feature in order, but this is just a brief overview of mixer features; Chapter 11 (Mixing Consoles) will describe each feature in more detail.

The *input connector* at the top left of the diagram in Fig. 2-5 is a connector for microphones and other signal sources. A mixer with four inputs can accept the signals of four microphones. Thus, the more inputs, the more mics you can use at one time. A *trim control, pad,* or *input attenuator* follows. This is a control to reduce the level of the microphone signal before it reaches the first stage of amplification (the mic preamplifier). This control prevents input-overload distortion. *LED overload indicators* are little lights that flash when distortion occurs in the mic preamp. They warn you of a need to switch in the input pad or adjust the trim control so that distortion will stop. A *fader* is a sliding volume control for each input signal. You use it during recording to set the recording levels on tape, and during mixdown to set the relative loudness balance among instruments.

An equalizer is shown next in Fig. 2-5 (center of sketch). Equalization (abbreviated EQ) means "tone control." With equalization, you can make an instrument sound more or less bassy, or more or less trebly, just by boosting or cutting certain frequencies. The simplest equalizer is just a bass and treble control. A multiple-frequency equalizer allows more control because you can select certain frequency ranges to boost or cut. A

Fig. 2-3. Tascam Model 244 Portastudio *(Courtesy of Tascam Corporation of America).*

Fig. 2-4. Audio-Technica Model AT-RMX64 mixing/ recording console *(Courtesy of Audio-Technica U.S. Inc.).*

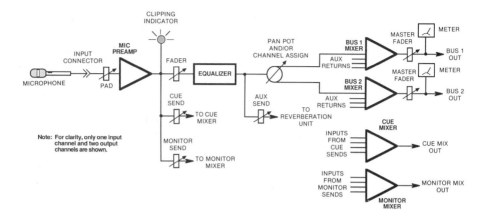

Fig. 2-5. Signal flow through a typical mixer.

Note: For clarity, only one input channel and two output channels are shown.

sweepable equalizer lets you "tune in" the exact frequency range you want to work on.

Channel-assign switches, shown next, let you send the signal of each instrument to the desired tape track, while a *pan pot* is a control that places the stereo image of each recorded track wherever desired between a stereo pair of loudspeakers. With a pan pot, you can locate an instrument at the left speaker, the right speaker, or anywhere in between.

Outputs or *buses* are signal channels that feed the tape tracks. A four-bus mixer provides four independent output channels; each channel carries a signal which may contain the sounds from one or more musical instruments. The four channels feed a 4-track cassette recorder. A mixer with only two output channels can be used with a 4-track recorder by recording two tracks at a time. A *direct output* is an output following the input fader. The fader controls the level at the direct-output jack. A direct output is used for recording one instrument per track. A pair of *master faders* control the overall level of the output channels.

An *auxiliary bus* or *effects bus* is a channel in the mixer used for sending a signal to and from an external signal processor, such as a reverberation or delay unit. By doing so, you can add a sense of room acoustics or spaciousness to an otherwise "dry" track. Some mixers have more than one such bus, allowing you to add a variety of special effects.

A *monitor mixer* is a submixer built into the larger mixer. It controls the balance of the instruments heard over the studio monitor speakers or headphones. The monitor mixer lets you hear an approximation of the final product without affecting the recording levels.

The *cue mixer* is another submixer that blends pre-recorded tape tracks and live microphone signals into a mix that is sent to the musicians' headphones in the studio. The musicians record new parts while listening to pre-recorded tracks over the cue headphones. Note that the *auxiliary sends* in the mixer can serve double duty as controls for a monitor mix or cue mix. In many recorder/mixers, the monitor mix and cue mix are identical.

Ping-ponging (bouncing tracks) allows you to mix several pre-recorded tracks with your mixer, and then record the result on an empty track. The original tracks are then erased, freeing them up for recording more instruments. For example, let's say you've recorded instruments on tracks 1, 2, and 3. With ping-ponging, you combine these tracks with your mixer and record the mix on track 4. Then you can record three different parts on tracks 1, 2, and 3.

Recorder/Mixer (Recorder Section)

Cassette and open-reel decks also have many features to investigate, such as overdubbing, synchronous recording, punch in/out, and noise reduction.

Overdubbing is recording a new track in sync with old tracks. When a musician overdubs, he or she listens with headphones to previously recorded tracks, plays along with them, and records a new musical part on a blank track. In this way, instruments can be recorded one at a time until all the parts are on tape. This provides maximum control and best sound quality. You can be a one-man band by overdubbing all the parts yourself. Overdubbing is a standard feature in all multitrack recorders.

The *synchronous recording* feature is used during overdubbing to keep pre-recorded tracks synchronized with new parts being added "live." Previously recorded tracks are played back from the record head, rather than the playback head. This keeps the timing of the old and new musical parts in sync. All multitrack recorders feature synchronous recording.

With a *punch in/out* feature, you can fix a mistake on a track without doing the whole track over. You insert the corrected musical parts into a previously recorded track. As the track is playing, you "punch in" the record button at the appropriate spot in the tune. Then, the musician plays a corrected version, and this is recorded over the previous performance on tape. When the musician has finished playing the corrected part, you "punch out" of record mode so the rest of the track is not erased. Many tape recorders accept a footswitch accessory so the musician can punch in and out while playing.

Noise reduction is a process that reduces tape hiss. The Dolby® and dbx® systems are commonly used. Noise reduction is essential with cassette recorders because the slow tape speed and narrow track width result in audible tape noise. Noise-reduction circuits clean up the signal.

Using a *return-to-zero* or *memory rewind* function, the recorder automatically rewinds to a preset point that is marked "000" on the tape counter. This function is useful for repeated practices of punch-ins and mixes.

With a *tape-speed option*, a cassette recorder operating at 1⅞-ips is compatible with commercial prerecorded cassettes, so you can play them on your recorder/mixer. A 3¾-ips recorder will not play standard prerecorded cassettes, and uses tape twice as fast, but it provides better sound quality (extended high-frequency response and less tape hiss). Some recorders offer selectable tape speeds.

Pitch control is a feature that varies the speed of the cassette recorder. This function lets you adjust the pitch of previously recorded tracks in order to match the tuning of new instruments that are to be added.

An *LED* (light-emitting diode) *bargraph level indicator* is a column of lights that shows recording level while an *LED peak indicator* is a light mounted in a VU meter. It flashes when the peak recording level is excessive.

The 8-Track Studio

This type of studio has a separate 8-track recorder and mixer. It can be used professionally. A possible list of equipment is as follows:

6-in, 4-out mixer	$1300
8-track open-reel recorder	1900
2-track open-reel recorder	775
6 microphones ($200 each)	1200
6 mike stands and booms	165
Microphone snake	200
4 cue headphones	160
Tape	75
Total	$5775

8-Track Open-Reel Recorder

An 8-track recorder, such as shown in Figs. 2-6 and 2-7, lets you record up to eight independent tracks, with each track containing the sound of one or more instruments. An 8-track unit for home-studio use can be bought for less than $2000 (including built-in noise reduction), while a 16-track recorder with built-in noise reduction can be bought for less

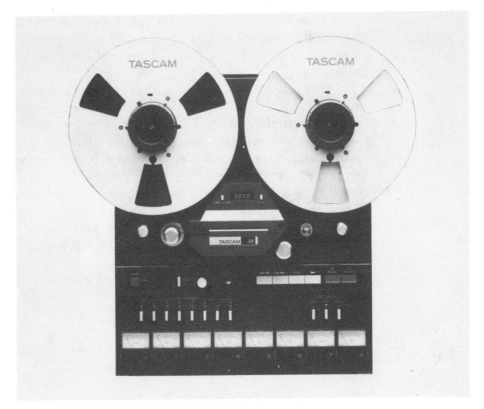

Fig. 2-6. Tascam 38 8-track recorder *(Courtesy Tascam Corporation of America).*

than $6000. Their sound quality is good enough to make master recordings.

An 8-track machine is much more convenient to use than a 4-track machine. You can record eight different instruments or groups of instruments without the chore of bouncing tracks. In addition, when you record a band on a 4-track unit, you often must combine several instruments on each track. As a result, you can't re-adjust the level, tone, or effects of each instrument independently within a recorded track. Eight tracks are usually enough to record each instrument on its own track, so you can control the sound of each instrument individually.

2-Track Open-Reel Recorder

This type of machine is used to record stereo mixes of the eight tracks that you recorded on the 8-track machine. An open-reel recorder is used rather than a cassette deck because the open-reel format has a higher quality, permits tape editing, and can be used to cut records. Fig. 2-8 shows an example of such a recorder.

Fig. 2-7. Fostex Model 80 8-track recorder *(Courtesy Fostex Corporation of America).*

8-In 4-Out Mixer

Although an 8-output mixer is commonly used with an 8-track recorder, a lower-cost alternative is a 4-output mixer, such as shown in Figs. 2-9 and 2-10. It can be used with an 8-track recorder by recording only four tracks at a time, or by using the direct-out jacks in the mixer. If the mixer has 8 inputs, you can record 8 tracks simultaneously (one instrument per track) from the direct outputs.

A combination 8-track open-reel recorder/mixer is shown in Fig. 2-11, and a 14-track cassette recorder/mixer is shown in Fig. 2-12. This unique 14-track format uses 12 tracks for audio, 1 track for the control track, and 1 track for the sync track.

Microphone Snake

If you try to monitor your recording in the studio where the musicians are playing, you won't be able to hear what you're recording because

Fig. 2-8. Fostex Model 20 2-track open-reel recorder
(Courtesy Fostex Corporation of America).

the sound of the live instruments will cover up the monitored sound. You need to place the mixer and the monitor system in a control room separate from the studio.

Long microphone cables are used to carry the mic signals from the studio to the control room. It's messy and time-consuming to run all these cables. Instead, you can use a *microphone snake*. The "snake" consists of several mic connectors mounted in a junction box and attached to a thick, multiconductor cable.

Blank Tape

Don't forget this expense! Buy the best, low-noise, high-output tape you can afford. If possible, use the brand recommended by the recorder manufacturer.

Fig. 2-9. Tascam M-308 mixing console *(Courtesy Tascam Corporation of America).*

Fig. 2-10. Fostex Model 450 mixing console *(Courtesy Fostex Corporation of America).*

Optional Extras

The following equipment is optional. Each piece of equipment enhances the sound or increases convenience of use.

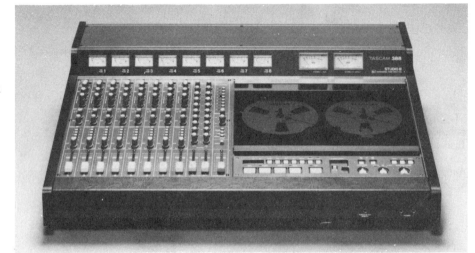

Fig. 2-11. Tascam Model 388 Studio 8 8-track recorder/mixer *(Courtesy Tascam Corporation of America).*

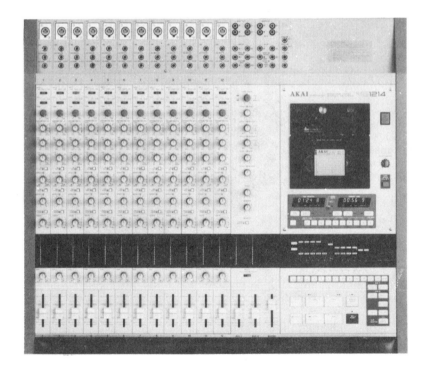

Fig. 2-12. Akai MG1214 12-channel mixer/ 12-track recorder *(Courtesy Akai Corp.).*

Reverberation Unit

Reverberation is the smooth decay of sound, such as heard in an empty gymnasium or a large cathedral. It's often described as "room acoustics" or "ambience."

Most recordings are made in a dead studio with little natural reverberation. To add a sense of spaciousness to recordings made in such a studio, an artificial reverberation device can be used. It electronically simulates room acoustics.

A stereo unit costs more than a mono unit, but it provides a more realistic sense of ambience. Good digital reverbs are available from about $250 and up.

Digital Delay

This device provides all sorts of effects, such as echo, chorus, doubling, and flanging. These effects add some "pizazz" to dry vocal tracks.

Compressor

A compressor keeps the loudness of the vocals (or any instrument) more constant, acting like an automatic volume control. Home-studio units start at about $400.

Rack/Patch Panel

All of the outboard equipment mentioned can be mounted in a rack—a wooden or metal enclosure with mounting holes for attaching equipment. You also may want to install a patch panel or patch bay, which is an array of connectors that are wired to equipment inputs and outputs. A rack with a patch panel is shown in Fig. 2-13. Using a patch panel and patch cords, you can change equipment connections easily. You also can bypass or patch around defective equipment. Fig. 2-14 shows the typical usage for various patch-panel jacks.

Acoustic Treatment

This is the use of material which is placed temporarily or permanently in the studio to absorb excessive sound reflections. It results in a cleaner recorded sound by controlling the room reverberation.

For budget studios, acoustic treatment is limited. Try surrounding the instrument being recorded with thick blankets or sleeping bags that are hung a few feet away. For some low-cost permanent acoustic treatment,

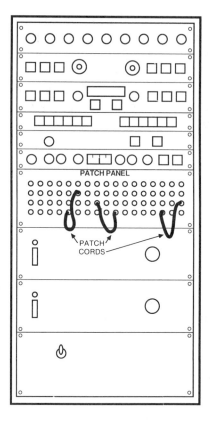

Fig. 2-13. A rack with a patch panel.

PATCH PANEL

PATCH CORDS

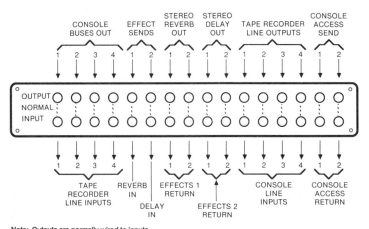

Fig. 2-14. Input/ output panel jacks.

CONSOLE BUSES OUT   EFFECT SENDS   STEREO REVERB OUT   STEREO DELAY OUT   TAPE RECORDER LINE OUTPUTS   CONSOLE ACCESS SEND

1 2 3 4   1 2   1 2   1 2   1 2 3 4   1 2

OUTPUT
NORMAL
INPUT

1 2 3 4   1 2   1 2   1 2   1 2 3 4   1 2

TAPE RECORDER LINE INPUTS   REVERB IN   EFFECTS 1 RETURN   EFFECTS 2 RETURN   CONSOLE LINE INPUTS   CONSOLE ACCESS RETURN

DELAY IN

Note: Outputs are normally wired to inputs behind the patch panel. Inserting a patch cord breaks the normal connection of the panel jack.

carpet the floor and attach patches of muslin-covered, thick, fiberglass insulation to the walls and ceiling. Add a little at a time until your recordings sound reasonably dry (free of audible room reverberation). More sophisticated room treatments are described in Chapter 3.

Conclusion

As we've shown, putting together a high-quality home studio needn't cost much. And, there is better equipment always being produced at lower prices. That dream of owning your own studio is within reach!

3 STUDIO ACOUSTICS

If you're designing a recording studio, or just looking for a good room to record in, it's essential to know how sound behaves in various rooms. The acoustics of a room greatly influence the sonic character of musical instruments in that room.

Poor recording-room acoustics can muddy your recordings, add noises, and color the tone qualities of instruments. In addition, overly dead (muffled) or overly live (reverberant) rooms are uncomfortable to play music in. It's important to understand and control room acoustics in order to provide a good recording environment. We'll divide "room acoustics" into several phenomena: sound waves, echoes, reverberation, room modes, leakage, and noise.

Sound-Wave Basics

To produce sound, most musical instruments vibrate against air molecules. The air molecules pick up the vibration and pass it along as a sound wave. When these vibrations strike our ears, we hear sound.

Let's examine how a sound wave is created. Suppose a speaker cone in a guitar amp is vibrating—moving rapidly in and out. When the cone moves out, it pushes the adjacent air molecules closer together. This forms a *compression*. When the cone moves in, it pulls the molecules farther apart, forming a *rarefaction*. As illustrated in Fig. 3-1, the compressions have a higher pressure than normal atmospheric pressure; the rarefactions have a lower pressure than normal.

These disturbances are passed from one molecule to the next in a spring-like motion; each molecule vibrates back and forth to pass the wave along. The sound waves travel outward from the sound source at 1130 feet per second.

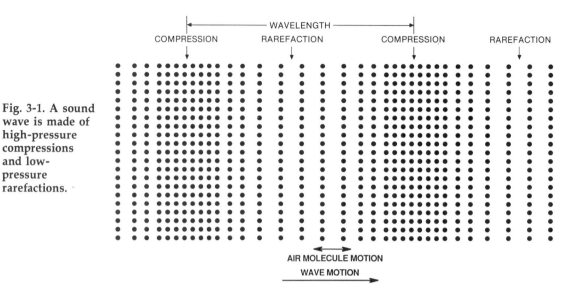

Fig. 3-1. A sound wave is made of high-pressure compressions and low-pressure rarefactions.

At some receiving point, such as an ear or a microphone, the air pressure varies up and down as the disturbance passes by. Fig. 3-2 is a graph showing how sound pressure varies with time. It fluctuates up and down like a wave; hence the term "sound wave." The high point of the graph is called a *peak*; the low point is called a *trough*. The horizontal center line of the graph is normal atmospheric pressure.

Fig. 3-2. Sound pressure vs. time of one cycle of a sound wave.

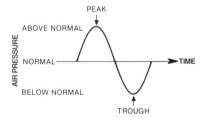

Sound-Wave Characteristics

Fig. 3-3 shows three waves in succession. One complete sequence—from normal pressure to peak, then back through zero to the trough, and, finally, back to normal pressure—is called one *cycle*. The time interval between any point on one wave and the identical point on the next wave is called the *period* of the wave. One cycle is one period long.

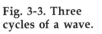

Fig. 3-3. Three cycles of a wave.

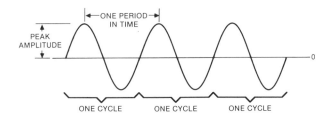

Amplitude

At any point on the wave, the vertical distance of the wave from the center line is called the *amplitude* of the wave. The amplitude of the peak is called the *peak amplitude*. The more intense the vibration, the greater the pressure variation, and the greater the peak amplitude. And, the greater the amplitude, the louder the sound.

Frequency

The sound source (in this case, the loudspeaker) vibrates back and forth many times a second. The number of cycles completed in one second is called the *frequency*. The faster the speaker vibrates, the higher the frequency of the sound. Frequency is measured in hertz (abbreviated Hz), which stands for cycles per second.

    The higher the frequency, the higher the perceived pitch of the sound. A low-frequency tone (say, 100 Hz) is low pitched; a high-frequency tone (say, 10,000 Hz) is high pitched. Doubling the frequency raises the pitch one octave.

Wavelength

When a sound wave travels through the air, the physical distance from one compression peak to the next is called the wavelength. This was shown in Fig. 3-1. Low frequencies have long wavelengths (several feet); high frequencies have short wavelengths (a few inches or less).

Phase and Phase Shift

Phase is measured in degrees, with 360° being one complete cycle. The beginning of a wave is at zero degrees; the peaks are at 90° (positive) and 270° (negative), while the end is 360°. Fig. 3-4 shows the phase of various points on the wave.

    If there are two identical waves, but one is delayed with respect to the other, there is a *phase shift* between the two waves. The more delay,

Fig. 3-4. The
phase of various
points on a
wave.

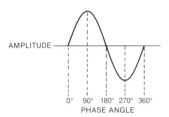

the more phase shift. Phase shift is measured in degrees. Fig. 3-5 shows
two waves which are separated by 90° (¼ cycle) of phase shift.

When there is a 180° phase shift between two identical waves, the
peak of one wave coincides with the trough of another. If these two
waves are combined, they cancel out. This phenomenon is called *phase
cancellation*.

Fig. 3-5. Two
waves that are
90° out-of-phase.
The dashed-line
wave lags the
solid-line wave
by 90°.

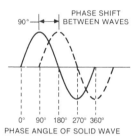

Harmonic Content

The waveforms seen in Figs. 3-2 through 3-5 are called *sine waves*. A
sine wave is a pure tone of a single frequency, such as produced by a
tone generator. However, most musical tones have more than one frequency component and have a complex waveform. Yet, no matter how
complex, all sounds are combinations of sine waves of different frequencies and amplitudes. Fig. 3-6 shows the sine waves of three frequencies which are combined to form a complex wave. The amplitudes
of the various waves are added algebraically at the same point in time
to obtain the final complex waveform.

The lowest frequency in a complex wave is called the *fundamental*
frequency. It determines the pitch of the sound. Higher frequencies in
the complex wave are called *overtones* or *upper partials*. If the overtones
are integral multiples of the fundamental frequency, they are called *harmonics*. For example, if the fundamental frequency is 200 Hz, the second
harmonic is 400 Hz, the third harmonic is 600 Hz, and so on.

The number of harmonics and their amplitudes, relative to the fundamental frequency, partly determine the tone quality or the *timbre* of a

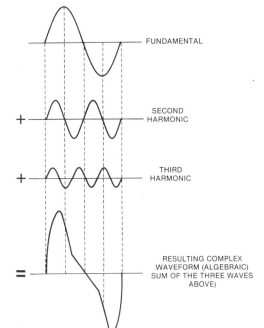

**Fig. 3-6.
Addition of
fundamental and
harmonic
waveforms to
form a complex
waveform.**

FUNDAMENTAL

+ SECOND
HARMONIC

+ THIRD
HARMONIC

= RESULTING COMPLEX
WAVEFORM (ALGEBRAIC)
SUM OF THE THREE WAVES
ABOVE)

sound. They identify the sound as being from a trumpet, piano, organ, voice, etc.

Noise, such as tape hiss, contains all frequencies and has an irregular non-periodic waveform.

Envelope

Another identifying characteristic of a sound is its *envelope*. This is the rise and fall in volume of one note. An envelope has four sections, as shown in Fig. 3-7: attack, decay, sustain, and release. During the *attack*, a note rises from silence to its maximum volume. Then, it *decays* from

**Fig. 3-7. The
four portions of
the envelope of
a note. The
envelope
connects the
peaks of
successive
waves.**

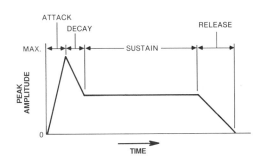

ATTACK
DECAY
RELEASE
MAX.
SUSTAIN
PEAK
AMPLITUDE
0
TIME

maximum to some midrange level. This midlevel is the *sustain* portion. During *release*, the note falls from its sustain level back to silence.

Percussive sounds, such as drum hits, are so short that they have only a rapid attack and decay. Other sounds, such as organ or violin notes, have slow attacks and long high-level sustains. Guitar plucks and cymbal crashes have quick attacks and slow releases.

Behavior of Sound in a Room

So far we've covered the characteristics of sound waves traveling in open space. But since most music is recorded in a room, we need to understand the acoustic phenomena created by the room interior surfaces.

Echoes

A musical instrument vibrates against air molecules, creating sound waves that travel outward in all directions. Some of the sound travels directly to the listener (or to a microphone) and is called *direct sound*. The rest strikes the walls, ceiling, floor, and the furnishings of the recording room. At those surfaces, some of the sound energy is absorbed, some is transmitted through the surface, and the rest is reflected back into the room.

Since a sound wave takes time to travel (about 1 foot per millisecond), the reflected sound arrives after the direct sound reaches the listener. The delayed arrival of a reflected sound causes a repetition of the original sound; this is called an *echo*, and is illustrated in Fig. 3-8. In large rooms, we sometimes hear discrete single echoes; in small rooms, we often hear a short, rapid, succession of echoes called *flutter echoes*.

Fig. 3-8. Echoes.

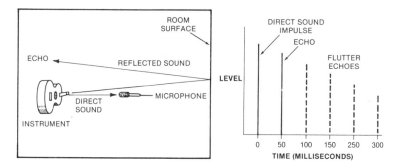

(A) Echo formation.

(B) Intensity vs. time of direct sound and its echoes.

Parallel walls or diagonally opposite corners create flutter echoes by reflecting sound back and forth between them many times. You can detect flutter echoes by clapping your hands next to one wall and listening for a fluttering sound. Since echoes can reduce the clarity of a recording, they should be eliminated by adding patches of absorbent material (cork, acoustic tile, carpet, fiberglass insulation) to one or both of the offending walls. Putting the material in patches, rather than all together in one piece, promotes an even distribution, or *diffusion*, of sound in the room.

Use enough acoustic damping to eliminate the flutter echoes, but do not deaden the room completely. The room still should have some *early* reflections (within 25 milliseconds) so that the room is comfortable to play in. Early reflections also enhance the apparent loudness, apparent transient response, and the timbre of acoustic instruments.

Reverberation

Sound reflects not just once but many times from all the surfaces in the room. These sonic reflections sustain the sound of the instrument in the room for a short time even after each note has stopped sounding. This phenomenon is called *reverberation*—the persistence of sound in a room after the original sound has ceased. For example, reverberation is the sound you hear just after you shout in an empty gymnasium. The sound of your shout persists in the room and gradually dies away (decays).

In physical terms, reverberation is a series of multiple echoes, decreasing in intensity with time. The echoes are so closely spaced in time as to merge into a single continuous sound, and eventually are completely absorbed by the inner surfaces of a room. The timing of the echoes is random, and the echoes increase in number as they decay. Fig. 3-9 il-

Fig. 3-9. Reverberation.

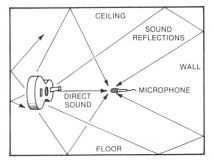

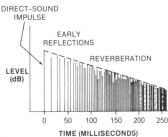

(A) Reverberation formation.

(B) Intensity vs. time of direct sound, early reflections, and reverberation.

lustrates reverberation as the decay of room reflections over a period of time.

Note that reverberation is a continuous fade-out of sound, while an echo is a discrete repetition of a sound.

Reverberation Time

The time it takes for sound to decay to 60 dB below the original steady-state sound level is called the *reverberation time* (abbreviated T_{60} or RT60). Reverberation time is typically measured at 500 Hz, and often at other frequencies.

Audibility of Reverberation

Reverberation comes to the listener from every direction since it is a pattern of multiple sound reflections off the walls, ceiling, and floor. Due to our ability to localize the direction of sounds in space, we can distinguish between the direct sound of an instrument which is coming to us from a single location, and the reverberation coming to us from everywhere else. Thus, we can ignore the reverberation and concentrate on the sound source. In fact, we normally are not aware of reverberation.

But a microphone does not have this ability to distinguish between the direct sound and the reverberation. In the playback of a recording, the recorded reverberation is no longer heard from all sides. Instead, it comes from the same point as the original sound (in front of the listener, between the playback speakers). As a result, the reverberation may seem much more noticeable on the tape playback than it was when heard live.

Desirable Reverberation Time for Recording

Too much reverberation in a recording gives a distant sound quality, with reduced clarity and presence. Consequently, popular-music recording requires a fairly nonreverberant studio, with a reverberation time of about 0.4 second or less. Classical music, however, should be recorded in a live, reverberant concert hall (RT60 about 1 to 3 seconds), because reverberation is a desirable part of the sound of classical music.

Controlling Reverberation

One way to reduce the amount of recorded reverberation is to mike the instruments closely. The closer a microphone is to its direct sound source, the less reverb or ambience is picked up. Why? As the microphone is placed closer to the sound source, the recorded level of the source gets louder, but the level of the reverberation stays constant. A microphone placed close to a source picks up a higher ratio of direct sound to reverberation than does a distant microphone.

To further minimize recorded reverberation, use microphones with a directional pickup pattern (such as a cardioid, supercardioid, or figure-8 mic). For example, a cardioid microphone is up to 4.8 dB less sensitive to reverberant sounds than an omnidirectional microphone placed at the same location.

Another effective technique is to record in a room that has little reverberation (an acoustically dead room). Since reverberation is caused by sound reflections off room surfaces, any surface that is highly sound-absorbent helps to reduce reverberation. High frequencies are best absorbed by porous, fibrous materials such as fiberglass insulation, acoustic tile, foam plastic, carpeting, and curtains. Spacing these materials several inches from the wall extends their absorption into the mid-bass region. Low-frequency absorbers called *bass traps* can be formed of flexible surfaces, such as wood paneling or linoleum mounted over a sealed air space (of several inches). Cavities such as closets, or air spaces behind couches, are also effective sound absorbers.

It's important to have equal sound absorption at all frequencies up to about 4000 Hz. Here's why: Suppose a room is highly absorbent at high frequencies, but not at low frequencies. The highs will be quickly absorbed but the lows will continue bouncing around the room. Consequently, the reverberation time will be short at high frequencies and long at low frequencies. If you record in such a room, both the live sound in the room and the recorded sound are likely to be bassy, boomy, and muddy, due to the persistence of low-frequency reverberation. Translated into material terms, if your home studio has an abundance of fibrous absorbent materials, but has no bass traps, you can expect dull and muddy sound. Tacking carpet to all the walls is not the way to create a good-sounding studio.

We don't want the room to be completely absorbent (dead) because such an environment is stifling—musicians feel they are playing in a vacuum; they get no reinforcement or enhancement from early reflections. Some reverberation and early reflections are beneficial, not only for the musicians' comfort, but for the sense of "air" and liveliness that they add to the recorded sound.

You can either look around for a good recording room, or take an existing room and treat it acoustically. Add absorption a little at a time until the recorded room acoustics sound good to you. Here's a list of some simple acoustic treatments that reduce reverberation.

- Open closet doors, and place couches and books a few inches from the walls.

- Carpet the floor.
- Hang canvas from the ceiling in deep folds.
- Hang thick curtains or blankets at least 2 feet from the walls, if possible.
- Attach open-cell acoustic-foam wedges (such as Sonex) on or near the walls. The thicker the foam, the better the low-frequency absorption. Four-inch-thick foam on the wall absorbs frequencies from about 400 Hz up.
- In a basement studio, nail acoustic tile to the ceiling joists, with fiberglass insulation in the air space between tiles and ceiling.
- For bass trapping, make some panel absorbers as follows: Nail ¼-inch- and ⅛-inch-thick plywood panels to 2-inch furring strips (battens). Put fiberglass insulation in the air space behind the panel, as illustrated in Fig. 3-10. Cover about half the wall area in this manner. Alternatively, you can buy ready-made tubular bass traps.
- For wide-range absorption, attach 2-inch- or 4-inch-thick pressed fiberglass board (Owens-Corning Type 703, 3 lb/cu ft) onto 2 × 6 studs, spaced 4 feet apart on the existing wall, with fiberglass insulation in the air space. Less effective but easier to find is standard fiberglass insulation. Cover it with muslin to keep the fibers intact.

Room Modes

If you play an amplified bass guitar through a speaker, inside a room, and do a bass run up the scale, you will hear some of the notes at which the room resonates, reinforcing the sound. These resonant frequencies, most noticeable below 300 Hz, are called *room modes* or *normal modes*. Resonance peaks of up to 10 dB can occur. They give a tubby or boomy coloration to musical instruments and should be minimized.

Room modes occur in physical patterns called *standing waves*. Standing waves are uneven sound-level distributions in a room that are caused

**Fig. 3-10.
Example of bass-trap construction:
a panel absorber.**

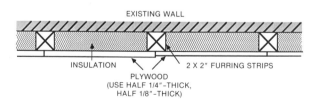

by sound waves continuously reinforcing themselves as they reflect between opposing surfaces. Opposite walls (or the ceiling and floor) can support standing waves between them, as illustrated in Fig. 3-11. Weaker modes can occur between other surfaces.

The frequencies at which a room resonates depend on the dimensions of the room—its length, width, and height. The formula for the most basic room-mode resonance frequencies is

$$f = \frac{N \times 565}{D}$$

where
  f is the resonance frequency, in Hz,
  N is the room mode (1, 2, 3, ...),
  D is the room dimension, in feet.

For example, a room 12-feet long will have room modes at 47 Hz, 94 Hz, and so on. These frequencies will be over-emphasized in the music unless there is sufficient bass trapping in the room to dissipate them.

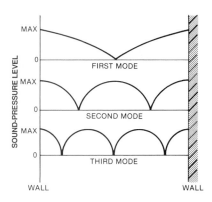

(A) Pressure distribution between two opposing walls, for the first three room modes.

Fig. 3-11. Standing-wave phenomena.

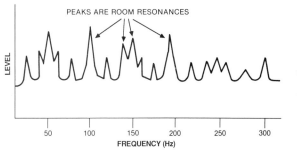

(B) Example of the frequency response of a room with standing waves.

Other frequencies will be reinforced by other room dimensions. If the height, width, and length of the room are identical, the same modal frequencies will be reinforced in all three dimensions, greatly emphasizing certain low frequencies. On the other hand, if the dimensions are not multiples of each other, the modes will be different for each dimension. Then, each room mode will be reinforced in only one dimension and there will be a more even distribution of resonance frequencies.

The following list gives several ratios of room dimensions that uniformly distribute the modal frequencies:

Height	Width	Length
1	1.14	1.39
1	1.17	1.47
1	1.26	1.41
1	1.28	1.54
1	1.45	2.10
1	1.47	1.70
1	1.60	2.33
1	1.62	2.62

Taking the top ratio as an example, if the ceiling height is 10 feet, the room width should be 11.4 feet and the length should be 13.9 feet for best distribution of modes.

Large rooms are generally preferred over small ones for recording because the room resonance frequencies are lower; hence, more likely to be below the musical range.

A common misconception is that nonparallel walls eliminate standing waves. Actually, low-frequency standing waves are not significantly affected by surface irregularities that are less than ¼ wavelength in size. For example, waveforms of frequencies below 280 Hz do not "see" a skew of 1 foot in a nonparallel wall. A better solution is to use bass traps that are tuned to the resonance frequencies of the room.

Leakage

Sound from an instrument travels to the nearest microphone, but it also "leaks" into the microphones intended for picking up other instruments. For example, a piano microphone may also pick up the drums, and the microphone intended for acoustic guitar may also hear the electric guitar amp. This overlap of one instrument's sound into the microphone of another instrument is called *leakage* (or *bleed* or *spill*).

It's very important to minimize leakage, and make sure that each microphone picks up only its intended instrument. Suppose the piano microphone hears a lot of drum leakage (Fig. 3-12)? The recorded mix of the instruments in Fig. 3-12 will contain not only the clean, tight sounds of the piano and the drums, as picked up by their microphones, but it will also have the delayed, distant, and muddy drum sound that leaked into the piano microphone. The *net* drum sound will be distant and dirty, rather than closeup and clean.

Leakage also lessens the ability to mix the various instruments independently. Increase the level of the piano microphone and the leaked drum sound also increases. Decrease the level of the drum microphones, and the bad-sounding drum leakage remains in the mix.

Fortunately, leakage can be minimized in several ways.

1. *Spread the musicians out in the studio—in moderation.* The sound of an instrument gets quieter as you move away from it. Specifically, the sound level drops 6 dB for each doubling of distance away from a point sound-source in a dead room. So, to decrease the loudness of the leakage, place the instruments farther apart.

There are limits to this separation, however. If the musicians are too far apart, they won't be able to play together in synchronization. Some closeness is needed for ensemble playing. In addition, the sound level of an instrument in a room decreases with distance only up to a point, and then it stays constant due to the room reverberation; so great spacing between instruments may not further improve sound separation. In addition, if instruments are placed too far apart, the delays present in the leakage are very long, making the leakage sound even more distant and muddy. You can sometimes achieve more apparent presence by placing the instruments closer to each other to shorten the delays (say 6 feet to 12 feet apart).

**Fig. 3-12.
Example of
sound leakage.**

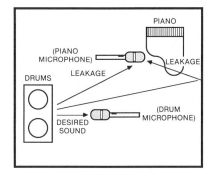

2. *Place microphones very close to instruments.* As a microphone is placed closer to a sound source, the recorded level of the source gets louder, but the level of the leakage does not. Thus, a microphone placed close to an instrument will pick up a high ratio of wanted-to-unwanted sound. With close miking, each microphone will probably hear little except the instrument it's aimed at.

3. *Use directional microphones.* A microphone with a directional pickup pattern (such as a cardioid, supercardioid, or bidirectional) discriminates against leakage approaching the microphone from the rear and/or sides. For example, a cardioid microphone is most sensitive to the sound source it is aimed at, and attenuates sounds coming from the sides by about 6 dB, and from the rear by about 20 dB. Such microphones reduce leakage pickup as long as the leakage is not coming from in front of the microphone, or is not reflected into the front of the microphone. The *bass boost* (proximity effect) of a closely placed directional microphone can be used to advantage: If you roll off the excess bass at the mixer, you also reduce low-frequency leakage.

4. *Record direct.* Amplified instruments, such as electric guitars, can be recorded direct by connecting their output directly to the mixing console through a transformer or a direct box. Since the microphone is eliminated, no leakage is picked up in (added to) the signal of an instrument fed directly to the mixer.

5. *Use acoustic baffles (goboes or flats) between and around instruments.* A *gobo* is a portable wall-like structure, usually built of several layers of wood (say, four inches thick) and covered with absorbent material on one or both sides. By preventing sound from passing through it, with proper placement, the gobo isolates the sound of one instrument from another.

Unfortunately, the gobo has several drawbacks. It colors the tone quality of the surrounded instrument by reflecting sound into the microphone. The direct sound and delayed reflections cause phase interference which cancels certain frequencies. It also dulls the sound of leakage because only the mid- to high frequencies are blocked by the gobo. Low frequencies travel around the gobo to the microphone, resulting in muddy-sounding leakage. A gobo also degrades the performance of a cardioid microphone by preventing leakage from entering the microphone from the rear, where cancellation is greatest. Because of these drawbacks, goboes should be used only as a last resort.

6. *Overdub instruments.* Leakage becomes a problem whenever loud instruments and quiet instruments are recorded at the same time. The signal from a microphone used on a quiet instrument must be turned up high at the console to get a sufficient level, and that makes it sensitive to leakage from the loud instruments. It may be best to record all the loud instruments (electric guitars and drums) at one time, and then go back and overdub (record later) the acoustic guitar, the strings, piano, and vocals. Or, record all the quiet instruments first, and then the loud ones. *Overdubbing* also lets you mike farther away to pick up a more natural timbre. Overdubbing is discussed in more detail in later chapters.

Some studios make a practice of overdubbing every instrument for perfect isolation and cleanest sound. However, this loses the emotional interaction among musicians that occurs when they all play together.

7. *Record in a large room.* This allows greater physical separation between players, and it also weakens leakage reflections due to the longer sound-travel paths to the walls.
8. *Record in a room that is acoustically dead.* The absence of reverberation in such a room prevents the reflections from various instruments from bouncing into microphones which are meant for other instruments. The lack of reverberation also reduces the loudness of the leakage.

If you use all these leakage-reducing tricks, except for treating the room acoustically, you may be able to make some very good recordings without spending any money on room treatment! Unless your recording room is very poor acoustically, you probably can avoid the expense and trouble of building a studio by following the previous suggestions.

A little leakage is not always a bad thing. *Creative leakage* is the use of some controlled leakage to achieve a "loose," "live," or "dirty" effect in the recording. The microphones are placed a little farther from the instruments than is normal to pick up some leakage.

Noise

Noise is unwanted sound, from such sources as appliances, air conditioning, traffic, airplanes, and noisy neighbors. Here are some suggestions to keep noise out of your home studio:

- Turn off appliances while recording.
- Pause for ambulances and airplanes to pass.
- Close windows; put on storm windows.
- Close doors; weather-strip doors all around, including underneath.
- Replace hollow doors with solid doors.
- Block openings in the room with thick plywood and caulking.
- Remove small objects that can rattle or buzz.
- Put several layers of plywood and carpet on the floor above the studio, and put insulation in the air space between the studio ceiling and the floor above.
- Place microphones close to the instruments, and use directional microphones. (This won't reduce noise in the studio, but it will reduce noise pickup by the microphones.)

When building a new studio, reduce noise transmission through the walls by using plastered concrete blocks, because massive walls reduce sound transmission. Nail gypsum board to 2 × 4 staggered studs on 2 × 6 footers, as seen in Fig. 3-13. Staggering the studs prevents sound transmission through the studs. Fill the airspace between walls with insulation.

Choosing a Recording Room

Let's summarize the requirements for a good pop music studio. Table 3-1 lists some important characteristics, and briefly notes how each is achieved.

So we need a large, well-sealed room with optimum dimensions. It should have some soft surfaces (carpet, acoustic-tile ceiling, drapes, couches) and some hard vibrating surfaces (wood or gypsum-board walls on studs). Ideally, this room is in a quiet neighborhood.

**Fig. 3-13.
Staggered-stud
construction to
reduce noise
transmission.**

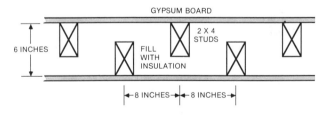

This Characteristic	Is Achieved By
No flutter echoes.	Nonparallel or absorbent walls.
Fairly low reverberation time (about 0.4 second).	Sufficient sound-absorbent surfaces on the walls, ceiling, and floor.
Equal reverberation time at all frequencies up to 4 kHz. (Equal absorption at all frequencies up to 4 kHz.)	Flexible panels, cavities, and fibrous materials, or fibrous materials spaced out from the walls and ceiling.
Some early reflections (to enhance the sound of acoustic instruments).	A few hard reflective room surfaces.
Minimized, well-distributed room modes.	Large rooms, optimum ratios of room dimensions, and bass traps tuned to room resonance frequencies.
Low leakage.	A large sound-absorbent room.
Good diffusion (an even distribution of sound).	Nonparallel walls, or sound absorbers in evenly distributed patches, rather than all together.
Low noise.	The suggestions offered earlier.

Table 3-1. Requirements for a Good Pop Music Studio

Because of its size, a club or auditorium where a band plays can be a suitable recording room. A large living room opening into other quiet rooms can also make a good studio. The openings act as effective sound absorbers, as do the couches, open closets, and bookshelves. The walls (on studs) help to absorb lows and provide early reflections, while the carpeting, stuffed furniture, and drapes help to absorb the highs.

We've explained the basics of sound and suggested methods to improve studio acoustics. With the proper recording environment, you can make cleaner, less muddy recordings.

4 MONITORING

One of the most exciting moments in recording comes when the finished mix is played over the big studio monitor speakers (Fig. 4-1). The sound is so clear that you can hear every detail, and so powerful that you can feel the deep bass throbbing in your chest.

The monitor system is used to listen to the output signals of the console or the tape recorders. It consists of the console monitor mixer, the power amplifiers, the crossovers, loudspeakers, and the listening room. Each power amplifier boosts the electrical power of a console signal to a sufficient level to drive a loudspeaker; the speaker converts the electrical signal into sound, and the listening-room acoustics affect the sound from the speaker.

The monitor system (Fig. 4-2) is a critical link in the recording-and-reproduction chain, for it provides the feedback that tells what you're doing to the recorded sound. According to what you hear, you adjust the mix and judge the effectiveness of your microphone technique. Clearly, the monitor system affects the settings of many controls on the console, as well as the microphone selection and placement. And all those settings affect the sound you're putting on tape. So, using inadequate monitors can result in a poor-sounding product coming out of your studio.

For example, if your monitor speakers are weak in the bass, you will tend to boost the bass in the mix until it sounds right over these monitors. But when that mix is played over speakers with a flatter response, it will sound too bassy because you boosted the bass in the control room. So, using monitors with weak bass results in bassy recordings; using monitors with exaggerated treble results in dull recordings, and so on. In general, colorations in the monitors will be inverted in the final tape. That's why it's so important to use an accurate monitor system—one with a wide, smooth frequency response. Such a system lets you hear exactly what's on the tape.

Monitors also have another function; they let you hear the program as the end listener will hear it. Since the purpose of a recording is to

Fig. 4-1. JBL Model 4430 (left) and 4435 (right) studio monitors *(Courtesy JBL Inc.).*

Fig. 4-2. UREI studio monitor loudspeakers *(Courtesy JBL Inc.).*

please the listener (as well as yourself), you must tailor the mix to sound pleasant over the kind of speakers that the end listener will have. Remember, when you're doing a mix over a particular monitor system, you're creating what the home listener will hear, assuming he or she has speakers and a listening room like yours.

Suppose all recording engineers and listeners at home had the same speakers, the same speaker placement, and the same listening-room acoustics. Then, engineers could rest assured that the sound they created over their monitors would be duplicated in everyone's home. Every home listener would hear what the engineer and the producer intended them to hear.

But everyone has different speakers, speaker placements, and listening rooms. A recording will sound different on every system it is played on. So, to please as many listeners as possible, you need to use a monitor system that sounds like a typical home system used by the intended audience.

We see a need for two kinds of monitors: *accurate* (to hear what's really on tape) and *typical* (possibly narrowband; to simulate a home listener's system). Two speaker systems are needed—one for your own accuracy, the other as a typical-user model.

Room Acoustics

The first step to make a monitor system accurate is to work on the control-room acoustics. Let's start by reviewing how room acoustics affect the monitored sound.

As described in Chapter 3, sound waves leaving the speaker strike the room surfaces. At those surfaces, some frequencies are absorbed while others are reflected. At the listener's ears, the sound waves reflected from the room surfaces combine with the direct sound. Only those reflections arriving within 20 to 65 milliseconds after the direct sound will blend or fuse with the direct sound to affect the perceived spectrum or tonal balance. After about 65 milliseconds, an echo is heard.

Suppose the walls are covered with carpet so that they absorb only the high frequencies; then the walls will reflect mainly the low frequencies. When you listen to a speaker playing in such a room, you hear the direct sound from the speaker plus the bassy wall reflections, giving a total sound that is bass-heavy. Now suppose the walls are made of wood paneling mounted on studs. Such a vibrating surface absorbs the lows and reflects the highs. The total sound you hear will probably be thin and overly bright.

Clearly, the room surfaces should reflect (or absorb) all frequencies about equally to avoid coloring the sound of the speakers. Equal absorption ($\pm$ 25%) from about 250 Hz to 4000 Hz is usually adequate. As described in the previous chapter, you can use flexible panels to absorb the lows, in combination with fibrous materials or foam to absorb the highs. Or, a thick fibrous material, spaced from the wall and ceiling, can be used.

Room resonances or *standing waves* can cause some notes to blare out and other notes to disappear. These resonances should be controlled as described in the previous chapter.

Room acoustics also affect the decay of the sound coming from the speakers. When a note in a reproduced program suddenly ends, the sound of that note continues to bounce around the room, causing echoes and reverberation that prolong the sound. This long decay of sound is not part of the program, so the control room should be relatively *dead*—that is, it should have a short reverberation time. A typical living room has a reverberation time of about 0.4 second; the control room should too, so that the engineer will hear about the same amount of ambience that a home listener will hear. A totally dead room is uncomfortable to listen in.

To absorb reflections, use sufficient sound-absorbent materials on the walls, ceiling, and floor. *Flutter echoes* can be eliminated by making the walls nonparallel or by adding sufficient absorption to at least one of the parallel walls.

Reducing wall reflections near the monitors also improves the stereo imaging of the monitors. All the information about sound-image location is in the direct sound coming from the speakers; wall reflections can only confuse the listener as to the correct location of the sound images.

The control room should be acoustically isolated from the studio so that you hear only the sound from the monitors, not the live sound from the studio musicians. In a home studio, you can achieve isolation simply by putting the control-room equipment in a room far removed from the studio, with the doors closed. To build a control room with good isolation near the studio, you may need to use double-wall construction with staggered studs, and with fiberglass insulation between the two walls. The door between the control room and studio should be solid wood and should be weatherstripped all around—including underneath. Use a double-pane window (mounted in rubber) between the control room and the studio.

Speakers and Crossovers

Most studio monitors are designed for high efficiency, typically using a ported 15-inch woofer for the low frequencies and a tweeter with a horn for the highs (Fig. 4-3). The horn efficiently couples the tweeter's sound to the air, like a megaphone. The port resonates at low frequencies to reinforce the bass. (An alternative to a port is a passive radiator, which is an electrically unconnected speaker cone.)

A *one-way* speaker system uses a single cone speaker. An example of such is a mini-monitor used to simulate compact stereos and car radios. A *two-way* system (the most popular) has a woofer and a tweeter. A *three-way* system uses a woofer, a mid-range driver (with or without a horn), and a tweeter. A *four-way* system covers the widest range by adding a super tweeter. Four models of JBL studio monitors are shown in Fig. 4-4.

A *crossover* or *dividing network* is a circuit that divides the monitor signal into two or more frequency bands. In the crossover network, a *low-pass filter* sends the low frequencies to the woofer, while a *high-pass filter* sends the high frequencies to the tweeter and keeps out the low-frequency components that could damage the tweeter. Some crossovers include a *bandpass filter* to route the middle frequencies to a mid-range driver.

The *crossover frequency* is the frequency above which the woofer stops working and the tweeter takes over. The low-pass filter passes frequencies below the crossover frequency; the high-pass filter passes frequencies above the crossover frequency. This frequency is set just below the upper limit of the woofer and above the lower limit of the tweeter—typically at

Fig. 4-3. UREI Model 809 studio monitor *(Courtesy JBL Inc.).*

Fig. 4-4. JBL Model 4406, 4408, 4410, and 4412 studio monitors *(Courtesy JBL Inc.).*

500 to 2500 Hz. However, there may be an additional crossover around 5000 Hz between a mid-range driver and a tweeter.

At the crossover frequency, the response is down 3 dB. The output of the crossover network does not suddenly cut off past the crossover frequency; rather, the output slopes down by 6, 12, or 18 dB per octave.

If the crossover is connected after the power amplifier, the crossover operates at high power levels and is called a *passive crossover* (Fig. 4-5). That is, it is made of passive (nonamplifying) components. If the crossover precedes the power amps, it operates at line level and is called an *active crossover* or *electronic dividing network* (shown in Fig. 4-6). It includes active (amplifying) components, such as transistors.

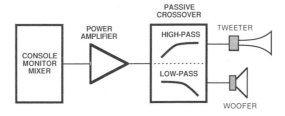

Fig. 4-5. Monitor system using a passive crossover.

An active crossover is used in a *bi-amped* system; in such a system, the woofer and tweeter are driven by separate power amplifiers. The active crossover is connected ahead of the power amps. Low-frequency signals from the crossover go to the power amp driving the woofer; the high-frequency signals from the crossover go to the power amp driving the tweeter. Because tweeters are more efficient than woofers, the tweeter amplifier can be about one-quarter of the power of the woofer amplifier.

Bi-amping has several advantages:

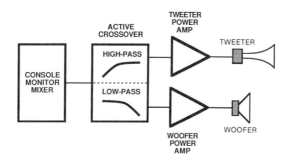

Fig. 4-6. Bi-amped monitor system using an active crossover.

- Distortion components caused by clipping the woofer power amplifier will not reach the tweeter, so there is less likelihood of tweeter burnout if the amplifier does clip. In addition, clipping distortion in the woofer amplifier is made less audible.

- Intermodulation distortion is reduced at high levels.

- Peak power output is greater than that of a single amplifier of equivalent power.

- Direct coupling of amplifiers to speakers improves the transient response—especially at low frequencies.

- Bi-amping reduces the inductive and capacitive loading of the power amplifier.

- The full power of the tweeter amplifier is available regardless of the power required by the woofer amplifier.

A three-way speaker system can be tri-amped, or it can be bi-amped by putting a passive crossover before the tweeter, as illustrated in Fig. 4-7.

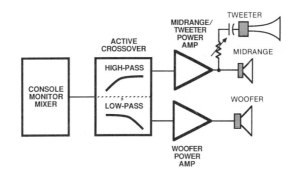

Fig. 4-7. Bi-amped monitor system using an active crossover and a passive crossover.

Speaker Requirements

The requirements for an accurate studio monitor are as follows:

1. *Wide, smooth frequency response.* The on-axis response of the direct sound should be within ± 4 dB from 40 Hz to 15 kHz to ensure accurate tonal reproduction. For a mini-monitor, the low end should extend to at least 70 Hz.

2. *Controlled dispersion.* A studio monitor should focus its sound on the listener and prevent radiation to the sides and rear of the speaker enclosure. This is to reduce reflections from nearby surfaces which can degrade the speaker's frequency response and stereo imaging. In monitoring a recording, we want to hear what's on the tape rather than hearing sound reflections from the room surfaces.

   Thus, a monitor should have *controlled dispersion*—a relatively narrow spread of sound leaving the loudspeaker. Dispersion is measured in *coverage angle*—the off-axis angle at which the speaker output is down 6 dB compared to the on-axis output. The horizontal coverage angle of a monitor should be about 60 to 90 degrees, or just wide enough to cover the console area evenly. Ideally, that angle should be maintained at all frequencies, so that people seated anywhere behind the console will hear the same tonal balance.

3. *Good transient response.* This is the ability of the speaker to accurately follow the attack and decay of musical sounds. Transient response is aided by aligning the acoustic centers of the woofer and tweeter so that their signals arrive at the listener at the same time.

4. *Clarity and detail.* The listener should be able to hear small differences in the sonic character of instruments, and should be able to sort them out in a complex musical passage.

5. *Low distortion.* This is a necessity for low listening fatigue.

6. *High efficiency.* Efficiency is the ratio of sound-power output to electrical-power input. A high-efficiency speaker is louder than a low-efficiency speaker, when both are driven by the same input power. High efficiency means less overheating because less power is needed for the same loudness.

7. *High sensitivity.* Sensitivity is the sound-pressure level that a speaker produces at 1 meter, when driven with 1 watt of pink noise. *Pink noise* is random noise with equal energy per octave.

This noise is either band-limited to the range of the speaker or is a ⅓-octave band centered at 1 kHz. A sensitivity specification of 93-dB SPL (Sound-Pressure Level) is considered high (typical of studio monitors); a specification of 85-dB SPL is considered low (typical of home bookshelf-type speakers).

8. *High output capability.* This is the ability of a speaker to play loudly without burning out. It's often necessary to monitor at high levels to hear the quiet details in the music. Plus, when you record musicians who play loudly in the studio, it can be a letdown for them to hear a quiet playback. Consequently, a maximum output capability of 110-dB SPL is typically required.

To calculate how loud a given speaker can play, use the following formula as a rule of thumb:

$$dB\ SPL = 10\ \log(P) + S + 10$$

where

dB SPL is the peak sound-pressure level obtainable at 1 meter,
P is the continuous sine-wave power rating of the speaker,
S is the sensitivity rating in dB SPL/1 watt/1 meter.

A factor of 10 is added to allow for 10-dB peaks in the music. At 2 meters from the speaker, the SPL will be up to 6 dB less.

More volume can be obtained by wiring an identical pair of speakers in parallel. That divides the power equally between them. Then you can double the amplifier power, which boosts the level 3 dB. Note that whenever identical speakers are wired in parallel, the total impedance is half the impedance of either speaker alone. Make sure that your power amplifier can drive the resulting low impedance.

Stacking the speakers vertically will result in an additional 2 dB at low frequencies due to coupling between the drivers, plus an additional 3 dB due to increased directivity.

Speaker Placement

Having a pair of quality speakers doesn't guarantee good sound reproduction; you have to install, equalize, and use them properly for best results. Let's start by considering where to put them in the control room.

The closer a loudspeaker is to the walls, ceiling, or floor, the more bass it produces. Why? If a speaker is placed in the middle of a room, it radiates low frequencies in all directions (into "full space"). But if the speaker is placed against a wall, the low-frequency energy is concentrated into half space, which boosts the lows by 3 dB. Putting a speaker in a corner maximizes the bass output by concentrating the low-frequency energy into one-quarter the space. The highs aren't much affected by speaker placement near a surface because the high frequencies radiate mainly out to the front. Check the speaker instructions for their recommended placement relative to the room surfaces.

There are several ways to install the monitor speakers, each with advantages and disadvantages. One way is to put them on shelves or platforms against a wall. Unfortunately, this arrangment can degrade the frequency response. Low-frequency sounds radiating around the speaker reflect off the rear wall, are delayed, and combine with the direct sound in front of the speaker, as shown in Fig. 4-8. This results in *phase cancellations* or a *comb-filter effect* in the mid-bass region.

One way to avoid reflections from the rear wall is to mount small wide-range monitors about three feet apart on top of the console meter bridge—very near the mixing position. This technique, developed by audio consultant Ed Long, is called *near-field monitoring*. Since the speakers are close to your ears, you hear mainly the direct sound of the speakers and tend to ignore the room acoustics. This can be an inexpensive monitoring arrangement for small home studios.

Another way to prevent rear-wall reflections is to flush-mount the monitors in the wall. They should be mechanically isolated from the wall by foam rubber, fiberglass insulation, or rubber shock mounts. That prevents sound from traveling through the wall and ceiling to the listener before the direct sound arrives through the air. If flush-mounting is impractical, you can weaken the wall reflections by placing the speakers at least three feet from the rear wall and four feet from the side walls.

Another arrangement is the "live end–dead end" room treatment (LEDE), invented by Don Davis and Chips Davis. The front half of the

Fig. 4-8. Speaker placement near a wall may cause phase cancellations due to delayed reflections combining with the direct sound.

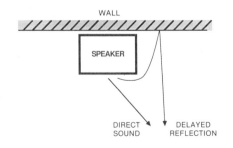

control room around the speakers is made very sound-absorbent (dead) by applying muslin-covered fiberglass insulation or Sonex acoustic foam to the walls and ceiling. That's to prevent reflections from the surfaces near the speakers. The wall behind the engineer is hard and reflective (live) to provide ambience and increase loudness. This surface is broken up, rather than flat, to diffuse the sound. Reflection Phase Gratings (RPG diffusers) are often used for this purpose.

An LEDE room is not necessarily all absorptive in the front and reflective in the rear. The speakers can be flush-mounted in a hard-wall array that is angled to eliminate early reflections at the listener's ears. The idea is to create a "reflection-free zone" at the mixing position.

A certified LEDE room has to meet certain criteria, but many control rooms can be improved simply by putting thick absorbent material on the walls behind and to the sides of the speakers. Some of the claimed benefits of an LEDE control room are:

- Mixes are easier and faster to do because it's easier to hear what's happening in the studio.
- The overall sound is clearer.
- Stereo imaging and depth are greatly improved.
- Frequency response is flatter.
- Boominess and overhang are reduced, and transient response is sharpened.
- LEDE-monitored recordings hold up well on many home hi-fi speakers.

In any control room, the speakers are mounted at ear height or slightly higher, so the sound path is not obstructed by the console. A typical arrangement is shown in Fig. 4-9. For best stereo imaging, align the speaker drivers vertically and mount the speakers symmetrically with respect to the side walls. Place the two speakers as far apart as you're sitting from them (about 8 feet); aim them toward you, and sit exactly between them.

Polarity and Stereo Balance

Of course, be sure to wire the speakers in-phase (same polarity) to obtain a sharp center image. Also, wire the speakers in correct *absolute* polarity so that their speaker cones vibrate in the same direction as the live

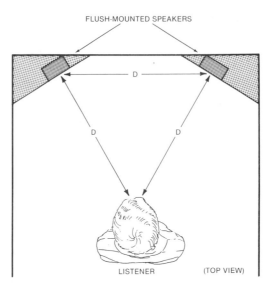

Fig. 4-9. Recommended speaker/listener relationship for best stereo imaging.

instrument at the onset of a note. The effect of absolute polarity is a subtle increase in clarity and solidity.

To determine whether a speaker is wired in correct absolute polarity, proceed as follows:

1. Place a microphone of standard polarity (pin 2 hot) inside a kick drum.

2. Have someone beat the drum while you watch the monitor-speaker woofer.

3. The woofer cone should go out (toward you) the instant that the drum is struck. If the opposite occurs, reverse the speaker leads of both speakers.

To adjust the stereo balance, play a mono musical signal and assign it to channels 1 and 2 in the console. Adjust the channel 1 and 2 master faders so that the signal reads the same on the channel 1 and channel 2 VU meters. Then, while sitting behind the console, exactly midway between the speakers, listen to the image of the sound between the speaker pair. It should be localized midway between the monitors—that is, straight ahead. If necessary, center the image by adjusting the monitor trim pots on the console, or by adjusting the volume control on the left- or right-channel power amplifier. Note that an off-center listener will hear the image shifted toward one side.

Power Requirements

Check the loudspeaker rating for the recommended amplifier power. A power amp of 150-watts continuous-average-power per channel should be sufficient for use with high-efficiency studio monitors (Fig. 4-10). A bi-amped system requires less total power than a single-amp system. For example, if a bi-amped system has a 100-watt amplifier for the woofer and a 25-watt amplifier for the tweeter, the peak power can equal that of a 225-watt amplifier driving a passive crossover.

Fig. 4-10. Two power amplifiers for studio monitoring use *(Courtesy Crown International).*

(A) Crown D-150A Series II.

(B) Crown DC-300A Series II.

Some performance requirements for a monitor power amplifier are:

1. Distortion under 0.05%.
2. Ability to drive any load.
3. Ability to control or damp the loudspeaker vibration (high damping factor).
4. Ability to amplify consistently over long periods.

Two valuable features are independent channel-level controls and an accurate indicator for distortion or clipping.

To avoid losing power in heating the speaker cables, put the power amplifiers close to the speakers and use short cables with thick conductors. The low resistance of these cables allows maximum damping of the speaker by the power amplifier. Use the following chart to select the cable gauge based on cable length:

Cable Length	Gauge
Less than 25 feet	#16
25 to 50 feet	#14
50 to 100 feet	#12

Room Equalization

Room equalization involves adjusting the frequency response of the monitor chain to flatten the speaker/room response at the listener's position. Equalization can correct for broad response errors in the anechoic frequency response of the speaker, and, partly, for unequal absorption versus frequency in the room treatment. Note that equalization is not effective against standing waves because they vary with the listener's position. Neither is equalization a cure for poor room acoustics or narrow-band speakers. Work on the room treatment and speaker placement first, and then apply as little equalization as possible. If a flat-response speaker is installed in a room with equal absorption at all frequencies, little or no equalization will be needed.

To equalize a monitor/listening room for flat response, you'll need a ⅓-octave real-time analyzer (RTA), a pink noise generator (usually built into the analyzer), a laboratory-calibrated instrumentation microphone, and a ⅓-octave equalizer (preferably a graphic type). The RTA and microphone can be rented from a sound-system dealer. Set up the test equipment as follows:

1. Connect the equalizer between the console monitor output and the power-amplifier input (or the active-crossover input if the system is bi-amped).

2. Set the controls of the graphic equalizer to their center (flat) positions.

3. Put the microphone at the listener's position and plug it into the analyzer.

4. Feed pink noise into the equalizer input. You'll see a frequency response curve on the RTA screen.

The final response curve after equalization should be flat from 40 Hz up to 5 or 8 kHz, and, then, it should gradually roll off to about -10 dB at 16 kHz. You'll probably need to do a final touch-up by ear. Rolling off the monitor high-frequency response will make the engineer boost the high frequencies in the mix. That boost is acceptable because most home-type hi-fi speakers roll off at high frequencies, making the end result sound natural. A mix made on monitors that are tuned flat up to the highest frequencies is likely to sound dull on most home systems.

Adjust the speaker's mid-range and tweeter controls to get the desired response curve. Or, if the system is bi-amped, adjust the volume control on the tweeter power amplifier. Finally, flatten the curve using the graphic equalizer. Pull down the highest peaks in the curve first—don't apply boost if you can help it.

If you need more than about 5 dB of boost or cut at any frequency, the speaker needs to be upgraded or the room treatment needs work. Add bass traps if the curve is raised at the low end. Add fiberglass insulation, carpet, or curtains if the curve is raised at the high end. A sharp dip at a certain frequency may be due to a vibrating wall panel— stiffen it. Some dips may be caused by sound reflections off the console; these can be detected by covering the console with a heavy blanket and looking for changes in the RTA display. Don't remove those dips with the equalizer. Instead, place the monitor speakers at a height that prevents them (according to Chips Davis, about 15° above ear level).

Lacking a real-time analyzer, you may be able to roughly equalize the monitor system by ear as follows: Place a flat-response omnidirectional microphone about one foot from some person in the studio, and record while this person is speaking. Play the recording through the monitor system at a natural level. Equalize the speaker so it sounds like the same person is speaking live in the control room near the speaker. This demonstrates the meaning of *accuracy*; the reproduced sound is similar to the original sound. As an alternative, play pre-recorded music through some top-quality headphones, and then through the monitor speakers. Equalize the speakers to sound like the headphones.

Using the Monitors

The listening level during mixdown should be maintained at about 85-dB SPL—a typical home-listening level. As discovered by Fletcher and Munson, we hear less bass in a program that is played quietly than in the same program played loudly. If you mix a program while monitoring at, say, 100-dB SPL, the same program will sound weak in the bass when heard at a lower listening level—which is likely in the home system. So, programs that are meant to be heard at 85-dB SPL should be mixed and monitored at that level.

There is another reason to avoid extreme monitor levels. Loud, sustained sound can damage your hearing or cause a temporary hearing loss at certain frequencies. If you must do a loud playback for the musicians, protect your ears by using earplugs or by leaving the room.

You can obtain an inexpensive sound-level meter from your local electronics distributor. Play a musical program at 0 VU on the console meters and adjust the monitor level to obtain an average reading of 85-dB SPL on the sound-level meter. Mark the monitor-level setting. While mixing, monitor the program alternately in stereo and mono to make sure that there are no out-of-phase components which cancel certain frequencies in mono. Also, beware of *center-channel buildup*. Instruments or vocals that are panned to center in the stereo mix will sound 3 dB louder when monitored in mono than they do in stereo. That is, the balance changes in mono—the center instruments are a little too loud. You may have to compromise the stereo and mono mixes so that both sound acceptable.

It helps to monitor with small cheap speakers in addition to the big, accurate, studio monitors. Single-driver mini-monitors (such as Auratone™) simulate the inexpensive car radios and compact stereos that the majority of consumers listen to. First, mix the program to sound good on the big monitors, and then switch to the small ones to see if anything is missing or if the mix changes drastically. Make sure that the bass instruments are recorded with enough harmonics to be audible on the smaller speakers.

Don't try to equalize the program so it sounds hi-fi over the cheap speakers. If you do, it will sound bad over the accurate monitors. Listeners who buy accurate stereo systems should not be penalized for their efforts!

Also, the recording will lack archival value if mixed to sound good only on a colored speaker. A recording monitored on an accurate system will sound better and better on home stereos as they improve in the future.

Many engineers like to do most of the mix on portable reference monitors which resemble home-style bookshelf speakers (Fig. 4-11). They are usually set up on the console meter bridge in a near-field arrangement.

Before doing a mix, you may want to play some familiar records over your monitors to become accustomed to a commercial spectral balance. But listen to several records since they vary widely.

Headphones

High-quality headphones are a low-cost alternative to loudspeakers for the home studio. You should be aware of their advantages and disadvantages when compared to loudspeakers.

The advantages of headphones are:

- Much lower cost than speakers and amplifiers.
- No room-acoustics coloration to worry about.
- Consistent tone quality in different environments.
- Ideal for on-location recording.

Fig. 4-11. Fostex RM765 reference monitor *(Courtesy Fostex Corporation of America).*

- Easier to hear small changes in the mix.
- No time smear due to room reflections.

The disadvantages of headphones are:

- May become uncomfortable after long listening sessions.
- The tone quality may not match that of speakers.
- You can't feel the bass notes through your body.
- Bass response varies with the headphone pressure against the head.
- The sound is in your head rather than out in front.
- No listening-room reverberation is heard, so you may mix in an inappropriate amount of artificial reverberation.
- For panned signals (or for coincident-pair stereo recording), the stereo spread between the ears is less than the spread between the speakers.

Even though headphones may not sound like speakers, you can do your mixes over headphones to match the commercial records heard over those same headphones. Then your mixes will sound commercial over speakers, too.

If you're monitoring as the musicians are playing, use the closed-cup type of headphone to block out sounds from the studio.

The Cue System

The *cue system* is a monitor system for musicians to use as they're recording. It consists of the cue mixer in the console, a cue amplifier, wiring to the headphone junction boxes, and the headphones. Musicians sometimes can't hear each other adequately in the studio (due to baffles and their own instruments), but by listening over headphones they can hear each other in a reasonable balance. They also can listen to previously recorded tracks while overdubbing.

A suggested cue system is shown in Fig. 4-12. A power amplifier connected to the cue output of the console drives several resistor-isolated headphones, which are in parallel. You may want to wire the headphones permanently to the cue lines to prevent theft.

Headphones for a cue system should be:

- Durable, with metal-jacket plugs.

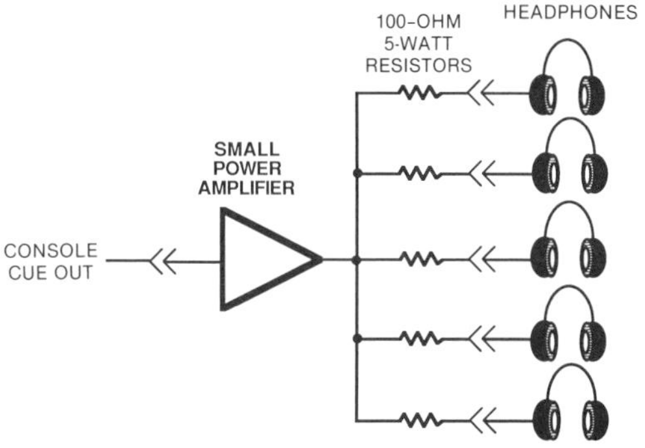

Fig. 4-12. A cue system.

- Comfortable.
- Closed-cup type (to avoid leakage into microphones).
- Wired mono (following the beat is easier in mono than in stereo).
- The smooth response type (to reduce listening fatigue).
- Capable of producing high levels without burning out.
- All the same model (so each musician hears the same mix and level).

Although some consoles can provide several independent cue mixes, the ideal situation is to set up individual cue mixers near each musician. Then, they can set their own cue mix and listening level. The inputs of these mixers are fed from the console output buses.

Conclusion

Ultimately, what you hear from the monitors influences your recording techniques and affects the quality of your recordings. So take the time to plan and adjust the control-room acoustics. Choose and install the speakers carefully; equalize them if necessary. Monitor at the proper levels and listen on several systems. You'll be rewarded with a monitor system you can trust.

5 HUM PREVENTION

Audio is often contaminated by a low-frequency tone (called *hum*) or by a higher-frequency buzz. *Hum frequencies* are 60 Hz (50 Hz in Europe) and multiples of that frequency. This annoying sound can be caused by many factors, such as cables picking up interference from power lines, noisy AC power (from wall outlets), and improper connections between the recording equipment. Fortunately, hum pickup can be prevented by following good wiring practices. This chapter explains several techniques to keep your audio clean and hum-free.

AC Power Wiring

Hum prevention starts with properly designed power wiring. Sound-system equipment should be powered on its own circuit separate from the lighting, air-conditioning, etc., which can put noise spikes on the AC line.

Here are four ways of powering the audio system. The first is most effective but it costs the most; the last is least effective but it costs the least:

1. Power the audio system from its own power transformer (located on a telephone pole outside the studio).
2. Get power from an independent breaker box.
3. Put the audio system on a different phase of the incoming AC mains than that which the other equipment is connected to. (*AC mains* is the 60-Hz, 120-volt AC power wiring that is supplied by the power company.)
4. Power the audio from its own circuit breaker.

In any case, all the audio equipment (including the guitar amps in the studio or on stage) should be on the same phase of the power line to prevent hum.

It helps to use *AC isolation transformers* between the AC power outlets and the audio-equipment power cords. These transformers remove any radio-frequency interference on the AC line that is generated by lightning, computers, motors, or other sources.

Avoid using fluorescent lights in the studio because they radiate strong magnetic fields. If fluorescent lights can't be removed, be sure that the lighting fixtures are grounded, and replace any faulty ballasts. Inside each fixture, install a noise filter (available from electronics supply houses). Also, avoid SCR dimmers (those that use silicon control rectifiers) as they put "hash" and buzzes on the AC line. Instead, use multi-way incandescent bulbs to vary the studio lighting levels. You may also want to enclose the power wiring in grounded metal conduit to prevent hum radiation from the power lines getting into audio circuits.

"Buzzes" in on-location work often are caused by interference from stage lighting circuits. Use AC isolation transformers or *line filters* (available from electronic supply houses). Keep the lighting cables and power wiring well away from the audio cables. If these cables must cross, cross them at right angles and separate them vertically.

Grounding Procedures

Once you've established a clean power feed, you should set up a solid grounding system. Before explaining how to do this, here are a few definitions:

1. A *ground* is the zero-signal reference point for a system of electronic components.
2. *Grounding* is the connecting of pieces of electronic equipment to this ground point.
3. *Earth ground* is a connection made to moist dirt (the ground we walk on). This connection usually is made through a copper ground rod or a cold-water pipe.

The purpose of grounding is to establish a zero-potential difference between any two metallic surfaces in the studio, and to make them all at zero potential with respect to earth ground. In other words, grounding eliminates any voltage differences between equipment chassis by connecting them all solidly to earth ground. Grounding also protects people from AC shorts to chassis.

Grounding for Small Studios

Modern AC outlets contain three wires: hot (black), neutral (white), and ground (bare or green). The ground wire goes to the U-shaped socket in the outlet. That ground wire connects back to the power company's earth ground, and establishes a *power ground* or *safety ground*. Many electrical/electronic devices have 3-wire power cords; the round ground pin on the cord connects the equipment chassis to safety ground. If a short-circuit occurs between the chassis and a hot power line, the chassis current will flow to safety ground rather than through someone who might be touching the chassis, thus preventing shocks.

In small studios which have short connecting cables and fewer than 20 power cords in use, the wall-outlet ground is usually adequate. Just plug the mixing console into a 3-wire grounded outlet. In many homes or buildings, which have older wiring, there is no third-wire power ground. In this case, you'll have to ground to a metallic cold-water pipe (which goes into the earth). Run a thick insulated wire (No. 4 gauge is ideal) from the mixer chassis to the pipe. Securely bond the ground wire to the pipe with a pipe clamp (available at hardware stores).

Ground Loops

Outlets on opposite sides of a room, or in different rooms, are often fed from different circuit breakers and often are at different ground potentials. If unbalanced equipment is plugged into these outlets and is connected together, ground loops can result and can cause hum.

A *ground loop* is a circuit formed out of ground leads. It is the circuit loop that is formed when equipment is connected to ground through more than one path. It occurs when two pieces of audio gear are connected to each other through a shield and also through the AC power ground.

To prevent ground loops, plug all components into one or more outlet strips that are fed from the same circuit breaker. First make sure that the current requirement of the system (the sum of the equipment fuse ratings) does not exceed the amperage rating for that circuit.

Orienting Power Cords for Minimum Hum

For each piece of audio gear, rotate the two-prong power-cord plug in its outlet to find the minimum-hum position. Proceed as follows:

1. Find an electrical ground, such as a cold-water pipe, the U-shaped hole in 3-hole wall outlets, or the metal screw that holds the cover plate to the wall outlet. Check to see whether the U-shaped hole or the metal screw is actually grounded by connecting a neon tester between the hole (or screw) and one of the other outlet sockets. If the tester glows in either of the sockets, the hole (or screw) is grounded. If not, use the cold-water-pipe ground for the following procedures.

2. Unplug all audio cables and ground leads from the component under test. Turn it on. Connect the neon tester between the component's chassis and the ground (from step 1). If the tester glows, reverse the AC power plug in the wall outlet. Mark the proper polarity on all the outlets and equipment plugs. Note: If the tester glows with both orientations of the plug, the chassis is electrically hot, and the piece of equipment should be repaired before use.

Grounding for Large Studios

The following suggestions are for large professional installations using balanced audio lines. If you have a small studio, you may want to skip this section (or just read it for the advice it contains).

Earth Ground

You can't always trust the wall-outlet grounds to have a low-resistance connection to earth ground. It's best to install your own earth ground by driving an 8-foot copper rod or pipe into moist earth outside the studio. Then, get some No. 2 gauge, or larger, stranded cable, and bolt this cable to the ground rod. In areas with radio-frequency interference, use a copper strap or braid that is 4 to 12 inches wide and as short as possible. Run the cable (or strap) up to the console *ground bus* (a terminal or plate). The entire ground system should be a very low resistance system because it carries heavy currents from all the audio shields.

An alternative earth ground is a metallic cold-water pipe (copper pipe is preferable to steel). Securely bond the ground wire to the pipe with a pipe clamp. However, a ground stake is preferable to a cold-water pipe because a water pipe may act as an RF antenna and introduce switching transients from adjacent lighting and motors into the sound system.

In less-critical applications, the ground plate in a circuit-breaker box will do because it is connected to the power company's earth ground. However, this power ground still may carry noise spikes and heavy currents. *Caution*: Make sure you know what you are doing before you start fooling around inside the circuit-breaker box.

Try all the earth-grounding methods described and use whatever works best.

Ground Wiring

Large studios require special ground connections in the power wiring. If you're unfamiliar with electrical wiring practices, hire an electrician. Be sure to check your local electrical code before doing any AC power wiring. Although studio power wiring meets code requirements, the ground wiring is nonstandard; so confer with the electrician to make sure the work is done as described in this section.

In most buildings, the safety ground wire is "daisy chained," or connected from one outlet to the next. This arrangement can cause hum problems because each outlet's ground terminal is at a different resistance to the earth ground. Consequently, hum currents may flow between two pieces of audio equipment plugged into separate outlets. To prevent this from occurring with new power wiring, run a separate insulated wire from each outlet ground back to the ground plate in the circuit-breaker box (or to the console ground bus). That way, all the outlet grounds are at the same potential. Then the audio equipment can be grounded through its 3-prong power-cord plugs.

A solid-copper, insulated No. 4-gauge ground wire is recommended for connecting the console ground bus to the ground-bus bar in the circuit-breaker box. Use No. 10-gauge wire for connections to the console ground bus (*or* whatever gauge your local electrical code requires).

Try to keep the lengths of all the ground leads about equal for equal resistance to earth ground. These ground wires should never short to the conduit, or you'll get ground loops. Use special wall outlets that *float* (isolate) the ground terminal from the wall box; the wall box is grounded through the conduit instead. Isolated-ground outlets are available from electronics supply houses. In studios where the power wiring is already installed, you can connect each chassis separately to the console ground bus, using No. 10-gauge insulated wire or a 1-inch wide copper braid. Then, the power-cord grounds are floated by using electrical 3-to-2 adapters with three sockets and two prongs. One ground wire goes from the console ground bus to a tape-deck chassis; another wire goes from the console ground bus to an equipment rack, and so on. The console ground bus is connected to earth ground. This is the single ground point for every major piece of equipment in the studio.

A proper grounding scheme resembles a tree (Fig. 5-1). The earth ground is the roots; the heavy cable from earth ground to the console

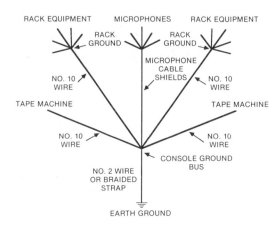

Fig. 5-1.
Recommended
grounding
layout.

ground bus is the trunk; and the ground leads from the console ground bus to the studio equipment are the branches. Some branches in a tree divide into smaller branches; this corresponds to the rack-grounding schemes described later in this chapter.

Power Distribution System

A touring sound company should carry its own single-phase power-distribution system because most building ground wiring is unreliable. The ground leads should be wired as just described. See Fig. 5-2 for a suggested AC-power distribution system.

Fig. 5-2. An
AC-power
distribution
system for a
touring
company's sound
system.

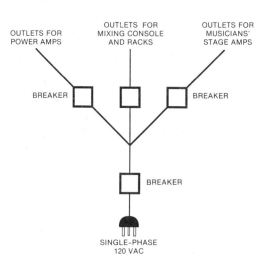

Rack Grounding

A *rack* is a grounded metal cabinet (or metal frame) used to hold signal processors and patch panels. The audio equipment bolts onto the rack channels, which are vertical metal strips with holes in them. Inside the rack is an AC-outlet strip that is used to power the rack equipment. Also inside the rack, near the bottom, is a *rack ground* which is securely bonded to the rack.

Connect the rack ground to the console ground bus using a heavy (No. 10) insulated wire, and float the rack power ground. Alternatively, ground the rack via the power ground from the rack's AC-outlet strip. There are several different approaches to grounding rack equipment:

1. *Unbalanced equipment grounded to the console ground bus.* Put all unbalanced equipment in a single rack to shorten the interconnecting cables. To prevent ground loops, isolate all the rack equipment from the rack (and from each other) by using nylon mounting bolts and washers (or a wooden rack). Then, run a separate insulated ground wire from each unit's chassis to the rack ground. For equipment with 3-prong plugs, put 3-to-2 adapters on the power cords.

2. *Unbalanced equipment grounded via the outlet-strip power ground.* Install the equipment as described above, with the following exception: For each piece of equipment having a 3-prong power plug, simply plug it into the rack's AC-outlet strip. This procedure grounds the chassis without you having to add a separate ground wire.

3. *Balanced equipment.* You can't always rely on the chassis making a good contact with the rack channels, so connect the chassis of each unit to the rack channels with a heavy cable or braided strap.

Audio Cables

Audio cables pick up hum from oscillating electrostatic and magnetic fields which are radiated from power lines in the walls. Let's see how this occurs.

Electrostatic Interference

Power lines act as one plate of a capacitor, while the conductors in the audio cables act as the other plate. An oscillating electrostatic field is set up between these two plates, causing hum to be transmitted (coupled) from the power lines to the cable conductors. An electrostatic field couples best at high frequencies, and so is heard as a buzz (including harmonics of 60 Hz).

The conductors can be protected from this electrostatic field by a surrounding shield. A *shield* is a conductive enclosure placed around signal-carrying conductors, and is used to keep out electrostatic hum fields and radio-frequency interference. In audio cables, a shield usually takes the form of a foil or metal-braid cylinder around one or two conductors. Metal racks, equipment chassis, and microphone handles also are shields. Shields must be connected to ground to be effective, because the ground provides a drain path for shield charges that are caused by the electrostatic fields. The greater the shield coverage, the better it rejects hum, so use cable with foil shielding for permanent wiring.

Audio cables should have an insulating jacket to prevent ground loops to the shield.

Magnetic Interference

Power lines also act like electromagnets, radiating magnetic lines of force that oscillate at 60 Hz. These lines of force cut the conductors in audio cables, causing the conductors to generate electricity at 60 Hz. Magnetic fields couple best at low frequencies, and so are heard as a low tone at 60 Hz. Note that shields do not block magnetic hum fields unless they are made of a magnetic material.

Balanced and Unbalanced Lines

Hum fields are rejected better by balanced lines than by unbalanced lines. A *balanced line* is a cable that uses two conductors, surrounded by a shield, to carry the signal, as shown in Fig. 5-3. The shield does not

Fig. 5-3. A balanced line.

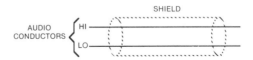

carry the signal; it is connected to ground and keeps electrostatic fields out of the conductors.

In a balanced line, each of the two conductors is at an equal impedance to ground. Consequently, the conductors pick up equal amounts of hum interference. The cable plugs into a balanced input, which is sensitive to the voltage difference between the two conductors. Since there is little or no difference in hum voltage between the two conductors, hum picked up by the cable is not amplified.

Twisted-pair cable creates less magnetically induced hum than does nontwisted-pair cable. This is because twisted-conductor pairs occupy the same point in space on the average, so they are the same distance from the hum source and receive equal hum interference.

An *unbalanced line* is a cable that uses a single conductor which is surrounded by a shield, as shown in Fig. 5-4. Both the conductor and the shield carry audio signals, so the shield isn't as effective in blocking electrostatic hum as it is in a balanced line. Also, the inner conductor and the outer shield are at different impedances to ground, so they pick up different amounts of hum interference. This difference in induced hum voltage is amplified by the equipment that the cable is plugged into. In spite of these drawbacks, unbalanced lines less than 10-feet long usually provide adequate hum rejection.

Fig. 5-4. An unbalanced line.

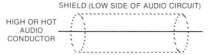

It's a good idea to bundle or group together the microphone cables separately from the line-level cables, and keep these separated from the speaker cables. Crosstalk or oscillations may occur if high-level and low-level signals are run together.

When connecting balanced equipment to unbalanced equipment, you may want to add a 1:1 audio isolation transformer at the unbalanced input or output (as shown in Fig. 5-5). This allows most of the interconnecting cable to be balanced.

Shield Connections

You should wire the cable shields to prevent ground loops, as follows: In each line-level balanced cable, connect the shield to ground at the input only as shown in Fig. 5-6. Solder the cable shield to pin 1 in the

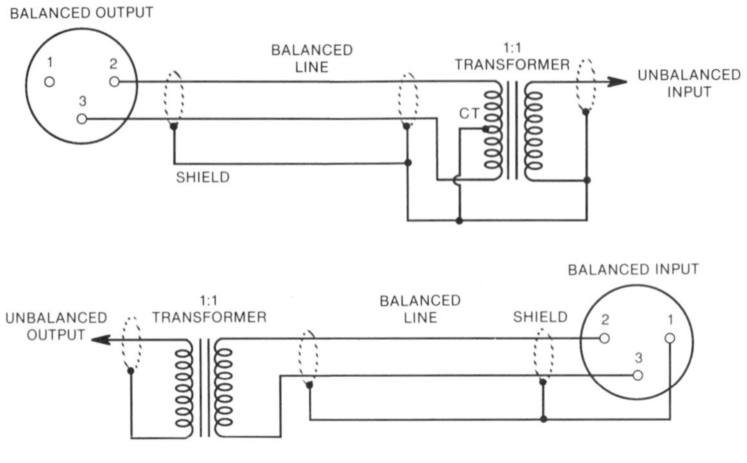

**Fig. 5-5.
Transformer
connections
between
balanced and
unbalanced
equipment.**

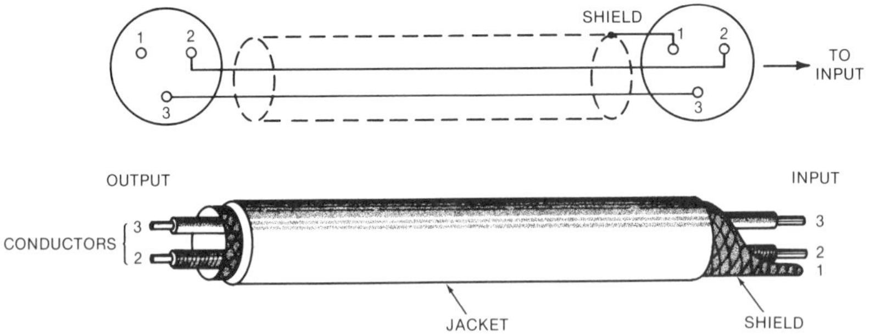

**Fig. 5-6. Proper
shield
connections for
balanced line-
level cables.**

input connector; leave it unsoldered (and cut short and shrink-tubed) in the output connector.

This arrangement is called a *telescoping shield* because the shield, being unconnected at one end, can be squeezed together, or collapsed like a telescope. The two conductors from pins 2 and 3 carry the audio signal. The shield still drains interference to ground through its single ground connection. If the shield were connected at both ends, a ground loop might be set up between the shield and the power-ground leads, causing hum. *Note:* A microphone cable is an exception to this rule. A microphone shield should be tied to pin 1 on both ends, otherwise the microphone housing won't be grounded.

As an alternative, tie the shield to pin 1 at both ends, and put two power diodes back-to-back in line with each safety-ground wire. That way, the safety-ground wire is out of the circuit (preventing ground loops) unless a chassis accidentally becomes hot.

In the unbalanced systems found in much home-studio equipment, the shield is usually connected at both ends and the power ground is not used (except at the console). In difficult locations, it may help to use 2-conductor shielded cable with a telescoping shield, as in Fig. 5-7. That way the conductors will be isolated somewhat from the shield currents.

Connections to Guitar Amps

At times, electric guitar players can receive a shock when they simultaneously touch their guitar and a sound-system microphone. This occurs when the guitar amp is plugged into an electrical outlet on stage, and the mixing console (to which the mics are grounded) is plugged into a separate outlet across the room. As stated before, these two power points may be at widely different ground potentials, so a current can flow between the grounded mic housing and the grounded guitar strings. This occurrence is especially dangerous when the guitar amp and the console are on different phases of the AC mains.

It helps to power all instrument amps and audio gear from the same AC distribution outlets. That is, run a heavy extension cord from the stage outlet back to the console (or vice versa). Plug all the power-cord ground pins into grounded outlets. That way, you can prevent shocks and hum at the same time.

An alternative is to force the instrument-amp chassis and the console chassis to be at the same ground potential by running a heavy insulated wire between them, and by floating the power-cord ground pin on the instrument amp. The console should be grounded to a power ground, earth ground, or cold-water pipe.

Some engineers prefer to use a 3-to-2 adapter to float the guitar amps in order to break up ground loops, and to use the direct-box cable for a safety ground. But, an audio-cable shield can't carry the heavy current present in the event of a power short to chassis, so the musician may get shocked anyway. It's better to ground the amp and use transformer-isolated direct boxes to prevent the ground loops.

Using a neon tester or a voltmeter, check the voltage between each stage amp and power ground. If there is a voltage, flip the polarity switch on the amp. Then, if you still measure a voltage, run a heavy wire between the amp chassis and power ground. Also, check the voltage

Fig. 5-7. Using 2-conductor shielded cable for unbalanced connections.

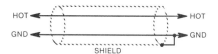

between the electric-guitar strings and the metal grille and handle of the microphones. If you measure a voltage, correct the situation before proceeding.

Interconnecting Multiple Sound Systems

When live concerts are recorded, three separate sound systems are commonly used: the house sound-reinforcement system, the stage-monitor system, and the recording system. These three systems share the stage-microphone signals by taking transformer-isolated balanced feeds from a 3-way *microphone splitter*, as shown in Fig. 5-8. To avoid ground loops between the three systems, only the cable shields going to the recording truck are connected at the splitter. The cable shields going to the house mixer and monitor mixer are disconnected at the splitter (say, by ground-lift switches).

The sound-reinforcement mixer and the monitor mixer can be powered from outlets at the recording truck. That way, the three systems share a common ground. Sometimes, a ground stake can be driven into the earth outside the recording truck and connected to the recording truck's ground bus.

Often, a radio station or video crew will take an audio feed from a studio's mixing console. In this case, you can prevent a hum problem by using a console with transformer-isolated inputs and outputs. Or, you can use a 1:1 audio-isolation transformer between the console and the feeds. Such a transformer is especially useful when interconnecting balanced and unbalanced equipment. It should have an electrostatic shield and should be able to handle +20 dBm. Mount it in a rack near the patch panel.

If you encounter an unknown system where balanced audio cables may be grounded at both ends, use some cable ground-lift adapters (Fig. 5-9) to float the extra ground connection at the equipment outputs.

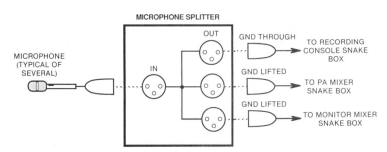

Fig. 5-8. Using a microphone splitter to feed three sound systems.

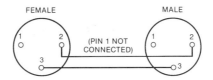

Fig. 5-9. Ground-lift adapter for signal cables.

Other Hum Reduction Techniques

Microphone Hum

Microphones and mic cables are especially sensitive to hum pickup because of the great amplification needed for mic-level signals. Here are some tips you can use to minimize microphone hum pickup:

- Use low-impedance microphones (150–600 ohms), which pick up less hum than high-impedance microphones.
- Use microphones with balanced outputs (3-pin connectors), which pick up less hum than unbalanced microphones (hot conductor plus shield).
- Use a balanced cable from the mic to the input and, if you have unbalanced microphone inputs on your recorder or mixer, unbalance the cable through a transformer that is plugged directly into the input.
- Use dynamic microphones with humbucking coils built in, if hum pickup is severe when using dynamic microphones.
- Use twisted-pair microphone cable to reduce the pickup of magnetically induced hum. The more shield coverage, the less pickup of electrostatically induced hum. *Braided shield* generally offers the best cable coverage; *double-spiral wrapped* is next best, and *spiral wrapped* is worst.
- Routinely check the microphone cables to make sure the shield is connected at both ends.
- Check that the mic connector is securely screwed clockwise into the mic handle. (Look for a set screw in the handle near the connector.)
- Tape over cracks between connectors to keep out dust and dirt (for outdoor work).

Also, to prevent ground loops, do not ground snake boxes. For microphone junction boxes located in the walls, do not ground them locally— only through the cable shield.

In addition, inside the mic-cable connector is a ground lug that makes contact with the connector shell. If the cable is used in a studio, solder the ground lug to pin 1 so that the shell is grounded and acts as a shield. If the cable is used in a remote or outdoor setup, do not connect the ground lug to pin 1, because ground loops may occur if the shell touches a metallic surface.

Electric Guitar Hum

Try the following suggestions to reduce hum associated with electric guitars:

- Replace or repair any guitar cords with broken shields; use only high-quality cords with metal-jacket plugs.
- Flip the polarity switch on the guitar amp to the lowest-hum position.
- Flip the ground-lift switch on direct boxes to the lowest-hum position.
- Have the guitarist turn up the volume of guitar all the way, and then turn down the gain on the guitar amp.
- Have the guitarist move around or turn around (rotate) to find a spot with minimum hum pickup.
- Replace any defective tubes in the guitar amp. If the power-supply filter capacitors in the guitar amp are corroded, replace them.
- Use guitars with humbucking pickups, or install modern humbuckers in the older guitars.
- Use a quieter amplifier.

If necessary, add extra shielding to the compartment that houses the tone and volume controls, and add aluminum tape grounded to (trapped under) the guitar output jack. Also, check the foil connections under the pickups.

In addition, with the guitar amp unplugged from the wall outlet, remove the 0.047-μF capacitors connected across the power-line input in the guitar amp (Fig. 5-10). They may create noise problems or cause a shock hazard.

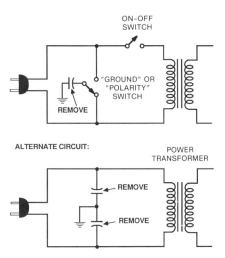

**Fig. 5-10.
Modifying the
guitar amplifier
power-supply
wiring.**

Reducing Radio-Frequency Interference (RFI)

This type of interference is heard as a buzz, as clicks, as radio programs, or "hash" in the audio signal. It's caused by Citizen's Band transmitters, computers, lightning, radar, radio and TV transmitters, industrial machines, auto ignitions, stage lighting, and other sources. To reduce RFI:

- Use wide copper straps or braids, rather than wires, for ground connections, to reduce the high ground resistance that is caused by *skin effect*.
- Install high-quality RFI filters in the AC power outlets. The cheap types available from local radio shops are generally ineffective.
- Physically separate the lighting power wiring from the audio cables.
- Avoid SCR dimmers—instead, use multiwatt incandescent bulbs to vary the studio lighting levels.
- Use enclosed equipment racks.
- Avoid long ground leads and unbalanced lines that are over ten feet long.

Also, for each unbalanced mic input, connect a 250-pF to 1000-pF capacitor between the hot terminal and ground (if the mixer doesn't already have such a capacitor). Then, if the mic-input shell isn't grounded to the chassis, connect a 0.001-μF Mylar capacitor between the shell terminal and the console chassis (if the console doesn't already have such a capacitor).

Long speaker cables can act as an RF antenna. Shunt the RF to ground at the power-amplifier speaker terminals. Connect a 0.01-μF to 0.03-μF disk capacitor between one speaker lead and the amplifier chassis ground; use one capacitor per channel.

If RFI is still a serious problem, connect the "unconnected" end of each telescoping cable shield to pin 1 through a 0.01-μF capacitor. Also, in microphone junction boxes, solder a 0.01 μF capacitor between pins 1 and 2, and between pins 1 and 3.

Summary

For balanced equipment in a large installation, the most important points to remember about hum prevention are:

- Put audio equipment on a separate power feed.
- Use AC isolation transformers or AC line filtering if necessary.
- Ground the chassis of each major piece of equipment to the console ground bus with a separate low-resistance wire. Connect the console ground bus to a single earth ground.
- Connect each chassis of rack equipment separately to rack ground, and connect the rack ground to the console ground bus.
- Connect all shields at the input end only (except in mic cables, and in one feed from a microphone splitter).

For unbalanced equipment in a small studio, and using short connecting cables,

- Plug the console into a 3-wire grounded outlet.
- Plug all equipment into outlet strips powered by the same breaker.
- Put unbalanced equipment in a single rack, isolated from the rack and from each other (say, by using a wooden rack).

6 MICROPHONES

What microphone is best for recording a symphonic band? What's a good piano mic? Should the microphone be a condenser or dynamic type, or an omni or cardioid type? These questions can be better answered once you understand the various types of microphones and their specifications. After learning a few definitions, you'll have a better idea of what microphone to use in a particular application.

A microphone is a *transducer*; a device that converts one form of energy into another. Specifically, a microphone converts acoustical energy (sound) into electrical energy (the signal). Then, the electrical signal is amplified and modified by the mixer. By controlling the signal, you also control the recorded sound quality.

Transducer Types

Recording microphones can be grouped into two types depending on their operating principle: *dynamic* or *condenser*. In a dynamic microphone, a moving conductor cuts the magnetic lines of force to produce electricity. Two types of dynamic microphones are the *moving-coil* microphone and the *ribbon* microphone.

A *moving-coil* microphone (popularly called a dynamic microphone) is diagrammed in Fig. 6-1. In this type of transducer, a coil of wire (attached to a diaphragm) is suspended in a magnetic field. When sound waves vibrate the diaphragm, the coil vibrates in the magnetic field and generates an electrical signal similar to the incoming sound wave. In a *ribbon* microphone, a thin metal foil, or ribbon, is suspended in a magnetic field. Sound waves vibrate the ribbon in the field and generate an electrical signal.

In the *condenser*, or *capacitor*, microphone (Fig. 6-2), a conductive diaphragm and an adjacent metallic disk (backplate) are charged to form

**Fig. 6-1.
Dynamic
moving-coil
transducer.**

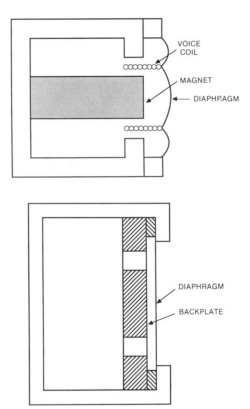

**Fig. 6-2.
Condenser
transducer.**

two plates of a capacitor. Sound waves striking the diaphragm vary the
spacing between the plates; this varies the capacitance and generates an
electrical signal similar to the incoming sound wave. The diaphragm and
backplate can be charged either by an externally applied voltage, or by
a permanently charged *electret* material in the diaphragm or on the backplate. Owing to its lower diaphragm mass and higher damping, a condenser microphone responds faster to rapidly changing sound waves
(transients) than does a dynamic microphone.

The condenser microphone (Figs. 6-3 and 6-4) generally provides a
smooth detailed sound with a very wide frequency response. With a
good condenser microphone, you can hear all the ''ting'' of the cymbals,
or the plucking of each string in a strummed guitar chord. This clear,
detailed sound quality makes the condenser microphone especially suitable for the miking of cymbals, snare drums, acoustic instruments, and
studio vocals.

A condenser microphone requires a power supply to operate, such
as a battery or an external *phantom* power supply. *Simplex phantom power*
is 12- to 48-volts DC applied to pins 2 and 3 of the microphone connector

Fig. 6-3. Audio-Technica AT813 unidirectional electret condenser microphone *(Courtesy Audio-Technica U.S., Inc.).*

Fig. 6-4. Shure SM81 unidirectional electret condenser microphone *(Courtesy Shure Brothers, Inc.).*

through two equal resistors. The microphone receives the phantom power and sends audio signals on the same two conductors. Many mixing consoles supply phantom powering at their mic input connectors; the microphone is simply plugged into the console for its power supply.

By contrast, the moving-coil microphone works without a power supply and provides a reliable signal under a wide range of environmental conditions. A well-designed moving-coil microphone is quite rugged and can accept very loud sounds without overloading. This ability suits it for miking guitar amps and drums.

The moving-coil microphone generally has a slower transient response than the condenser type, so it can be used to soften the fine detail that the condenser picks up. A flat-response moving-coil microphone might be a good choice for woodwinds or brass if you want to take the "edge" off the sound. Moving-coil microphones generally have a rougher response than condenser or ribbon mics, although excellent quality moving-coil units are available.

Ribbon microphones (Fig. 6-5), while more delicate than the moving-coil variety, are often prized for their warm, smooth tone quality. They are typically used on brass instruments to mellow the tone.

Microphone Characteristics

The following section describes several characteristics of microphones to further explain their differences.

Directional Patterns (Polar Patterns)

Microphones differ in the way they respond to sounds coming from different directions. An *omnidirectional* microphone is equally sensitive to sounds arriving from all directions. A *unidirectional* microphone (Fig. 6-6) is most sensitive to sounds arriving from in front of the microphone, but discriminates against sounds entering the sides or rear of the microphone. A *bidirectional* microphone is most sensitive to sounds arriving from in front of and from behind the microphone, but rejects sounds

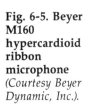

Fig. 6-5. Beyer M160 hypercardioid ribbon microphone *(Courtesy Beyer Dynamic, Inc.).*

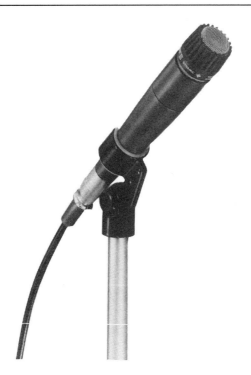

Fig. 6-6. Shure Model SM57 unidirectional dynamic microphone *(Courtesy Shure Brothers, Inc.).*

entering the sides. Fig. 6-7 shows various polar patterns, while Fig. 6-8 shows a multipattern microphone.

The unidirectional classification can be further divided into *cardioid*, *supercardioid*, and *hypercardioid* pickup characteristics. A microphone with a *cardioid* pattern is sensitive to sounds arriving from a broad angle in front of the microphone. It is about 6 dB less sensitive at the sides, and about 15 to 25 dB less sensitive at the rear. The *supercardioid* pattern is 8.5 dB down at the sides and has two nulls of least pickup at 127° off axis. The *hypercardioid* pattern is 12 dB down at the sides and has two nulls of least pickup at 110° off axis. This pattern has the most rejection of leakage and room reverberation of any of the three types.

To hear how a cardioid pickup pattern works, talk into a cardioid microphone from all sides while listening to its output. Your reproduced voice will be the loudest when you talk into the front of the microphone and softest when you talk into the rear. Because they discriminate against sounds that are to the sides and rear, cardioid mics help to reject unwanted sounds, such as room acoustics (reverberation), feedback, or leakage (off-mic sounds from other instruments). Cardioids are the most popular choice for this reason. They provide good isolation or separation between recorded tracks.

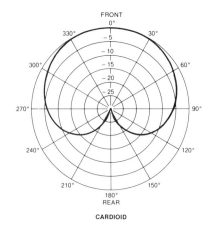

OMNIDIRECTIONAL

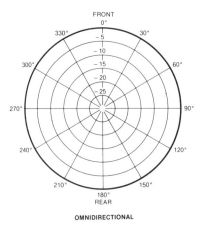

CARDIOID

Fig. 6-7. Various polar patterns. Sensitivity is plotted vs. angle of sound incidence.

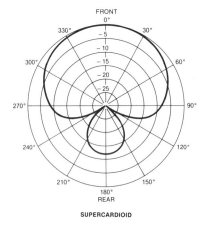

SUPERCARDIOID

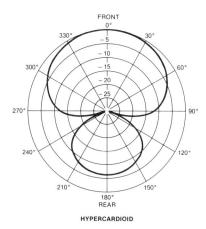

HYPERCARDIOID

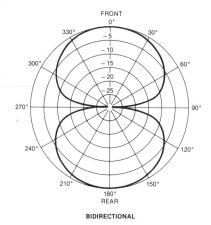

BIDIRECTIONAL

**Fig. 6-8. AKG
C-414EB/P48
multipattern
dual-diaphragm
condenser
microphone**
*(Courtesy AKG
Acoustics Inc.).*

Proximity Effect

Most unidirectional and bidirectional microphones boost the bass when used within a few inches of a sound source. You've heard how the sound gets bassy when a vocalist sings right into the mic. This bass boost related to close mic placement is called *proximity effect*. It occurs in *single-D directional* microphones which have a single distance between the front and rear sound entries.

The warmth created by proximity effect adds a pleasing fullness to the drums. In most recording situations, however, the proximity effect lends an unnatural boomy or bassy sound to the instrument or voice that is picked up by the mic. To minimize proximity effect, some microphones (*multiple-D* or *variable-D* types) are specially designed to reduce it; others have a bass rolloff switch to compensate for the bass boost. Alternatively, you can roll off the excess bass with your mixer's equalizer until the sound is natural. By doing so, you also reduce the low-frequency leakage picked up by the microphone.

Omnidirectional microphones have some characteristics that make them especially useful for certain applications. Use omnidirectional microphones when you need:

- All-around pickup
- Pickup of room reverberation
- Low sensitivity to pop (explosive breath sounds)
- Low handling noise
- No proximity effect (no close-up bass boost)
- Extended low-frequency response (in condenser mics)
- Lower cost in general

Use directional microphones when you need:

- Selective pickup

- Rejection of room acoustics, background noise, and leakage
- Close-up bass boost
- Better gain-before-feedback in a sound-reinforcement system

Note that the condenser or moving-coil types mentioned earlier can be obtained with any kind of directional pattern (except bidirectional moving coil). Ribbon mics are either bidirectional or hypercardioid.

Fig. 6-9 classifies microphones according to transducer type and polar pattern.

Frequency Response

Frequency response is the range of frequencies that a microphone will reproduce at an equal level (within a tolerance, such as ± 3 dB). A frequency response from 50 to 15,000 Hz is good, from 40 to 18,000 Hz is very good, and from 20 to 20,000 Hz is excellent.

If an accurate or natural sound is desired, the frequency response of the microphone should cover the frequency range of the instrument. For example, a trombone radiates frequencies from about 80 Hz to 8000 Hz, so a microphone with a frequency response covering at least this range will pick up all the sounds that a trombone can make. Similarly, an orchestra produces a very wide frequency span, from about 40 Hz (bass drum and bass viol) to 15 kHz or higher (cymbals and other percussion instruments). So, microphones used to record an orchestra (or other large ensemble) should have a wide, flat, frequency response covering most of the audible spectrum.

**Fig. 6-9.
Microphone
categories.**

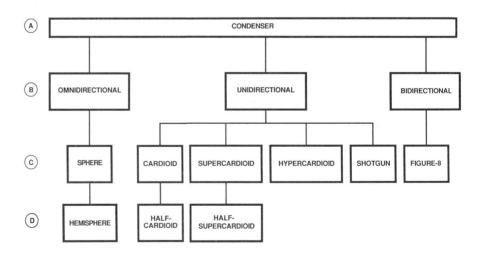

A frequency response from 80 Hz to 15 kHz is adequate for most instruments and a response from 40 Hz to 9 kHz covers the range of the bass instruments, while a high-end response up to 12 kHz is sufficient for brass, voice, and piano. However, a response out to 15 or 20 kHz is necessary for cymbals and some percussion instruments.

The low-frequency response of the microphone should be limited to the lowest fundamental frequency of the instrument to be recorded, if possible. For example, the frequency of the low E string on an acoustic guitar is 82.41 Hz. A mic used on the acoustic guitar should roll off below that frequency to avoid picking up low-frequency noise and room rumble. Some microphones provide a low-frequency cutoff switch for this purpose. Or, you can filter out the unneeded lows at the mixer.

A *frequency-response curve* is a graph of the output level, in dB, at various frequencies. For a microphone, the output level at 1 kHz is placed at the 0-dB line on the graph, and the levels produced at other frequencies are so many dB above or below that reference level. The shape of the response curve usually indicates how the microphone sounds at about 2 to 3 feet. For example, a microphone with a flat extended response reproduces the fundamental frequencies and harmonics in the same proportion as the sound source. Thus, a flat-response mic tends to provide accurate, natural reproduction at that distance.

A microphone with a rising high end or a "presence peak" around 5 to 10 kHz emphasizes the higher harmonics (Fig. 6-10). The subjective effect is a crisp articulate sound. This type of response is sometimes called a "tailored" or "contoured" response. It's popular for guitar amps and drums because it adds punch and emphasizes attack.

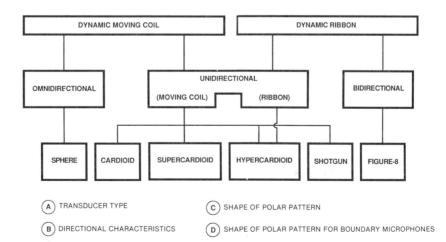

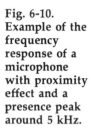

Fig. 6-10.
Example of the
frequency
response of a
microphone
with proximity
effect and a
presence peak
around 5 kHz.

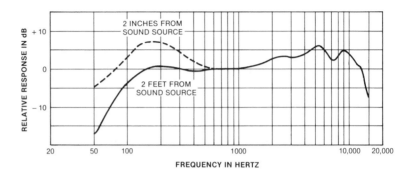

Note that microphone placement can greatly affect the recorded tone quality. A flat-response microphone does not always guarantee high-fidelity sound, because mic placement has such a strong influence. Tonal effects of microphone placement are covered later in the next chapter.

Sensitivity

Sensitivity is a measure of the efficiency of a microphone. A very sensitive microphone produces a relatively high output voltage for a sound source of a given loudness. The sensitivity of a microphone doesn't affect its sound quality. Rather, sensitivity affects the audibility of the mixing-console noise (hiss). To achieve the same recording level, a low-sensitivity mic requires more mixer gain than a high-sensitivity mic. More gain usually results in more noise.

If you record quiet distant instruments, such as a classical guitar or chamber music, you'll hear more mixer noise with a low-sensitivity mic than with a high-sensitivity mic, all else being equal. With close-miked pop music, however, sensitivity matters little because the microphone signal level is well above the mixer noise floor. That is, the signal-to-noise ratio is high.

Microphone sensitivity is often stated in "dB re 1 volt per microbar." This figure tells what voltage the microphone produces (in dB relative to 1 volt) when picking up a 1000-Hz tone at a 74-dB sound-pressure level. The following is a list of the typical sensitivity specs for the three transducer types:

Condenser: −65 dB (high sensitivity)
Moving coil: −75 dB (medium sensitivity)
Ribbon or small moving coil: −85 dB (low sensitivity)

Differences of a few dB among microphones are not critical.

The louder the sound source, the higher the signal voltage that the microphone produces. Very loud sources, such as kick drums or guitar amps, can cause a microphone to generate a signal strong enough to overload the mic preamp in your mixer. That's why input attenuators or pads are included in mixers to reduce the mic signal level from a loud source.

Impedance

The *impedance* of a microphone is its effective output resistance at 1 kHz. A microphone impedance between 150 and 600 ohms is considered low, while 1000 to 4000 ohms is medium, and above 25 kilohms is high. Low-impedance microphones are preferred for recording because they allow long cable runs without causing hum pickup or high-frequency loss. Nearly all solid-state mixers are designed to accept low-impedance mics.

Maximum Sound-Pressure Level

Another microphone specification is *maximum SPL*. To clarify this specification, we first need to explain the term "SPL." SPL or *sound pressure level* is a measure of the intensity of a sound. The quietest sound we can hear, the threshold of hearing, measures 0-dB SPL. Normal conversation at one foot measures about 70-dB SPL; painfully loud sound is above 120-dB SPL.

Maximum SPL is the point at which a microphone's output signal starts to distort; usually, this is the SPL at which the microphone produces 3% total harmonic distortion (THD). If a microphone has a maximum SPL specification of 125-dB SPL, it means that the microphone starts to distort audibly when the sound-pressure level produced by the source reaches 125-dB SPL. A maximum SPL specification of 120 dB is good, while 135 dB is very good, and 150 dB is excellent. Any well-designed dynamic microphone can handle SPLs in excess of 150-dB SPL.

Self-Noise

Self-noise, or *equivalent noise level*, is the electrical noise a microphone produces—equivalent to what a sound source would produce in dB SPL. This figure is usually *A-weighted*, meaning that the noise is measured through a filter that rolls off the low and high frequencies to simulate the frequency response of the ear. A self-noise specification of 20-dB SPL, or less, is excellent (quiet); a specification around 30-dB SPL is good, and a specification around 40-dB SPL is fair.

Output Signal Polarity

Most microphones produce a positive voltage at pin 2 with respect to pin 3 when the sound pressure pushes the diaphragm in (positive pressure). If a microphone is wired in the opposite polarity (check the microphone data sheet) and combined to the same channel, low frequencies in the sound pickup are attenuated or completely cancelled out. To prevent this from happening, check that all your microphones are wired identically, using the following procedure:

1. Choose one microphone as a polarity reference. Plug it into your mixer. Talk into it from about 3 inches away and set the meter to peak around 0 VU. Do the same with a second microphone (and cable) plugged into another input.

2. With both microphones mixed to the same channel, hold the mics together and talk into them again at a distance of 3 inches. If the meter reading is lower, the polarity of the second mic (or cable) is reversed with respect to the reference mic. In that case, remove the connector shell from the second mic's cable and reverse the connections to pins 2 and 3 (in one connector only). Mark the cable and use only that cable with that microphone.

If you can remove the connector in the microphone itself, reverse the connections to pins 2 and 3 for mics that are opposite in polarity to the reference. However, check a few mics before doing this to make sure the reference mic itself isn't backwards.

Special Microphones

The following section describes several types of microphones used for special purposes. These are *boundary* microphones, *miniature* microphones, and *stereo* microphones.

Boundary Microphones

A new kind of microphone is the *boundary microphone*. It's designed to be used on surfaces such as a floor, wall, table, piano lid, baffle, or panel.

One example of such a microphone is the Crown Pressure Zone Microphone PZM®-30F illustrated in Fig. 6-11. It includes a miniature electret condenser capsule that is mounted facedown next to a sound-reflecting plate or boundary. Due to this construction, the microphone diaphragm receives both direct and reflected sounds in-phase at all frequencies, thus avoiding phase interference between them. Fig. 6-12 is a diagram of the construction of a PZM microphone. The claimed benefits are a wide smooth frequency response that is free of phase cancellations, excellent clarity and "reach," a hemispherical polar pattern, and a uniform frequency response anywhere around the microphone.

Fig. 6-11. The Crown PZM®-30F, a boundary microphone *(Courtesy Crown International).*

Fig. 6-12. Typical PZM construction.

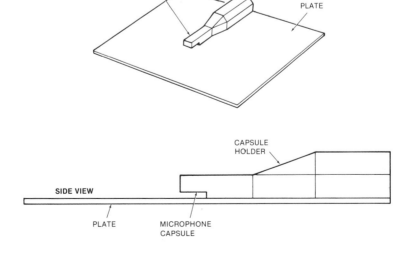

In the studio, a boundary microphone is typically taped to the underside of a piano lid or to a wall for pickup of room ambience. It can be used on hard baffles between instruments, or on a panel to make it directional.

Boundary microphones are also available with a unidirectional polar pattern. They have the benefits of both boundary mounting and the unidirectional pattern. Such microphones are well suited for lecterns, news desks, and the stage-floor pickup of drama or musicals.

Miniature Condenser Microphones

These microphones can be attached to drum rims, flutes, horns, guitars, and so on. Their sound quality is on par with larger studio microphones. With these tiny units (Fig. 6-13), you can mike a live band for recording without cluttering up the stage with boom stands. One or two mini mics can cover a small drum set.

Stereo Condenser Microphone

A *stereo microphone* combines two directional mic capsules in a single housing for convenient stereo recording (Fig. 6-14). Simply place the mic about 10 to 15 feet in front of a band, choir, or orchestra, and you'll get a stereo recording with little fuss. Since there is no spacing between the mic capsules, there also is no delay or phase shift between their signals. Consequently, stereo microphones are mono-compatible; the frequency response is the same in mono and stereo, because there are no phase cancellations if the two channels are combined.

Fig. 6-13. The Crown GLM-100, a miniature condenser microphone *(Courtesy Crown International).*

Fig. 6-14. AKG C422 stereo condenser microphone *(Courtesy AKG Acoustics Inc.).*

Selection Chart

Taking into consideration the various microphone characteristics mentioned previously, the listing in Table 6-1 is a microphone selection guide based on your requirements.

Find your requirements in the left-hand column. For each one, read across horizontally to determine the recommended microphone characteristic. Write down all the recommendations to describe the microphone best suited for your application.

Let's run through some examples to see how the table is used. Suppose you want to record a grand piano, that is playing with several other instruments. You need a microphone to reduce leakage, so you find this requirement in the left column. The table recommends a unidirectional mic or a close-up omnidirectional mic. For this particular piano, you want a natural sound—the table suggests a mic with a flat response. You also want a detailed sound, so a condenser mic is the choice. Thus, a microphone with all these characteristics is a flat-response, unidirectional, condenser mic. If you're miking close to a surface (the piano lid), a boundary mic is recommended.

Now, suppose you're recording an acoustic guitar on stage, where the guitarist roams around. This is a moving sound source, for which the table recommends a miniature microphone attached to the guitar. Since you're miking close, feedback and leakage are not a problem, so you can use an omni mic.

You try an omnidirectional condenser mic. On this particular guitar, it sounds too detailed (too much pick noise and string noise). You want a less detailed sound, so you finally choose a miniature omnidirectional dynamic mic—a good choice for this particular application.

Requirement	Recommended Mic Characteristic
Natural, smooth, tone quality.	Flat frequency response.
Bright, present, tone quality.	Rising frequency response.
Extended lows.	Omnidirectional condenser, or dynamic with extended low-frequency response.
Extended highs (detailed sound).	Condenser.
Reduced "edge" or detail.	Dynamic.
Boosted bass (up close).	Single-D cardioid.
Flat bass response (up close).	Omnidirectional, multiple-D cardioid, or single-D cardioid with bass rolloff.
Reduced pickup of leakage, feedback, and room acoustics.	Unidirectional (or close-up omnidirectional).
Enhanced pickup of room acoustics.	Omnidirectional (or unidirectional farther away).
Miking close to a surface; Even coverage of moving sources or large sources; Inconspicuous microphone.	Boundary mic or miniature mic.
Coincident or near-coincident stereo (see Chapter 18).	Unidirectional mic or stereo mic.
Extra ruggedness.	Moving coil.
Reduced handling noise.	Omni (or unidirectional with shock mount).
Reduced breath popping.	Omni (or unidirectional with pop filter).
Distortion-free pickup of very loud sounds.	Condenser with high maximum-SPL specification, or dynamic.
Noise-free pickup of quiet sounds.	Low self-noise, high sensitivity.

**Table 6-1.
Microphone
Selection Chart**

Microphone Accessories

There are many devices used with microphones to route their signals or to make them more useful. This section describes some of these accessories.

Pop Filter

A much needed accessory for a vocalist's microphone is a foam *pop filter* or *windscreen*. When a vocalist sings a word and emphasizes "p," "b," or "t" sounds, a turbulent puff of air is forced from the mouth. A microphone placed close to the mouth is hit by this air puff, resulting in a "thump" or little explosion called a *pop*. The windscreen reduces this problem. Some microphones have pop filters or ball-shaped grilles built in.

Pop is also reduced by placing the vocalist's mic above or to the side of the mouth, or by using an omnidirectional microphone.

Microphone Stands and Booms

These adjustable devices hold the microphones and let you position them as desired. A *microphone stand* has a heavy metal base that supports a vertical pipe. At the top of the pipe is a rotating clutch that lets you adjust the height of a smaller telescoping pipe inside the larger one. The top of the small pipe has a standard 5/8"-27 thread, which screws into a microphone stand adapter.

A *boom* is a long horizontal pipe that attaches to the small vertical pipe. The angle and length of the boom are adjustable. The end of the boom is threaded to accept a microphone stand adapter, and the opposite end is weighted to balance the weight of the microphone.

Shock Mount

This device mounts on a microphone stand and holds a microphone in a resilient suspension to isolate the microphone from mechanical vibrations, such as stand and floor thumps. The shock mount acts as a spring which resonates at a subaudible frequency with the mass of the microphone. This mass-spring system attenuates mechanical vibrations above its resonance frequency.

Many microphones have an internal shock mount which isolates the microphone capsule from its housing; this reduces handling noise as well as stand thumps.

Cables and Connectors

Microphone cables carry the electrical signal from the microphone to the mixing console or tape recorder. With low-impedance microphones, you can use hundreds of feet of cable with little or no signal degradation. Some microphones have a permanently attached cable for convenience and low cost; others have a connector in the handle to accept a separate microphone cable. The second method is preferred for serious recording because you have to repair or replace only the cable, if the cable breaks, not the whole microphone.

Microphone cables are made of one or two insulated conductors surrounded by a fine-wire shield designed to keep out electrostatic hum. If you hear a loud buzz when you plug in a microphone, check to see that the shield is securely soldered in place.

After acquiring a microphone, you may need to wire its 2-conductor, shielded, balanced-line cable to a 3-pin audio connector. Here's how: Solder the shield to pin 1, solder the hot conductor to pin 2, and then solder the other conductor to pin 3. The hot conductor (specified in the data sheet) produces a positive voltage at the instant that sound pressure pushes the diaphragm inward.

If the microphone output is 3-pin balanced, but your recorder or mixer mic input is an unbalanced phone jack, then a different wiring is needed. Solder the hot conductor to the tip terminal of the phone plug, and solder both the shield and the other conductor to the long ground lug of the phone plug.

Junction Boxes and Snakes

It is messy and time-consuming to run several individual mic cables from the many microphones all the way back to a mixer. Instead, you can plug all the mics in the studio into a junction box that has multiple connectors. Then, a single, thick, multiconductor cable (called a *snake*) carries the signals to the mixer. At the mixer end, the cable is divided into several mic connectors that plug into the mixer.

Splitters

When recording a live band, you need to have each microphone feed its signal simultaneously to your recording mixer and the band's sound-reinforcement mixer. A *microphone splitter* does the job. It has one input for each microphone and two or three isolated outputs per microphone to feed each mixer.

Summary

We've discussed some microphone types, specifications, and accessories. You should now have a better idea about what kind of microphone to choose for your own applications.

There is no one "correct" microphone to use on any particular instrument, because you choose the microphone that sounds best to you. Quality recordings, however, always require quality microphones which have a smooth wide-range response, low noise, and low distortion.

7 MICROPHONE-TECHNIQUE BASICS

Microphone selection and placement—mic technique—greatly affects the sound of a recording. Even if your tape recorder and mixer are the best available, the final result will be poor unless you choose and place your microphones carefully. This chapter covers the general fundamentals; the following chapter will describe techniques for individual instruments.

Microphone Selection

Is there a correct microphone to use in each application? No. Every microphone sounds different, and you choose the microphone that gives you the sound you want. Still, there are some guidelines that apply in most situations, and these were covered in the previous chapter.

To summarize these guidelines, the next two sections give a brief description of how to choose a microphone—based on its frequency response and polar pattern.

Frequency Response

The frequency response of a microphone affects the reproduced tone quality. A flat-response microphone tends to sound natural; a mic with an emphasized high-frequency response sounds brighter or more trebly. A microphone that rolls off below the range of the instrument minimizes pickup of room rumble; a mic that rolls off low frequencies within the range of the instrument tends to sound weak in the bass.

Most condenser microphones have an extended high-frequency response, making them suitable for use with cymbals or other instruments requiring a detailed sound, such as an acoustic guitar, strings, piano, or voice. Dynamic moving-coil microphones have a response that is adequate for drums, guitar amps, horns, and woodwinds.

Polar Pattern

The more ambience that is recorded along with an instrument, the more distant that instrument sounds. And, the more the leakage of an instrument is recorded by other mics, the more distant that instrument sounds. The polar pattern of a microphone affects the amount of leakage and ambience (room reflections) that are picked up.

Because of its greater pickup of ambience and leakage, an omnidirectional microphone sounds more distant than a directional microphone when both are placed the same distance from an instrument. Stated another way, an omnidirectional microphone must be placed closer to an instrument than does a directional microphone to reproduce the same sense of distance.

Quantity of Microphones

The number of microphones required in a session varies with the recording situation. Use just two microphones (or a stereo microphone), as shown in Fig. 7-1, when you want to record an overall acoustic blend of

Fig. 7-1. Overall miking of a musical ensemble using two distant microphones.

the instruments and the room ambience. Many ensembles can be recorded quite well this way. The technique is usually effective for classical orchestras, marching bands, choirs, string quartets, pipe organs, small folk groups, and vocal quartets.

On the other hand, pop-music groups are usually recorded with multiple microphones: one or more for each instrument or instrumental section. Miking every instrument lets you control the *balance* (relative loudness) among the instruments by adjusting the volume control for each microphone at your mixer, as illustrated in Fig. 7-2.

For greatest clarity in a multi-mic recording, use as few microphones as are necessary to get a good sound. Don't use two microphones when one will do the job. To achieve this, you can sometimes cover two or more sound sources with a single microphone, as shown in Fig. 7-3. A brass section of four players can be covered with just one microphone on four players, or with one microphone on every two players.

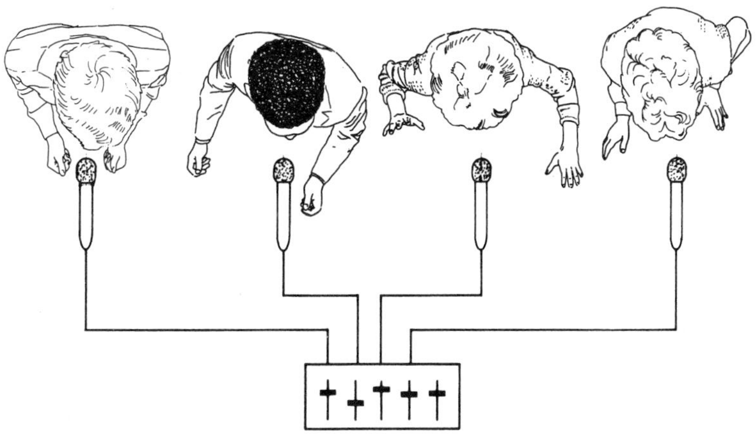

**Fig. 7-2.
Individual
miking using
multiple close-
up microphones
and a mixer.**

**Fig. 7-3.
Multiple miking
with several
sources on each
microphone.**

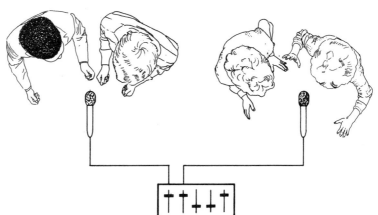

There's a disadvantage, however, in picking up several instruments with one microphone. During mixdown, you can't adjust the balance among instruments recorded on the same track. For a proper blend, the instruments must be balanced acoustically in the studio while making the recording. Instruments that are too quiet should be moved closer to the mic, and vice-versa.

Miking Distance

Suppose you're going to mike a musical instrument. How close do you put the microphone? Let's consider the pro-and-cons of close miking and distant miking.

Close Miking

With close miking, you place the microphone nearer the sound source than the source is big—say, a few inches away.

Close-Miking Advantages

If you put the microphone close, it picks up very little room reverberation, leakage, and background noise. Here's why. The levels of reverberation, leakage, and background noise in a studio are fairly constant with microphone position. But, the closer you place a microphone to a sound source, the louder that source is at the microphone. The direct-sound level increases rapidly as the mic approaches the instrument. Consequently, close mic placement picks up a high ratio of desired signal (the instrument) to undesired signal (ambience, leakage, and noise). The result is a tight, close-up sound with *presence*. This is illustrated in Fig.7-4.

Close-Miking Disadvantages

Although close miking has several benefits, you should place each microphone only as close as necessary, not as close as possible. Miking too close can color the recorded tone quality of an instrument. Why does this occur?

Most instruments are designed to sound best at a distance (at, say, 1½ or more feet away). So, a flat-response microphone placed at that distance tends to pick up a natural or well-balanced timbre (tone quality). But when leakage or poor room acoustics forces you to mike in close, you emphasize the part of the instrument that the microphone is near.

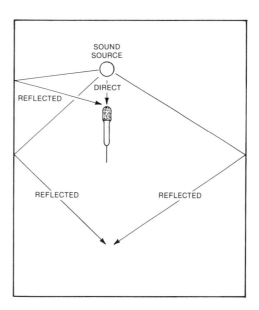

Fig. 7-4. A close microphone picks up mainly direct sound, resulting in a "close" sound quality.

The tone quality that is picked up very close may not reflect the tone quality of the entire instrument.

The sound hole of an acoustic guitar, for example, strongly resonates at around 80 to 100 Hz. A microphone placed close to the sound hole hears and emphasizes this low-frequency resonance, producing a bassy, boomy, recorded timbre that does not exist at a greater miking distance. To make the guitar sound more natural when miked close to the sound hole, you need to roll off the excess bass on your mixer, or use a microphone with a bass rolloff in its frequency response.

In general, close miking may give a tonal imbalance, which you can partially correct with equalization or with careful microphone selection and placement.

Distant Miking

With distant miking, you place the microphone farther from the sound source than the source is big—say, 1½ feet or more away.

Distant-Miking Advantages

Distant mic placement adds a live, loose, airy feeling to a recording. This technique is often used when overdubbing strings and horns, and is sometimes applied to overdubbed vocals, electric-guitar solos, drums, and pianos. Classical music is always recorded at a distance because concert-hall reverberation is a desirable part of the sound.

If you carry distant miking to the extreme, the microphone is called an *ambience microphone*. Such a microphone is placed about 10 feet or more from an instrument in order to pick up more *ambience* (room echoes and reverberation). The microphone is often omnidirectional. Its output is mixed with the usual close-placed microphones, adding an airy or spacious feeling to the sound of the instrument being recorded. Two mics are often used for stereo. In live concert recording, ambience microphones placed over the audience pick up the audience reaction and the concert-hall acoustics.

A natural tonal balance usually can be found at a miking distance that is equal to the size of the instrument. If the situation allows, place the microphone as far from the instrument as the instrument is big. That way, the mic picks up all the sound-radiating parts of the instrument about equally. For example, if the body of an acoustic guitar is 18 inches long, place the mic 18 inches away from the guitar for a natural tonal balance.

Distant-Miking Disadvantages

Suppose the studio acoustics sound bad—the room reflections make the recorded instrument sound muddy. Distant miking picks up a lot of these bad-sounding reflections because the relative level of the direct sound decreases with distance. This is illustrated in Fig. 7-5.

If you want a close up, tight sound with presence, you can't get it with distant miking because of the high ratio of reverberation to direct sound in the recording.

Suppose you're close-miking several instruments simultaneously. Each microphone picks up its own instrument with a close, clear, sound quality. Unfortunately, each microphone also picks up leakage from distant instruments. That nice, tight sound you hear on each mic, alone, may degrade into a distant, muddy sound when all the mics are heard together, due to this leakage. This is illustrated in Fig. 7-6.

When miking many instruments at once, you can reduce leakage pickup by miking each instrument very closely. If you do this, the sound-pressure level at each microphone is high. Then, you can turn down the mixer gain of each microphone signal, which reduces leakage at the same time.

Achieving Depth

By miking each instrument or vocalist at a different distance, you can create a sense of depth in the recording. A close-miked instrument sounds

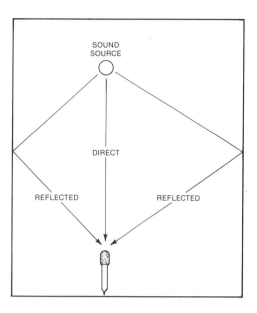

Fig. 7-5. A distant microphone picks up mainly reflected sound, resulting in a "distant" sound quality.

close to the listener (that is, it has presence), while a distant-miked instrument sounds far away.

Using Microphone Placement for Tone Control

A musical instrument radiates different tone qualities in different directions, and produces different tone qualities from different parts of the instrument. Thus, you can partly control the recorded tone quality simply by changing the position of the microphone relative to the instrument. For example, Fig. 7-7 shows the tonal balances picked up at various microphone positions near a guitar.

Other instruments show the same phenomenon. A trumpet radiates strong highs directly out of the bell, but does not project them to the sides. Thus, a recorded trumpet will sound bright when miked on-axis to the bell and will sound more natural or mellow when miked off to one side. A piano miked one foot over the middle strings sounds fairly natural; under the soundboard, it sounds bassy and dull, and, in a sound hole, sounds constricted.

It pays to experiment with all sorts of microphone positions until you find a sound that you like. There is no single right way to place the microphones because you place them to achieve your desired tonal balance.

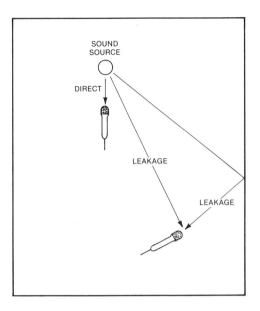

Fig. 7-6. A distant microphone may pick up leakage, changing the "close" sound quality to "distant."

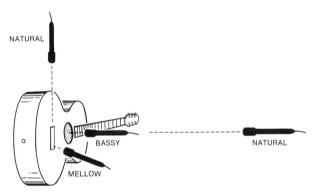

Fig. 7-7. Microphone placement affects the recorded tonal balance.

To determine a good starting microphone position, try closing one ear with your finger. Listen to the instrument with the other ear and move around until you find a spot that sounds good. Put the microphone there. Then, make a recording and see if it sounds the same as what you heard live.

On-Surface Techniques

Sometimes you're forced to place a microphone near a hard reflecting surface. Applications where this might occur include the recording of drama or opera with the microphones near the stage floor, recording an instrument that is surrounded by reflective baffles, or recording a piano with the microphone close to the lid. An unnatural, filtered, tone quality can result. Here's why: In these situations, sound travels to the microphone via two paths: directly from the sound source, and reflected off the nearby surface. Because of its longer travel path, the reflected sound is delayed relative to the direct sound. The direct and delayed sound waves combine at the microphone, resulting in phase cancellations of various frequencies, as shown in Fig. 7-8. The series of peaks and dips in the net frequency response is called a *comb-filter* effect. The recorded tone quality, in this case, can be quite colored; it is similar to that achieved by phasing or flanging.

To avoid the tonal coloration caused by microphones placed near a surface, *boundary microphones* (such as the Crown Pressure Zone Microphone series) have been specially designed for on-surface mounting. They are constructed with the microphone diaphragm very close to the reflecting surface so that there is no delay in the reflected sound. Direct and reflected sounds combine in-phase over the audible range of frequencies, resulting in a flat response (as shown Fig. 7-9).

An omnidirectional boundary mic is often taped to the underside of a piano lid, to a hard-surfaced panel, or to a wall for ambience pickup. A unidirectional boundary mic is commonly used on the stage floor near the footlights, on a lectern, or on a news desk.

The 3:1 Rule

When multiple microphones are mixed to one channel, the distance between microphones should be at least three times the mic-to-source dis-

Fig. 7-8. A microphone placed near a surface picks up direct sound and delayed reflections. The resulting phase interference gives a "comb-filter" frequency response.

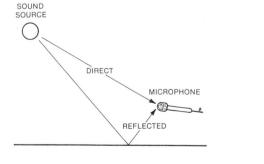

(A) Direct and reflected sound waves.

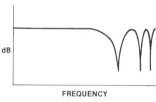

(B) Response curve.

Fig. 7-9. A boundary microphone on a surface picks up direct and reflected sound waves in phase. The resulting lack of phase interference gives a flat response.

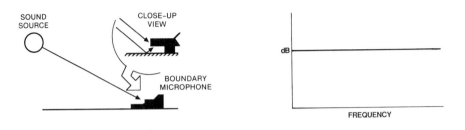

(A) Direct and reflected sound waves.   *(B) Response curve.*

Fig. 7-10. The 3:1 rule of microphone placement avoids phase interference between microphone signals.

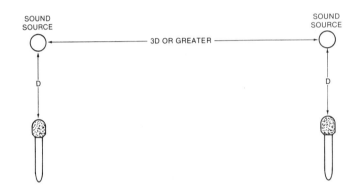

tance. This is called the *3:1 rule* and is illustrated in Fig. 7-10. For example, if two microphones are each placed 1 foot from their sound sources, the microphones should be at least 3 feet apart. Following this rule will prevent phase cancellations and the resulting blurred, colored, sound quality.

If the 3:1 rule is violated (many mics at a distance), clarity is reduced. If the 3:1 rule is followed (fewer mics at a distance, or many mics up close), clarity is enhanced.

Minimizing Off-Axis Coloration

Some microphones have *off-axis coloration*; this is a dull or colored tone quality for those sources that are not directly in front of the microphone. Try to keep the sound source as on-axis as possible, especially if the source radiates strong high frequencies. For a wide-angle sound source, use a microphone that has uniform response over a wide angle. Boundary microphones and miniature microphones have almost no off-axis coloration.

Summary of Mic Techniques

Microphone selection and placement affect two aspects of recorded sound: tonal balance and sense of distance. The frequency response and placement of a microphone affect the recorded tonal balance. The polar pattern and miking distance affect the recorded sense of distance. Follow the 3:1 rule to prevent phase cancellations between microphones, and use boundary microphones to prevent phase cancellations caused by surface reflections. Be aware of off-axis coloration when selecting and placing microphones.

Stereo Microphone Techniques

Stereo microphone techniques capture the sound of a musical ensemble as a whole, using only two or three microphones, and are frequently used to record classical-music ensembles and soloists. During playback of a stereo recording, *phantom images* of the instruments are heard in various locations between the stereo speakers. These image locations—left to right, front to back—correspond to the instrument locations during the recording session.

Stereo miking is also used in the studio for background singers, piano, drum-set cymbals, vibraphone, or other large sound sources.

Goals of Stereo Miking

In stereo miking a large musical ensemble, one objective is *accurate localization*. When this is achieved, instruments in the center of the ensemble are accurately reproduced midway between the two playback speakers. Instruments at the sides of the ensemble are reproduced from either the left or right speaker. Instruments located halfway to one side are reproduced halfway to one side, and so on.

Fig. 7-11 shows three stereo localization effects. In Fig. 7-11A, various instrument positions in an orchestra are shown: left, left-center, center, right-center, right. In Fig. 7-11B, the reproduced images of these instru-

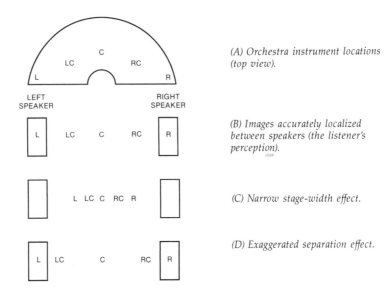

(A) *Orchestra instrument locations (top view).*

Fig. 7-11. Stereo localization effects.

(B) *Images accurately localized between speakers (the listener's perception).*

(C) *Narrow stage-width effect.*

(D) *Exaggerated separation effect.*

ments are accurately localized between the stereo pair of speakers. The *stereo spread*, or stage width, extends from speaker to speaker.

If the microphones are placed improperly, the effect is either the narrow stage width shown in Fig. 7-11C, or the exaggerated separation shown in Fig. 7-11D. (Note that a large ensemble should spread from speaker to speaker, while a quartet can have a narrower spread.)

To judge these stereo localization effects, it's important to position yourself properly with respect to the monitor speakers. Sit as far from the speakers are they are spaced apart. Then, the speakers will appear to be 60° apart, which is about the same angle that an orchestra fills when viewed from the typical ideal seat in the audience (say, tenth row center). Sit exactly between the speakers (equidistant from them); otherwise the images will shift toward the side on which you're sitting and will become less sharp.

Types of Stereo Microphone Techniques

There are three microphone techniques commonly used for stereo recording: the coincident-pair, the spaced-pair, and the near-coincident-pair technique. Let's look at each in detail.

Coincident Pair

With the coincident-pair (or X-Y) method, two directional microphones are mounted with their grilles touching and their diaphragms placed one above the other, angled apart to aim approximately toward the left and right sides of the ensemble, as illustrated in Fig. 7-12. For example, two cardioid microphones can be mounted so that their grilles are touching but angled apart. Other directional patterns can be used, too. The greater the angle between microphones, the wider the stereo spread.

Now, let's examine how the coincident-pair technique produces localizable images. As described in Chapter 6 on microphones, a directional microphone is most sensitive to sounds in front of the microphone (on-axis) and progressively less sensitive to sounds arriving off-axis. That is, a directional mic produces a relatively high-level signal from the sound source it's aimed at, and produces a relatively low-level signal for all other sound sources.

The coincident-pair method uses two directional mics symmetrically angled from the center line, as shown in Fig. 7-12. Instruments in the center of the ensemble produce an identical signal from each microphone. During playback, a phantom image of the center instruments is heard midway between the stereo pair of loudspeakers. That's because identical signals in each channel produce a centrally located image.

If an instrument is off-center to your right, it is more on-axis to the right-aiming mic than to the left-aiming mic. So the right mic will produce a higher-level signal than the left mic. During playback of this recording, the right speaker will play at a higher level than the left speaker; this reproduces the image off-center to your right—where the instrument was during recording.

The coincident array codes instrument positions into level differences between channels. During playback, the brain decodes these level differences back into corresponding image locations. A pan pot in a mixing console works on the same principle. If one channel is 15 to 20 dB louder

Fig. 7-12. Coincident-pair technique.

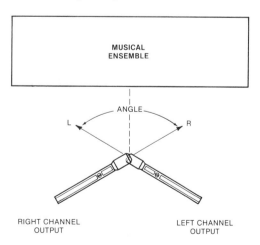

than the other, the image shifts all the way to the louder speaker. So, if we want the right side of the orchestra to be reproduced at the right speaker, the right side of the orchestra must produce a signal level 20 dB higher from the right mic than from the left mic. This occurs when the mics are angled apart sufficiently. The correct angle depends on the polar pattern.

Instruments part-way off center produce interchannel level differences less than 20 dB, so they are reproduced part-way off center.

Listening tests have shown that *coincident cardioid microphones* tend to reproduce the musical ensemble with a narrow stereo spread. That is, the reproduced ensemble does not spread all the way between speakers.

A coincident-pair method with excellent localization is the *Blumlein array*, which uses two bidirectional mics angled 90° apart and facing the left and right sides of the ensemble.

A special form of the coincident-pair technique is the *Mid-Side (MS) recording method* illustrated in Fig. 7-13. A unidirectional, omnidirectional, or bidirectional microphone facing the middle of the orchestra is summed and differenced with a bidirectional microphone aiming to the sides. This produces left- and right-channel signals. With this technique, the stereo spread can be remote controlled by varying the ratio of the mid signal to the side signal. This remote control is useful at live concerts, where you can't physically adjust the microphones during the concert. MS localization accuracy is excellent.

To make coincident recordings sound more spacious, boost the bass 4 dB (+2 dB at 600 Hz) in the L-R or side signal. [1]

Stereo microphones include two coincident microphone capsules mounted in a single housing for convenience. A recording made with

Fig. 7-13. Mid-side technique.

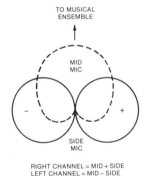

TO MUSICAL ENSEMBLE

MID MIC

SIDE MIC

RIGHT CHANNEL = MID + SIDE
LEFT CHANNEL = MID − SIDE

1. David Griesinger, "Spaciousness and Localization in Listening Rooms and Their Effects on the Recording Technique," *Journal of the Audio Engineering Society*, Vol. 34, No. 4, April, 1986, pp. 255-268.

coincident techniques is *mono-compatible;* i.e., the frequency response is the same in mono or stereo. Because of the coincident placement, there is no time or phase difference between channels to degrade the frequency response if both channels are combined to mono. If you expect your recordings to be heard in mono (say, on the radio), then consider coincident methods.

Spaced Pair

With the spaced-pair (or A-B) technique, two identical microphones are placed several feet apart, and aimed straight ahead toward the musical ensemble, as in Fig. 7-14. The mics can have any polar pattern, but the omnidirectional pattern is most popular for this method. The greater the spacing between microphones, the greater the stereo spread.

When using the spaced-pair technique, instruments in the center of the ensemble produce an identical signal from each microphone. During playback of the recording, a phantom image of the center instruments is heard midway between the stereo pair of loudspeakers.

If an instrument is off-center, it is closer to one mic than the other, so its sound reaches the closer microphone before it reaches the farther mic. Consequently, the microphones produce approximately an identical signal, except that one mic signal is delayed with respect to the other. If you send an identical signal to two stereo speakers with one channel delayed, the sound image shifts off center. With a spaced-pair recording, off-center instruments produce a delay in one mic channel, so they are reproduced off center.

The spaced-pair array codes instrument positions into time differences between channels. During playback, the brain decodes these time differences back into corresponding image locations.

It takes only one to two milliseconds of delay to shift an image all the way to one speaker. So, if we want the right side of the orchestra to be reproduced at the right speaker, its sound must arrive at the right mic

**Fig. 7-14.
Spaced-pair
technique.**

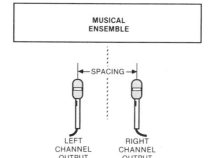

about one to two milliseconds before the sound reaches the left mic. In other words, the mics should be spaced about two to three feet apart, because this spacing produces the appropriate delay needed to place right-side instruments at the right speaker. Instruments that are partway off center produce interchannel delays of less than one to two milliseconds, so they are reproduced partway off-center.

If the spacing between microphones is, say, 12 feet, then instruments slightly off-center will produce interchannel delays greater than one millisecond, which places their images at the left or right speaker. This could be called an "exaggerated separation" or "ping pong" effect. On the other hand, if the mics are too close together, the delays produced will be inadequate to provide much stereo spread. In addition, the mics will tend to favor the center of the ensemble because the mics are closest to the center instruments. Therefore, we need to place the mics about 10 or 12 feet apart to record a good musical balance, but such a spacing results in exaggerated separation. One solution is to place a third microphone midway between the outer pair and mix its output to both channels. That way, the ensemble is recorded with a good balance and the stereo spread is not exaggerated.

The spaced-pair method tends to make off-center images relatively unfocused or hard-to-localize, because spaced-microphone recordings have time differences between channels, and stereo images that are produced solely by time differences are unfocused. Centered instruments are still heard clearly in the center, but off-center instruments are difficult to pinpoint between the speakers. This method is useful, however, if you prefer the sonic images to be diffused, rather than sharply focused (say, for a blended effect).

There's another problem with spaced microphones. The large time differences between channels correspond to gross phase differences between channels. Out-of-phase low-frequency signals can cause excessive vertical modulation of the record groove, making records difficult to cut unless the cutting level or stereo separation is reduced. In addition, combining both mics to mono sometimes causes phase cancellations of various frequencies, which may or may not be audible.

There is an advantage with spaced miking, however. Spaced microphones are said to provide a "warm" sense of ambience in which concert-hall reverberation seems to surround the instruments and, sometimes, the listener. Here's why: The two channels of recorded reverberant sound are *incoherent*; that is, they have random phase relationships. Incoherent signals from stereo loudspeakers sound diffuse and spacious. Since reverberation is picked up and reproduced incoherently by spaced microphones, it sounds diffuse and spacious. The simulated spaciousness caused by out-of-phase signals is not necessarily realistic, but it is pleasant to many listeners.

Another advantage of the spaced-microphone technique is the ability to use omnidirectional microphones. An omnidirectional condenser microphone has more extended low-frequency response than a unidirectional condenser microphone, and it tends to have less off-axis coloration.

Near-Coincident Pair

As shown in Fig. 7-15, the near-coincident technique uses two directional microphones angled apart, with their grilles horizontally spaced a few inches apart. Even a few inches of spacing increases the stereo spread and adds a sense of ambient "warmth" or "air" to the recording. The greater the angle or spacing between mics, the greater the stereo spread. This method works by angling the directional mics, which produces level differences between the channels, and by spacing the mics, which produces time differences. The interchannel level differences and time differences combine to create the stereo effect. If the angling or spacing is too great, exaggerated separation results. If the angling or spacing is too small, the result is a narrow stereo spread.

The most common example of the near-coincident method is the ORTF system, which uses two cardioid mics angled 110° apart and spaced 7 inches (17 cm) apart horizontally. ORTF stands for *Office de Radiodiffusion-Television Française,* or French Broadcasting Network. This method tends to provide accurate localization; instruments at the sides of the orchestra are reproduced at or very near the speakers, and instruments halfway to one side tend to be reproduced halfway to one side.

Fig. 7-15. Near-coincident-pair technique.

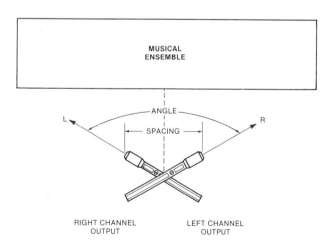

Comparing the Three Techniques

The coincident-pair technique has the following features:

- Uses two directional mics that are angled apart, with grilles touching.
- Level differences between channels produce a stereo effect.
- Images are sharp.
- Stereo spread ranges from narrow to accurate.
- Signals are mono compatible.

The spaced-pair technique has these features:

- Uses two mics that are spaced several feet apart.
- Time differences between channels produce the stereo effect.
- Off-center images are diffused.
- Stereo spread tends to be exaggerated unless a third center mic is used.
- Provides a warm sense of ambience.
- May cause record-cutting problems.

The near-coincident-pair technique has these features:

- Uses two directional mics that are angled apart and spaced a few inches apart.
- Level and time differences between the channels produce the stereo effect.
- Images are sharp.
- Stereo spread tends to be accurate.
- Provides a greater sense of "air" than the coincident methods do.

Mounting Hardware

When you use coincident and near-coincident techniques, the microphones should be rigidly mounted with respect to each other so that they can be moved as a unit without disturbing their arrangement. A device used for this purpose is called a *stereo microphone adapter* or *stereo bar*. It mounts two microphones on a single stand; microphone angling and spacing are adjustable.

Microphone Requirements

The sound source dictates the requirements of the recording microphones. Most acoustic instruments produce frequencies from about 40 Hz (string bass and bass drum) to about 20,000 Hz (cymbals, castanets, triangles). A microphone with uniform response between these frequency limits will do full justice to the music. The highest octave from 10 kHz to 20 kHz adds transparency, air, and realism to the recording. You may need to roll off frequencies below 80 Hz to eliminate rumble from trucks and air conditioning, unless you want to record organ or bass drum fundamentals.

Sound from an orchestra or a band approaches each microphone from a broad range of angles. To reproduce all the instruments' timbres equally well, the microphone should have a broad, flat response at all angles of incidence within at least ±90°. Stated another way, the polar pattern should be uniform with frequency. For sharp imaging, the microphone pair should be well matched in frequency response, phase response, and polar pattern.

We've investigated several microphone arrangements for recording in stereo. Each has its advantages and disadvantages. Which method you choose depends on the sonic compromises you are willing to make.

8 MICROPHONE TECHNIQUES

This chapter explores various recording techniques for musical instruments and vocals. After trying these suggestions, experiment with your own techniques. From time to time, this chapter will refer to various signal-processing devices, such as noise gates, etc. These are discussed in detail in Chapter 10.

Electric Guitar

The electric guitar can be recorded in many ways, as shown in Fig. 8-1:

- With a microphone placed in front of the guitar amp
- With a direct box
- Both miked and direct
- Through a signal processor.

The style of music you're recording suggests the appropriate method. Miking the amp is best when you want a rough, raw sound, including the tube distortion and speaker coloration. Rock 'n' roll or Heavy Metal music usually sounds best with a miked amp. Recording with a direct box, on the other hand, sounds clean and clear, with extended highs and lows. It might be the best method for quiet jazz or R&B. Use whatever sounds right for the particular song being recorded.

The recorded guitar should sound full-range, so that you will have something to work with later in the mixdown. The highs should be bright, but not too bright; the lows should be warm, but not muddy.

Work first on reducing any hum heard through the guitar amp. Set the guitar volume and treble controls up full for the best signal-to-noise ratio. Have the guitarist move around to find a null spot in the room where hum disappears. Flip the polarity switch on the amp to the lowest

**Fig. 8-1.
Recording an
amplified-
instrument
system.**

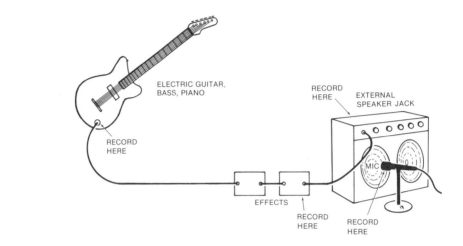

hum position. Also, you may want to try a noise gate to remove buzzes between guitar notes.

Miking the Amp

Small practice amplifiers are generally better for recording than large, noisy, stage amplifiers. If you use a small amp, place it on a chair to avoid picking up reflections from the floor.

The most popular microphone choice for an electric guitar is a cardioid dynamic type with a presence peak in the frequency response (a boost around 5 kHz). The cardioid pattern reduces leakage; the dynamic transducer withstands high sound-pressure levels without distorting, and the presence peak adds punch. Of course, you can use any mic that sounds good to you. A flat-response condenser mic provides a natural sound for quieter guitar parts.

For starters, mike the amp from about one inch to one foot away, with the microphone aimed at the center of one of the speaker cones. The closer the mic is placed to the amp, the bassier is the tone, and the less ambience and leakage are picked up. Placement in front of the center of the speaker cone sounds bright; off-center placement sounds more mellow and reduces amplifier hiss.

You may want to put three mics side-by-side in front of the amp, plus a boundary microphone on the floor. Then, switch between the mics while listening to the guitarist play, and choose the best-sounding microphone. Another method is to mike the speaker front-and-back with a polarity reversal in the second mic line.

If you're overdubbing a lead guitar that is played through a huge stack of speakers in an acoustically live room, you may want to mike the amp at a distance. A dynamic microphone placed five feet away can be mixed with boundary microphones on the control-room window for ambience.

During overdubs, communications are easier if the musician is in the control room with the engineer. You still can record the guitar amp in the studio while the guitarist is playing in the control room. Here's how:

1. Plug the guitar directly into the mixing console or through a direct box into a console mic input.

2. Then, use the cue knob of that input to send the guitar signal to the headphone junction box in the studio.

3. Patch the junction box into the guitar-amp input (keeping the cue level moderate).

4. Mike the amp.

5. Monitor and record the microphone signal.

Recording Direct

Now let's consider recording *direct* (also known as *direct injection* or *DI*). The electric guitar produces an electrical signal, so it can be plugged right into the mixing console—no microphone is needed. Since the mic and guitar amp are bypassed, the sound is clean and clear; it lacks the distortion and coloration of the amp. But remember that amplifier distortion is desirable in some songs.

If you can use a short cable from the guitar to the mixer, and your mixer has a high-impedance unbalanced mic input, you can then plug directly into the mixer. If your mixer has 3-pin balanced mic inputs, you will need a *direct box*, such as illustrated in Fig. 8-2. This converts the

Fig. 8-2. Sketch of a typical direct box front panel.

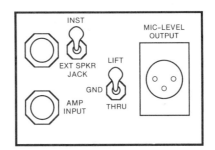

high-impedance unbalanced guitar signal to the low-impedance balanced signal required by the mixer.

Plug the electric guitar into the direct box, and plug the direct box into a microphone input. Some direct boxes let you record off the amplifier's external-speaker jack to pick up distortion. These boxes often include a low-pass filter to simulate the frequency response of the guitar-amp speaker. The direct box should have a ground-lift switch to prevent ground loops and hum. Set it to the lowest hum position (usually lifted).

An inexpensive direct-connection cable was described in Chapter 2. This cable connects between the amplifier speaker jack and a mixer mic input. When you use such a cable, roll off the highs at your mixer to take the edge off the sound (as the guitar-amp loudspeaker does).

Recording Direct from the Guitarist's Effects Boxes

If you want to record the guitarist's special effects, connect the output of the effects boxes into the direct box input. Some engineers like to record a combination of direct sound and miked sound.

Studio Effects with an Electric Guitar

Often a thick or spacious lead-guitar sound is desired. One way to get it is to send the guitar signal through a delay unit that is set for a few milliseconds delay. Pan the direct signal left and the delayed signal right. Or, send the guitar signal to a harmonizer for a slight pitch change. Delay the pitch-shifted signal by 15 to 20 msec, and then pan it to the right, and pan the direct signal to the left. Adjust the direct and delayed levels to spread the guitar between your monitor speakers.

Still another way to thicken the sound is to double the guitar. Have the player re-record the same part in sync with the original part. Pan the original part left and pan the doubled part right. Or, plug the guitar cord into a "Y" adapter that feeds both the guitar amp recorded on a track panned left and the amplifier input of a Leslie organ speaker recorded on another track which is panned right. You'll hear a spacious, swirling sound. Other popular effects are reverberation, stereo chorus, and extreme compression.

There are guitar-level signal processors (such as The Rockman by Tom Scholz) that add many different effects to an electric guitar, such as distortion, equalization, chorus, and compression. You simply plug the electric guitar straight into the Rockman, adjust the switches for the desired sound, and record the signal direct from the Rockman. You wind up with a fully produced sound with a minimum of effort.

Electric Bass

Now let's consider the electric bass guitar. As always, you first work on the sound of the instrument itself. Put on new strings if the old ones have become dull-sounding. Adjust the pickup screws (if any) for equal output from each string. Also adjust the intonation and tuning.

The electric bass is almost always recorded direct for the cleanest possible sound. A direct pickup provides deeper lows than a miked amp, but the amp gives more midrange punch. A combination of direct and miked sound provides clarity and a deep low end. The microphone can be a condenser or dynamic type, with a good low-frequency response, and placed one inch to one foot away from the amplifier/speaker.

When combining a direct signal with a microphone signal, make sure they are in-phase with each other. To do this, set them to equal levels and reverse the polarity of either the direct signal or the microphone signal. The polarity that gives the most bass is correct.

Once you're satisfied with the basic pickup, have the musician play some scales to see if any notes are louder than the rest. You may be able to set a parametric equalizer to reduce the level of those notes.

The bass guitar should be fairly constant in level (a dynamic range of about 6 dB) to be audible throughout the song, and to avoid saturating the tape on loud peaks. To achieve this, the bass guitar signal is often run through a compressor, as described in Chapter 10. Set the compression ratio to about 4:1; set the attack time fairly slow (8–20 milliseconds) to preserve the attack transient, and set the release time to fairly fast (¼ to ½ second). If the release time is too fast, however, harmonic distortion will occur.

Equalization can increase the clarity of the bass guitar. It often helps to cut at 125 Hz to 400 Hz, and/or boost at 1500 Hz to 2000 Hz.

Here are some tips on keeping the bass sound both clean and well defined:

- Record the bass direct.
- Use no reverb or echo on the bass.
- Try not to record a lot of extreme low frequencies—they are difficult to put on a record and won't be heard on most systems.

- Have the bass player turn down the bass amp in the studio; adjust it to just loud enough to play adequately. This reduces muddy-sounding bass leakage into other microphones.
- Better yet, don't use the amp. Instead, have the musicians monitor the bass (and each other) with headphones.
- Have the bass player try new strings or a different guitar.
- If it suits the song, the bass player can mute the strings with the side of the hand and play with a pick for extra definition.
- Ask the bass player to use the treble pickup near the bridge.

If the bass part is full and sustained, it's probably best to de-emphasize the "pluck" and let the kick drum define the rhythmic pattern. But if the bass and kick drum both are rhythmic and work independently, then the plucks should be audible. Listen to the song first, and then get a bass sound appropriate for the music.

To make an electric bass sound like an acoustic bass, mike the amp to pick up cabinet vibrations and use a noise gate or expander with a rapid decay, as described later in Chapter 10.

You might also want to try a bass guitar signal processor, such as the Bass Rockman. It has separate 3-position switches for equalization, chorus, and sustain, as well as a high-frequency compressor and a peak clipper.

Leslie Organ Speaker

This device contains a rotating horn on top for highs and a woofer on the bottom for lows. A typical recording technique is to mike the top and bottom separately, from a few inches to a foot away. Aim the top mic into the louvers. It's often effective to record the rotating horn in stereo with a microphone on either side, or by using boundary microphones inside the cabinet.

Electric Keyboards

Electric pianos, synthesizers, and drum machines are usually recorded direct for maximum clarity. If the instrument has an unbalanced high-impedance output, use a direct box into a mixer mic input. Note that some inexpensive mixers and recorder/mixers have unbalanced high-impedance inputs, which can accept a keyboard signal through an ordinary cable. If the instrument has a balanced low-impedance output, use a microphone cable with appropriate adapters between the instrument and mixer. Record both outputs of stereo keyboards.

If the keyboard player has several keyboards plugged into his or her own mixer, you may want to record a premixed signal from that mixer's output.

The Drums

Let's look at some recording techniques for a drum set next. The first step is to make the live sound of the drums sound good in the studio. If the set itself sounds bad, you'll have a hard time making it sound good in the control room.

The drum set is often put on a 1½-foot-high riser to reduce bass leakage and to provide better eye contact between the drummer and the rest of the band. To reduce drum leakage into other mics, 4-foot-tall goboes are often placed around the drum set. For more isolation, the set is placed in a *drum booth*—a small padded room with large windows.

Tuning

One secret of creating a good drum sound lies in careful tuning. Getting a good sound onto tape will be much easier if you tune the set to sound right in the studio before miking it.

Drum Heads

First, a word about drum heads. Plain heads have maximum ring or sustain, while hydraulic heads or heads with sound dots dampen the ring. Thin heads provide a sharp attack, good sustain, and weak projection. Thick heads have a duller attack, rapid decay, and strong projection. Old used heads tend to become dull and muffled, while new heads sound crisp.

Tom-Toms

The following is one suggested tuning procedure for tom-toms. First, take off the heads and remove the damping mechanism—a possible source of rattles. Put just the top head back on and hand-tighten the lugs. Then, using a drum key, tighten opposite pairs of lugs one at a time, one full turn. After all lugs have been tightened in this manner, repeat the process, tightening one-half turn. Then, apply heavy pressure to the head to stretch it. Continue tightening one-half turn at a time until you reach the desired pitch.

You'll get the most pleasing tone when the heads are tuned within the range of the shell reinforcement. One popular tuning procedure sets the pitch just below the middle of the range of the drum.

Leave the bottom head off the drum if you want best projection and the broadest range of tuning. In this case, pack the bottom lugs with felt to prevent rattles.

However, you may want to add the bottom head for extra control of the sound. Projection is best if the bottom head is tighter than the top head—say, tuned a fourth above the top head. There will be a muted attack, an "open" tone, and some note bending. If you tune the bottom head looser than the top head, the tone will be more "closed," with good attack.

Kick Drum

For the kick drum (bass drum), a loose head gives lots of slap and attack, and almost no tone. The opposite is true for a tight head. Tune the head to complement the style of music. A hard beater also adds attack.

Snare Drum

Tune the snare drum with the snares off. A loose batter head or top head gives a deep, fat sound. A tight batter head sounds bright and crisp. With the snare head or bottom head loose, the tone is deep with little snare buzz, while a tight snare head yields a crisp snare response. Set the snare tension just to the point where the snare wires begin to "choke" the sound, and then back off a little.

Sometimes a snare drum buzzes in sympathetic vibration with a bass guitar passage or a tom-tom fill. You may be able to control the buzz by wedging a thick cotton wad between the snares and the drum stand. Experiment with the position and thickness of the wad for best results.

Damping and Noise Prevention

If the tom-toms or snare drum ring excessively, tape some gauze pads or folded handkerchieves to the edge of the heads. Put the tape on three sides of the pad so that the untaped edge is free to vibrate and dampen the head motion. Don't overdo the damping, or the drum set will sound like cardboard boxes.

To reduce excessive cymbal ringing, apply drafting tape in radial strips from the bell to the rim. Also, oil the kick-drum pedal to prevent squeaks, and tape rattling hardware in place with drafting tape.

Miking the Drum Set

Now you're ready to mike the set. For a tight sound, place the mics very close to the edge of each drum head. For a more open airy sound, move the mics back a few inches, use fewer mics, or mix in some room mics (such as boundary mics or omni condensers) placed several feet away. Sometimes a jazz drum set can be miked adequately with two overhead mics and one kick-drum mic. Fig. 8-3 shows typical microphone placements for a drum set. This figure will be referred to often in the following text.

The following is a detailed description of typical miking techniques for each element of the drum set.

Snare Drum

Bring the mic in on a boom from the front of the set. Place it about one inch above the rim (or one inch in from the rim), and angled down to aim at the spot where the drummer hits (as shown in Fig. 8-4).

You may want to aim the snare mic partly toward the hi hat to pick up both instruments on one microphone. *Caution:* Every time the hi hat closes, it produces a puff of air that can "pop" the snare drum mic. Place the snare drum mic so that it is not hit by this air puff. Either a cardioid condenser or cardioid dynamic microphone will work fine—use whichever sounds best for the tune being recorded. Most mics with a cardioid pattern have proximity effect, which boosts the bass up close and adds fullness to the snare beat.

If you want to mike the snare and hi hat separately, bring the boom in under the hi hat, and aim the snare mic away from the hi hat for better isolation.

An alternative technique is to tape a miniature condenser mic to the side of the snare drum so it "looks at" the top head over the rim.

Some engineers like to mike both the top and bottom heads of the snare drum, with the microphones in opposite polarity. A mic under the snare drum gives a zippy sound; a mic over the snare drum gives a fuller sound.

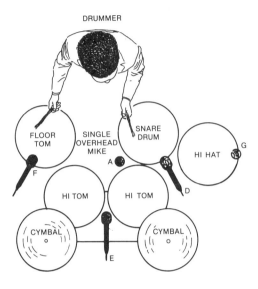

Fig. 8-3. Typical microphone placements for a drum set.

(A) Top view.

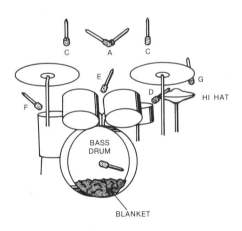

(B) Front view.

Hi Hat

Usually, the snare mic or ambience mics pick up enough hi hat sound, but if you want to mike the hi hat separately, try placing a cardioid condenser microphone about 6 inches above the edge of the hi hat, and aimed at the side farthest from the drummer (Fig. 8-5). To avoid the air puff just mentioned, don't mike the hi hat off of its edge; mike it from above, while aiming down.

If the hi hat needs more sizzle, try boosting a little at 10 or 12 kHz.

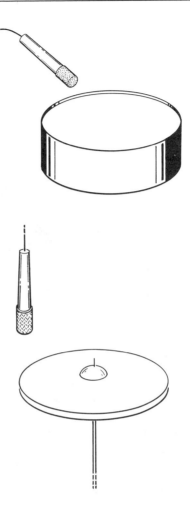

Fig. 8-4. Typical mic placement for a snare drum.

Fig. 8-5. Typical mic placement for a hi hat.

Toms-Toms

Tom-toms can either be miked individually, or with one mic between each pair of toms. One typical technique uses a cardioid dynamic or condenser mic, which is placed one inch above the rim (or about two inches in from the rim), and angled down about 45° toward the drum head, as shown in Fig. 8-6. Again, the cardioid's proximity effect gives a full sound. An alternative setup is to tape mini condenser mics to the toms, and have them just peeking over the top rim of each drum. Or, you might try a bidirectional microphone placed between two tom-toms.

Tom-tom mics often pick up too much leakage from the cymbals, and this is sometimes heard as a low tone. To reduce cymbal leakage and improve isolation, take the cardioid tom-tom mics and aim their "dead" rear ends at the cymbals. Note that a supercardioid or hyper-

Fig. 8-6. Typical mic placement for a tom-tom.

cardioid mic is partially sensitive to sounds arriving from the rear, and should be placed so that the null of greatest rejection aims at the cymbals.

Another way to reduce cymbal leakage is to remove the bottom heads from the toms and mike them inside, a few inches from the head and off-center, as shown in Fig. 8-7. This also keeps the mics out of the drummer's way. The sound picked up inside the tom-tom has less attack and more tone than the sound picked up outside.

Fig. 8-7. Mic placement for a tom-tom that is miked inside.

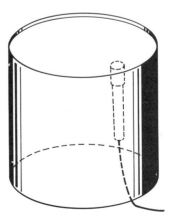

Kick Drum

Place a blanket inside the drum, pressing against the beater head to dampen the vibration and tighten the beat. The blanket shortens the decay portion of the kick drum envelope.

The microphone commonly used in the kick drum is a cardioid dynamic type with an extended low-frequency response. For starters, place it inside the drum, on a boom, and just a few inches from where the beater hits, as illustrated in Fig. 8-8. Mic placement that is close to the beater picks up a hard beater sound; off-center placement picks up more skin tone, and a mic placed farther away picks up a boomier shell sound.

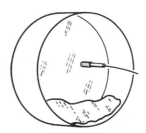

Fig. 8-8. Typical mic placement for a kick drum.

Alternatively, a miniature omnidirectional condenser microphone can be hung inside near the beater for a clearly defined attack.

Cutting equalization at 300 to 600 Hz helps to remove the "cardboard" sound, and boosting the signal several dB at 2.5–5 kHz adds attack, "click," or "snap."

How should the recorded kick drum sound? Well, they don't call it *kick* drum for nothing. *THUNK!*—a powerful low-end thump plus an attack transient.

Cymbals

Place overhead mics (cardioid condenser types) about one to three feet above the cymbal edges; closer miking will pick up a low-frequency ring. Two mics placed overhead can aim straight down, or can be angled apart for better isolation, as in Fig. 8-9. For mono compatibility, mount the mic grilles together and angle the mics apart, as in Fig. 8-3, position "A."

Place the cymbal microphones to pick up all the cymbals equally. Usually not much gain is needed on the overhead mics, since the cymbals leak into the drum mics. Recorded cymbals should sound crisp and smooth, not sizzly or harsh.

Ambience

In addition to the close-up drum microphones, you might want to use a distant ambience microphone when recording drum overdubs. Place the

Fig. 8-9. Typical cymbal overhead mic placement.

mic about 10 to 20 feet from the set to pick up room reverberation. When mixed with the close-up mics, this gives an open, loose, airy sound to the drums. Two microphones are usually used for stereo. You can use omnidirectional condenser microphones or boundary mics attached to the control-room window. Sometimes ambience mics are heavily compressed for special effect.

Boundary Microphone Techniques

Boundary microphones permit some unusual arrangements for drum-set miking. You can strap one onto the drummer's chest to pick up the set as the drummer hears it, or tape them to hard-surfaced goboes surrounding the drummer, or put them on the floor under the toms and near the kick drum.

Recording with Three Microphones

If you're limited in the number of microphones you can spare for the drums, the setup illustrated in Fig. 8-10 uses only two miniature omnidirectional condenser mics and one kick drum mic. This method works well for small drum sets.

1. Tape or clip one mini microphone near the left-rack tom and the snare drum. (This mic picks up the hi hat, the snare drum, the left-rack tom, and the cymbals.)

2. Tape or clip another mini mic near the right-rack tom and the floor toms. (This mic picks up the right-rack tom, the floor tom, and the cymbals.)

3. Place the third mic inside the kick drum.

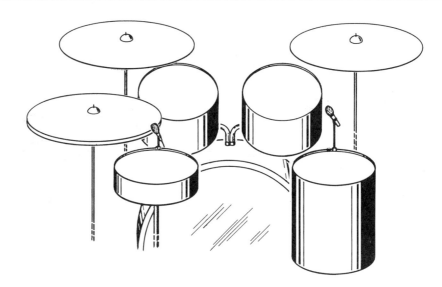

Fig. 8-10. Miking a small drum set with three microphones (one microphone goes inside the kick drum).

With a little bass and treble boost, you'll be surprised at the good sound and even coverage achieved with this simple setup.

Recording with Two Microphones

Here's an even simpler method for mono miking a small set. With some bass and treble boost, the sound can be quite adequate.

Clip a miniature omnidirectional condenser mic to the snare drum rim. Locate it about four inches above the rim, in the center of the set, and aimed at the hi hat, as seen in Fig. 8-11. Put another mic inside the kick drum.

Drum Recording Tips

After all the drum microphones are set up, ask the drummer to play. Listen for rattles and leakage by soloing each microphone. Try not to spend more than 10 or 20 minutes getting a sound on the drums; otherwise, you waste the other musicians' time and wear out the drummer.

To keep the drum sound tight, turn off all the mics not in use in a particular tune, or use a noise gate on each drum mic.

An interesting effect on the snare drum is gated reverberation. There is a short splash of bright-sounding reverberation, which is rapidly cut off by the noise gate or expander. (This is described in Chapter 10.) To gate the reverberation, patch a noise gate into the reverberation-return signal line and adjust the gate for the desired effect.

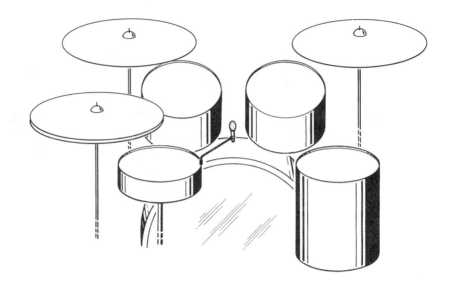

Fig. 8-11. Miking a drum set with two microphones. One is clipped onto the snare drum rim. The other goes inside the kick drum.

Electronic drums (such as Simmons) or drum machines (such as LinnDrum) are recorded direct into the console for maximum clarity. If the drum machine sounds too mechanical, you can make the sound more interesting by combining real drum sounds with the machine's signal. The machine can play a steady background while the drummer does other things.

When miking drums on stage for sound reinforcement, you don't need a forest of unsightly mic stands and booms. Instead, you can use short microphone holders that clip onto drum rims and cymbal stands, or you can use miniature condenser microphones.

Various equalizer settings can enhance the recorded sound of the drums:

- Boost at around 200 Hz for fullness on the snare drum and high toms, and at around 100 Hz on the floor toms. Or, use a cardioid microphone up close for its bass-boosting proximity effect.

- Roll off some bass on the snare for extra clarity.

- Boost at 5 kHz (or use a mike with a presence peak) on the snare and toms for attack and crispness.

- Boost at 10 kHz or higher on the cymbals for brilliance and sizzle, and filter out the frequencies below about 500 Hz on the cymbals to minimize the pickup of low-frequency leakage.

- Boost around 2.5 kHz on the bass drum for punch, and filter out the frequencies above about 5 kHz on the bass drum to reduce leakage from the cymbals.

Drum Set Leakage Comparisons

As an experiment, try miking the drum set with a single microphone in various positions, and note the level of the high tom-tom in each position. The following results were obtained in one such test:

Microphone Placement	Tom-Tom Level
2 feet over the cymbals	0 dB
In the center of the set near the snare	+8 dB
2 inches over the tom-tom rim	+18 dB
Inside the tom-tom on the shell, 1 inch from the head	+36 dB

As these measurements indicate, miking a drum set from overhead with a single microphone provides poor isolation from the other instruments. That is, if a single overhead mic is used, the pickup of the drum set is relatively weak compared to the leakage. Miking from the center of the set, near the snare drum, rejects leakage and ambience by 8 dB compared to overhead miking. The result is a tighter sound. Thus, this near-the-snare pickup with one microphone might be a simple, inexpensive way to mike the drum set for demo recording or sound reinforcement.

Miking the tom-tom from just over the rim reduces leakage by another 10 dB (because the tom-tom is 10 dB louder there), and miking it inside reduces leakage by an additional 18 dB.

Percussion

Percussion instruments in addition to the drum set are a challenge to record accurately. Miking techniques for several of these instruments are described next.

Triangle, Tambourine, Guiro, Maracas, and Claves

The transient clarity of a quality condenser microphone makes it a good choice for many percussion instruments. Mike them from at least one foot away to prevent overloading the mic, itself, or use a dynamic microphone with an extended high-frequency response.

Congas, Bongos, and Timbales

These double drums can be covered using a single microphone between the pair of drums. A single-D moving-coil microphone, with a presence peak, gives a full sound with a clear attack.

Xylophone and Vibraphone

A popular mic technique for these instruments uses two cardioid microphones (condenser or dynamic) aimed at the instrument from about 1½ feet above it, either crossed at about 135° or spaced about 2 feet apart. This arrangement allows a stereo effect and provides good coverage of the entire instrument. Miking the instrument from underneath loses attack and picks up leakage.

Acoustic Guitar

The acoustic guitar has a delicate timbre which we try to capture through careful microphone selection and placement.

Preparation

First prepare the guitar for recording. Use strings designed to reduce finger squeaks, if possible. For maximum brilliance, replace old strings with new ones. Experiment with different kinds of guitars, picks, and finger picking to achieve a timbre suitable for the song.

Microphone Choice

A condenser microphone with a smooth, extended frequency response (from 80 Hz up) is often preferred for the acoustic guitar. Such a microphone typically gives a clear, detailed quality, in which the plucking of each string is audible within a strummed chord. The reproduced sound usually has all the crispness of the live instrument.

The clear pickup of string noise, however, can be distracting in some songs. You can diminish this fine detail by using a dynamic microphone, which usually has a slower *transient response* (the ability to follow sudden changes in acoustic pressure).

Effects of Various Microphone Positions

Miking Near the Sound Hole

If you've ever miked an acoustic guitar close to the sound hole (as in Fig. 8-12)—a popular microphone position—you've probably noticed that the recorded guitar doesn't sound much like the real thing. The recording sounds too bassy, boomy, and thumpy. This is mainly because the sound hole and the air inside the guitar resonate at low frequencies (around 80 to 100 Hz). A microphone placed close to the sound hole (or in it) picks up and emphasizes this resonance, giving a bassy character to the recorded guitar.

**Fig. 8-12.
Acoustic guitar
miked close to
the sound hole.**

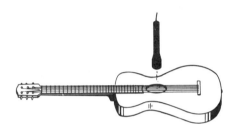

Why, then, is a guitar commonly miked close to the sound hole? On stage, this microphone position provides maximum loudness before feedback occurs. In the studio, it provides maximum isolation (minimum leakage pickup). The acoustic guitar, being a relatively quiet instrument, often requires such a technique to prevent feedback and to reject leakage.

To achieve a more natural sound in this microphone position, roll off the low frequencies on your mixer (say, about 10 dB or more at 100 Hz).

Contact Pickups

Best isolation—sometimes at the expense of fidelity—is achieved with a contact pickup, which attaches to the body of the guitar. For a starting point, place the pickup on or next to the bridge and adjust the position from there. Positioning a contact pickup is critical; a movement of a fraction of an inch can change the sound drastically. Each instrument has a different best location for the pickup, and every brand of pickup sounds different. Multiple pickups, or a pickup and a microphone, can be mixed.

Miniature Microphone Placement

A miniature omni condenser microphone taped to the guitar provides good fidelity. A typical mounting position is halfway between the sound hole and the bridge, near the low E string (as illustrated in Fig. 8-13). For more isolation, tape a miniature directional mic in the sound hole and roll off the bass on your mixer.

Miking for a Natural Timbre

If leakage is not a problem (as during an overdub), a more natural sound can be achieved by miking the guitar at a distance—say, 1½ feet from the sound hole (as in Fig. 8-14). At this position, the microphone picks up a well-balanced blend of all the parts of the guitar: strings, soundboard, and sound hole. A closer placement that also provides a bright, realistic sound is 6 inches over the top of the guitar, over the bridge, and even with the front soundboard, as shown in Fig. 8-15. You may be pleasantly surprised with the sound you get with this technique.

Miking for a Mellow Timbre

A woody, mellow, tone quality is picked up by a microphone that is placed about 4 inches in front of the bridge (as in Fig. 8-16). Here the vibrations

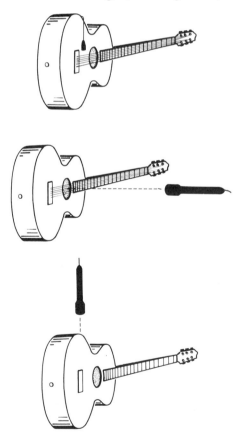

Fig. 8-13. Suggested placement of a mini microphone for recording an acoustic guitar.

Fig. 8-14. An acoustic guitar miked at 1½ feet from the sound hole.

Fig. 8-15. An acoustic guitar miked from 6 inches over the top, over the bridge, and even with the front soundboard.

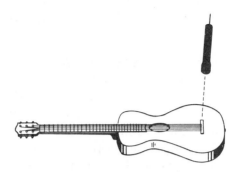

Fig. 8-16. An acoustic guitar miked from 4 inches in front of the bridge.

of the soundboard are emphasized, starting around 200 Hz. This position also reduces the pickup of string and pick noise.

Classical Guitar Solos

When recording a classical guitar solo, use distant microphone placement to capture the room acoustics or the reverberation—a desirable part of the sound of classical music. Record in a recital hall or another warmly reverberant room. Place the microphone about 3 to 8 feet away—closer to reduce reverberation, farther to increase it.

For a more realistic sense of space or "air" surrounding the soloist, record in stereo. Angle two cardioid microphones 90° apart and space their grilles about 8 inches apart, as shown in Fig. 8-17. If you are forced to record a classical guitar in an acoustically dead room, try miking the guitar as shown in Figs. 8-13, 8-14, and 8-15. Add artificial reverberation with your mixer.

Fig. 8-17. A stereo miking technique.

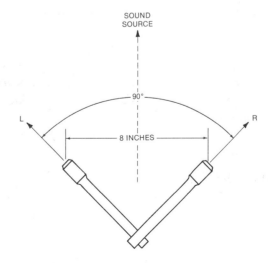

The Banjo

The banjo uses a "drum head" to couple the string vibrations to the air. The center of the head vibrates mainly at the head's fundamental frequency, while the harmonics of the head vibration are strongest near the edge. Sometimes, the lower notes are reinforced by holes in the flange surrounding the head. To pick up a natural blend of all the parts of the banjo, place a flat-response microphone about 1 foot away. Positioning the microphone close to the center of the head produces a rather harsh, thumpy sound (unless you roll off the bass), but provides good isolation. The sound becomes thinner toward the edge of the head.

You can tape a miniature omni condenser microphone to the drum head, about 1 inch in from the bottom edge for maximum isolation, or you can clip the microphone onto the tailpiece, aiming toward the bridge. As a starting placement for a contact pickup, wedge the pickup between the strings and the head, behind the bridge. The pickup should be flat against the banjo head.

Mandolin, Dobro, and Fiddle

These instruments are constructed somewhat like the acoustic guitar, so many of the microphone techniques for the guitar are applicable.

When played, the fiddle or violin radiates high frequencies upward best. Consequently, the audience usually hears a duller sound from the violin than the violinist hears. When close miking the violin, you can avoid the harsh, bright sound that the violinist hears by aiming the microphone at the side of the violin. A microphone with a response down to 200 Hz is sufficient.

Another technique that works very well is to clip a miniature microphone to the violin's tailpiece and mount it a few inches from an f-hole or over the bridge. You can even clip it to the strings on the player's side of the bridge. A suggested pickup placement for a fiddle is on the left side of the top (player's view), on the player's side of the bridge.

The Grand Piano

The piano is difficult to record so that it sounds realistic. One reason is that it is such a big, complex sound source (5 to 9 feet long). The natural sound of a piano, as heard at a distance, is a blend of the individual sounds of its many parts: the strings, hammers, soundboard, and lid. Close miking, however, emphasizes the part of the piano that the microphone is near. An unnatural recorded timbre can result.

To further complicate matters, combinations of sounds from various areas and the sound reflections from the lid cause acoustic phase cancellations that vary with microphone placement. Lid reflections arrive off-axis at the microphone, sometimes producing coloration. In addition, a piano has sharp attack transients that can saturate the recording tape unless it is recorded at lower than normal levels. All these factors make the piano a challenge to record without distortion or coloration.

Distant Miking

Here's one way to record the piano as an audience hears it: Set the piano lid on the long stick. Place a pair of flat-response cardioid condenser microphones, as in Fig. 8-17, about 6 to 12 feet away from the open lid, and at a height of about 6 feet. Then, record in stereo. This method is useful for taping either piano solos or overdubs. A classical piano solo should be recorded in a reverberant locale, such as a recital hall or concert hall.

Close Miking

In pop-music recording, the piano is miked closer, to increase clarity and reduce pickup of room acoustics and leakage. But try not to mike the strings closer than from 8 inches away, since doing so emphasizes the strings closest to the microphone. You want equal coverage of all the notes that the pianist plays.

There are many ways to close mike a piano. Experiment to see which works best for the particular song and instrument you're recording.

Spaced Microphones

One popular miking method uses two spaced microphones inside the piano, with the lid raised on the long stick (or even removed). One microphone goes about 8 inches over the treble strings and about 8 inches horizontally from the hammers. The other microphone is placed over the bass strings, at a height of about 8 inches and about 2 to 4 feet from the hammers (as noted in Fig. 8-18 by position A). These microphone signals are panned partly toward the left and right for a stereo effect.

Fig. 8-18. Some close-miking positions for a piano.

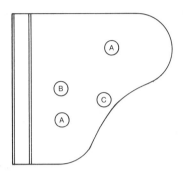

Alternatively, two boundary microphones can be taped to the underside of the piano lid—over the bass and treble strings, or they can be taped to the inside of the front edge. Close the lid, if necessary, for more isolation.

Coincident Microphones

The spaced microphones can cause phase cancellations when mixed to mono, so you might want to try coincident miking. Mount a single microphone or a pair of cardioids that are crossed at 120°, and position them about 1 foot over the middle of the piano, at about 8 inches from the hammers (as in Fig. 8-18, position B). The closer to the hammers that the microphones are placed, the more percussive the attack and the greater the isolation. So, if the sound is too "bangy" and lacks tone, move the microphones away from the hammers and toward the tail of the piano.

Again, you might want to tape a boundary microphone to the underside of the piano lid (in the middle), and close the lid if leakage is excessive.

Sound-Hole Miking

Putting a microphone over a sound hole, with the piano lid on the long stick, provides good isolation and yields a punchy, constricted sound which can be effective for rock music (position C, Fig. 8-18,). Each hole emphasizes the strings closest to it.

For best isolation, aim a microphone into a sound hole, close the lid, and cover the piano with heavy blankets. The tone quality will be unnatural, so you'll have to experiment with equalization if you want a more realistic sound. Special contact pickups for pianos are available to further increase isolation.

Bright Sound

Often a bright piano sound is desired. You can improve clarity, sharpness, and attack by boosting frequencies around 5 kHz on your mixer, by using a microphone with a presence peak, or by sticking thumbtacks into the hammer felt. This last method gives a tinkly, player piano sound.

The Upright Piano

As with a grand piano, each microphone placement for the upright piano produces a different tone quality. The following suggestions are just a few of the possible miking locations.

Distant Miking

The upright piano is not normally miked at a distance because it is not a classical music instrument. Distant miking of an upright piano, in a small room, tends to sound muddy.

Close Miking

The following suggestions provide a variety of piano tonal balances, all with a clear close-up perspective. Experiment to find the method most suited to the particular song you're recording.

Miking the Kick-Board Area

For a natural sound, remove the kick board in front of the piano to expose the strings. Place one mic near the bass strings and one near the treble strings, at about 8 inches away. Record in stereo and pan the signals left and right for the desired piano width. If you can spare only one microphone for the piano, just cover the treble strings.

Miking Over the Top

Place two microphones just over the open top, one over the bass strings and one over the treble strings. The tone quality is somewhat colored with this technique.

Boundary Miking

Place a boundary microphone about 1 foot from the soundboard on the floor, either on the player's side or on the back side.

Miking the Soundboard

To reduce excessive hammer attack, place a pair of microphones about 8 inches from the soundboard, covering the bass and treble sides. The soundboard should be facing into the room, not into a wall.

Miking for Isolation

For extra isolation, place two microphones inside the open top of the piano. Or tape two mini omnidirectional condenser mics to the soundboard and experiment with their positioning for best results. Another alternative is to tape two boundary microphones to the wall—one inch from the soundboard.

The Strings

Not many home studios record string sections. But if you want to add some string sweetening during an overdub session, here are some suggested techniques.

String Section

Place the strings in a large hard-surfaced room that has noticeable reverberation, and mike the strings at a distance to pick up a natural acoustic sound. Condenser microphones with a flat-frequency response are usually preferred. For two violins, try one microphone about 6 feet off the floor, aiming down between the players. The viola and cello can each be miked from the side, at about 2 feet from the f-hole. For added definition on the cello, mike it about 1 foot from the bridge.

Acoustic Bass

The acoustic bass (string bass, double bass, upright bass, or bass viol) can be recorded in several ways. This instrument produces frequencies as low as 41 Hz, so use a microphone with an extended low-frequency response. For a well-defined sound, place the microphone a few inches out front, above the bridge. Aim it into the treble f-hole for a fuller sound. As always, watch out for *proximity effect* with a closely placed cardioid microphone.

Here are several techniques to increase isolation and allow the performer freedom of movement. They are useful in sound-reinforcement situations:

- Wrap a miniature omni condenser microphone in foam rubber (or in a foam windscreen) and mount it in an f-hole.

- Wrap a regular microphone in foam padding (except for the front grille) and squeeze it behind the bridge or between the tailpiece and the body.

- Try a direct feed from a pickup. This method provides clarity and "bite," but has an "electric" sound. Also wrap a condenser lavalier mic in foam and stuff it in an f-hole. Mix this microphone with the pickup to round out the tone. You may need to roll off the bass of the f-hole microphone. Try flipping the polarity of the mic and use whichever polarity sounds best.

Large Ensembles

Large string ensembles can be covered with one microphone for every four violins and violas, one for every two celli, and one for the acoustic bass. For miking a string section on-location with minimal leakage, try a bidirectional mic over the section aiming down.

Achieving Stereo Spread

When you mix all the signals of the strings to stereo, pan them evenly between the monitor speakers. Spread them left, center, and right to achieve a "curtain of sound." A simpler stereo recording method uses just two microphones which are spaced 3 to 5 feet apart to pick up the whole ensemble. If you can spare only one track for the strings, you can make that track simulated-stereo in the mixdown. To do this:

1. Pan the track to the left channel.
2. Simultaneously send it through a 20-millisecond delay.
3. Pan the delayed signal to the right channel.
4. Adjust the relative levels of the direct and delayed signals to achieve a stereo spread from speaker to speaker.

String Quartet

A string quartet can be recorded in stereo using the microphone place-ment illustrated in Fig. 8-17. Place the microphones about 6 to 10 feet away from the quartet to capture the room ambience. A limited stereo spread, rather than a speaker-to-speaker spread, is sometimes preferred for a string quartet. To reduce the width of the stereo stage, reduce the angle or spacing between the microphones.

Bluegrass Band

A small Bluegrass or Old-Time Music string band might be covered with a stereo microphone or with two cardioid mics placed as shown in Fig. 8-17. Arrange the group in a semi-circle with the microphone(s) about 3 feet away. Try to record in an acoustically dead room for clarity, and adjust balances by moving the musicians toward or away from the mics. If the results are poor, try miking the instruments and voices individually, up close, and use a mixer.

The Harp

A harp can be covered by a microphone aimed toward the treble part of the soundboard from the front, at a distance of about 1½ feet (if the harp is playing with an orchestra), or at a greater distance for a harp solo.

For best isolation, tape a miniature omni condenser microphone to the soundboard. Or, put some C-Ducer tape on the soundboard with some added reverberation. (C-Ducer tape is a strip of plastic that picks up mechanical vibrations and produces a corresponding electrical signal.) Also, try a bidirectional mic and orient it vertically along the axis of the strings, with the null of the bidirectional pattern pointing at the undesired source.

The Brass

These instruments (trumpets, cornets, trombones, and tubas) radiate strong high-frequency harmonics directly out of the bell, but do not project them to the sides. A microphone placed close to, and in front of, the bell picks up a brighter, more "edgy" tone than what the audience usually hears. To soften the tone and restore the natural horn sound, try miking the bell at an angle with a flat-response microphone, as illustrated in Fig. 8-19. Or mike it on-axis with a ribbon microphone, which typically provides a smooth sound. Use a condenser microphone to reproduce a lot of sizzle.

The waveform of a trumpet on-axis has strong spikes that can overload a condenser mic and saturate recording tape. This is another reason for miking the trumpet off-axis. Close microphone placement (about 1 foot) gives a tight sound; distant placement (about 5 feet) yields a fuller, more dramatic sound.

Fig. 8-19. Miking for trumpet tone control (top view).

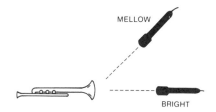

MELLOW

BRIGHT

It's common to mike two or more horns with one microphone. Several players can be grouped around a single omnidirectional microphone, or around a cardioid microphone placed below the group and aimed upwards. Alternatively, the musicians can play to a boundary microphone taped on the control-room window or on a large panel.

The Woodwinds

With woodwinds, most of the sound radiates not from the bell, but from the holes. So, aim a microphone at the holes from about 1 foot away. A flat-response dynamic microphone is typically used.

When miking a woodwind section within an orchestra, you need to reject the nearby leakage from other instruments. To do this, try aiming a bidirectional mic down over the woodwind section. The side nulls of the microphone minimize leakage.

The Saxophone

A sax miked very near the bell, as in Fig. 8-20, sounds bright, breathy, and rather hard. Mike it there for best isolation. A mic placed off to the

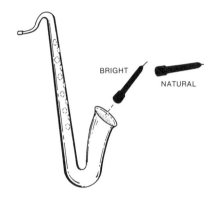

Fig. 8-20. Two
ways to mike a
saxophone.

Fig. 8-21. One
effective
microphone
arrangement for
flute miking.

side picks up a quiet sound with poor isolation. For a natural tonal balance, mike the sax from about 1½ feet away, aiming at the player's left hand, and about one-third to one-half of the way down the wind column. Don't mike too close or else the level varies when the player moves. A compromise position for a close-up microphone might be just above the bell, aiming at the holes. A sax section can be grouped around a single microphone.

The Flute

One effective microphone placement for the flute, as shown in Fig. 8-21, is a few inches from the area between the mouthpiece and the first set of finger holes. However, a pop filter may be needed. If you want to reduce breath noises, roll off the high frequencies or mike from farther away. For classical music solos, try a stereo pair of microphones placed 5 to 8 feet away.

The Harmonica

A popular technique for the harmonica uses a cardioid dynamic microphone (with a ball grille) placed very close to the harmonica. (Sometimes, the mic is held by the player.) For a bluesy, dirty sound, use a "bullet" type of harmonica mic or play the harmonica through a miked guitar amp. A condenser mic placed about 1 foot away yields a natural sound.

Vocals

Vocal recording presents a number of problems. Among these are proximity effect, pop, wide dynamic range, sibilance, and sound reflections from the lyric sheet. Let's look at these in detail.

Minimizing Proximity Effect

A vocalist on stage has to sing with his or her lips touching the microphone grille to reduce feedback. Singing or talking close to a cardioid microphone boosts the low frequencies due to proximity effect. The result is a bassy, boomy tone quality that we've come to accept as a standard sound-reinforcement vocal sound. During a recording session, this effect may add robustness to a weak voice; but, normally, the vocalist should back off at least 8 inches from the microphone to restore the natural tone quality. Vocals are typically overdubbed at a distance of about 8 to 24 inches with a flat-response condenser microphone, as shown in Fig. 8-22.

Close Miking

If you must record the vocalist simultaneously with the instruments, as in a live recording, you'll probably have to mike him or her very close so that the accompanying musical instruments don't leak into the vocal microphone. A cardioid microphone with a pop filter is useful here. To reduce the boominess caused by a close-up mic placement, roll off the excess bass on your mixer (typically -8 dB at 100 Hz). Some microphones have a built-in bass rolloff switch for this purpose. Aiming the microphone up toward the singer's nose will avoid a nasal or "closed-nose" effect.

Fig. 8-22.
Typical miking
technique for a
lead vocalist.

Minimizing Pop

When a vocalist sings a word with "p" or "t" sounds in it, a turbulent puff of air is forced from the mouth. A microphone placed near the mouth is hit by this air puff and generates an undesirable thump or little explosion called a *pop*. It can be reduced by placing a foam-plastic *pop filter* (*windscreen*) on the microphone. Some microphones have a built-in ball grille screen for pop suppression.

Although these devices reduce pop, they do little to minimize breathing sounds or lip noises. Distant miking or some high-frequency rolloff can help with these problems.

Foam pop filters should be made of special open-cell foam to allow high frequencies to pass through. For this reason, it's better to use a commercially made foam screen than to make one yourself from packing foam, cloth, or socks. Allow a little air space between the foam front and the microphone grille for best pop rejection.

Since most pop filters slightly change the frequency response of a microphone, they should be left off of microphones intended for instruments, except when used for outdoor recording or dust protection.

A very effective way to eliminate popping is to place the microphone well above the singer's mouth level, as in Fig. 8-22. This way the puffs of air shoot under the microphone and miss it. Or, you can place the microphone off to one side of the mouth, as shown in Fig. 8-23.

Reducing Wide Dynamic Range

Vocalists often sing too loudly or too softly during a song, either blasting the listener or getting buried in the mix. That is, singers generally have

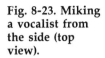

Fig. 8-23. Miking a vocalist from the side (top view).

MUSIC SHEET IS
ANGLED AWAY FROM
MICROPHONE

a wider dynamic range than their instrumental backup. To even out these extreme level variations, the vocalist should use proper mic technique; backing away from the microphone on loud notes, coming in closer for soft ones. Or, you can *ride gain* on the vocalist: gently turn him down as he gets louder, and vice versa. The best solution is to pass the vocal signal through a *compressor*, a device that automatically reduces the dynamic range. (Compressors are described in greater detail in Chapter 10.)

A microphone placed close to the mouth is very sensitive to small changes in miking distance. The singer's loudness will fluctuate if he fails to keep a constant distance from the microphone, or if he fails to use the mic technique mentioned above. For this reason, it's better to mike the singer from at least 8 inches away. Small movements of the singer cause less change in loudness at that distance. If you must mike close to prevent leakage, have the singer's lips touch the pop filter to maintain a constant distance to the microphone.

Minimizing Sibilance

Sibilance is the emphasis of "s" or "sh" sounds. These sounds are strongest in the 5- to 10-kHz range, and can easily saturate a tape running at 7½ ips if not controlled.

To reduce excessive sibilance, use a microphone with a flat response—rather than one with a presence peak—or reduce the highs at around 5 kHz on your mixer. A *de-esser* device does this automatically whenever sibilant sounds occur. As an alternative, mike the vocalist from the side rather than in front, as illustrated in Fig. 8-23. The "s" sounds are projected more out front than they are to the sides.

Reducing Reflections from the Lyric Sheet

Sound reflections from the lyric sheet and music stand can bounce into the microphone along with the direct sound from the vocalist, as shown in Fig. 8-24. The reflections interfere with the direct sound, creating a colored tone quality similar to mild phasing or flanging.

To eliminate this effect, place or tape the lyric sheet at the rear of the vocalist's cardioid microphone, perpendicular to the microphone axis, as shown in Fig. 8-22. Or, mike the vocalist from the side, and angle the lyric sheet slightly away from the microphone, as shown in Fig. 8-23. In the first arrangement, reflections entering the rear of the cardioid microphone are rejected. The second method makes reflections bounce away from the microphone.

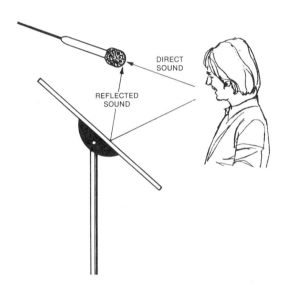

Fig. 8-24.
Reflections from
a music stand
can cause
interference.

Vocal Effects

Some effects often used on lead vocals are reverberation, echo, and doubling. Room reverberation sometimes can be recorded live by miking the singer at a distance in a hard-surfaced, echoey room. Tape echo (or slap echo on a delay unit) gives a 1950's rock 'n' roll effect. It sounds less mechanical if some highs are rolled off the echo signal.

Doubling a vocal provides a fuller sound than does a single vocal track. Record a second take of the vocal on an empty track at a slightly different miking distance. During mixdown, mix the second vocal take with the original, at a slightly lower level than the original. Or, you can run the vocal signal through a delay device to double it (as described in Chapter 10).

Equalization

Vocals typically are boosted slightly in the presence range between 2 kHz and 5 kHz to help them stand out against an instrumental track. This boost may increase sibilance as well.

Classical Solos

When recording a classical music singer, place the microphone(s) about 3 to 8 feet away to pick up the room reverberation. You may also want to use a boundary microphone on the floor.

Background Vocals

When overdubbing background vocals, you can group two or three singers in front of a microphone. The farther they are from the microphone, the more distant they will sound in the recording. Barbershop or gospel quartets with a good natural blend can be recorded with the stereo setup seen in Fig. 8-17 (or with a stereo microphone). Mike from about 2 to 4 feet away. If their balance is poor, try miking them individually up close, with omnidirectional microphones, and balance them with your mixer.

Summary

Microphone placement can be summed up as follows. In general, if leakage or feedback is a problem, you place the microphone close to where the sound output is loudest. Otherwise, you place the microphone in several different positions until you find a location where you can monitor the desired tone quality and desired amount of ambience.

There is no single "correct" microphone technique for any instrument because you place the mic where you hear a tonal balance and ambience pickup that you like. You can find that spot more quickly if you understand microphone characteristics and instrument sound-radiation patterns.

We've covered some typical microphone techniques for musical instruments and vocals. These are just suggestions to serve as a starting point. After trying them out, invent your own techniques. If you can capture the power and excitement of amplified instruments and drums, if you can capture the beautiful timbre of acoustic instruments and vocals, you've made a successful recording.

9 TAPE RECORDING

Thanks to the tape recorder, an event as fleeting as a musical performance can be permanently captured and relived. This chapter explains several areas related to tape recording:

1. The analog tape recorder; its parts, functions, and operation, plus preventive maintenance.
2. Noise-reduction systems.
3. Tape handling, storage, and editing.
4. The digital tape recorder.

The Analog Tape Recorder

During the recording process, a tape recorder converts electrical signals into permanent magnetic signals on magnetic tape. The tape itself is a strip of plastic, usually mylar, with a thin coating of ferric oxide or chromium dioxide particles. These particles have a random magnetic orientation, but they can be aligned into magnetic patterns by the external magnetic field that is applied during recording. During playback, the tape machine converts the magnetic field of the particles on the tape back into an electrical signal.

Recorder Parts and Functions

The tape recorder has three main parts: the heads, the electronics, and the transport.

- The *heads* are electromagnets that convert electrical signals to magnetic fields, and vice versa.

- The *electronics* amplify and equalize the signals going to and from the heads.

- The *transport* pulls the tape past the heads, which contact the tape.

Let's look at each of the three main parts in detail.

The Heads

Most tape recorders include three heads (Fig. 9-1) placed left to right as follows: erase, record, and playback. Some recorders have a single head that combines the record and playback functions.

The *erase head* produces an ultrasonic, oscillating, magnetic field. As the tape passes over the erase head, the tape is exposed to a gradually decreasing magnetic field. This orients the magnetic particles randomly and erases any signal on the tape.

The *record head* converts the incoming electrical signal into an analogous varying magnetic field. As the tape passes the record head, the head magnetizes or aligns the tape particles in a pattern that corresponds to the audio signal. This pattern is then stored permanently on the tape.

The pattern stored on a tape is a magnetic field. As the tape passes the *playback head*, the head picks up this magnetic field pattern and converts it back into a corresponding electrical signal. This electrical signal is amplified and sent to speakers, the mixing console, or another tape deck.

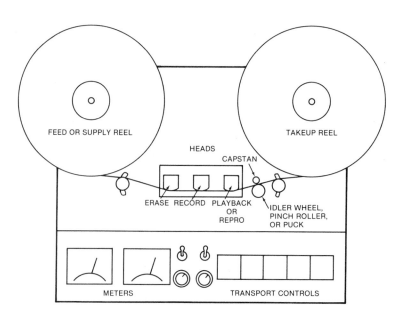

Fig. 9-1. Major parts of a typical tape recorder.

There are limits to the signal level that can be recorded. *Tape saturation* occurs when all the magnetic particles are aligned, so that further increases in recording level do not increase the magnetic signal on tape. If the recording level is too low, tape noise (hiss) becomes audible because the recorded signal is weak in comparison to the random-noise signals generated by nonaligned magnetic particles.

It's very important that the heads be correctly aligned with respect to the tape and to each other. The *gap* in each head (the break in the front of the electromagnet) must be exactly at a right angle to the tape for best high-frequency response. This is called the *azimuth alignment*, and is illustrated in Fig. 9-2. Heads are aligned with the aid of a *standard alignment tape* (described later in the chapter).

**Fig. 9-2.
Azimuth
alignment.**

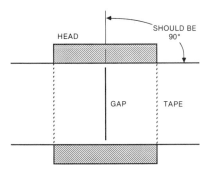

The Electronics

Tape recorder electronics perform the following functions; they

- Amplify and equalize the incoming audio signal
- Send the audio signal to the record head
- Amplify and equalize the signal from the playback head

The equalization provided by the electronics is called *record equalization* and *playback equalization*. Record equalization is a slight boost at low and high frequencies to improve the signal-to-noise ratio at these frequencies. Playback equalization occurs during playback, when the output from the playback head rises 6 dB per octave because the head's output depends on the rate of change of magnetic flux, which doubles with frequency. To compensate for this rise, playback equalization falls 6 dB per octave. In addition, playback equalization includes a bass cut to compensate for the bass boost during recording, plus a high-frequency boost to compensate for self-erasure of the tape and losses within the head.

The frequency response of the playback equalization has been standardized in the United States to a curve called the NAB (National Association of Broadcasters) curve. Other countries may use different playback equalization.

Also in the electronics is an ultrasonic oscillator that drives the erase head. The ultrasonic signal, called *bias*, is mixed with the audio that is fed to the record head. The addition of bias is necessary to reduce distortion. The amount of bias, which is adjustable, affects the recording's audio level, frequency response, distortion, and *drop-outs* (temporary signal loss).

The bias setting is critical. Too high a setting reduces the level recorded on tape and rolls off the high frequencies. Too low a setting also reduces the level on tape, results in distortion and drop-outs, and raises the high-frequency response. Bias-setting procedures are covered later in this chapter in the section on alignment.

The Tape Transport

The job of the transport is to move the tape past the heads. During recording and playback, the transport should move the tape at a constant speed and with constant tape tension. During rewind or fast forward, the tape shuttles rapidly from one reel to the other.

Most professional machines have three motors in the transport mechanism: two for shuttling and tape tension, and a third for driving the capstan. The *capstan* is a post that rotates against a *pinch roller*. The tape is pressed between the capstan and pinch roller. As the capstan rotates, it pulls the tape past the heads. The transport also includes rollers that reduce tape-speed variations (*wow* and *flutter*).

The *tape counter* usually shows the elapsed time on tape. A particular point on tape—say, the beginning of a song—can be marked by resetting the tape counter to zero. On some machines, a *return-to-zero* button shuttles the tape to the zero point and then stops automatically. This function is useful for repeated practices of an overdub or a mix.

A professional tape deck moves tape at 7½, 15, or 30 ips (inches per second). As tape speed is increased, high-frequency headroom increases, and wow and flutter (speed variations) decrease. By contrast, a slower tape speed consumes less tape and allows more running time.

Tracks

A *track* is a path on tape containing a single channel of audio. The wider the track (that is, the more tape width it covers), the greater the signal-to-noise ratio. Doubling the track width improves the signal-to-noise ratio by 3 dB.

Track Width

Tape recorder heads are available in different configurations. Some record over the full width of the tape; some are divided so that they can record two or more independent tracks on the tape width. Heads are available in the track formats described below. Fig. 9-3 shows some track-width standards for ¼-inch tape.

- A *full-track mono* head records over nearly the full width of the tape in one direction (Fig. 9-3A).
- A *half-track mono* head records one track in one direction and one track in the opposite direction when the tape is flipped over (Fig. 9-3B). Each track covers approximately one-third of the tape. The unused third between the tracks is a guard band to prevent crosstalk between tracks.

Fig. 9-3. Some track-width standards for ¼-inch tape.

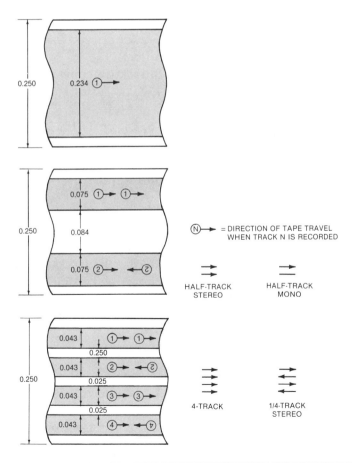

- A *2-track stereo* head records two tracks in one direction (Fig. 9-3B). This format is used for stereo master tapes. Track widths are the same as half-track mono.

- A *quarter-track stereo* head records two tracks in one direction and two tracks in the opposite direction when the tape has been flipped over (Fig. 9-3C).

- A *multitrack* head (4, 8, 16, 24, or 32 track) records four or more tracks in one direction (Fig. 9-3C).

Tape Widths

Magnetic recording tape comes in various widths to accommodate the various track formats.

Tape Width	Usage/Number of Tracks
1/8 inch	Cassettes
1/4 inch	Full-track mono
	Half-track mono
	Quarter-track stereo
	2-track stereo
	4-track
	8-track (in some semi-professional recorders)
1/2 inch	4, 8, or 16 tracks
1 inch	8 or 16 tracks
2 inch	16, 24, or 32 tracks

Multitrack and Synchronous Recording

A multitrack machine records 4, 8, 16, 24, or 32 tracks on a single tape. Each track contains the signal of a different instrument, or a different mix of instruments. The tracks can be recorded all at once, one at a time, or in any combination. After the tracks are recorded, they are combined and balanced through a mixing console. Unlike 2-track recording, multitrack recording lets you fine-tune the mix after the recording session. You can practice the changes in the mix until you get them right.

Overdubbing

Tape tracks can be recorded at different times. To illustrate, suppose that several tracks of music have been recorded on a particular tape. A musician can listen to these recorded tracks, play along with them, and then record his or her part on an unused, or open, track.

Let's say the musician listens to the recorded tracks off the playback head, and overdubs a new part. During playback, the new part will be delayed relative to the original tracks. Here's why: The playback head is a small distance from the record head. The signal on tape travels from the record head to the playback head, and this travel time delays the monitored sound relative to the part being overdubbed. To remove this delay and to synchronize the original tracks with the overdub, the original tracks are played through the record head. At the same time, the record head records the overdub on an open track. This process is called *simul-sync*, *selsync*, or *synchronous recording*. It's usually enabled by setting each track's tape-monitor switch to the SYNC position.

Multitrack recording offers the potential of clearer sound than recording live to 2-track, because you can overdub instruments (without leakage) rather than recording them all at once. If you record several instruments and vocals simultaneously, leakage or off-mic sound can introduce a muddy, loose sound to the mix. But when you overdub, there is no leakage, so the final mix can be cleaner.

Note, however, that multitrack recording requires an extra generation, since you must record the multitrack mix onto a 2-track tape. Each *generation*, or tape copy, adds 3 dB of tape hiss. In addition, every time the number of tracks used in the mix doubles, the noise increases 3 dB.

Meters and Level Setting

Meters on the tape recorder (one per track) show the record and playback levels. These meters may be VU meters, VU meters with built-in peak LEDs (light-emitting diodes), or LED bargraph indicators showing peak levels.

The VU Meter

A VU meter is a voltmeter of specified transient response. It shows approximately the relative volume or loudness of the audio signal. The meter is calibrated in *VU*, or *Volume Units*. The Volume Unit corresponds to the decibel only when measuring a steady-state sine-wave tone. That is, 1 VU = 1 dB only when a steady tone is applied.

A *0-VU recording level* (0 on the record level meter) is the normal operating level of a recorder. It produces the desired recorded flux (magnetic field strength) on a tape. With a VU meter, 0 VU corresponds to a recording level that is 8 dB below the level that will produce 3% third-harmonic distortion on a tape at 400 Hz. Distortion at 0 VU is typically below 1%.

Excessive recording levels (greater than $+3$ VU) saturate the tape, causing distortion. Levels which are too low (say, consistently below -10 VU) result in an audible tape hiss.

When a complex waveform is applied to a VU meter, the meter reads less than the peak voltage of the waveform. This is because the response of a VU meter is not fast enough to track rapid transients accurately. This inaccuracy can cause problems with level setting. For example, if you record drums at 0 VU on the meter, the peaks may be 8 to 14 dB higher, resulting in tape distortion.

So, whenever you record instruments having transient attacks or a high peak-to-average ratio (such as drums, piano, percussion, or horns), record at -6 to -8 VU to prevent tape distortion. Note that mild distortion on drum peaks (recording "hot") may give a desirable effect. Instruments with a low peak-to-average ratio, such as an organ or flute, can be recorded around $+3$ VU without audible distortion.

Peak Indicators

Unlike the VU meter, the peak indicator shows peak recording levels more accurately because it responds very rapidly. If your recorder has LED (light-emitting diode) peak indicators, set the levels for all the tracks so that the LEDs only flash occasionally. For setting recording levels, an LED flash takes precedence over the meter reading. If the recorder has LED bargraph peak indicators, set all tracks to peak at 0 to $+6$ dB, depending on the sound source.

Cleaning the Tape Path

Oxide shed from the tape accumulates on the recorder heads. This layer of oxide deposit separates the tape from the heads, causing high-frequency loss and drop-outs. In addition, buildup of oxide on the tape guides, capstan, and pinch roller can cause flutter. So it's very important to clean the entire tape path frequently.

Use the cleaning agent recommended by the tape recorder manufacturer. Denatured alcohol (from hardware stores or drugstores) and a dense-packed cotton swab are often used. *Note*: Some manufacturers recommend using rubber cleaner rather than alcohol for rubber parts to prevent swelling or cracking. Clean your machines after every eight hours of use, before alignment, and before every recording session. Allow the cleaning fluid to dry before threading tape through the recorder.

Demagnetizing the Tape Path

Tape heads and tape guides can accumulate residual magnetism which can partially erase high frequencies, add tape hiss, and cause clicks at splices in the tape. This residual magnetism can be eliminated with a tape-head *demagnetizer*, or *degausser*, available from any sound system dealer.

Essentially an electromagnet with a probe-type tip, the demagnetizer produces a 60-Hz oscillating magnetic field. By touching the probe tip to the heads and the tape guides, you magnetize them; by slowly pulling the tip away, you diminish the induced magnetization until no magnetic field is left. Generally, only the gapped types are strong enough to be effective.

Cover the probe tip with electrical tape, if necessary, to avoid scratching the heads.

The technique of using a demagnetizer is critical. Proceed as follows:

1. Turn off the recorder.

2. Plug in the demagnetizer at least 3 feet from the machine.

3. Bring the demagnetizer slowly to the part to be demagnetized.

4. After touching the part with the probe tip, slowly move the demagnetizer to 3 feet away so that the induced magnetic field gradually diminishes to zero. Touching the demagnetizer to a head and then quickly removing it may magnetize the head worse than it was when you started.

5. Demagnetize each tape head and tape guide in this manner, one unit at a time.

6. Turn off the demagnetizer only when it's at least 3 feet from the machine.

Demagnetize your machines after every 8 hours of use and before playing an alignment tape. The same precautions about slow operation and 3-foot turn-off distance apply to a bulk tape eraser as well.

Alignment

Alignment or *calibration* is the adjustment of tape-recorder circuitry and tape-head azimuth for optimum performance from the particular type of tape being used. It's a complicated procedure not recommended for beginners. Professional recording engineers align their machines periodically to ensure flat frequency response, maximum signal-to-noise ratio, and lowest distortion.

Some home and semi-pro recorders are not designed for easy alignment. The internal pots that need to be adjusted may not be easily accessible. In that case, the alignment is usually left alone, and you use the brand of tape for which the machine was adjusted.

To perform a complete alignment, you'll need a small screwdriver, an audio-frequency generator, and a standard playback alignment tape. Information about such tapes is available from Ampex, 2201 Lunt Avenue, Elk Grove Village, IL 60007; Magnetic Reference Laboratory, 999 Commercial Street, Palo Alto, CA 94303, and from various tape-recorder manufacturers.

Follow the instructions that come with the tape recorder regarding calibration. Clean and demagnetize the tape heads before starting. Basically, you'll perform the following operations:

1. Using the alignment tape, play the 15-kHz tone and adjust the playback-head azimuth for maximum output or for best phase match between channels (using an oscilloscope).

2. Adjust the high-frequency playback equalization (if any) to achieve the same output level at 700 Hz and at 10 kHz. Or try for the flattest overall response if several tones are on the tape. Don't adjust the low-frequency equalization yet.

3. The magnetic field strength on tape (the *fluxivity*) is measured in nanowebers per meter (nWb/m). If you're using an alignment tape that has a standard operating level of 185 nWb/m (old Ampex standard level), set the playback level to read −3 VU or −6 VU as recommended by the recording tape manufacturer. If you're using an elevated-level alignment tape that uses a standard operating level of 250 nWb/m or 320 nWb/m, set the playback level to read 0 VU (or as recommended by the recording-tape manufacturer and recorder manufacturer). *Note:* Do not touch the playback level for the rest of the calibration.

4. Thread some blank tape of the desired brand onto the machine.

5. Record a 15-kHz tone and adjust the record-head azimuth for maximum playback output, or for best phase match between channels. *Note:* Skip this step if your recorder combines the record and playback functions in a single head.

6. While recording a 1-kHz tone, set the bias to achieve maximum playback level. Then, go back to 10 kHz, and turn up the bias

past that point (*overbias*) until the output drops 0.5 to 1 dB. Overbiasing reduces drop-outs and modulation noise. Consult the tape manufacturer's specifications for alternative overbias settings.

7. While recording tones of 10 kHz, 100 Hz, and 700 Hz, adjust the high-frequency record equalization and low-frequency playback equalization (if any) to achieve the same playback output level at all frequencies. Or, use many tones to achieve the flattest overall response. Record the tones at 0 VU for 15 ips, −10 VU for 7½ ips, and −20 VU for cassettes.

8. Feed a 1-kHz tone at 0 VU from the mixing console to the recorder. Record the tone. Set the record level so the recorder reads 0 VU on playback.

9. Set the "record cal" or "meter cal" so that the meter reads 0 VU on "input" or "source."

After calibration, your tape machine will operate as well as possible with the particular type of tape you're using. The playback signal should sound identical to the input signal (except for some added tape hiss).

Reducing Print-Through

Print-through is the transfer of a magnetic signal from one layer of tape to the next, causing an echo. If the echo follows the program, it is called *post-echo*. If the echo precedes the program, it is called *pre-echo*. Print-through is especially audible in recordings with many silent passages, such as narration. To minimize print-through:

- Demagnetize the tape path (stray magnetic fields increase print-through).
- Use 1½-mil tape (thinner tapes increase print-through).
- Use noise-reduction devices (discussed later in this chapter).
- Store tapes at temperatures under 80° Fahrenheit, and don't leave tapes on a hot machine (heat increases print-through).
- Rewind tapes in storage at least once a year to allow print-through to decay.
- Store tapes *tail out*. That is, after playing or recording a tape, leave it on the take-up reel. Rewinding a tape about 15 minutes before playing helps to reduce any print-through that may have occurred during storage. (This measure becomes less effective as

the storage time increases.) In addition, tail-out storage results mainly in post-echo, which is less audible than the pre-echo that is emphasized in tapes which were rewound before being stored.

Operating Precautions

The following are some operating tips for tape recorders which may prevent some accidents.

1. Don't put the machine in record mode until levels are set. If you record an extremely high-level high-frequency signal, the crosstalk within the head might erase other tracks.

2. Keep the tape away from the recorder heads when turning the machine on or off. Many recorders generate a *field spike* which may put a click on the tape.

3. Keep degaussers and bulk-tape erasers several feet away from tapes you don't want to erase.

4. Before you start recording on a track, make sure you won't be erasing something you wanted to keep. Listen to the track first, or refer to your track sheet.

5. Edge tracks of multitrack tapes are prone to drop-outs due to edge damage. Since drop-outs occur mostly at high frequencies, use the edge tracks only to record those instruments with little high-frequency output (such as the bass or kick drum).

6. Repeated passes of a recording past the heads may gradually erase the high frequencies. You may want to make a copy of the multitrack tape (or a quick two-track mix) for musicians to practice overdubs with. Then, go back to the original tape when the musicians are ready to record.

7. *Bouncing* or *ping-ponging* is the process of mixing several tape tracks and recording the mix on a single open track. Then you can erase the original tracks to free them up for recording new instruments. Bouncing or copying tracks tends to lose high-frequency response, so try to limit bounced tracks to the bass or midrange instruments.

Noise Reduction

The analog tape recorder adds undesirable tape hiss and print-through to the recorded signal, degrading its clarity. Tape hiss becomes especially audible during a multitrack mixdown because every track that is mixed in adds to the overall noise level.

Noise increases 3 dB whenever the number of tracks in use are doubled, assuming they are mixed at equal levels. Fortunately, *noise-reduction* devices, such as Dolby® or dbx®, are available to reduce the noise and print-through added by the tape recorder. However, these units do not remove noise in the original signal coming from the console.

One channel of noise reduction is needed per tape track. Noise-reduction units connect between the console output buses and the corresponding tape track inputs, and also between the tape track outputs and the console tape inputs, as shown Fig. 9-4. Some multitrack recorders have built-in noise reduction.

These noise-reduction devices compress the signal during recording and expand it in a complementary fashion during playback. The compressor part of the circuit boosts the recorded level of quiet musical passages. The expander part works in a complementary way during play-

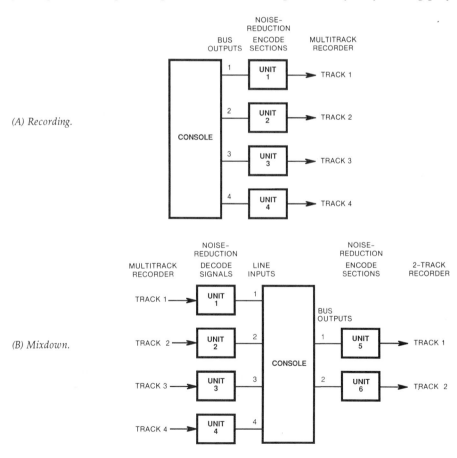

Fig. 9-4. Noise reduction applied to multitrack tape and to 2-track master tape.

(A) Recording.

(B) Mixdown.

back, turning down the volume during quiet passages, and thereby reducing noise added by the tape. During loud passages, when noise is masked by the program, the gain returns to normal.

A compressed tape is described as *encoded*; the expanded tape is called *decoded*. If an encoded tape is played without decoding, the dynamic range and frequency response are altered.

It's important that the encode and decode sections track each other. For example, a 10-dB level change at the input of the encode section should yield a 10-dB level change at the output of the decode section. Otherwise, dynamics sound unnatural.

The Two Major Noise-Reduction Systems: dbx® and Dolby®

dbx

With dbx noise reduction, the compression ratio is 2:1. That is, a program with a 90-dB dynamic range is compressed to 45 dB, which is easily handled by a tape recorder with a 60-dB signal-to-noise ratio. Then, during playback, the dynamic range is expanded back to the original 90 dB. Use of the dbx process improves the signal-to-noise ratio by 30 dB and increases headroom by 10 dB. The dbx circuit also includes pre-emphasis (treble boost) of 12 dB during recording and complementary de-emphasis (treble cut), during playback, to reduce modulation noise. dbx operates at all signal levels and across the entire audible spectrum. Fig. 9-5 shows the dbx 224X Type II Noise Reduction System.

Dolby

The Dolby® A system divides the audible spectrum into four separate frequency bands which are compressed and expanded independently. In addition, Dolby operates only on quiet passages—those below about −10 VU. High-level passages do not need noise reduction since the program masks the noise. This system reduces noise by 10 dB below 5 kHz, and up to 15 dB at 15 kHz.

Dolby® B, a lower-cost system for cassette decks, operates only at high frequencies to reduce tape hiss by up to 10 dB. Dolby® C works over a slightly wider range and reduces noise by up to 20 dB.

Fig. 9-5. The dbx 224X Type II Noise Reduction System (*Courtesy dbx, a Division of BSR North America, Ltd.*).

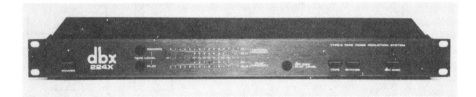

Dolby® SR (for Spectral Recording System) is the most effective Dolby system, reducing noise by more than 25 dB over most of the audible spectrum. As a result, a recorder operated at 15 ips with Dolby SR can have a maximum signal-to-noise ratio exceeding 105 dB. During recording, Dolby SR boosts the gain of those regions of the spectrum that are low to medium in level. During playback, it reduces the gain of the same regions in a complementary fashion.

When using Dolby A, you must record a calibration signal called a *Dolby® tone* on the tape before the regular program. This tone is generated by an oscillator in the Dolby unit. During playback, the level of the recorded Dolby tone is indicated on a Dolby® meter. You set the Dolby input level so that the meter indication lines up with the Dolby-level mark on the meter. Then the expander circuitry will track the recording properly.

If the level is set improperly, the frequency response and dynamic range are slightly altered. Fortunately, there is room for error since these alterations occur in low-level signals and, consequently, are hard to hear.

Dolby® vs. dbx®

Both Dolby and dbx have advantages and disadvantages. Compared to Dolby A, B, and C, dbx provides more noise reduction and requires no calibration tone or careful level setting. On the other hand, dbx exaggerates drop-outs more than Dolby does. Dolbyized recordings are relatively free of noise "breathing," which is sometimes audible on a dbx-encoded tape as fuzziness accompanying bass solos or bass-drum solos.

Using Noise Reduction

Dolby-encoded and dbx-encoded tapes are not compatible with each other, and cannot be played properly without decoding through the appropriate unit. So, if you plan to send your master tapes to another studio, check that the studio has the same type of noise reduction that you want to use.

When using noise reduction, avoid saturating the tape while recording. Otherwise, the attack transients may be altered during playback through the noise-reduction unit. If you are using dbx noise reduction, you can record at 3 VU lower than normal for 3 dB more headroom.

Encoded tapes should be copied by decoding first, and then re-encoding while recording onto the second machine. Be sure to copy the Dolby tone if the master tape has one.

Matching Mixer and Recorder Meters

It's common practice to set the mixer meters and recorder meters to track each other. That way you have to watch only the mixer meters while recording. Also, when the mixer and recorder are both peaking around 0 VU, they are operating at an optimum level for distortion and noise performance. However, if dbx noise reduction is used, matching the meters becomes confusing because the encoded signal from the dbx is compressed.

First, let's describe how to match meter readings without dbx:

1. Calibrate the recorder as described earlier in this chapter (if necessary).

2. If a test oscillator (tone generator) is not built into your mixing console, get an external oscillator. Set it to 1 kHz and at about a −50-dB level. Plug the oscillator into a mixer mic input and bring up the level to read 0 VU on all the console meters. An alternative to a 1-kHz tone generator is a continuous sine-wave synthesizer note. Note "C," two octaves above middle C (1046.52 Hz), or note "B" (987.8 Hz) can be used.

3. Send the 0-VU tone from the console to the recorder.

4. Put the recorder in record mode and set the record level to obtain 0 VU during playback on all the recorder meters.

If dbx is used, the procedure is as follows:

1. Turn on a 1-kHz tone and set it to 0 VU on all the console meters.

2. Put the recorder in record mode. With dbx switched OUT, set the record level to read 0 VU during playback on track 1 of the multitrack recorder.

3. With dbx switched IN, adjust the record-trim potentiometer on the dbx so that the recorder meter still reads 0 VU. Don't touch the record level on the recorder. *Note:* Since dbx operation varies with frequency, you must use a 1-kHz tone. If you don't have a 1-kHz tone, just calibrate with the dbx switched out.

4. Repeat the preceding steps for all of the recorder tracks.

5. With the dbx function of the 2-track recorder switched OUT, feed a 0-VU tone to buses 1 and 2 of your mixer (or the stereo mixdown buses), and set the record levels on the 2-track machine to read 0 VU on playback. Repeat the preceding steps for dbx adjustments.

Now that the mixer and recorders are calibrated to match each other at 0 VU, leave the recorder controls alone. Set levels with the mixer faders only.

The encoded signal that the dbx process feeds to the tape recorder is compressed, so the needles of the recorder meters will wiggle less than the mixer meters. This makes it difficult to set recording levels by watching the mixer meters, so you'll have to watch the recorder meters instead when dbx is used.

Tape Handling and Storage

Careful handling and storage of tape reels is essential to avoid damaging the tape and the signals recorded on it. If you examine a reel of used recording tape, you may see some edges or layers of tape sticking out of the tape pack. These edges can be crushed by pressure from the reel flanges, causing drop-outs and high-frequency loss. For this reason, never hold a reel of tape by squeezing the flanges together. Instead, hold the reel in one hand by putting your fingers in the hub and your thumb on the flange edges, as shown in Fig. 9-6. When using two hands, hold the reel with extended fingers on the flange edges.

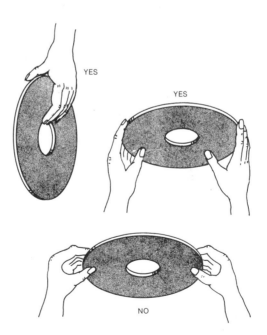

**Fig. 9-6.
Handling tape
reels.**

To prevent edge damage during storage, leave tapes tail out after playing or recording to ensure a smooth tape pack. Repair or discard reels with a bent flange. Reels left out in the open can collect dust, so keep them in boxes. Store tape boxes vertically—not stacked. The preferred storage conditions are 60° to 75° Fahrenheit, with 35–50% relative humidity. Keep tapes away from magnetic fields, such as those caused by speakers or telephones.

Editing

Editing is the cutting and rejoining of magnetic tape to delete unwanted material, to insert leader tape, or to rearrange material into a desired sequence.

Equipment and Preparation

Editing requires the following materials: demagnetized single-edge razor blades, a light-colored grease pencil, splicing tape, leader tape, and an editing block.

Leader tape is plastic or paper tape without an oxide coating, which is used for a spacer between takes (i.e., silence between recorded songs). Plastic leader is preferred over paper leader because paper can absorb humidity during long storage, and can become warped. An *editing block* holds the tape during the splicing operation. It's easier to use than a tape splicer with hold-down tabs and it allows more precise cuts.

Before editing, wash your hands to avoid getting oily spots on the tape. Cut several 1-inch pieces of splicing tape and stick them on the edge of the tape deck or table so they are handy. Also cut several sections of leader at a 45° angle using the 45° slot in the editing block. A typical leader length between songs is four seconds, which is 60 inches long for 15 ips or 30 inches long for 7½ ips. While editing, try to hold the magnetic tape lightly by the edges.

Leadering

Suppose you've recorded a reel full of takes and you want to remove the out-takes, count-offs, and noises between the good takes. You also want to insert leader between each song. This process, called *leadering*, can be done as follows.

First, wind several turns of leader onto an empty take-up reel and cut the leader at a 45° angle using the 45° slot in the editing block. Remove this take-up reel, put on an empty one, and play the tape to be edited. Locate the beginning of the first song's best take. Stop the tape there. Put the machine in cue or edit mode so that the tape presses against the heads. While monitoring the tape-recorder output, rock the tape back and forth over the heads by rotating both reels by hand; first rapidly, and then more and more slowly. You'll hear the music slowed down and low in pitch. Find the exact point on the tape where the song starts; that is, where it passes over the playback-head gap. Align the beginning sound with the gap. Using the grease pencil, mark the tape about ½ inch to the right of the gap (that is, at a point on the tape just before the song starts).

Next, loosen or "dump" the tape by simultaneously rotating the supply reel counterclockwise and the take-up reel clockwise. Remove the tape from the tape path and press it into the splicing block, oxide side down. Align the grease-pencil mark with the 45° angled slot on the editing block, as shown in Fig. 9-7A. Slice through the tape with a razor blade, drawing the blade toward you. Don't use the 90° slot because such an abrupt cut can cause a pop noise at the splice.

Fig. 9-7. Aligning edit marks with cutting slot.

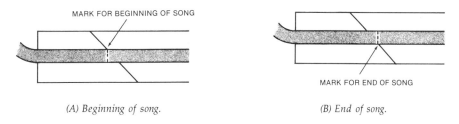

MARK FOR BEGINNING OF SONG

MARK FOR END OF SONG

(A) Beginning of song.   *(B) End of song.*

Remove the unwanted tape to the right of the cut and put the take-up reel aside. Slide the cut end of the tape to the right in the editing-block slot, as in Fig. 9-8. Put on the take-up reel containing the turns of leader tape, and insert the end of the leader into the right half of the block. Shove together the ends of the leader tape and magnetic tape so that they butt or touch together with no overlap.

Fig. 9-8. Applying splicing tape.

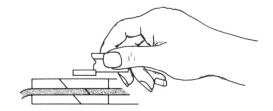

Now, take a piece of splicing tape and stick a corner of it onto a hand-held razor blade. Align the piece of splicing tape parallel to the recording tape, as shown in Fig. 9-8. Apply the piece over the cut on the nonoxide side, and press it down by rubbing with your fingernail.

Slide the splice out of the block. Gently pop the tape out of the block by pulling up on the ends of the tape that extend from both sides of the block. Twist the tape toward you while pulling. Check that there is no gap or overlap at the splice.

Now wind the tape onto the take-up reel and locate the ending of the first song. As it ends, turn up the monitors and listen for the point where the reverberant "tail" of the music fades into tape hiss. Stop the tape there and mark it lightly—at the playback-head gap (at the center line of the head).

After inserting the tape into the editing block, cut the tape at the pencil mark, as noted in Fig. 9-7B. Remove the tape on the left-hand side of the cut. Splice the end of the first song to a four-second length of leader and again check the splice. Wind the first song and the leader onto the take-up reel and remove the reel. Then, put on the take-up reel containing the unwanted material that you previously set aside. Splice it to the rest of the master tape.

Next, locate the beginning of the next good take you want in the program. Mark it and cut the tape. Put the reel containing the first song on the take-up spindle. Splice the tail end of the leader onto the beginning of the second song, and then wind the second song onto the take-up reel. You now have two songs joined by leader tape.

Repeat this process until all the good takes are joined by leader. Then you will have a reel of tape with several songs separated by white leader, which makes it easy to find the desired selection.

Joining Different Takes

What if you want to join the verse of Take 1 to the chorus of Take 2? You'll have to cut into both takes at the same point in the song, then join them. It takes practice to make an inaudible splice in this manner, but it's done every day in professional studios.

The two takes must match in tempo, balance, and level for the edit to be undetectable. To mask any clicks occurring at the splice, cut the tape just before a beat—say, at the beginning of a drum attack. An alternative is to cut into a silent pause. If you cut into a continuous sound, such as a steady chord, a cymbal ring, or reverberation, the splice will be noticeable.

Let's run through the procedure. First play Take 1 and locate the point where you want Take 1 to stop and Take 2 to start—say, at the beginning of the chorus. Stop the tape there. Then, put the recorder in cue or edit mode, rock the tape, and try to identify a beat or attack transient. At the point on the tape where this beat just starts to cross the playback-head gap, mark the tape. Cut the tape at the mark and remove the take-up reel containing the verse of Take 1.

Next, put on an empty take-up reel, thread the master tape, and fast-wind to Take 2. Find the same spot in Take 2 that you marked in Take 1. Mark and cut it. Using splicing tape, join Take 2 (on the supply reel) to Take 1 (on the take-up reel you just set aside). Again, check that there is no gap and no overlap at the splice.

Play the spliced area of the tape to see if the edit is detectable. If not, congratulations! It should sound like a single take. If Take 2 comes in a little late, carefully remove the splice and cut out just a little tape surrounding the cut. Re-splice and listen again.

More Editing Tips

Suppose you've recorded most of a good take, but then the musicians make a mistake and stop playing. Rather than repeating the entire song, the musicians can start playing a little before the point where they stopped, and then finish the song. Then you can splice the two segments into a complete and perfect take. Editing is also useful for interjecting comments or sound effects into the middle of a song, or for making tape loops. You can even record a difficult mixdown in segments, and then edit the segments together.

The Digital Recorder

The type of recorder described earlier is an analog recorder. That is, the magnetic particles on the tape are oriented in patterns analogous to the audio waveform. The drawbacks of this system are tape hiss, tape distortion, frequency-response errors, and speed variations (wow and flutter). Recently, digital recorders have been developed that eliminate these problems.

A complete discussion of the digital recorder is beyond the scope of this book, but here is a brief overview. During recording, a digital recorder measures or samples the voltage of the incoming waveform about 48,000

Fig. 9-9. A digital audio processor, the Sony PCM-F1 *(Courtesy Sony Corporation of America).*

times a second. Numbers are assigned to these voltage samples. This process is called *analog-to-digital (A/D) conversion*. The machine then records the numbers on tape in binary code (1s and 0s). This code is accurate to 16 digits (bits). The binary numbers are in the form of a modulated square wave recorded at maximum level.

During playback, the binary numbers are read and converted back into the original sampled voltages—a process called *digital-to-analog (D/A) conversion*. Finally, the varying voltage levels are smoothed back into the original audio waveform by a low-pass filter.

Since the digital playback head reads only two binary numbers (bits), it is insensitive to tape hiss and tape distortion. Numbers are read into a buffer memory and read out at a constant rate, eliminating speed variations. The resulting freedom from noise, distortion, print-through, wow, and flutter makes digital recordings sound extremely clean and clear. Unlike analog recordings, digital recordings can be copied with little or no degradation in quality. Lost data is restored by error-correction circuitry.

Currently, digital recorders are quite expensive. For stereo mastering, there's an alternative to a digital recorder: a *digital audio processor* with pulse code modulation (PCM), such as shown in Fig. 9-9. This device digitally encodes the audio and records it onto a standard video cassette tape. You connect the analog signal to be recorded to the processor inputs, and connect the processor outputs (a modulated radio-frequency signal) to the inputs of any video cassette recorder. Then you set levels and start recording. During playback, the modulated video signal feeds the processor, and analog audio comes out.

Thanks to digital recording, the original goal of tape recording has finally been achieved: *to accurately store and reproduce our audio creations.*

10 SIGNAL PROCESSORS

You can create special sonic effects, enhance the music you record, and improve sound quality through the use of signal processors. Usually external to the mixing console, this outboard equipment takes a signal fed from the console and modifies it in a controlled way. Then, the modified signal is returned to the console for routing to the appropriate channels. The result is a recording that sounds more like a production and less like a bland documentation.

This chapter describes the most popular signal processors and tells how to use them. Fig. 10-1 is a diagram that shows how signal processors are classified.

The Equalizer

An equalizer (usually in the mixing console) is a sophisticated tone control, something like the bass and treble controls on a hi-fi set. Equalization affects tone quality by boosting or cutting selected frequency bands. That is, it alters the frequency response. EQ (pronounced "E.Q.") is studio jargon for "equalization."

To understand how an equalizer works, we first need to know what a *spectrum* is. A musical instrument produces a wide range of frequencies, even when a single note is sounded. These frequencies, including the fundamental and the harmonics, are the spectrum of the instrument, and they give the instrument its own distinctive *tone quality* or *timbre*.

Tone quality is affected by a change in the level of any portion of the spectrum. An equalizer raises or lowers the level of a particular range of frequencies (a frequency band), and so controls the tone quality. For example, a boost (a level increase) at 10 kHz makes many instruments sound bright and crisp. A cut at the same frequency dulls the sound.

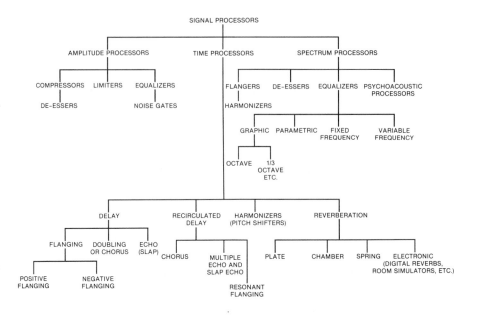

Fig. 10-1. Signal-processor categories.

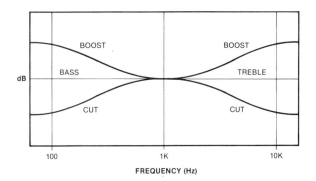

Fig. 10-2. Effect of the bass and treble control.

Types of Equalizers

Let's examine several types of equalizers, ranging from the simple to the complex.

Bass and Treble Control

The most basic equalizer is a bass and treble control. Its effect on frequency response is illustrated in Fig. 10-2. Typically, such a device provides up to 15 dB of boost or cut at 100 Hz (for the low-frequency equalization knob) and at 10 kHz (for the high-frequency equalization knob).

Multiple-Frequency Equalizer

A multiple-frequency equalizer allows boost or cut at several preset frequencies, as diagrammed in Fig. 10-3.

Sweepable Equalizer

A sweepable equalizer lets you tune in the exact frequency range that you wish to boost or cut. This is illustrated by the curves in Fig. 10-4.

Parametric Equalizer

The most complex equalizer of all is the parametric equalizer, which allows continuous adjustment of frequency, boost or cut, and *bandwidth*—the range of frequencies affected. The curves of Fig. 10-5 show how a parametric equalizer varies the bandwidth of the boosted portion of the spectrum.

Peaking or Shelving

An equalizer is described as either peaking or shelving depending on how it affects the frequency response. With a peaking equalizer set for a boost, the shape of the frequency response resembles a hill or peak,

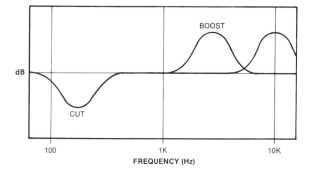

Fig. 10-3. Effect of multiple-frequency equalization.

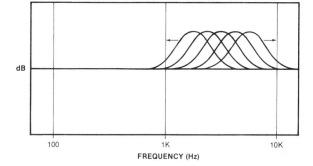

Fig. 10-4. Effect of sweepable equalization.

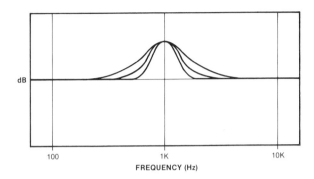

Fig. 10-5. Curves that illustrate varying the bandwidth of a parametric equalizer.

Fig. 10-6. Peaking equalization at 7 kHz.

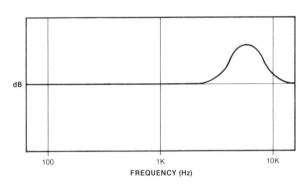

Fig. 10-7. Shelving equalization at 7 kHz.

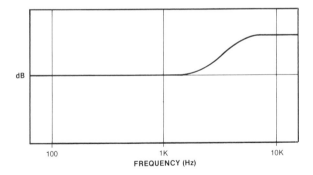

as shown in Fig. 10-6. With a shelving equalizer, the shape of the frequency response resembles a shelf, as shown in Fig. 10-7.

Graphic Equalizer

A graphic equalizer has a row of slide potentiometers which divide the audible spectrum into five to thirty-one bands. When the controls are adjusted, their positions graphically indicate the resulting frequency response. Usually, a graphic equalizer is used for monitor-speaker equalization.

Filters

A filter is a form of equalizer that sharply rejects (attenuates) frequencies above or below a certain frequency. For example, a 10-kHz *low-pass filter*, or *high-cut filter*, removes frequencies above 10 kHz (as shown in Fig. 10-8). This reduces hiss-type noise without affecting tone quality as much as a gradual treble rolloff would. A 100-Hz *high-pass filter*, or *low-cut filter*, attenuates frequencies below 100 Hz, reducing rumble from air conditioning, trucks, etc. Filtering out frequencies above and below the spectral range of a musical instrument reduces leakage at those frequencies.

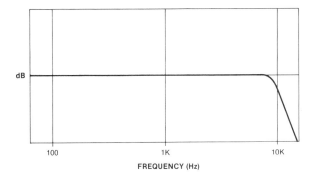

Fig. 10-8. A 10-kHz low-pass filter (−3 dB at 10 kHz).

Setting Equalization

The following is one way to set an equalizer. First, set it to the approximate frequency range that you need to work on (you'll soon know where by experience). Then apply full boost so the effect is easily audible. Finally, fine-tune the frequency and the amount of boost or cut until the tonal balance is the way you like it. For example, if a close-miked vocal sounds unnaturally bassy, reach for the low-frequency equalization knob (say, 100 Hz) and turn it down, adjusting the amount of cut for the desired tonal balance.

If you hear a strong coloration in the tone quality of an instrument, set a sweepable equalizer for extreme boost to find the frequency range matching the coloration. Then cut that range by the amount that sounds right.

It's very instructive to spend some time using a graphic equalizer. Play a musical program through it to hear the tonal effect of each frequency band. Also play individual tracks of different instruments through it, and note how a boost at a certain frequency has a different effect on each instrument. Then you'll know what frequency to boost or cut to correct a tonal coloration. With a little experimentation, you'll also get a better idea of what knob to turn on any equalizer to get a "woody" sound or a "brassy" sound.

At the end of this chapter, there is a descriptive listing of sound qualities. Among other things, the listing suggests some equalizer settings to achieve various sonic effects.

When To Equalize

Should equalization be applied during recording or during mixdown? If you're mixing the instruments live to 2-track tape as the music is performed, there is no separate mixdown session, so you must apply equalization during recording. Also, if you're assigning several instruments to one track, you must equalize these instruments during recording because you can't equalize them individually during mixdown. The same restriction is true for adding reverberation or other effects to instruments assigned to the same track. However, if you assign each instrument to its own track, the usual practice is to record *flat* (without equalization) and then equalize the track during mixdown.

If the equalization used is a bass cut or a treble boost, you can obtain a better signal-to-noise ratio by applying equalization during recording, rather than during mixdown. Similarly, if the equalization used is a treble cut, applying it during mixdown will reduce tape hiss.

Uses of Equalization

The following is a list of some ways that equalization is used.

Improving Tone Quality

Equalization can make an instrument sound better tonally. For example, you might use a high-frequency rolloff on a singer to reduce sibilance, or on a direct-recorded electric guitar to take the "edge" off the sound. As another example, boosting 100 Hz on a floor tom gives a fuller sound, or cutting around 250 Hz on a bass guitar aids clarity. The frequency response and placement of each microphone affects tone quality as well.

Special Production Effects

Extreme equalization reduces fidelity, but it also can make interesting sound effects. Sharply rolling off the lows and highs on a voice, for instance, gives it a "telephone" sound. An extreme boost at 5 kHz can accent the impact of a snare drum.

Helping a Track Stand Out

The recorded track of an instrument heard by itself may sound very clear, but when it's mixed with other tracks, the clarity may disappear. Certain frequencies of the instrument can be covered up or *masked* by frequencies produced by other instruments. A boost in the presence range, say, 1.5 kHz–6 kHz, can help restore presence and clarity. Vocals, typically, are boosted in this range to help them stand out against an instrumental background.

Compensating for Response Deficiencies

The microphones, tape recorder, monitor speakers, and the mixing board, itself, may not have a flat frequency response. Equalization can partly compensate for these deficiencies. If a microphone has a gradual high-frequency rolloff, for example, a high-frequency boost on the console may help restore a flat response. On the other hand, if a microphone "dies" above a certain frequency, no amount of boost can help it. Some directional microphones have proximity effect—a bass boost when used up close. A bass rolloff on the console can compensate for this boost.

Compensating for Microphone Placement

Often, you must place a microphone very close to an instrument to reject the background sounds and leakage. Unfortunately, a close-placed microphone tends to emphasize the part of the instrument that the microphone is near; the tone quality picked up may not be the same as that of the instrument as a whole. Equalization can partly compensate for this effect. For example, a guitar miked next to the sound hole sounds bassy because the sound hole radiates strong low frequencies, but a complementary low-frequency rolloff on the console can restore the natural tonal balance.

Reducing Noise and Leakage

By filtering out frequencies that are above and below the spectral range of an instrument, you can reject noise and leakage at those frequencies. For instance, a kick drum has little or no output above 5 kHz, so you can filter out the highs above 5 kHz on the kick drum to reduce cymbal leakage. If this filtering is done during mixdown, it will also reduce tape hiss. Filtering out frequencies below 100 Hz on most instruments reduces air-conditioning rumble and muddy bass.

Compensating for the Fletcher-Munson Effect

As discovered by Fletcher and Munson, the ear is less sensitive to bass and treble at low volumes than at high volumes. So, when you record a very loud instrument and play it back at a lower level, it might lack bass and treble. To restore these, you may need to boost the lows (around 100 Hz) and the highs (around 4 kHz) when recording loud rock groups. The louder the group, the more boost is needed. As an alternative, use cardioid microphones with proximity effect (for bass boost) and a presence peak (for treble boost).

Making a Pleasing Blend

When several instruments are heard together, they sometimes "crowd" or overlap each other in the frequency spectrum. That is, it may be difficult to distinguish the instruments by tonal differences. But by equalizing various instruments at different frequencies, you can make their timbres distinct, which results in a more pleasing blend. This procedure also evens out the contribution of each frequency band to the total spectrum, yielding a mix that is tonally well balanced.

The Compressor

This device acts like an automatic volume control, turning down the volume if the signal gets too loud. Here's why it's necessary.

When you record a vocalist, he sometimes sings too softly and gets buried in the mix; other times, he hits loud notes, blasting the listener and saturating the tape. Or, he may move toward and away from the microphone while singing, so that the average recording level fluctuates.

To control this problem, you can *ride gain* on the vocalist—turn him down when he gets too loud, turn him up when he gets too quiet. Or you can use a *compressor*, an amplifier that performs the same function automatically. It reduces the gain (amplification) when the input signal exceeds a preset level (called the *threshold*). The greater the input level, the less the gain. As a result, quiet passages are made louder, loud passages are made softer, and, thus, the dynamic range is reduced. This is illustrated in the sketch of Fig. 10-9.

Compression keeps the level of a vocal or an instrument more constant, making it easier to hear throughout the mix and preventing loud notes which may saturate the tape. With extreme control settings, a compressor can also be used for special effects—say, to make drums sound

**Fig. 10-9.
Compression.**

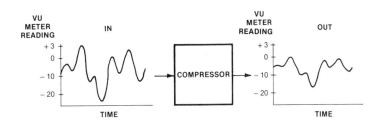

"fatter." Compression is applied nearly always to vocals, often to bass guitar and drums, and sometimes to piano and lead guitar.

Using a Compressor

Normally, you compress individual instruments or tracks rather than the entire mix. That procedure makes the effect less audible by applying compression only to those instruments needing it.

Compressing instrument signals during recording improves the signal-to-noise ratio of the tape tracks, but forces you to decide on compressor settings during the recording session. Compressing tape tracks during mixdown allows you to change the settings at will, but it can make tape hiss audible by raising the gain during quiet passages.

Several controls on the compressor need careful adjustment. Some of the parameters described next are preset internally on various models.

Compression Ratio or Slope

This parameter is the ratio of the change in input level to the change in output level. For example, a 2:1 ratio means that for every 2-dB change in input level, the output changes 1 dB. A 20-dB change in input level results in a 10-dB change in the output, and so on. Ratio settings of 1.5:1 to 4:1 are typical.

Gain Reduction

This is the amount, or number of decibels, that the gain is reduced below unity gain. It varies with the audio level. You set the ratio and threshold controls so that the gain is reduced on loud notes by an amount that sounds right, or looks right on the gain-reduction meter.

Attack Time

The *attack time setting* controls how fast the gain reduction occurs in response to a musical attack. Typical attack times range from 0.25 to 10 milliseconds. Some compressors adjust attack time automatically to suit the program material; others have an attack time that was set at the factory. The longer the attack time, the larger the peaks that are passed before gain reduction occurs. Thus, a long attack time emphasizes percussive attack transients; a short attack time reduces punch by attenuating the attack.

Release Time

The *release time* or *recovery time control* affects how fast the gain returns to its normal value after a loud passage. It can be adjusted from about 50 milliseconds to several seconds. Release time must be longer than about 0.4 second for bass instruments to prevent harmonic distortion.

As the gain returns to normal, noise is increased along with the signal, resulting in a "pumping" or "breathing" sound. Release time usually is set for the least objectionable effect, depending on program material. Shorter release times make the compressor follow faster dynamic changes in the music, and keep the average level higher. In some units, the release time is adjusted automatically, or is factory-set to a useful value.

Threshold

Threshold is the input level above which compression occurs. You set the threshold high (near 0 VU) to compress only the loudest notes; you set it low (-10 or -20 VU) to bring up quiet passages as well as to attenuate the loud ones. If the compressor has a fixed threshold, the input level control is used to adjust the amount of compression.

Output Level Control

The *output level control* sets the signal strength coming out of the compressor to the proper level for the input section of the console (usually around 1.23 volts). Some units automatically maintain a constant output level when other controls are varied.

Connecting a Compressor

You connect a compressor in series with the signal you want to compress, in one of the following ways:

- If you want to compress a single instrument or voice, and your console has access jacks, locate the console input module controlling the instrument you want to compress. Connect the compressor between the access jacks.

- If you want to compress the signal of a console output channel (bus) while recording, locate the bus output containing the signal of the instrument(s) you want to compress. Connect this output to the compressor input. Connect the compressor output to the desired tape-track input.

- If you want to compress a particular tape track during mixdown, connect the tape-track output to the compressor input. Connect the compressor output to the console line input normally used for that track. Alternatively, locate that track's input module in the console, and connect the compressor between the access jacks for that input module.

The Limiter

A *limiter* is an amplifier whose output is practically constant above a preset input level. The compression ratio in a limiter is very high—10:1 or greater—and the threshold is usually set just below the point of tape saturation or amplifier clipping. The output of the limiter is virtually constant for input signals above that level, so tape saturation or amplifier clipping is prevented.

While a compressor reduces the overall dynamic range of the program, a limiter controls only the level of attack transients or peaks, as shown in Fig. 10-10. To act on these rapid peaks, limiters have a much faster attack time than compressors—typically, 1 microsecond to 1 millisecond.

Compressors are sometimes called "limiters," but the setting of the ratio or slope tells what the device is really doing. A compressor/limiter combines both functions by compressing the average signal levels over a wide range, and by limiting peaks to prevent overload. It has two thresholds: one relatively low for the compressor and one relatively high for the limiter.

Fig. 10-10.
Limiting.

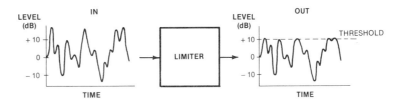

The Noise Gate

A *noise gate* (*expander*) is patched between a tape-track output and a mixing-board line input. The gate acts like an on-off switch to eliminate noises during pauses in an audio signal. It does this by reducing the gain when the input level falls below a preset threshold. That is, when an instrument momentarily stops playing, the signal level is low enough so that the noise gate turns off—removing any noise and leakage during the pause, as illustrated in Fig. 10-11.

Fig. 10-11. Noise gating.

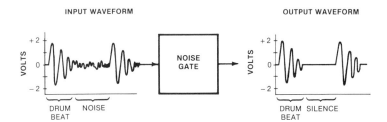

The noise gate helps to clean up drum tracks by removing leakage between beats. It also can be used for special effect to shorten the decay time of the drums, giving a very tight sound. During a mixdown, a gate is sometimes used on each output of the multitrack recorder to reduce tape hiss. The noise-gate threshold should be set high enough to chop off tape hiss during pauses, but low enough so as not to remove any program material (unless that is the desired effect). The release time should be very fast for drums and longer for more sustained instruments.

Some signal processors combine compression, limiting, and noise gating in a single package.

The Delay Unit

A wide variety of special effects can be created by delaying a signal. Some of these effects are echo, multiple echo, doubling, chorus, and flanging. Before explaining these, let's look at the device that performs all these wonders: the delay unit.

A *delay unit* or *digital delay* accepts an input signal, holds it in an electronic memory, then plays it back after a short delay of from about 1 millisecond to 1 second. (This is illustrated in Fig. 10-12.) *Delay* is the

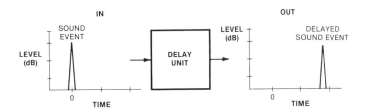

Fig. 10-12. Delaying the signal.

time interval between the input signal and its repetition at the output of the delay device.

Delay Unit Specifications

The *bandwidth* of the delay unit is the frequency range or upper-frequency limit of the delayed signal. A 12-kHz bandwidth is good, 16 kHz is excellent, and 20 kHz is icing on the cake.

The *signal-to-noise ratio* (S/N) of the delay unit is the ratio in dB between the level of the delayed signal and the noise level. In general, the longer the delay, the poorer the signal-to-noise ratio. A ratio of 70 dB is considered fair for delay units; 80 dB is good, and 90 dB is very good.

Echo

Delay by itself is not an audible effect. However, if we delay the incoming signal by 50 milliseconds to 1 second, and combine the undelayed and delayed signals, we will hear two distinct sounds: a signal and its repetition. The delayed repetition of a sound is called an *echo*. This is illustrated in Fig. 10-13 by the two pulses. Echoes occur acoustically when sound waves travel to a room surface, bounce off, and return later—repeating the original sound. A delay unit can mimic this effect.

The direct (undelayed) and delayed signals can be combined in the delay device by setting its direct/delay mix control part-way up.

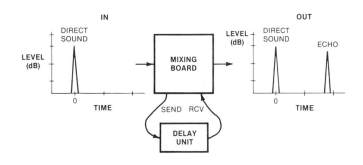

Fig. 10-13. Echo, the repetition of a sound.

There's another way to mix the delayed signal with the undelayed signal to make an echo: through the mixing console. Proceed as follows:

1. Plug the signal to be delayed into your mixing console.

2. Set the direct/delay mix control on the delay unit all the way to "delay."

3. On the mixing console, locate the *echo-send output* (also called *aux send* or *effects send*). Connect it to the delay unit input.

4. Connect the delay unit's output to the console *echo-return connector* (also called *aux return* or *effects return*).

5. Set the echo-return knob about half-way up.

6. Locate the input module where you plugged in the signal to be delayed. The fader in this module controls the level of the undelayed sound; the echo-send knob in this module controls the level of the delayed sound. Mix the two in the desired proportion.

Slap Echo

A delay of around 50 to 200 milliseconds results in a *slap echo* or *slapback echo*—often used in 1950s rock 'n' roll tunes, and still used today.

If you don't have a delay unit, you can achieve slap echo with a tape recorder that has separate record and playback heads. The recorder can be set up to delay an input signal as follows:

1. Connect the recorder to the console (in place of the delay unit) as just described.

2. Set the source/tape switch on the recorder to "tape" so that you hear the signal coming from the playback head.

3. Set the record-level control on the tape recorder about three quarters up.

4. Find the echo-send knob for the instrument you want to delay. This knob controls the signal level sent to the tape recorder, because you plugged the echo-send output into the recorder.

5. Set the echo-send knob to achieve a normal recording level (around 0 VU on the recorder meter).

6. Set the tape machine in record mode.

7. While the tape is moving, turn up the echo-return knob on your mixer to hear the delayed signal mixed with the original signal. There's your slap echo. The faster the tape speed, the shorter the delay.

Multiple Echo

Many delay units have a feature called *recirculation* or *regeneration*. With this feature, some of the delayed output is fed back into the input, so that the signal is re-delayed many times. This creates a *multiple echo*—several repetitions that are evenly spaced in time (Fig. 10-14 illustrates this).

Fig. 10-14. Multiple echo from a delay unit.

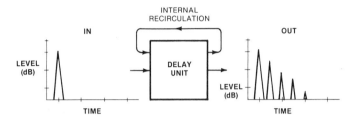

You recirculate the delayed sound simply by turning up the recirculation control on the delay unit. If the unit has no such control, you can make it recirculate externally. Patch the unit's output into a spare console-line input, and turn up the effects-send control of that input for the desired effect, as shown in Fig. 10-15. The higher the recirculation level, the longer the repeats last.

Fig. 10-15. Setup for creating a multiple echo using external recirculation.

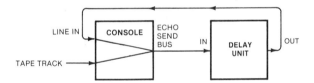

A tape recorder with separate record and playback heads also can produce multiple echoes. You set the tape/source switch on the recorder to "tape," and patch the recorder's output back into its input as described earlier. The faster the tape speed, the faster the echoes repeat.

Multiple echo is most musical if you set the delay time to create an echo rhythm that fits the tempo of the song. A slow repeating echo—say, 0.5 second between repeats—gives an outer-space or haunted-house effect.

Doubling

If the delay is set to around 15 to 35 milliseconds, the effect is called *doubling* or *automatic double tracking (ADT)*. It gives an instrument or voice a fatter, stronger sound, especially if the original signal is panned left and the delayed signal is panned right. The short delays used in doubling sound like early sound reflections in a studio—thus, they add a sense of "air" or ambience to close-miked instruments that would otherwise sound too dead.

Doubling a vocal can be done without a delay unit as follows:

1. Record a vocal part.
2. Rewind the tape to the beginning.
3. Set the tape recorder in sync mode so the singer can hear the performance just recorded and can sing along with it.
4. On an unused track, re-record another performance of the same vocal part.
5. Rewind the tape and play back the two synchronized performances. The doubled vocal sounds fuller than a single vocal track.

Chorus

If the delay used in doubling is modulated (swept) or varied randomly, it produces a wavy or shimmering effect called *chorus*. Feeding some of the delayed output back into the input (regeneration) adds extra fullness. Chorus can make a single voice sound like a chorus of voices singing in unison, or can give a lead guitar a spacious, "singing" quality. Stereo chorus is an especially beautiful effect.

The time modulation of the delayed signal causes frequency modulation (pitch bending) as a side effect. That's because frequency equals cycles per unit of time. If the unit of time varies, so does the frequency. The slight pitch bending of the delayed signal creates the wavy effect.

Flanging

If the delay is set to around 0 to 20 milliseconds, the ear is usually unable to resolve the direct and delayed signals into two separate and distinct sounds. Instead, a single sound with an unusual frequency response is heard. Due to phase cancellations of the combined direct and delayed signals, there results a series of peaks and dips in the net frequency response that is called the *comb-filter effect* (this is shown in Fig. 10-16).

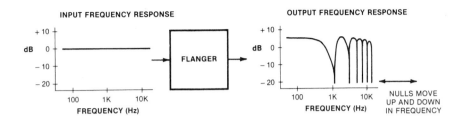

Fig. 10-16. Flanging (or positive flanging).

It gives a very colored, filtered, tone quality. The shorter the delay, the farther apart the peaks and dips are spaced in frequency.

In a flanger (or in a digital delay set to flanging mode), the delay is automatically varied (swept) from about 0 to 20 milliseconds. This causes the comb-filter nulls to sweep up and down the spectrum. The resulting sound quality is hollow, swishing, and ethereal, as if the music was being played through a variable-length pipe. Flanging is applied most effectively to broadband signals, such as cymbals, but can be used on any instrument.

Positive and Negative Flanging

Positive flanging refers to flanging in which the delayed signal is the same polarity as the direct signal. With *negative flanging*, the delayed signal is opposite in polarity to the direct signal, creating a stronger effect. The low frequencies are cancelled (the bass rolls off), and the "knee" of the bass rolloff moves up and down the spectrum as the delay is varied; the high frequencies are still comb-filtered, as shown in Fig. 10-17. Negative flanging makes the music sound like it is turning inside out!

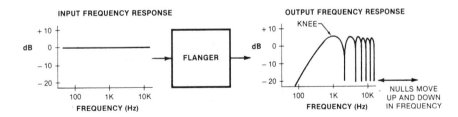

Fig. 10-17. Negative flanging.

Resonant Flanging

By feeding some of the output of the flanger back into the input, the peaks and dips are reinforced, creating a powerful "science-fiction" effect called *resonant flanging*.

Phasing

Phasing is similar to flanging except that a phase-shift network replaces the time-delay circuit. The resulting peaks and dips are spaced more widely and irregularly in the frequency spectrum.

The Reverberation Unit

A reverberation unit adds a sense of room acoustics, ambience, or space surrounding the instruments and voices. It works as follows.

Acoustic reverberation is a series of multiple sound reflections which make the original sound persist and gradually die away or decay. These reflections tell the ear that you're listening in a large or hard-surfaced room. An artificial reverberation unit simulates the sound of an acoustic environment—a club, auditorium, or concert hall—by generating random multiple echoes that are too numerous and rapid for the ear to resolve. Reverberation is illustrated in Fig. 10-18.

**Fig. 10-18.
Reverberation.**

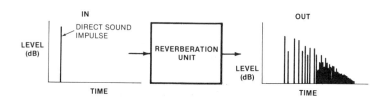

Types of Artificial Reverberation

The random multiple echoes that form reverberation can be created *acoustically* by sending a signal to a speaker in a hard-surfaced room—an *echo chamber*—where the reverberant sound is picked up by a distant microphone and returned to the console. Or, the reverberation can be generated *mechanically* by vibrating a spring or a metal-foil plate with an electromagnetic driver, and detecting the response of the spring or plate with one or two pickups. Reverberation also can be produced *electronically* through multiple electronic delays and regeneration.

Plate Reverberation

The plate or foil type of reverberation device has the brightest sound and has traditionally been the most popular type used in major studios.

Digital Reverberation

Rapidly becoming the new standard, the all-electronic device offers the most control and greatest variety of reverberation sounds (Figs. 10-19 and 10-20). One type of digital reverberation unit is the *room simulator*. It uses sophisticated programs that mimic the early and late sound-reflection patterns of various-size rooms. It even can duplicate the sound of plate reverberation. Unnatural effects are also available, such as non-linear decay, reverse reverberation that builds up before decaying, and gated reverberation.

With *gated reverberation*, the reverberation suddenly cuts off shortly after a note is hit. It's often used on snare drums. To produce this effect, you either use a reverberation unit with a gated-reverb program, or feed the reverberation-return signal through a noise gate that is set to cut off the end of the reverberant "tail."

Spring Reverberation

For home studios, spring units are very cost-effective and vary from mediocre to excellent. A cheap, "twangy," spring reverb is worse than no reverberation at all—a slow tape echo might be a better alternative. Low-cost digital reverbs may obsolete the spring units.

Fig. 10-19. The Yamaha® REV7 Digital Reverberator *(Courtesy Yamaha Electronic Corporation USA).*

Fig. 10-20. The Alesis Microverb digital reverberator—a low-cost, professional-quality unit with a variety of reverberation programs *(Courtesy Alesis Corp.).*

Other Reverberation-Unit Features

Stereo Reverberation

A unit with a *stereo-reverberation* feature has two different outputs for a stereo effect. When the echo-return signals from these outputs are panned full left and right, the reproduced reverberation spreads out around the instruments, much as it does in real life.

Tone Controls

Tone controls affect the tonal balance of the reverberation. Bass rolloff, for example, is used to reduce muddiness.

Adjustable Reverberation Time

In some reverberation devices, the reverberation time (decay time) can be adjusted. Sophisticated units permit different decay times at different frequencies.

Pre-delay (Pre-reverberation Delay)

A more realistic reverberation sound can be created by putting a pre-delay (say, 30 to 100 milliseconds) before the reverberation to simulate the delay that occurs in real rooms before the onset of reverberation. You connect the delay unit between the console echo-send output and the reverb-unit input. Some digital reverbs have a built-in pre-delay. In real rooms, there are a few delayed early reflections following the original sound, just before the reverberation starts, and, by simulating these reflections with pre-delay, you can create a sense of room size.

Reverberation vs. Echo

Note that reverberation is sometimes called "echo," although an echo is a distinct repetition of a sound, rather than a continuous decay of sound. In fact, the echo-send and echo-return controls on the console are normally used to adjust the amount of recorded reverberation. The echo-send output on the console connects to the input of the reverberation unit, and the output of the reverb unit connects to the echo-return input on the console.

The Pitch Shifter

A *pitch shifter* is a special kind of delay device that can actually change the pitch of a signal in real time without changing its duration. In one such device (The Marshall Time Modulator), the delay is varied in repetitive sweeps every 20 milliseconds. This results in a Doppler-shift effect which varies the pitch. In another device (The Eventide Harmonizer), the signal is read into an electronic memory and is read out at a different rate, varying the pitch. Changes in pitch—up to two octaves up or down—are possible, which lets you create harmony parts or correct out-of-tune notes!

The Psychoacoustic Processor

A *psychoacoustic processor* increases brilliance not by equalization, but by adding harmonics not present in the original signal. One example is the Aphex Aural Exciter, which adds a special low-level signal to the original signal to enhance the sound. The subjective effect has been described as an open, airy, defined sound with greater brilliance or presence.

To process a signal with the Aphex Exciter, you send some of a track's signal to the Exciter via the echo send or aux send, and then bring it back to the console via the echo return or aux return. Inside the Aphex Exciter, the signal is high-pass filtered at 500 Hz, distorted mainly by even-order harmonic distortion, and phase-shifted by an amount that varies with frequency. You mix in the "Aphexed" signal about 20 dB below the original unprocessed signal.

The subjective brilliance is probably due to the added "edge" of the distortion. The device also is said to make signal peaks louder by increasing their duration.

Summary of Signal-Processor Effects

The following is a brief definition of each effect that we have discussed:

- *Equalization*—Adjusting the frequency response to affect the tonal balance.

- *Compression*—Reducing the dynamic range while passing the transient peaks.
- *Limiting*—Applying extreme compression to transient peaks without affecting the dynamic range.
- *Noise Gating*—Removing noise and leakage during pauses.
- *Echo*—Repetition of a sound after a delay of 50 milliseconds to 1 second.
- *Multiple Echo*—Recirculating an echo (several repetitions).
- *Doubling*—Delaying a signal 15 to 35 milliseconds for ambience and fullness.
- *Chorus*—Varying or sweeping the delay used in doubling (possibly with regeneration). This produces a wavy multiple-voice effect.
- *Flanging*—Sweeping a delay from 0 to 20 milliseconds. This gives the sound of a variable-length pipe.
- *Reverberation*—Same as multiple echo, but with random, recirculated, short delays. This simulates room acoustics and adds spaciousness.
- *Pitch Shifting*—Raising or lowering the pitch of the signal.
- *Psychoacoustic Processing*—This is the high-pass filtering and distorting of a signal (in the Aphex Aural Exciter) and, then, the combining of it at a low level with the original unprocessed signal. This adds brilliance.

Multiprocessors

Recently available are devices called *digital programmable processors (multiprocessors)*, such as shown in Fig. 10-21. These multipurpose units can be programmed to create most or all of the effects listed above.

The first signal processors that a home-studio owner should purchase are a good reverberation unit and a compressor. These devices are practically indispensable in producing a commercial sound.

Special effects help define the characteristic recorded sound of an era. The 1950s had the "tube sound" and slap echo; the 1960s used fuzz, wah-wah, and flanging; the 1970s and early 1980s popularized delay and psychoacoustic processors; and today's sound emphasizes MIDI keyboards, drum machines, and ambience. You make contemporary-sounding recordings by using the latest effects and musical instruments on the market, and by inventing new sounds. It's the creative usage of these

Low-Frequency Boost (below about 500 Hz)

Positive	*Negative*
Powerful (under 200 Hz)	Muddy
Ballsy (under 200 Hz)	Tubby (200–300 Hz)
Heavy (under 200 Hz)	Thumpy
Fat	Boomy
Thick	Barrel-like
Warm	Woody (200–400 Hz)
Robust	
Mellow	
Full	
Woody (200–400 Hz)	

Flat, Extended, Low Frequencies

Positive	*Negative*
Full	Rumbly
Full-bodied	
Rich	
Solid	
Natural	

Low-Frequency Rolloff

Positive	*Negative*
Clean	Thin
	Cold, cool
	Tinny
	Anemic

Mid-Frequency Boost (500 Hz to 7 kHz)

(5-kHz area for most instruments, 1.5–2.5-kHz for bass instruments.)

Positive	*Negative*
Present (Presence)	Hollow, muffled (500 Hz)
Punchy	Muddy, horn-like
Edgy	"Aw" sound (500–800 Hz)
Clear	Tinny, telephone-like (1 kHz)
Intelligible	"Er" sound (1.5 kHz)
Articulate	Nasal, honky (500 Hz to 3 kHz)
Defined	Hard (2 kHz to 4 kHz)
Projected (2 kHz to 3 kHz)	Harsh, strident, piercing (2 kHz to 5 kHz)
Forward (2 kHz to 3 kHz)	Metallic (3 kHz to 5 kHz, especially 3 kHz)
	Twangy (3 kHz)
	Edgy (3 kHz to 7 kHz)
	Sibilant (4 kHz to 7 kHz)

Chart 10-1. Translation of Audio-Engineering Terms

Flat Mid-Frequencies

Positive   *Negative*

Natural   No Punch
Neutral   "Flat" (lacking character or color)
Smooth
Musical

Mid-Frequency Dip

Positive   *Negative*

Mellow   Hollow (500 to 1000 Hz)
                                                        Disembodied (500 to 1000 Hz)
                                                        Muffled (5 kHz)
                                                        Muddy (5 kHz)

High-Frequency Boost (above about 7 kHz)

Positive   *Negative*

Trebly   Trebly
Bright   Sizzly (voice)
Crisp   Edgy
Articulate   Glassy
Etched   "Essy" Sibilant
Hot   Steely
Sizzly (cymbals)   String Noise

**Chart 10-1
(cont).
Translation of
Audio-
Engineering
Terms**

Flat, Extended High Frequencies

Positive   *Negative*

Open   Too detailed
Airy   Too close
Transparent
Clear
Natural
Neutral
Smooth
Effortless
Detailed

High-Frequency Rolloff

Positive   *Negative*

Mellow   Dull
Round   Restricted
Smooth   Muffled
Easy-on-the-ears   Veiled
Concert-hall-like   Muddy
Dark   Distant

Overall Response

Positive (all flat response)	*Negative*
Natural	Rough, peaky, harsh, colored (non-flat, peaks and dips)
Accurate	
Neutral	Phasey (sharp dips)
Smooth	Cheap (narrow-band)
Transparent	Flat (lacking character—too neutral)
Effortless	
Musical	
Uncolored	
Liquid	

Reverberation or Leakage

Too Little	*Well-Controlled*	*Pleasant*	*Too Much*
Sterile	Clean	Warm	Echoey
Dry	Tight	Rich	Bathroom-sound
Dead		Sumptuous	Muddy
Muffled		Airy	Loose
Thin		Having depth	Washed-out
		"Live"	Barrel-like
		Spacious	Cavernous
		Open	In another room
		Full	Distant
		Bright	Trashy

Noise and Distortion

Absent	*Present*
Clean	Veiled (mild distortion)
Clear	Hard
Smooth	Harsh
Open	Grainy
	Gritty
	Dirty (positive or negative)
	Distorted
	Fuzzy
	Sputtering
	Raunchy
	Noisy
	Hissy

Transient Response

Good	*Bad*
Clean	Smeared
Tight	Blurred
Crisp	Veiled
Sharp	Muffled

Chart 10-1 (cont). Translation of Audio-Engineering Terms

Chart 10-1 (cont). Translation of Audio-Engineering Terms

Stereo Imaging

Sharp	*Diffuse*
Focused	Vague
Pin-pointed	Unfocused
Easy-to-localize	Hard-to-localize
Fused	Smeared
Defined	Spread
Pan-potted	Directionless
	Spacious
	Hole-in-the-middle
	Phasey
	Fat
	Big

Relative Loudness in the Mix

Loud	*Quiet*
Up front	Distant
On top	Subtle
Present	In the background
Hot	Recessed
Forward	Lost
Dominating	Covered
Covering	

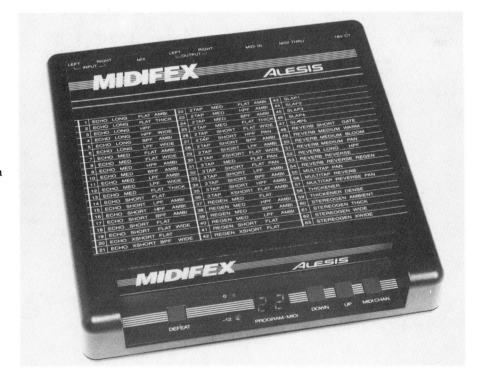

Fig. 10-21. The Alesis Midifex, a multiprocessor with several delay-related effects *(Courtesy Alesis Corp.)*

effects—combining and using them in unusual ways—that leads to ear-grabbing recordings.

Sound-Quality Descriptions

All these signal processors produce sonic effects that may be difficult to describe in technical terms. For example, what equalization should be used to get a "fat" sound or a "thin" sound? What physical conditions may be causing a "muddy" sound or a "metallic" sound? In general, which knob do you turn to achieve a certain sonic effect?

Chart 10-1 answers these questions. It translates audio-engineering terms (such as equalization settings) into subjective descriptions of sound quality. *Note:* These definitions are not universally agreed upon, but they are probably the most common meanings. The positive terms are used when you like the effect; the negative terms are used when you don't!

11 MIXERS AND MIXING CONSOLES

The mixing console (also called the "board" or the "desk") is the control center of the studio. A large complex device, the console accepts electrical signals from the studio microphones, tape recorders, and signal processors. The operator manipulates these signals with an array of switches and knobs, and then routes the signals to tape machines, signal processors, and monitor power amplifiers.

The mixing console may appear complicated and intimidating at first, but it is straightforward to operate once the functions of the various parts are understood. This chapter describes some of the console systems and components. More specific information is available in manufacturers' data sheets and operation manuals.

Mixers

Before describing an elaborate mixing console, let's briefly explain what a mixer does. A mixer performs the following functions:

- Amplifies signals from microphones or other sources plugged into its inputs.
- Controls the relative volume or level of each microphone signal.
- Combines or mixes the microphone signals into one or more composite signals.
- Feeds a tape recorder or power amplifier from its outputs.

Inputs and Outputs

A mixer or console can be specified by the number of inputs and outputs it has. For example, an 8-in, 2-out mixer (8×2 mixer) has 8 inputs for microphones, which can be mixed into 2 output channels (*buses*) for stereo recording. Similarly, a 16-in, 8-out (16x8) mixing board has 16 microphone inputs and 8 output channels for multitrack recording. A $16 \times 4 \times 2$ mixer has 16 inputs, 4 submixes (explained later), and 2 main outputs. There also may be connectors for external equipment, such as reverberation units and monitor amplifiers.

Most mixers and consoles accept line-level inputs (about 0.3 to 1.2 volts) as well as microphone-level inputs (nominally about 2 millivolts). Typically, the line inputs are fed from the outputs of a multitrack tape recorder.

A microphone input may be either low impedance or high impedance. A *low-impedance* input is intended to be used with a low-impedance microphone (150 to 600 ohms); a *high-impedance* input should be used with a high-impedance microphone (about 40 kilohms). Low-impedance microphones are preferred for serious recording because they allow long cable runs without causing hum pickup or high-frequency loss.

Some consoles have *simplex phantom powering* to power condenser microphones. This is a 12- to 48-volt DC voltage that is applied through resistors equally to pins 2 and 3 of the mic-input connectors. The microphone uses the same two conductors to receive phantom power and send audio.

Signal Flow

The signal from each microphone flows in the console through circuits that modify the signal or route it to various other channels. There is a signal flow or signal path from input to output. Let's first look at each stage of the signal path in a simple mono mixer; then, we'll examine the signal paths in a multichannel console. We'll use this method because a knowledge of the simpler units is needed to understand a complex console.

Mono Mixer

The signal flow in a typical mono mixer is shown in Fig. 11-1. First, the signal from each microphone is amplified by a *preamplifier* (one for each

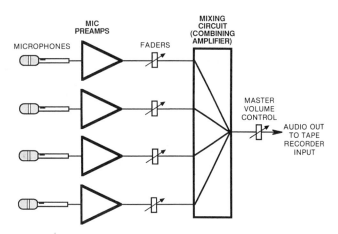

Fig.11-1. Signal paths in a typical mono mixer.

microphone). Then, the amplified signal goes to a *potentiometer* (*pot* or *fader*) that controls the level of the signal. You adjust the pots independently to make some instruments louder, some softer, so that they blend in a pleasing balance.

Then, the signals are combined by a *combining amplifier*—also called a *summing network* or an *active combining network* (ACN). Finally the level of the composite signal is adjusted by a *master volume control*. This composite signal goes to the mixer output for connection to a tape recorder or a monitor system.

2-Channel Stereo Mixer

Fig. 11-2 shows the signal flow in a typical 2-channel stereo mixer. For clarity, only two microphone input channels are shown.

The microphone signals are amplified and adjusted in level as before. Then, each signal is run through a *pan pot*, which divides the signal between output channels 1 and 2. Channel 1 goes to the left speaker and channel 2 goes to the right speaker. If the pan pot is rotated all the way to the left, the signal goes just to channel 1 (the left speaker). If the pan pot is rotated full right, the signal goes just to channel 2 (the right speaker). If the pan pot is set in the middle, the signal divides equally to both channels, producing a sonic image centered between the two speakers. Other settings produce corresponding sound-image locations between the speaker pair for any position desired.

In other words, the pan pot creates a stereo effect by assigning each instrument to a particular left-right location within the stereo spread. Note that the listener must be exactly between the two stereo speakers

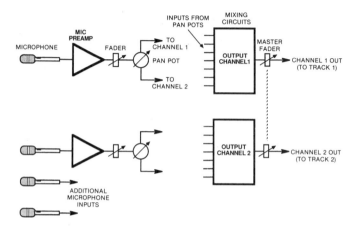

Fig. 11-2. Signal paths in a typical 2-channel mixer.

for this to work as described. In some mixers, a 2- or 3-position channel-assign switch is used instead of a pan pot.

2-Channel Mixing Console

The signal flow in a typical 2-channel mixing console is shown in Fig. 11-3. For clarity, only one microphone input channel is shown. Every console is a little different, but most include the features described here.

Fig. 11-3. Signal paths in a typical 2-channel console (or in a typical multichannel console during mixdown).

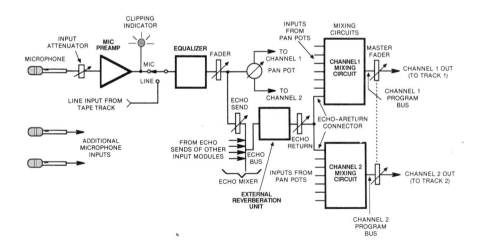

The microphone signal goes first to a *pad* or *input attenuator*. This reduces the voltage of the microphone signal. A pad is used only when the microphone voltage is so high that it overloads the microphone preamp. A preamp driven by too strong a signal clips the signal waveform and produces audible distortion—a gritty sound. As an example of the need for a pad, a typical dynamic microphone placed in a kick drum may generate 0.4 volt. This voltage can drive the microphone preamp into clipping. The pad solves this problem by attenuating the microphone signal before it reaches the preamp.

Some consoles also include a *gain-trim* pot which adjusts the gain of the mic preamp to prevent distortion. A light-emitting diode (LED) follows each preamp and flashes when the preamp distorts. This is a warning to switch in the pad or reduce the preamp gain.

After the microphone signal is properly attenuated and amplified, it goes to an *equalizer*. This is a sophisticated tone control, something like the bass and treble controls on a hi-fi set. Equalization affects tone quality by boosting or cutting selected frequency bands. That is, it alters the frequency response. See Chapter 10 for more detailed information on equalization.

The equalized signal then goes to a *fader* for level adjustment, and then to a *pan pot* for division between the channels. Each output channel feeding a tape track is called a *program bus*.

The signal leaving the fader also may be sent to an *external reverberation unit*. The reverberated signal is returned to the console where it blends with the original signal, adding a sense of room acoustics or spaciousness.

The console controls associated with this process are the *echo-send control*, which adjusts the signal level feeding the reverberation unit, and the *echo-return control*, which adjusts the signal level from the reverberation unit. This reverberated signal enters the *echo-return connector* in the console, where the reverberated signal blends with the program bus signal. The echo-send control affects the amount of reverberation added to each instrument, while the echo-return control affects the overall level of reverberation added to all instruments.

An *echo mixer* combines the signals from all the echo-send controls in the console into a signal in the *echo bus*, which feeds the reverberation unit.

Note that echo send may also be called "effects send" or "aux send." Similarly, echo return may be called "effects return" or "aux return." Echo send and echo return may be used with a wide variety of effects devices, not just reverberation.

Multichannel Console

Fig. 11-4 shows the signal paths in a typical multichannel console. This console is similar to the 2-channel console described above, but with the addition of a *channel assignment switch* (or *track assignment switch*). This switch feeds the signal of each microphone to the desired track of a multitrack tape recorder. For example, you can assign (route or send) the bass-guitar signal to track 1, a drum machine to track 2, a vocal to track 3, a guitar to track 4, and so on. Or, you can assign a single microphone to two tracks and pan it between those tracks.

You also can assign several microphones (say, for a drum set) to the same track. Then, all those microphones are mixed to that track. Using the faders assigned to each common channel, you can create various *submixes* to record on different tape tracks. A *submix*, or *group* is a small preset mix within a larger mix, such as a drum mix, keyboard mix, vocal mix, etc.

From the channel-assign switch, the signal goes to the output channels or buses to connect to tape recorders. The level of each output

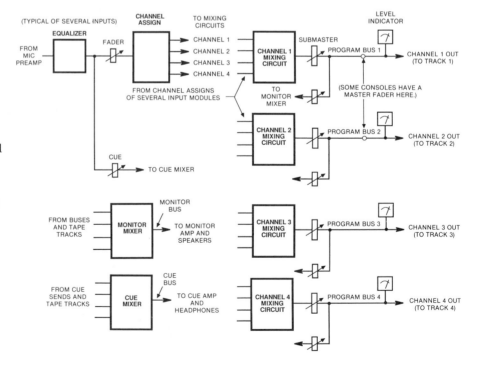

Fig. 11-4. Signal paths in a typical multichannel console (during recording).

channel is measured by an indicator, such as a *VU meter* (volume unit meter) or *LED bargraph indicator*.

The set of controls that affect a single input is called an *input module*; this is a vertical panel in the console control surface. Each input module in the mixer has an identical set of these controls. Fig. 11-5 shows a simple input module with the features just mentioned. Fig. 11-6 shows several modules in a row; they comprise a simple mixer. Input modules in a mixer are numbered consecutively from left to right.

So far, we've examined only the *program mixer*, which creates the mixes that are recorded onto tape tracks. Its inputs are the signals from the input modules; its output is the program bus. But, also shown in Fig. 11-4 are two smaller mixers that are built into the console: the *monitor mixer* and the *cue mixer*.

The *monitor mixer* creates the mix heard over the monitor speakers. The monitor-mixer output bus feeds a stereo power amplifier and the monitor speakers. You can monitor (listen to) the instruments as you

Fig. 11-5. Diagram of a typical input module.

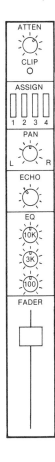

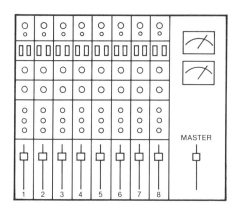

**Fig. 11-6.
Diagram of a
typical mixer—
comprised of
several input
modules and one
2-channel output
module.**

record them. The monitor mixer lets you balance the channels (control
their relative levels) for a good-sounding mix without affecting the signals
going on tape. In other words, the monitor mixer is used during recording
to set up a well-balanced blend of the instruments, to simulate the sound
of the final tape. It's not being recorded that way; you're just listening
to it that way.

The *cue mixer* blends pre-recorded tape tracks and live microphone
signals into a mix that is sent to the musicians' headphones in the studio.
This mixer's input levels are controlled by *cue pots*; its output is called
the *cue bus*.

Some small mixing boards include a multipurpose *submixer* to be
used for whatever purpose you might need. Instead of providing a set
of pots labeled "cue," the board may provide a submixer that can be
used as a cue mixer, a monitor mixer, or whatever. Often, you need only
one function at a time. Larger consoles permit simultaneous cue, monitor,
and other mixes for maximum flexibility.

Recording and Overdubbing Summary

So far we've looked at the signal path through the console during the
recording stage. The signal is attenuated, amplified, equalized, assigned,
submixed, metered, and monitored. During overdubbing, the signal path
is the same, except that the recorded tape tracks are fed into the monitor
mixer and cue mixer along with the microphone signal of the instrument
you're overdubbing. That way, the musician can hear the tape tracks that
they must play along with.

Mixdown

Some consoles have a separate *stereo mixdown bus*. This is the final 2-channel mix that is recorded onto a 2-track tape. Other consoles just use program buses 1 and 2 for the stereo mix.

For a mixdown, the tape-track signals enter the console line inputs via the *mic/line selector* in each input module. The signal flow for the mixdown stage is similar to that shown in Fig. 11-3, except that each mic/line switch is in the line position to accept a recorded tape-track signal, rather than a microphone signal.

During mixdown, you either monitor channels 1 and 2, or if available, the separate stereo mixdown bus. You add equalization, reverberation, and effects to the tracks; you mix them, and then pan them between channels 1 and 2. These channels feed a 2-track tape recorder. The tape made on that machine is the final product.

Mixing Console Sections

Mixing consoles can be divided into three main sections: INPUT, OUTPUT, and MONITOR.

The *INPUT section* is a series of input modules. Each module includes an input connector, microphone preamplifier, input attenuator, fader, equalization, echo send, channel assign, and other functions.

The *OUTPUT section* controls the output of the console. It includes a series of *bus master modules* (or *submaster modules*), each with a *submaster fader*. The master faders control the overall level of all the buses. Also in the output section are the echo-return circuits. Output-level indicators, such as VU meters, are used to set the recording levels.

The *MONITOR section* controls what you're monitoring or listening to. It typically includes a monitor mixer, a cue mixer (for headphones in the studio), a monitor-level control, a cue-level control, switches to choose control room or studio speakers for playback, mono/stereo select, solo buttons, solo level, etc. Fig. 11-7 shows a hypothetical mixing console arranged in clearly defined sections.

Control Layouts

Although there are three main sections, each with its own set of controls, some of these controls are scattered around the mixing console, rather

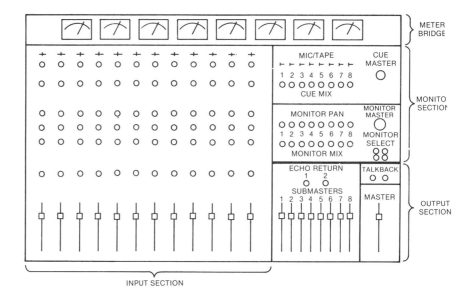

Fig. 11-7. A hypothetical mixing console arranged in clearly defined sections.

than being grouped together. For example, if you look for a group of pots labeled "cue mix," you might not find them. The cue-mixer pots are usually distributed among the input modules. That is, each input module includes a cue-mixer pot that adjusts the level of that input in the cue mix. The same goes for the monitor mixer, whose pots might be located in the bus master modules.

Actually, this arrangement is convenient. Suppose you need to turn up the cue level of the bass guitar. You just look for the bass-guitar input module, and then find its cue pot within that module.

Not all consoles are laid out as just described; some do have separate monitor and cue mixers. Others have multipurpose submixers to be used for whatever purpose you need: monitor mix, cue mix, or effects mix. Similarly, there might be no separate submaster section. Some consoles use an *Input/Output (I/O)* type of construction (also called *in-line*). In this type of console, each module (other than the monitor section) contains one input channel and one output channel.

Input Module Functions

Let's examine each console function in detail, starting with those in the input module. Each input module includes some or all of the following functions or connectors.

MIC INPUT Connector

The microphone input is either an unbalanced phone jack or a balanced 3-pin connector.

Phone-Jack Connector

This unbalanced input might be for a low-impedance microphone, a high-impedance source (such as an electric guitar), or a line-level source.

DIRECT Output

This output connector follows the microphone preamp to feed an individual track of a tape machine. This connector bypasses the combining amps in the program-bus (output) section, thus providing a cleaner signal for recording one mic per track.

There is another use of the direct-out jack. Suppose you have an 8-track recorder which you want to use with a 4-channel mixer. If the mixer has 8 inputs with a DIRECT OUT on each input, you can record 8 tracks simultaneously from the direct-out jacks.

CUE Jack

Some inexpensive mixers have a cue jack on the back of each input module. These jacks can be used to feed an external cue mixer.

AUX IN Jack

On some consoles, this jack accepts the output of a 2-track tape machine. On other units, it functions as an echo-return or effects-return jack.

ACCESS Jacks

These jacks allow access to various points in the signal path, like a patch point. Usually, each input module has a pair of access jacks—send and receive—which you can connect to the input and output of a compressor or limiter. Plugging into the access jacks breaks the signal flow and allows you to insert a signal processor in series with the signal. Many mixers also include access jacks in each program-bus module.

TRIM (GAIN)

On an input module, this pot provides a continuously variable gain adjustment of the mic preamplifier. High gain is needed for low-level signals; low gain is needed for high-level signals to prevent input-overload distortion (also see INPUT ATTENUATOR).

In many consoles, TRIM affects the input level of the mic, line, and tape signals. During mixdown, TRIM is sometimes used to fine-tune the levels coming from the multitrack tape for optimum console gain staging.

INPUT ATTENUATOR (PAD)

This is a resistive network placed ahead of the mic input transformer (if any). The input attenuator prevents overload of the transformer, as well as the mic preamp, by inserting fixed amounts of loss. The TRIM control (just described) prevents input overload by adjusting the gain of the mic preamp.

Since the pad decreases signal-to-noise ratio, use it only when the trim pot can't stop distortion. For example, suppose a mic is in input 1, and the fader is set in its optimum position for noise and headroom (about three quarters up). If the overload LED is flashing, first turn down the TRIM until the flashing stops. If the LED still flashes, switch in the PAD. Now, if the VU meter reads too low, turn up the TRIM until you read 0 VU (average).

EQUALIZATION (EQ)

An equalizer is a sophisticated tone control. (It is explained in detail in Chapter 10.)

ECHO SEND (AUX SEND, EFFECTS SEND)

The term "echo send" is a misnomer that stuck. The echo-send control usually is used to adjust the amount of reverberation on an instrument, rather than the amount of echo. As explained in detail in Chapter 3, reverberation is a continuous decay of sound, such as is heard in an empty gymnasium or a large cathedral. Echo is a discrete repetition of a sound, such as that produced by a digital delay.

The echo-send knob might be called "aux send" or "effects send." There may be several such channels in your console, called AUX1, AUX2, etc.

Whatever this function is named, it can be used to create any submix you wish. Suppose you need to run four vocal mics through a compressor, and you don't have a submaster section. You can turn up the echo sends for the four vocal-mic channels, and then feed the ECHO SEND output to the compressor input. Connect the compressor output to a line input on the console. That input module can be used as a "submaster" module that controls all the compressed vocals.

In other words, even though a knob is labeled ECHO SEND, you can use it for whatever submix you need to set up. Similarly, the cue-mix bus and the monitor-mix bus can be used for submixes other than what their name describes.

PRE-FADER/POST-FADER Switch

When used with an echo-send pot, the PRE/POST switch selects whether the echo send is derived pre-fader (before the fader) or post-fader (following the fader). A pre-fader echo send is not affected by the input's fader; if you turn down the input fader, the echo remains. A post-fader echo send follows the fader action; if you turn down the fader, the echo send level goes down too.

Use the POST position when you want the recorded instrument to sound close (high direct-to-reverberation ratio). Use the PRE position when you want the instrument to sound far away (low direct-to-reverberation ratio). That is, adjust the relative levels of the pre-fader echo send and the input-module fader for the desired sense of distance. Remember the rhyme, "POST sounds close, PRE sounds awee" (away, or distant).

Other functions, such as the AUX SEND, may be pre- or post-fader.

CUE (FOLDBACK or FB)

In each input module, the CUE pot controls the level of that input in the cue mix. The cue mix is the mix heard over headphones in the studio.

When overdubbing, musicians need to hear their own instruments over headphones, as well as the previously recorded tracks they must play along with. The headphone levels of the live instruments that are being recorded are controlled by the MIC CUE or CUE pots; the levels of the pre-recorded tracks are controlled by the TAPE CUE pots.

Some consoles have two CUE buses in order to provide two independent cue mixes or a single stereo cue mix.

CHANNEL ASSIGN (BUS ASSIGN)

This is a set of switches used to assign input signals to various output channels. For example, suppose inputs 1 through 6 are drum microphone signals, and you want to feed them all to track 2 of a 4-track recorder. On input modules 1 through 6, you'd punch in the channel 2 assignment button. Then, all the drum mics would be routed to track 2 of your recorder (assuming you connected console channel 2 to tape track 2).

If you assign a single input to two channels, the input feeds both channels. The PAN control then varies the relative level that is fed to each of those two channels. Typically, 2-channel assignments are used for stereo piano, stereo background harmonies, and stereo drum mixes.

In a stereo drum mix, you pan each drum to its desired location between the monitor speakers.

SOLO (PFL)

The SOLO button in an input module lets you monitor only that input, without affecting other console functions. More than one input can be soloed at one time. On British consoles, the SOLO function is called "PFL," which stands for PRE FADER LISTEN; you listen to or monitor the signal before the fader.

In consoles that have both PFL and SOLO, PFL is a pre-fader and is used mainly to listen for distortion during tracking. SOLO is a post-fader and is used for soloing during mixdown.

Here's an example of how to use the SOLO button. Suppose you hear a buzz in the audio and suspect it may be in the bass-guitar signal. Push the SOLO button in the input module for the bass-guitar, and you'll monitor only the bass guitar. Then, you can easily hear whether or not the buzz is in that input.

MUTE

This turns off the input by disconnecting the input-module output from CHANNEL ASSIGN and DIRECT OUT. During mixdown, you can reduce noise by muting those tracks that have nothing playing at the moment. In some mixers, MUTE is called "CHANNEL ON/OFF."

PHASE (POLARITY INVERT)

This switch inverts the polarity of the input signal. That is, it switches the pin 2 and 3 connections to flip the phase 180°. You might use it to correct for a miswired microphone cable whose polarity is reversed.

+48

This button turns on 48 volts of phantom power at the mic input connector for powering condenser microphones.

Automated Mixing Controls

These controls (Read, Write, Update, etc.) are beyond the scope of this book. Basically, they control the functions of a computer-assisted mixing system. The computer memory remembers and updates the console settings so that a mix can be performed and refined in several stages.

Output Module Functions

Output modules are also called *group, submix, submaster,* or *bus master* modules. Each output module includes a combining network (fed by the input modules) and a submaster fader that controls the overall level of the submix feeding each program bus. The submaster fader might also be called a *group master* or *bus master* fader.

As decribed earlier, small submixes, such as a drum mix, keyboard mix, vocal mix, etc., can be set up on the console. The level of each mix or group is controlled by a SUBMASTER fader.

A 16×4×2 console has 16 input modules, 4 submaster modules, and 2 master output channels. The following items are some of the other connectors and functions found in an output module.

ECHO RETURN (ECHO RECEIVE, EFFECTS RETURN, AUX RETURN)

As explained earlier in this chapter, the output of the reverberation unit (or other effects device) returns to the echo-return connector in a program-bus module, where the reverberated signal blends with the program-bus signal. The ECHO RETURN knob controls the level of the signal coming from the reverberation unit.

BUS IN Jack

This is a line-level input to a program bus. It is used as an echo return or an effects return.

Effects Panning

Effects panning places the images of the effects or echo signals wherever desired between the monitor speakers.

FOLDBACK Connectors

These connectors are in parallel with the TAPE IN jacks. The output of each tape track is connected to a TAPE IN jack, so the FOLDBACK connector parallels, or "mults," the tape-machine output. The FOLD-BACK jacks can be be used to send the tape outputs to an outboard device in addition to the console, such as an external cue mixer.

BUS TRIM

This rotary pot provides fine tuning of the bus level, and is used together with the bus master (or submaster) fader.

BUS/MONITOR/CUE Switch for ECHO RETURN

This is a switch that feeds the echo-return signal to your choice of three destinations: the program bus (for mixdown), the monitor mix, or the cue mix.

Level Indicators

These are a VU meter or a column of LEDs, which are connected to each bus, to indicate the signal level (voltage) being sent to the tape recorder.

Meter Switches

In many consoles, the VU meters can measure signal levels other than console output levels. Switches near the meters can be set so that the meters indicate bus level, echo-send level, echo-return level, monitor-mix level, etc.

Those readings help you set optimum levels for the outboard devices receiving those signals. Too low a level results in noise; too high a level causes distortion in the outboard unit. For example, if the echo-return signal sounds garbled or distorted, the cause may be an excessive echo-send level. That condition can be verified by checking the VU meters which are switched to read the ECHO or EFFECTS bus.

Monitor-Section Functions

In the monitor section, we have the following switches and functions.

Monitor Mixer

This is a submixer that controls the balance of the instruments heard over the monitor speakers. The monitor mixer lets you hear an approximation of the final product without affecting the recording levels. Monitor-mixer pots typically are distributed among the submaster (bus master) modules. The monitor mixer might also include panning and echo sends for the monitored signals.

BUS/TAPE Switch

This switch lets you monitor either the program buses or the tape machine. When the source/tape switch on a tape machine is set to "tape," the BUS/TAPE switch on the console lets you monitor off-tape to check for tape distortion.

MONITOR SELECT Switches

These switches allow monitoring of various signals, such as LINE (for 2-track recorders), AUX (such as cue or echo), or MON (the monitor mix of the buses).

DIM

This is a switch that reduces the monitor level by a preset amount (as in "Dim the lights").

ECHO RETURN TO CUE

This is an echo-return level control that affects the amount of echo or reverberation heard in the studio headphone mix. This echo is independent of any echo being recorded on tape.

ECHO RETURN TO MONITOR

This echo-return control affects the amount of echo or reverberation heard in the monitor mix. This echo is independent of any echo being recorded on tape.

Talkback, Slate, and Oscillator

TALKBACK

The TALKBACK function lets the people in the control room talk to the musicians in the studio. A small microphone often is built into the console for this purpose.

SLATE

The SLATE function routes the control-room microphone signal to all the buses for announcing on tape the name of the tune and take number. In some consoles, a low-frequency tone is recorded on tape during slating; thus, the beginning of the take can be quickly located by listening for tape tones during fast-forward or rewind.

OSCILLATOR

An OSCILLATOR is used to put alignment tones on tape, and to reference the tape recorder's meters to those on the console.

Conclusion

We've covered the most common mixing-console functions. The next time you encounter an unfamiliar console, you may have a better idea of what those strange labels mean. With some knowledge of console functions, you're ready to set knobs, flip switches, and push buttons to control the sound of music.

12 SESSION PROCEDURES

"We're rolling. Take One." With those words begins the recording session. It can be an exhilarating or an exasperating experience, depending on how smoothly you run the session.

The musicians need an engineer who works quickly, yet carefully. Otherwise, they may lose their creative inspiration while waiting for the engineer to get his act together. And the client, paying by the hour, wastes money unless the engineer has prepared for the session in advance. This chapter describes how to conduct a multitrack recording session. These procedures should help you keep track of things and run the session efficiently.

There are some spontaneous sessions—especially in home studios—that just "grow organically" without advance planning. The instrumentation is not known until the song is done! You just try out different musical ideas and instruments until you find a pleasing combination. Using this method, a band that has its own recording gear can afford to take the time to find out what works musically before going into a professional studio. In addition, if the band is recording itself where it practices, the microphone setup and some of the console settings can be more-or-less permanent. This chapter, however, describes those procedures normally followed at professional studios, where time is money.

Pre-production

Long before the session starts, you're deeply involved in *pre-production*—the planning in advance of what you're going to do at the session, in terms of overdubbing, track assignments, instrument layout, and microphone selection.

Planning the Production Schedule

The first step is to find out from the producer what the instrumentation will be and how many tracks will be needed. Make a list of the instruments and vocals that will be used in each song. Include such details as the number of tom toms, whether acoustic or electric guitars will be used, and so on.

Next, decide which of these instruments will be recorded at the same time and which will be overdubbed one at a time. It's common to record the instruments in the following order, but there are always exceptions:

1. Loud rhythm instruments—bass, drums, electric guitar, and electric keyboards. The lead vocalist usually sings a *reference vocal* or a *scratch vocal* along with the rhythm section so the musicians can get a feel for the tune and keep track of where they are in the song. The vocalist's performance in this case is recorded but probably will be redone later.
2. Quiet rhythm instruments—acoustic guitar and piano.
3. Lead vocal; doubled lead vocal (if desired).
4. Backup vocals (in stereo).
5. Overdubs—solos, percussion, synthesizer, and sound effects.
6. Sweetening—horns and strings.

The planned sequence of recording basic tracks and overdubs is listed on a *production schedule*. An example is shown in Fig. 12-1.

Track Assignments

Once the instrumentation and the order of recording are clearly understood, you can plan your track assignments. Decide what instruments will go on which tracks of the multitrack recorder, and write this information on a *track sheet*, as shown in Fig. 12-2. Note that the outer tracks are most prone to drop-outs at high frequencies, and so they are usually reserved for bass and kick drum.

You may have more instruments than tracks, in which case, you'll have to decide what groups of instruments to put on each track. In a 4-track recording, for example, you might record a stereo mix of the rhythm section on tracks 1 and 2, and then overdub the vocals and solos on tracks 3 and 4. Or, you might put guitars on track 1, bass and drums on track 2, vocals on track 3, and keyboards on track 4.

```
         Tape Speed:  15 ips              Artist:  Muffin
         8 Track                          Producer:  B. Brauning
         Noise Reduction:  dbx


      1.  Song:  "Mr. Potato Head."
          Instrumentation:  Bass, drums, electric rhythm guitar,
          electric lead guitar, acoustic piano, sax, lead vocal.
          Comments:  Record rhythm section together with reference
          vocal. Overdub sax, acoustic, piano, and lead vocal later.

      2.  Song:  "Sambatina."
          Instrumentation:  Bass, drums, acoustic guitar, percussion,
          synthesizer.
          Comments:  Record rhythm section with scratch acoustic
          guitar. Overdub acoustic guitar, percussion, and
          synthesizer.

      3.  Song:  "Mr. Potato Head."
          Overdubs:  (1) acoustic piano, (2) lead vocal, (3) sax.

      4.  Song:  "Sambatina."
          Overdubs:  (1) acoustic guitar, (2) synthesizer,
          (3) percussion.

      5.  Mix:  "Mr. Potato Head."
          Comments:  Add 80-msec delay to toms.
                     Double lead guitar in stereo.
                     Increase reverb on sax during solo.

      6.  Mix:  "Sambatina."
          Comments:  Add flanger to bass on intro only.
                     Manually flange percussion.
```

Fig. 12-1. Production schedule for a multitrack recording session.

Remember that when several instruments are assigned to the same track, you can't separate their images in the stereo stage. That is, you can't pan them to different positions; all the instruments on one track will sound like they're occupying the same point in space. For this reason, you may want to do a stereo mix of the rhythm section on, say, tracks 1 and 2, and then overdub the vocals and solos on tracks 3 and 4.

It's possible to overdub more than four parts on a 4-track tape recorder. To do this, you re-record several tracks onto one track—a procedure called *bouncing* or *ping-ponging*. The following is an example of this process:

1. Record bass, rhythm guitar, and drums on tracks 1, 2, and 3, as shown in Fig. 12-3A.

Fig. 12-2. A track sheet.

```
                    TRACK SHEET

        Studio: SUBLIMINAL SOUND
        Client: MR. PACKETS PRODUCTIONS
        Artist: THE TROLLS
        Producer: FLAKEY FOONT
        Engineer: B. BARTLETT
        Album title: SIT-DOWN MUSIC
        Speed: 15 IPS
        Noise reduction: DOLBY C

        Song title: DIG UP NEBRASKA

        Track 1: BASS
              2: RHYTHM GUITAR
              3: LEAD GUITAR
              4: PIANO
              5: LEAD VOCAL
              6: DRUMS L
              7: DRUMS R
              8: KICK

        Song title: SIDEWALK BLUES (EXPERIMENTAL)

        Track 1: BANJO-BASS
              2: VOCAL
              3: DOUBLED VOCAL
              4: EXPONENTIAL HORNS
              5: TINKER TOYS (PERCUSSION)
              6: SLINKY (PERCUSSION)
              7: FOOT STOMPS
              8: SPARE
```

2. Play the tape, mix these tracks through the console, and record the mix onto track 4, as in Fig. 12-3B.

3. While monitoring track 4 in sync mode, record lead vocal and backup vocals on tracks 1 and 2, as illustrated in Fig. 12-3C.

4. Bounce tracks 1 and 2 to track 3, as shown in Fig. 12-3D.

5. Record the lead guitar on track 1 and the piano on track 2, as in Fig. 12-3E. More instruments can be added by mixing them in "live" along with the tracks you're bouncing.

6. Finally, mix the four tracks down to a 2-track recorder, as shown in Fig. 12-3F.

When playing back off the record head, try not to bounce a track to an adjacent track—otherwise, the crosstalk between tracks may create a high-frequency squeal. Keep in mind that tape hiss and distortion increase slightly every time a track is re-recorded. This is called *generation loss*. Fortunately, noise-reduction systems, such as Dolby® or dbx®, can keep the noise down. When doing extensive bouncing, record the background instruments first; record the instruments that need to be crisp and clean last (such as the lead vocal and drums).

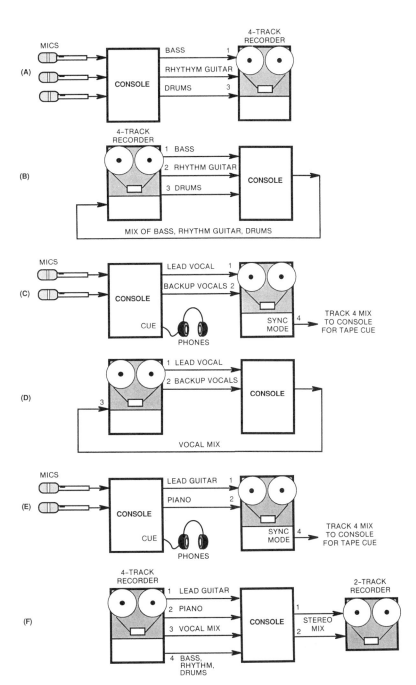

Fig. 12-3.
Example
procedure for
bouncing tracks.

If you have many tracks available, leave several tracks open for experimentation. For example, you can *stack* the vocals—record several takes of a vocal part using a separate track for each take, so that no take is lost. Then, you can combine the best parts of each take into a single final performance on one track. It's also a good idea to record the monitor mix on one or two unused tracks. The recorded monitor mix can be used to make a *work-print* tape for the client to take home and evaluate, or for a cue mix that is used for overdubs.

Microphone Input List

Now make up a *microphone input list* similar to the following list.

Microphone Input List

Input	Instrument	Microphone
1	Bass	Direct
2	Kick	EV RE-20
3	Snare/Hi-Hat	AKG C451
4	Drums Overhead L	Shure SM81
5	Drums Overhead R	Shure SM81
6	Hi Toms	Sennheiser MD421
7	Low Toms	Sennheiser MD421
8	Electric Lead Guitar	Shure SM57
9	Electric Lead Guitar	Direct
10	Piano	Crown PZM-30R
11	Reference Vocal	Beyer M500
12	Spare	—

Write down a column of numbers at the left side of the list corresponding to each numbered console input. Next to each input number write the name of the instrument assigned to that input. Finally, write down next to each instrument the microphone(s) or direct box that you plan to use on that instrument.

Be flexible in your microphone choices. You may need to experiment with various microphones during the session to find the one giving the best sound with the least console equalization. During the lead guitar overdubs, for example, you can set up a direct box, three close-up microphones, and one distant microphone, and, then, find the combination that sounds best.

Find out from the producer what kind of sound he or she wants—a "tight" sound, a "loose, live" sound, an accurate, realistic sound, or whatever. Ask to hear records having the kind of sound that the producer desires. Try to determine what techniques were used to create the sounds on those records, and plan your microphone techniques and effects accordingly. (Tips on choosing a microphone were given in Chapter 6.)

Instrument Layout Chart

Next, work out an *instrument layout chart*, indicating where each instrument will be located in the studio, and where baffles and isolation booths will be used (if any). In planning the layout, make sure that all the musicians can see each other and are close enough together to play as an ensemble.

Setting Up the Studio

About an hour before the session starts, clean up the studio so that you promote a professional atmosphere. Lay down rugs and place AC power boxes according to your layout chart. Run cue cables from each artist's location to the cue panel in the studio.

Now, position the baffles on top of what has gone before. Put out chairs and stools according to the layout. Add music stands and music-stand lights.

Place microphone stands approximately where they will be used. Wrap one end of a microphone cable around each microphone-stand boom, leaving a few extra coils of cable near the microphone-stand base to allow slack for moving the microphone stand. Run the rest of the cable back to the microphone input panel. Plug each cable into the appropriate wall-panel input, according to your microphone input list. Some engineers prefer to run cables in reverse order, connecting to the input panel first and running the cable out to the microphone stand. That procedure leaves less of a confusing tangle at the input panel where connections might be changed.

Now bring out the microphones. Check each microphone to make sure that its switches are in the desired positions. Put the microphones in their stand adapters, connect the cables, and balance the weight of the boom against the microphone.

Finally, connect the musicians' headphones for cueing. Set up a spare cue line and microphone to allow for last-minute changes.

Setting Up the Control Room

The following is a step-by-step procedure for setting up the control room.

1. If necessary, patch console bus 1 to tape track 1, bus 2 to track 2, and so on.

2. Check out all the equipment to make sure that it's working properly.

3. Clean and demagnetize the tape machines.

4. Thread some blank tape onto the machines.

5. Put some calibration tones on tape, as described later in this chapter under "calibration tones."

6. Pull all the patch cords from the patch panel.

7. Normalize or zero the console by setting all the switches and knobs to "off," "zero," or "flat," so as to have no effect. That's to establish a point of reference and to avoid surprises later on.

8. Feed a 1-kHz tone to all of the console outputs so that the console meters read 0 VU. Adjust the record levels of the multitrack machine so the recorder meters also read 0 VU. This procedure matches the recorder meters to the console meters, so that you only have to watch the console meters while recording. If you're using noise-reduction equipment, refer to Chapter 9 for meter calibration and Dolby®-tone recording.

9. Switch on phantom powering for the condenser microphones.

10. Set the console input-selector switches to "mic."

11. Attach a *designation strip* of paper leader across the front of the console so that you can write down the name of the instrument each fader affects. Also, label the submasters and monitor-mixer pots according to what is assigned to them.

12. Turn up the monitor system. Carefully bring up each fader, one at a time, and solo each microphone. You should hear normal studio noise. If you hear sounds of any problems, such as dead or noisy microphones, hum, bad cables, or faulty power supplies, correct them before the session. To verify the correctness of the microphone input list, have an assistant scratch each microphone grille with a fingernail and identify the instrument that the microphone is intended to pick up.

Check all the cue headphones by playing a tone through them and listening while wiggling the cable.

This should complete your checklist.

After the musicians arrive, they typically are allowed from 30 minutes to 1 hour of free setup time for seating, tuning, and microphone placement. Show them where to sit, and work out new seating arrangements, if necessary, to make them more comfortable. Set up the drums first and tune them. Add tissues and tape, if necessary, to dampen the drums.

Once the instruments are set up, you may want to listen to their live sound in the studio and do what you can to improve it. A dull-sounding guitar may need new strings; a noisy guitar amp may need new tubes, and so on.

Session Overview

Let's return to the control room now and get started. Usually, the upcoming sequence of events is as follows:

1. For efficiency, the basic rhythm tracks for several songs are recorded on the first session.
2. The out-takes are edited out.
3. The overdubs for all the songs are done in a dubbing session.
4. All the tunes are mixed down.
5. The master tape is assembled and leadered.

Recording

In recording the basic rhythm tracks, the main concerns are to assign instruments to tracks, adjust attenuation and recording levels, set submixes, set the cue mix, and set the monitor mix. Let's describe these procedures in detail.

Turn Up the Cue Potentiometers

Turn the cue mixer pots up about halfway so the musicians can hear themselves over the headphones. The cue mix will be adjusted later after the input attenuators are set.

Assign Microphone Signals to the Channels

Next, assign each microphone to the desired output channel (bus) as specified on your track sheet. Each channel is connected to the correspondingly numbered tape track on the multitrack recorder.

If only one instrument is assigned to a track, you can eliminate the noise of the console combining amplifier by patching the instrument's signal directly to the tape track. To do this, locate the *direct output jack* of the input module for that instrument and patch it to the desired track. Some mixing boards also require pressing a *direct button* on the input module.

Set Master and Submaster Faders to Design Center

Once the channel assignments are made, turn the master and submaster faders up about three quarters of the way (10 to 15 dB from the top). This portion of the fader travel, usually shaded, is called the *design center*. When the faders are at design center, the console gain is distributed for optimum headroom and signal-to-noise ratio.

Turn Up the Monitor System

Turn up the monitor-mixer pots and monitor the console program buses. For tape tracks receiving a direct-patched signal, monitor the tape-track input rather than the bus.

Set Input Attenuation

Next, listen to one instrument at a time by turning up the fader for that instrument, or by pushing the solo button for that input. Have the musician play the loudest part of the song. If necessary, adjust the input attenuation (gain trim) as follows: Starting with no attenuation, gradually increase attenuation (that is, reduce the level) just to the point where there is no trace of distortion or until the LED clipping indicator stops flashing. Repeat this procedure for each input module in use. (Some consoles have switchable pads instead of gain-trim controls.)

Readjust the Microphones

Listen to each instrument alone to make sure it sounds reasonably clean and accurate. Work out the instrument's sound with the producer, adjusting microphone positions as needed.

Set Equalization

You may, at this point, want to apply equalization to each instrument heard individually. Filter out frequencies which are above and below the range of the instrument. However, don't spend too much time on equalization until all the instruments are mixed together, because the equalization that sounds right on an individual instrument may not sound right when all the instruments are heard together. In creating the desired tonal balance, use equalization as a last resort, after experimenting with microphone selection and placement.

Set Recording Levels

Now you're ready to "get a level." Have each instrument play—one at a time. Using the fader on the instrument's input module, set the recording level as high as possible without causing tape distortion. Repeat this procedure for each instrument.

Normally, you'd watch the console meters to set levels, because you previously had matched the recorder meters to the console meters. However, you'll have to watch the recorder meters for tracks that are patched direct, or if you're using dbx® noise reduction.

If your recorder uses VU meters, different instruments will require different recording levels, as described in Chapter 9.

Set Submixes

If you have several microphones assigned to one channel, monitor that channel and turn up the faders for those microphones. As the band plays, set the desired balance between microphones with the faders while maintaining a proper recording level. The submaster fader for that channel controls the overall level of the submix.

Readjust Attenuators and Recording Levels

Next, have the entire band play the loudest part of the song, and touch up the attenuator and level settings. You might want to work from the first fader to the last, soloing each one in turn.

Set Monitor Mix and Cue Mix

Adjust the monitor volume controls for a rough mix, as heard from the monitor speakers. Then monitor the cue mix and adjust it according to what the musicians want to hear. These mixes are independent of the levels going onto the tape.

Record a Work-Print Tape

Get set to record a work-print tape of the studio monitor mix, either on two left-over tracks or on a 2-track machine. This tape is for the producer to take home so he or she can evaluate the performance.

Start Recording

Now you're ready to record the tune. Briefly play a metronome to the group at the desired tempo, or play a click track through the cue system.

Start the tape in record mode. Hit the slate button and announce the name of the tune and the take number.

The piano player plays the keynote of the song (for tuning other instruments later). Then the group leader or the drummer counts off the beat, and the group starts playing.

The producer listens to the musical performance while the engineer watches levels and listens for audio problems. As the song progresses, you may need to make small level adjustments. As stated before, the recording levels are set as high as possible without causing distortion. Balancing the instruments at this time is done with the monitor mixer. The monitor mix affects only what is being heard, not what is going on tape.

The assistant engineer (if any) runs the tape machine and keeps track of the takes on a *take sheet*. He or she notes the name of the tune, the take number, and whether the take was complete. A code is often used to indicate whether the take was a false start, nearly completed, a "keeper," etc. Fig. 12-4 shows a sample take sheet.

Fig. 12-4. A take sheet.

```
                        TAKE SHEET

        C       Complete take
        ©       Choice take (best take)
        INC     Incomplete take (nearly finished)
        FS      False start
        LFS     Long false start

        1.  Song title:  "DIGITAL GOO"
            Takes:  1-FS, 2-©, 3-©
            Comments:  USE INTRO OF TAKE 3, USE REST OF TAKE 2.

        2.  Song title:  "HWEE-HWOW"
            Takes:  1-FS, 2-FS, 3-LFS, 4-INC, 5-FS, 6-INC, 7-LFS
            Comments:  FORGET IT!

        3.  Song title: "BUSTED PAN-POT BLUES"
            Takes:  1-C, 2-FS,  3-©, 4-C
            Comments:  MONO.
```

As the song is in progress, don't use the solo function because the abrupt monitoring change may disturb the producer. The producer should stop the performance if a major fluff (mistake) occurs but should let the minor ones pass.

At the end of the song, the musicians should be silent for several seconds after the last note. Or, if the song will end in a fade-out, the musicians should continue playing for about a minute so there will be enough material for a fade-out during mixdown.

After the tune is done, you can either play it back or go on to a second take. The musicians will catch their fluffed notes during playback; you should just listen for audio quality.

Now, record other takes or tunes. It's usually less tiring to do only three or four takes of a single song, and then run through another song. If a song is not working, you can come back to it later. Try to limit tracking sessions to four hours or less; five hours maximum.

Breaking Down

When the session is over, take down the microphones, microphone stands, and cables. Put the microphones back in their protective boxes and bags. Wipe off the cables with a damp rag if necessary.

Wrap each cable around your arm (between palm and elbow) and coil the last two feet or so around the cable loops. Some studios hang the cable in big loops on the microphone stand. However, another way to wrap a cable so that it uncoils easily is as follows:

1. Connect the two XLR connectors together.

2. Hold the connectors vertically in one hand so that the cable hangs in two lengths.

3. Fold the cable two lengths at a time, accordion-style, to the length of the connectors.

4. Stuff the folded cable in a cardboard tube.

When you undo the cable the next time it's used, it will open out without any kinks or knots.

Put the track sheet and take sheet in the multitrack tape box along with the tape (stored tail out). Label the box and the tape for their contents. Normally, the studio keeps the multitrack master unless the recording group wants to buy it.

You may want to edit out the out-takes and splice them together on a separate reel. Then, put one foot of paper leader between each of the keeper takes on the master tape. Write new tape logs indicating each of the reels' contents.

Log the console settings by reading them slowly into a portable cassette recorder. At a future session, you can play back the tape and reset the console just the way it was for the original session.

Overdubbing

After the basic or rhythm tracks for all the tunes are recorded, *overdubs* are added. To do this, a musician listens to previously recorded tracks over headphones, and records a new part on an open track.

First, however, set up the studio for the instrument that is to be overdubbed. You'll have more freedom in microphone placement here because there will be no leakage from other instruments.

Setting Up the Console and Tape Machine

Here's how to set up the console for overdubbing: First, re-label the inputs if necessary. Set the recorded tape tracks to "sync" mode and set the tracks to be recorded to "record ready" mode. Assign the new instrument to the desired tape track, turn up its fader(s), and adjust the input attenuation, level, and equalization, as needed. Find the section of the song (on the tape) that needs overdubs. Play the previously recorded rhythm tracks in sync mode.

Setting the Cue Mix and Monitor Mix

Set the cue mix and monitor mix for a good balance between the pre-recorded tracks and the live microphone signals you're adding. For example, suppose you've already recorded drums, bass, and guitars, and you're ready to add a vocal. While monitoring the cue bus, play the tape and set up a cue mix so that the vocalist can hear himself and the previously recorded tracks in his headphones. Mix the tape tracks with the *tape-cue* pots, and mix in the vocalist with the *cue* pot on his input module.

Set a mix on the monitor mixer too. Remember, the monitor mix and cue mix are not going onto tape—they just allow you to hear how the vocalist blends with the other tracks.

Recording the Overdub

When you're happy with the cue mix and the monitor mix, record the new track(s). The musician should be quiet when not playing so that extraneous noises are not recorded.

The new part is recorded and re-recorded until it is correct. This re-recording does not affect previously recorded tracks.

Punching In

Sometimes overdubs are used to correct only a few notes of a musical line or solo. A useful technique in this case is called *punching in*. You rewind the tape to a point several bars before the spot where the mistake was made. Play the tape in sync mode and have the musician play along. You *punch in* the record button just before the mistake, wherever there is a convenient space between notes. Then, you *punch out* of record mode at an appropriate point as the tape is running. The musician can signal the engineer where to punch in by jabbing his finger toward the engineer. Better yet, the musician can punch in and out by using a foot pedal that is wired to the record-mode relay.

Often it's difficult for a musician to get all the way through a long difficult solo or musical line without making a mistake. In this case, you can punch in and out to record the part in successive segments. Another use of overdubbing is to re-do individual tracks that were unsatisfactory in sound or performance at the original recording session.

With care, overdubbing can be used to record a few more instruments on a completely full tape. By punching in and out, you can overdub new instruments in the pauses on previously recorded tracks. For example, suppose all the tracks are full but you want to add a cymbal roll at the beginning of the chorus. Find a track that has nothing playing at that moment, and punch in the cymbal roll there.

Stacking Tracks

If several open tracks are available, you can record a solo overdub in several takes, each on a separate track. This procedure is called *stacking tracks*. After recording all the takes, play back the solo (in sync mode) and assign all the overdubbed tracks to a remaining open track set in record mode. Match the levels of the different takes. Then, switch the overdubbed tracks on and off (using muting), recording just the best parts of each take. Finally, erase the old overdubbed tracks to free them up for other instruments.

Drum Overdubs

Drum overdubs are usually done right after the rhythm session because the microphones are already set up, and the overdubbed sound will match the sound of the original drum track.

Overdubbing in the Control Room

To aid in communications among the engineer, producer, and musician, you can have the musician play in the control room while overdubbing. A synthesizer or electric guitar can be patched into the console through a direct box, and the direct signal can be fed to a guitar amp in the studio via a cue line. Pick up the amp with a microphone, and record and monitor the microphone's signal.

Mixdown

After all the parts are recorded, you're ready for mixdown. You prepare the console and tape decks, record tones, erase noises, and play the multi-track tape through the console while adjusting balances, panning, equalization, reverberation, and effects. Once you've rehearsed the mix to perfection, you record it onto a 2-track recorder. Let's look at these procedures in detail.

Preparing for Mixdown

If necessary, connect console buses 1 and 2 to tracks 1 and 2 of the 2-track recorder which you will be using to record the mixdown. Clean, demagnetize, and align the tape machines. Normalize or zero the console.

Tape a designation strip of paper leader tape along the front of the console to write down the names of the instrument(s) that each fader affects. Keep this strip with the multitrack master tape so you can use it each time the master is played.

Calibration Tones

Calibration tones should be recorded on the ¼-inch master tape just before recording the mixes. After cleaning, degaussing, and aligning your tape machine, record the following tones on both channels simultaneously with NO noise reduction (20 seconds each):

1. 1 kHz at 0 VU.
2. 1 kHz, 15 kHz, 10 kHz, 100 Hz, and 50 Hz at 0 VU for 15 ips, or at −10 VU for 7½ ips.
3. If Dolby® A noise reduction is used, record an encoded Dolby® tone at 0 VU, followed by an encoded 1-kHz tone at 0 VU. Dolby® A tones should be generated by each track's encoder.
4. If dbx® Type-1 noise reduction is used, record an encoded 1-kHz tone at 0 VU. If a zero offset is used, note the offset level (e.g., 0-VU program = −3 VU on tape).

The duplicating engineer or record-mastering engineer will use the 15-kHz tone to align the playback head, the 1-kHz 0-VU tone to set the overall level and channel balance, and the other tones to set playback equalization. Then the engineer's tape machine will play back the same tonal balance and stereo balance that you recorded during mixdown.

If you don't have access to a multifrequency generator, just put a 1-kHz tone or a sine-wave synthesizer note (2 octaves above middle C) at 0 VU on both channels.

Setting the Input-Selector Switches

Flip the input-selector switch on each input to the appropriate position so the tape tracks will play through the console for mixing.

Monitoring the 2-Track Mix Bus

Since you're mixing to two-channel stereo, monitor only channels 1 and 2 (the 2-track mix bus), with their monitor pan pots set to the extreme left and right. Assign each track to channel 1 (left), channel 2 (right), or both (for panning between left and right).

Setting the Pan Pots

Set the pan pot for each recorded track to a position that will place its sonic image in the desired location between the pair of monitor speakers.

Try to achieve a stereo stage that is well-balanced from left to right. For ease of record cutting, the bass, kick drum, and lead vocal should go to the center (pan pot set straight up). The other instruments can go equally to left or right, or to half-left and half-right.

You may want to pan the extreme left and right tracks slightly toward the center; this makes record-cutting easier and keeps the tracks from sounding too isolated in space. However, try not to pan everything to the middle—you'll wind up with a mono tape.

Erasing Unwanted Program Material

Turn up the master fader and play the multitrack tape. Listen to each track by itself. Erase any unwanted noises or out-takes so that you won't be surprised during the mixdown. You may want to erase entire tracks, or segments, that don't add to the song.

If a noise occurs just before the musician starts playing, erasing the noise may accidentally erase the musical part. This can be prevented as follows: Turn the tape upside down by reversing the reels, and then find the track of the desired instrument, playing backwards. Play the tape section which came just after the noise. You'll hear it playing in reverse. Just after the reverse part ends, punch that track into record mode, erasing the noise. That way, you avoid erasing part of the musical line.

Starting the Mixdown

Now you're ready to mix. Set the master fader and submaster faders about three quarters of the way up (10 to 15 dB from the top). Play the multitrack tape and adjust the faders for a pleasing balance of the instruments.

Setting the Mix

As a starting point, you may want to set the mix so that all the instruments and vocals sound equally loud, and then turn up the most important tracks and turn down the background instruments. Or, you can bring up one track at a time and blend it with the other tracks. For example, first bring up the kick drum, and then add bass and balance the two together. Next, add drums, guitars, keyboards, and then the vocals. To reduce tape noise, mute any track that has nothing playing on it at the moment.

Pop Music Mix

Here's a mixdown method for pop music. Set the kick-drum level to -10 VU on the VU meters. Turn up the monitor level until the kick drum is as loud as you like to hear it; then leave the monitor level alone. Bring up the other tracks, one at a time, and mix them relative to the kick drum.

Country Music Mix

The following is another method of doing a mixdown. It's for country music, where the vocal is most prominent. Set the lead-vocal level to peak at −5 VU. Bring up the monitor level so that the vocal is as loud as you like to hear it, and then leave the monitor level alone. Bring in the other tracks, one at a time, and mix them relative to the vocal track.

Setting Equalization

Next, adjust equalization as desired. The procedure for this was described in Chapter 10.

Setting Echo-Send and Echo-Receive

Set the echo-receive or effects-receive controls about half-way up. Adjust the echo-send and effects-send knobs for each track for the desired results. The bass and kick drum usually get little or no reverberation so that they retain their clarity.

Fine-Tuning the Mix

As you're adjusting the mix, set the input faders and master fader to achieve a 0-VU recording level (+3 VU maximum) on the meters for buses 1 and 2. Try to keep the input faders, submaster faders, and master faders near design center. If level changes are required during the mix-down, mark on the faders the settings for each change.

Make a *cue sheet* that notes the mixer changes required at various tape-counter times. For example:

1:10   Bring up lead-guitar solo to +3 dB.
1:49   Bring down lead guitar to −2 dB.
2:42   Add +6 dB at 12 kHz to synthesizer bell effect.
3:05   Start fade, out at 3:15.

Don't mix in too much bass. Sometimes it's hard to tell how much bass is appropriate, owing to variables in the monitoring system. Typically, the bass is mixed in at about −8 to −4 VU when metered alone. You normally mix by ear, of course, rather than by watching the meters.

Using the tape recorder's return-to-zero function, play the multitrack tape several times to perfect and practice the mix. Set the balances, equalization, and effects as desired.

You may want to set them to achieve a mix that sounds like records you've heard through the monitors you're using. It's a good idea to play a record with tunes like those you're recording to hear a typical mix for that particular style of music.

When you mix, your attention scans the inputs, briefly listening to each instrument in turn, and to the mix as a whole. Take your hands off the console and listen. If you hear something you don't like, fix it. Is the vocal too tubby? Roll off the bass on the vocal track. Is the kick drum too quiet? Turn it up. Is the lead-guitar solo too dead? Turn up its echo send.

Recording the Mix

When you're satisfied with the mix, sound quality, and recording levels, slate the tape and record the mix on your 2-track machine.

You may want to *fade out* the end of the tune by slowly pulling down the master fader. The slower the song, the slower the fade should be. Start the fade relatively quickly, then slow down as you fade. The mixdown is now complete.

Read the console settings slowly into a cassette tape recorder for future reference.

Repeat the mixdown procedure for all the best takes on the multitrack reels.

Summary of the Console Operating Procedures

The following lists are the step-by-step procedures you will use. They are summarized here for easy reference.

Recording

1. Turn up the cue system.
2. Assign the instruments to their tracks.
3. Turn up the monitor system.
4. Turn up the submasters and master to design center.

5. Adjust the input attenuators.
6. Set the submixes and recording levels.
7. Set the monitor mix and cue mix.
8. Record onto the multitrack tape.

Overdubbing

1. Assign the instruments to be recorded to open tracks.
2. Turn up the monitor system and cue system.
3. Turn up the submasters and master to design center.
4. Play the multitrack tape in sync mode and set up a cue mix and a monitor mix.
5. While a live musician is playing, adjust his or her input attenuation and recording level.
6. Set the cue mix and monitor mix to include the sound of the instrument being added.
7. Record the new parts on open tracks.

Mixdown

1. Set the input selectors to accept the multitrack tape signals.
2. Monitor channels 1 and 2 (2-track mix bus). Pan the monitor channels to extreme left and right.
3. Assign tape tracks to channel 1, channel 2, or both (using pan pots).
4. Turn up the master fader to design center. In some consoles, the submasters should also be up.
5. Set a rough mix with the input faders.
6. Set equalization, reverberation, and effects.
7. Perfect the mix and set the recording levels.
8. Record onto the 2-track tape.

Assembling the Master Reels

Now you're ready to assemble the 2-track tape into a finished format for tape duplication or for record cutting. It will contain the songs in the desired order, plus the leader tape for banding the record. In addition, it will have calibration tones so that the playback deck used for record cutting can be aligned for flat response from your tape.

Sequencing

Decide what sequence you want the songs to be in on the record. For the first song on Side 1, use a strong, accessible, up-tempo tune. Follow it with something quieter. Alternate keys or tempos from song to song. To leave a good final impression, the last tune should be as good as or better than the first.

Try to keep the total time per side under 18 minutes for maximum level, maximum bass, and lowest distortion on the record. A maximum of 24 minutes per side is recommended. Also, try to keep the total times for Side 1 and Side 2 about equal, to conserve cassette tape.

Leader Length

The length of leader between songs depends on how long a pause you want between them. Four seconds is typical. Use a longer leader if you want the listener to get out of the mood of the piece just heard before going on to the next. Use a shorter leader to either change the mood abruptly or to make similar song flow together. Or, using two 2-track machines, you can crossfade between the two final mixes, copy the result on a third machine, and edit the copy into the rest of the program.

Master-Reel Assembly

You'll be making a separate reel for Side 1 and Side 2 of the record or cassette. To assemble the master tapes, wind onto the take-up reel the following material in this order:

1. Tones.
2. At least ten seconds of leader.
3. First song.
4. Leader.
5. Second song.
6. Leader, etc.
7. Last song on Side 1 of album.

8. At least ten seconds of leader.

Then rewind the tape. Play it and time it from the beginning of the first song to the end of the last song (including the leaders between songs). This is called the *running time*. Also, time each selection.

Using a piece of masking tape, fasten the leader tail to the reel and print "TAIL OUT" on the masking tape. Type or print a neat label for the tape reel, and include the title, artist, "Side 1," and the running time.

Using another take-up reel, assemble Side 2 of the album (but without tones). Time Side 2 and label the reel.

Labeling

Include the following information on the tape-box label:

1. Tape-head format, stereo/mono, tape speed, playback equalization (usually NAB), noise reduction, "tail-out" designation.

2. The location of the test tones (usually at the beginning of Reel 1), tone frequencies, and level as recorded.

3. The flux level corresponding to 0 VU (e.g., 0 VU = 250 nWb/m).

4. The location on tape of the highest peak level in the program.

5. Album title, artist, studio, engineer, and producer.

6. Song titles and timing, plus the total running time per side.

7. Suggestions for equalization or level settings for each song, if desired.

Safety Copy

Be sure to make a safety copy of the master before sending the master tape, in case it is lost or damaged. When copying the master, set the 0-VU tone from the playback machine to read 0 VU on the recording machine. There's no need to reset the program levels because you already set them when recording the master tape.

Note that the master tape doesn't leave the studio until all studio time has been paid for!

Documentation

Send the tape to the record mastering company insured for the whole cost of the production. Include the song lyrics, producer's notes, the address and phone number of the engineer and producer, and the record-label information (such as the composers, arrangers, and publishers).

There is your finished product. It's amazing how the long hours of work with lots of complex equipment have been concentrated into that little tape. But it's been fun. You have created a craftsmanlike product you can be proud of. When played, it will re-create a musical experience in the ears and mind of the listener—no small achievement.

13 CREATIVE SONIC EFFECTS

Probably the most creative part of recording engineering is "getting a sound." This means taking the raw sound from instruments in the studio and shaping it, playing with it, until you create a pleasing new effect.

For example, some producers and engineers work for hours getting a good drum sound. They experiment with various microphones, and with microphone placements, ambience mics, drum synthesizers, delays, equalization, reverberation, and so on, until they achieve a musical illusion that is interesting and colorful.

In this chapter, we'll reveal several ways to play with sound creatively. By experimenting with your equipment and by connecting it in unusual ways, you can invent new sounds to intrigue the listener and enhance the music.

Modifying Room Acoustics and Instruments

Try to manipulate the environment around an instrument to affect the acoustics. For instance, make an acoustic instrument sound more brilliant and "live" by surrounding it with hard reflective panels. For a bright sound, record a sax player standing on a hard floor. Record the sax in a carpeted area for a mellow sound.

Move a hard panel both toward and away from a microphone while recording an instrument. The changing delays of the sound reflections off the panel will give a flanging effect.

You can stick tacks in the felt of the piano hammers for a bright attack.

Use a $40.00 kiddie drum set in place of a regular set. Find one with rivets in the cymbals. When played with regular sticks or brushes, a child's set can sound surprisingly good and can yield some interesting effects.

In fact, such a drum set can substitute for a real set on a home demo tape if a regular set isn't available.

Bounce a basketball near a microphone to simulate a kick drum. Slam books on a table top for that extra "sock" during a clap track. Use a "Slinky" toy or baby rattle for a percussion instrument (these are good for Latin tunes).

Microphone Techniques

For a different microphone technique, place a cardboard tube in front of a microphone for a strong coloration. The tube resonates and puts a complex series of peaks and dips in the frequency response. The longer the tube, the lower the pitch of the coloration.

Move the microphones around as you record with them. Swing two mics by their cables while taping a lead guitar solo. If the recording is heard in mono, you'll hear phasing effects. If you monitor in stereo, the sound will be all over the place.

Place the microphones in unusual positions. Try miking a guitar amp from inside the cabinet for a hollow sound. Mike a grand piano underneath the soundboard for a full, mellow tone. Try recording a rock group at a distance with just two microphones. Mike the drums or guitar solos from across the room for a "live" and "roomy" effect.

You can combine several microphones on a single instrument, or can combine a direct box or a pickup with a microphone. Mike different areas of an instrument up close, and then mix the microphone outputs.

For an unusual reverberation sound, mike a piano with the sustain pedal on, and blow a sax into the piano.

Record some segments of a song binaurally. *Binaural recording* uses two miniature omnidirectional condenser microphones placed on the head, one in each ear (as shown in Fig. 13-1). These microphones capture what each ear is hearing. When this recording is played back over headphones, each ear hears the signal of the microphone that was in it. That is, the original sound at each ear is reproduced. The accurate re-creation of room ambience is startling. You may be fooled into thinking that you're hearing a real instrument playing in your listening room.

When making a binaural recording with mics in your ears, be sure to keep your head very still so that the reproduced images remain stable.

Another way to record binaurally is to place two omnidirectional microphones on either side of a head-sized cushion. This gives a smoother

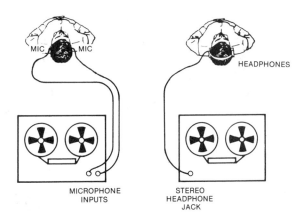

**Fig. 13-1.
Binaural
recording and
playback.**

response than the on-head method. Also available for binaural recording
are dummy heads that contain a microphone in each ear.

Edit some binaural recordings of conversations or solos into recordings made with the usual close-miking techniques. You'll surprise a listener who is wearing headphones when these passages come up, because
their realism is striking.

If you have some rugged and expendable microphones, use them for
drumsticks while recording with them. That is, play the drums with the
microphones and record their output. It's the ultimate in close miking!
Cymbals sound especially strange this way.

Occasionally, try using some very cheap microphones. They may give
a trashy sound that is just right for a particular song.

Try recording with microphones near the players' ears. After all, they
are hearing a sound that they like—it may sound good to the microphones
too.

Instead of using faders to balance the instruments, use microphone
techniques. Normally a track is made more prominent by boosting its
fader. Try the following method instead:

1. Close-mike instruments that you want to stand out.

2. Mike background instruments at a greater distance.

Then, on playback, the close-miked instruments will tend to stand out
with greater definition, while the distant-miked instruments will tend to
stay in the background.

This technique applies well to the lead vocal and the background
harmony vocals. If all the singers are miked at the same distance, it will
be hard to audibly separate them or distinguish them. You'll have to
boost the level of the lead singer to make that track prominent. But if
you mike the lead singer closer than the harmony singers, the lead vocal
will sound up front and the harmony will sound in the background.

You can use microphone frequency response as a tool to make instruments distinct. Suppose you record a lead acoustic guitar that is playing with a rhythm guitar. Use a condenser mic on the lead guitar for clarity, and use a dynamic mic on the rhythm to soften the detail. The differences in timbre will help keep the instruments distinct. If you use the same microphone on both instruments, they will tend to mask each other.

Playing with Reverberation and Echo

There are several ways to change your sound. Vary the echo-send or echo-receive levels during a mixdown. Turn them up just after a loud isolated crash in the music, and then turn them back down. The same can be done with an ambience track.

Adjust the reverberation to follow the phrases in the vocals. Turn the reverberation up during the singing, and then cut it off whenever the singing stops. This is a totally unnatural effect, but it will attract a listener's attention.

If your console has pre-fader echo sends (reverberation sends), you can make an instrument recede into the distance. Play the instrument's track through the console. Set the appropriate fader up, set the echo-send to "pre-fader," and then set the echo-send about three quarters up. Gradually pull down the fader. The direct sound of the instrument (as controlled by the fader) will diminish, but the reverberation will remain. The effect is as if the instrument were moving farther away from you into space.

The opposite effect was heard on Lou Reed's "Walk on the Wild Side," where the background vocals start in the distance and end up very close to the listener. You can duplicate this effect as follows: Play a track through your mixer. Start with the fader slightly up, the echo-send set to "pre-fader," and the echo-send up full. Gradually boost the fader and turn down the echo-send. The track will seem to approach you.

This technique can also be applied to a 2-track master tape of a song. Play the tape through your console and record the console output on another 2-track machine. Set the controls as previously described. At the beginning of the song, slowly turn up the faders and turn down the echo-sends. The song will begin swamped in reverb, and then will gradually become more coherent and clear, like bringing order out of chaos.

To add acoustic ambience to dry tracks, feed an echo-send mix of the tracks to a loudspeaker in the studio or in some other room. Pick up the loudspeaker sound with one or two distant microphones. Return this signal to the board and use it as an ambience signal. Fig. 13-2 shows the setup.

Have a vocalist and lead guitar play identical melody lines at the same time, and record them on two separate tracks. Feed the guitar track through the console to your reverberation unit pre-fader, with the fader down. Feed the vocal track to a fader with no reverberation. You'll hear a vocal that has the guitar's reverberation behind it.

Filter out everything below 5 kHz in the reverb-return signal Try this reverberation on vocals to brighten the sound, or on a snare drum to add a "splash."

You can make a stereo echo that moves back and forth between the speakers (refer to Fig. 13-3). Suppose you're using a 2-track tape deck for tape echo. Set the source/tape switch on the deck to "tape" for both channels. Patch Tape Channel 1 OUT to a mixer input, and assign that input's echo-send to Tape Channel 2 IN. Patch Tape Channel 2 OUT to another mixer input, and assign that input's echo-send to Tape Channel 1 IN. Set the recorder in record mode and adjust the echo-sends for the desired number of repetitions. The echo should bounce from side to side, giving a spacious effect. A digital delay can be used in place of the tape machine if the delay can be set to around 0.2 to 0.5 second.

For other effects, vary the speed of a tape deck as it's echoing to vary the pitch of the echo. Do the same by varying the delay on a digital delay unit. Try routing the echo-send signal through a pitch shifter. Also, turn up the echo-send on a particular track, with the echo-send feeding a tape

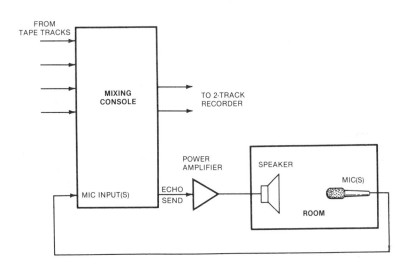

Fig. 13-2. Setup for adding acoustic ambience to dry tracks.

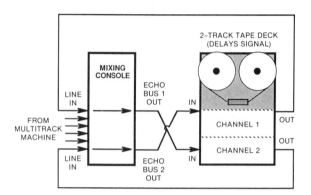

**Fig. 13-3.
Arrangement for
stereo echo.**

delay or digital delay. Bring the echo-return signal back through a spare input module. Turn up that input's echo-send to recirculate the echo. Equalize this signal. The equalization will double each time the sound repeats.

For a quadruple echo effect that uses a 4-track tape recorder, see the equipment arrangement shown in Fig. 13-4. Set all the source/tape switches on the recorder to "tape." Patch track 1 OUT to track 3 IN. Patch track 2 OUT to track 4 IN. Patch 4 OUT to 1 IN. Set all tracks in record mode, and record an instrument on track 2.

"Mult" or "Y" the track outputs so that you can bring them up on individual faders on the console, and monitor all four tracks in mono. By carefully adjusting the four faders, you will achieve four equal repeats of each note. Try this on a drum solo. Even if the drummer is playing very slowly, the quadruple echo will make him sound like his sticks are made of lightning.

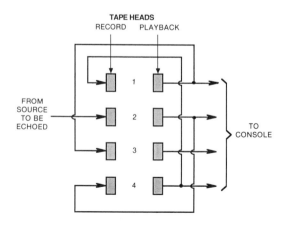

**Fig. 13-4. Setup
for quadruple
tape echo.**

Try setting the faders so that each successive echo gets louder—a most unusual effect. Pan each track to a different stereo location for a moving echo.

Console Tricks

Record a guitar direct on track 1. Using a microphone, record its amp on track 2. Combine the two tracks to mono in the mixdown, or pan them left and right for a larger ("fatter") sound. Also, if an electric guitar is played through a chain of effects boxes, you can pan the clean guitar signal to the left and pan the effects output to the right.

Here are some more fattening effects. First, record a drum set on track 1, and feed the track-1 signal to a guitar amp in a separate room. Then, mike the guitar amp and record it on track 2. During mixdown, combine and pan the tracks as desired. Do the same with a lead guitar or a vocal, but route the signal to a Leslie organ speaker.

For another console trick, place two microphones side-by-side near an instrument, with one mic a few inches farther away than the other. Assign the mics to two faders. As the instrument is being recorded, rapidly alternate the gain between the faders (push one up while pulling the other one down, and then reverse). The effect is like subtle phasing.

Finally, try this trick. Ride several faders slightly up and down in time with the music. This will add a subconscious emphasis to push the tune along.

Recorder Tricks

There are several ways to use a recorder. First, for a fat snare-drum sound, record the snare with some tape distortion, and mix the track with a drum-machine snare. Then, add gated reverb.

Using the varispeed feature, record a floor-tom lick at a speed slightly faster than normal. Play it back at normal speed. The pitch of the toms will be lowered, making them sound thunderous.

After recording a lead-vocal part, record a second take at half speed. Then play it back at normal speed for a chipmunk effect. Mix the chipmunk voice at low level with the regular voice at normal level to add "edge" to the vocal.

For something unusual, you can form a *tape loop* by splicing together the head and tail of a short length of tape. Route the tape past the heads and between the capstan and pinch roller. Insert a pencil in the loop to stretch the tape taut. Set the tape machine in record mode, and record a second or two of random sounds in the studio—say, someone dropping a box of junk. Then, stop the tape loop and play it back. The repetition of the loop will impart a rhythm to the random noises.

Alternatively, you can record a single lead-guitar note on the loop. Then during mixdown, turn up the loop's signal at an appropriate point in the lead-guitar solo. It will sound like the guitar has infinite sustain.

During mixdown, play some of the recorded tracks in sync mode (off the record head). Those tracks will be heard out-of-sync with the rest of the program. To add wow and flutter to a track, applying pressure to the feed-reel flange (or wrap some tape around the capstan). Then, record the instrument you want to hear. Be careful not to damage the tape or tape machine. *Caution:* Don't do this on a servo-controlled machine.

Try using two identical 2-track recorders. Set their outputs to "tape." Patch their outputs to two console inputs as shown in Fig. 13-5. Assign these two inputs to the same console output bus, and connect the bus to both recorder inputs. Set both recorders in record mode. Gradually increase their fader levels on the console until an echo occurs, then feedback. Using varispeed or pressure on the feed reel, vary the speed of one recorder. You'll hear an outer-space feedback tone that shifts pitch, echoes, and flanges all at the same time.

How does this work? Both recorders delay the signal by the same amount. Looping the delayed signal from tape output back around to tape input creates an echo. Varying the speed of one recorder causes a time difference between the recorders that makes the flanging effect.

With this next effect, you can make echo or reverberation precede the attack of each note. It's called *reverse echo* or *preverb*. Referring to Fig. 13-6, proceed as follows:

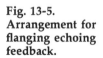

Fig. 13-5. Arrangement for flanging echoing feedback.

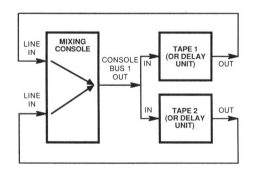

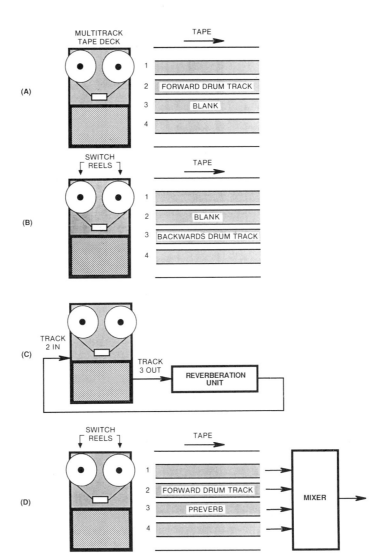

Fig. 13-6. Setup for *reverse echo,* **or** *preverb.*

1. Let's say you want to add preverb to a drum track. The track format might be as shown in Fig. 13-6A.

2. On your multitrack machine, reverse the tape reels so that the tape plays backwards. That is, put the take-up reel where the supply reel was, and vice versa. Play the tape in sync mode. You'll hear the tracks playing backwards (as illustrated in Fig. 13-6B). Since the tape is upside down, the instruments will be on different tracks than they were originally.

3. Now, add reverberation or echo to the desired track, and record the reverberated signal on an open track (as shown in Fig. 13-6C).

4. Again reverse the reels and play the desired track along with the newly recorded reverberation track (as illustrated in Fig. 13-6D).

You can also make an instrument or voice play backwards in the mix. This effect, called *backwards tracks*, has been used for overdubbing lead-guitar solos and for adding secret messages. To do this, reverse the reels as just described, and then record the new part on an open track. The musician should monitor the other tracks which are playing backwards in sync mode. Then, reverse the reels, play the tape, and mix the tracks as desired.

Outboard Equipment

There are various other pieces of equipment you can use. For example, connect several equalizers in series and boost them at the same frequency. The result is a screaming peak which can add a sense of pitch to un-pitched instruments (such as drums and cymbals). Also, play a tape track through a graphic equalizer or parametric equalizer. Boost a single frequency and vary the frequency as the track is playing. The tone color of the instrument will change as you adjust the frequency. Try patching a track to two console inputs. Equalize each input differently and then pan them left and right.

Set a compressor for a high compression ratio. Record a drum set with crashing cymbals, and run the drum track (including the kick drum) through the compressor. Every time the kick drum beats, the cymbals will get "sucked down" in level. This effect was heard on "Come Together" by the Beatles. For a drum sound with sustain, apply bass boost to a drum track before compression. Apply a complementary bass rolloff after compression to restore the tonal balance. Only the lows will be compressed. Try other complementary equalization schemes.

Leave a signal Dolby-encoded for special effect. This is effective on snare drum and acoustic guitar. Also, patch a signal through several tube-type amplifiers in series to get a "soft distortion" tube sound. Use old tube-type microphone preamps or tube limiters.

Try recording a signal with a polarity reversal between the left and right channels. However, this requires studio equipment that has balanced lines. Make a polarity-reversing adapter as shown in Fig. 13-7.

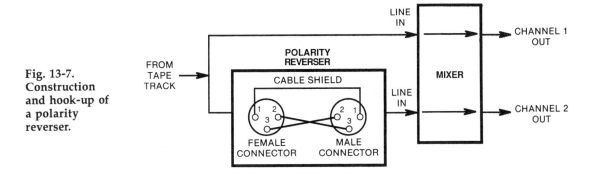

Fig. 13-7.
Construction
and hook-up of
a polarity
reverser.

"Mult" or "Y" the tape track output. Feed one leg of the Y into your console. Feed the other leg through the polarity reverser, and then into another console input. If your console has polarity-reverse switches, simply run the track into two console inputs with the polarity reversed on one input.

Pan the in-phase signal full left and pan the out-of-phase signal full right. The sound image produced will be diffuse, directionless, and hard to localize. It may even sound like it's behind you. This is effective for ambience, audience-reaction tracks, and lead-guitar solos. *Caution:* The out-of-phase tracks will cancel if the recording is heard in mono (both channels combined).

Conclusion

This chapter has presented several suggestions for sonic effects that should be fun to try. Invent your own, too. Most of this book describes typical recording techniques that are in common use today; if you try something entirely different, you may end up with a novel sound.

Basically, new effects are created by:

- Using recording equipment in unusual ways
- Connecting equipment in unusual ways
- Playing instruments in unusual ways

- Playing unusual instruments.

Let's illustrate these methods with a description of the ultimate special effect. Record a vocalist in a bathroom using a small loudspeaker for a microphone. Route the signal to a guitar amp and mike the amp both front and back with a dynamic and condenser microphone. Using a graphic equalizer, boost these signals 15 dB at every other octave and cut in-between. Send the equalized signal to a reverberation unit and flange and compress the reverberation. Record the result on a 4-track recorder while varying the speed and the bias settings. *Finally*, run the tape through a bulk tape eraser.

You may not want to take my final suggestion too seriously. But what you should take seriously is that *creative sonic effects* are fun to make and exciting to hear.

14 RECORDING THE SPOKEN WORD

Many studios record narration as well as music for documentary films, slide shows, educational programs, radio dramas, commercials, and books on tape. In fact, many studio recording engineers record nothing but speech. Others start with speech recording to learn the ropes, and then move on to music.

In this chapter, we'll cover some ways to record the spoken word most effectively. It's not as simple as it seems!

Consistency

One of the most important qualities of a speech recording is *consistency*. The tone quality, average recording level, average pitch, and average tempo of the voice should not change noticeably throughout the recording (except for dramatic effect).

Often a complete script is recorded in a single session. Then, a *proof copy* of the tape is sent to the script's publisher to check for errors. After corrections are received, the announcer is called back into the studio to record *inserts* or corrected sentences and paragraphs. These inserts are edited back into the original recording. If the sound of the inserts doesn't match the sound of the original, the listener will hear jarring changes in the voice quality as the recording plays. So it's important to duplicate the recording setup every time that the announcer is recorded.

Several factors can vary from one session to the next: recording level, microphone choice, microphone placement, text position, announcer's position, equalization, noise reduction, and even the announcer's voice itself. You need to keep all these factors constant by documenting the setup.

Take notes on the type of microphone used, its switch positions (if any), and its distance and position relative to the announcer. Also, note any equalization or noise reduction used. To reduce the number of variables, many engineers record without any equalization. You may want to settle on a standard setup so you can record a predictable sound.

Microphones

Let's start with the microphone. Four types of microphones are commonly used for voice recording:

1. A top-quality lavalier condenser microphone.
2. A flat-response cardioid microphone (condenser or dynamic).
3. A ribbon microphone.
4. A "multiple-D" dynamic microphone. ("Multiple-D" is explained in the discussion on microphones in Chapter 6.)

A *lavalier microphone* is a miniature unit (like TV newscasters use) that clips onto the announcer's tie or shirt. Most of the major microphone manufacturers have excellent models in the $200 price range. Don't skimp on this microphone, or the sound quality will suffer. Since the microphone is worn by the user, it remains a constant distance from the mouth, which aids consistency. And there's no problem with breath pops.

A cardioid condenser microphone provides a luxurious, big-budget sound—one with full lows and detailed highs. A ribbon microphone offers a warm and smooth sound. Unfortunately, the bass response of these microphones varies with the announcer's distance from the mic. The closer the announcer is to the microphone, the more bass is heard in the recording. Unless the announcer can remain a constant distance away, the voice tone quality will vary.

This close-up bass boost (called *proximity effect*) occurs with a single-D directional microphone. A multiple-D microphone is designed to compensate for proximity effect, with a bass response that varies only slightly with distance.

Microphone Placement

The placement of a microphone for speech recording affects the pickup of room acoustics, breath and lip noises, table thumps, and sound reflections. Let's examine how microphone placement can be used to prevent each of these unwanted sounds.

Distance

It helps to standardize on a distance between the microphone and the announcer's mouth—one that provides the best sound quality. A typical distance might be 8 to 12 inches; a too-distant placement picks up excessive room acoustics. In general, little or no room sound should be audible in a narration recording. Too close a placement emphasizes lip and tongue noises, and allows the voice level to vary greatly with small changes in the announcer's position. Find a workable distance somewhere in the middle and stick with it. This applies to lavalier microphones too.

An exception to this rule might be in drama recording. The actors often vary miking distance for special effect.

Some studios set the miking distance with a spacer or ruler. Alternatively, announcers can set the spacing with their hands. They spread their fingers, place their thumb on their mouth, and place their little finger on the microphone grille.

Minimizing Pop

Microphones should also be placed to avoid popping. When a person says words containing the letters "p," "t," or "b," a turbulent puff of air is forced from the mouth. If this air puff hits a microphone grille, a little thump or explosion called a *pop* is heard in the microphone signal. Since a pop disturbance leaves the mouth within a narrow conical angle, you can prevent popping by placing the microphone above, below, or to the side of the mouth. It also helps to put a foam pop filter or windscreen on the microphone.

Minimizing Table Thumps

Mount the microphone on a boom stand, and place the base of the stand on the floor. This arrangement reduces the pickup of table thumps. It also helps to use a shock-mounted microphone-stand adapter (available from your microphone dealer). Many studios pad the announcer's table with cloth or foam to prevent noises.

Minimizing Sound Reflections

You also should place the microphone so as to avoid picking up sound reflections from the script or the announcer's table. When these reflections combine at the microphone with direct sound from the announcer, phase interference occurs, resulting in a filtered tone quality. In addition, the tone quality changes as the announcer moves.

Figs. 14-1 through 14-6 show several right and wrong ways to position microphones. In Fig. 14-1, a lavalier microphone is used. Sound reflects off the script and into the microphone, causing phase interference. But, in Fig. 14-2, the script is angled flatter so that the reflections bounce away from the microphone.

In Fig. 14-3, a cardioid microphone is improperly positioned because reflections off the script stand enter the microphone. But, in Fig. 14-4, the reflections approach the "dead" back side of the cardioid microphone,

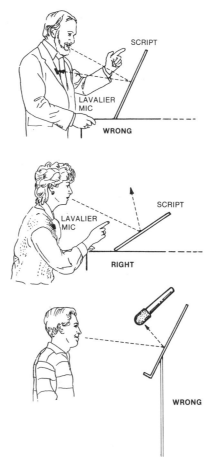

Fig. 14-1. The wrong way. Sound reflects off the script and into the microphone, causing phase interference.

Fig. 14-2. The right way. Sound reflects away from the microphone.

Fig. 14-3. The wrong way. Sound reflects off the script stand and into the microphone, causing phase interference.

and are attenuated. Paper noise is reduced as well. Figs. 14-5 and 14-6 show two other good methods.

If you record more than one announcer at the same time, seat them at least four feet apart to prevent phase interference between the microphones.

Controlling the Announcer's Position and Voice

Provide the announcer with a comfortable, fixed-frame chair, with a back that promotes a consistent sitting position. Advise the announcer to move as little as possible, and to not slump over the table.

Fig. 14-4. The right way. Sound reflects into the "dead" back side of the cardioid microphone.

RIGHT

Fig. 14-5. Sound reflects off angled script and away from the microphone.

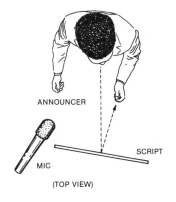

ANNOUNCER

SCRIPT

MIC

(TOP VIEW)

Fig. 14-6. A boundary microphone mounted on a 2-foot-square script stand.

The announcer's head motion can change the recorded tone quality. Here's why: Low frequencies radiate from the mouth in all directions, but high frequencies radiate mostly straight out. So, if an announcer moves his or her head while talking, the high frequencies ("s" sounds) may miss the microphone occasionally. This occurs with lavalier microphones as well. Ask announcers to move only their eyes while reading, not their head.

Actually, we're asking the announcer to become a frozen robot. A microphone worn on the head (and in front of the mouth) allows more freedom of movement. These mics may be a useful alternative if you are satisfied with the sound and can position the microphone consistently.

The average pitch and speed of an announcer's voice can change from day to day. It even varies from the beginning to the end of a recording session. So, whenever you record inserts, play back some of the original tape to the announcer for voice matching. Also, let the announcer warm up by reading for a few minutes while you set the recording level.

Reducing Sibilance

Another factor to keep under control is *sibilance*: the emphasis of "s" and "sh" sounds. These sounds have strong high-frequency components at 5 to 10 kHz, which can saturate the recording tape and cause distortion. You can reduce sibilance by using flat-response microphones, miking off axis to the mouth, or cutting around 5 kHz with an equalizer.

A better solution is to use a *de-esser*. This is a signal processor that removes excessive sibilance without affecting tone quality. Actually, it's a compressor with a high-frequency boost before compression and a complementary cut after compression. That way, only excessive high frequencies (sibilant sounds) are compressed. To work effectively, a de-esser should not be used in conjunction with another compressor.

Reducing Print-Through

A tape recording of narration may contain unwanted echoes or pre-echoes of speech during pauses between words. These echoes are called *print-through*. In the tape reel, the magnetic signal transfers or "prints" from one layer of tape to the next. This causes a repetition of the program.

Print-through is a major problem with narration recording because speech contains many silent pauses where print-through can be heard. Tips on reducing print-through were given in Chapter 9.

Recording-Session Procedures

Now that you've taken all the precautions to assure consistent, clean sound, you're ready to record a script. The announcer is seated the proper distance from the microphone, with the script ready to read. Some announcers fold up the bottom corners of their script pages to form a handle for turning pages without causing noise.

The engineer or producer has an identical script on which to mark *edit points*—spots where the announcer misreads a sentence.

After a level check, you start recording. The announcer reads the script, and you or the producer follows along in your own script, marking edit points with a pen. You just leave the tape rolling when mistakes occur.

If the announcer misreads a word or makes a paper noise, he or she goes back to the beginning of the sentence where the error occurred, and starts over. The announcer should not attempt to correct the error in mid-sentence and continue through the sentence. That kind of correction is too hard to edit. Also, the speech rhythm may be off, making an edit impossible. It's much easier to make an undetectable tape splice if you have a long pause between words (say, between sentences).

Fig. 14-7 shows a typical script with edit marks. Instead of marking the words that were flubbed, the producer marked the beginning of the sentences containing the errors. Those marks correspond to the edit points on the tape. Two marks indicate a second re-take.

Editing

After the recording is done, you're ready to edit out the mistakes. Play the tape and follow the marked-up script. When you come to an edit point, stop the tape. Put the recorder into cue or edit mode. Rock the tape back and forth over the playback head to find the exact beginning of the flubbed sentence. Mark the tape at the playback-head gap with a grease pencil. Then, using a razor blade and a splicing block, cut the tape about ½ inch to the right of the mark.

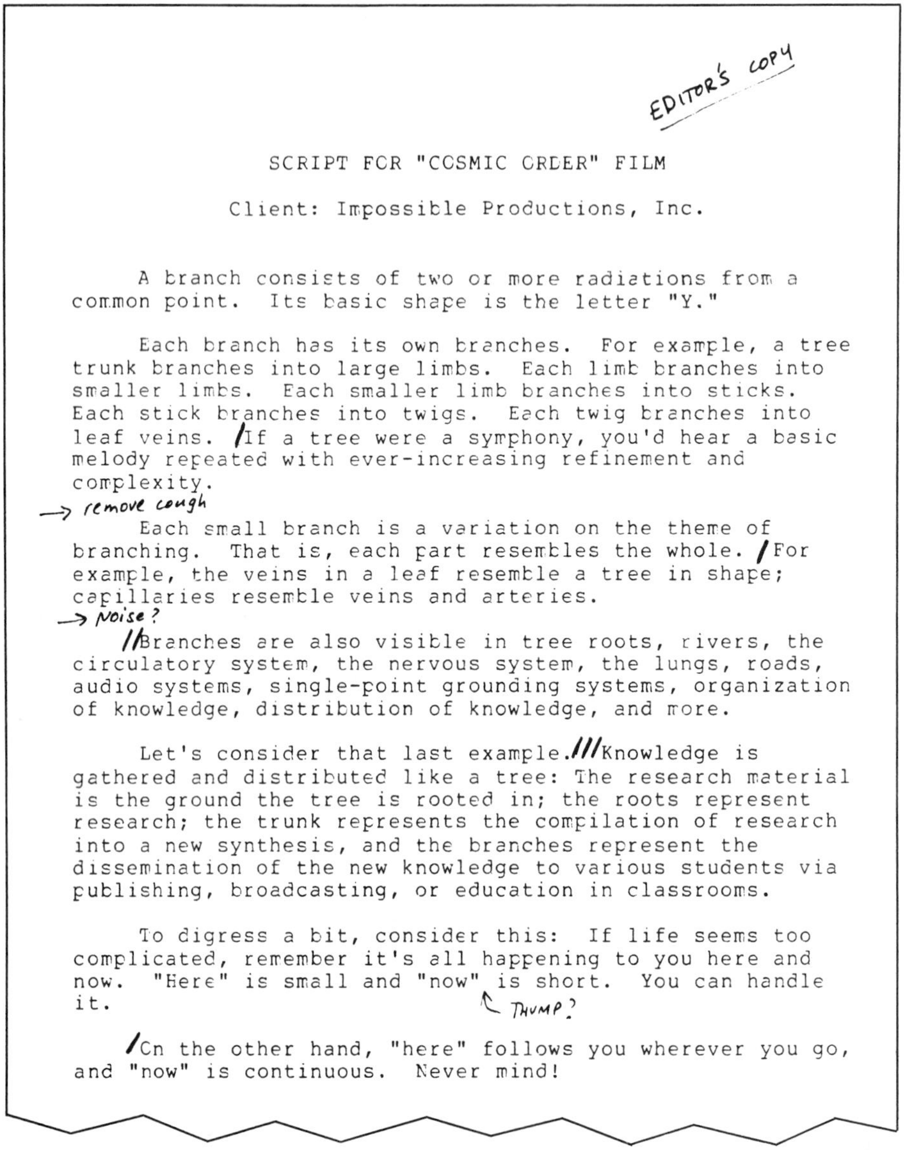

EDITOR's COPY

```
            SCRIPT FOR "COSMIC ORDER" FILM

         Client: Impossible Productions, Inc.


     A branch consists of two or more radiations from a
common point.  Its basic shape is the letter "Y."

     Each branch has its own branches.  For example, a tree
trunk branches into large limbs.  Each limb branches into
smaller limbs.  Each smaller limb branches into sticks.
Each stick branches into twigs.  Each twig branches into
leaf veins. /If a tree were a symphony, you'd hear a basic
melody repeated with ever-increasing refinement and
complexity.
```
→ *remove cough*
```
     Each small branch is a variation on the theme of
branching.  That is, each part resembles the whole. /For
example, the veins in a leaf resemble a tree in shape;
capillaries resemble veins and arteries.
```
→ *Noise?*
```
     //Branches are also visible in tree roots, rivers, the
circulatory system, the nervous system, the lungs, roads,
audio systems, single-point grounding systems, organization
of knowledge, distribution of knowledge, and more.

     Let's consider that last example.///Knowledge is
gathered and distributed like a tree: The research material
is the ground the tree is rooted in; the roots represent
research; the trunk represents the compilation of research
into a new synthesis, and the branches represent the
dissemination of the new knowledge to various students via
publishing, broadcasting, or education in classrooms.

     To digress a bit, consider this:  If life seems too
complicated, remember it's all happening to you here and
now.  "Here" is small and "now" is short.  You can handle
it.                                      ⌐ THUMP?

     /On the other hand, "here" follows you wherever you go,
and "now" is continuous.  Never mind!
```

Fig. 14-7. Script with edit marks.

Next, put the feed-reel tape back into the tape-path slot, and pull the tape past the heads. You'll hear the flubbed sentence. The announcer will stop, and then restart the sentence. Mark and cut the tape at the beginning of the corrected sentence.

After removing the flubbed section of tape, splice the two remaining tape ends together. Play the edited portion to check it. You should hear no double breaths between sentences. Also edit out paper noises and table thumps.

Here's an alternative method of editing: Mark the two edit points (the beginning of the flubbed sentence and the beginning of the good re-take) before cutting the tape. Then, align both edit marks in your splicing block, cut both at once, and splice the ends together.

Once the tape is edited, add leader tape, label the reel and tape box, and store the tape tail out.

Proof Cassettes and Inserts

You might want to make a proof cassette copy of the tape to send to the script publisher for approval. The publisher may notice reading errors that you missed during the recording session. They'll send back a marked-up script showing the errors. The next time that the announcer is back in your studio, have him or her re-record the sentences or paragraphs needing corrections.

Be sure to match the recording levels, microphone position, etc., with those of the original tape. Otherwise, the inserts may sound like another person is talking. Play some of the original tape to the announcer so he or she can duplicate the pitch and tempo. You may need to equalize the inserts to match the original take.

When the inserts are edited into place, make and send another proof tape to the publisher. If it's error-free, you can add sound effects or music as needed.

Sound Effects and Music

Many scripts require certain sound effects to accompany the narration. If you record the speech on track 1 of a 2-track tape recorder, you can record the sound effects on track 2 in the spots where the script calls for them. After the effects are recorded, mix the 2-track tape of narration and effects to mono, and record the mix on another deck. Or, you can use a 4-track machine for the master recording to record music or effects in stereo.

Libraries of sound effects and mood music are available from several record companies, and are advertised in recording-industry magazines and audio-visual publications. Many require royalty payments for each use of the material. Some sound-effects records found in the Schwann catalog can be ordered through record stores. You can even record the sound effects yourself, in some cases.

Sound effects can be pre-recorded on broadcast cartridges, which can be played and mixed in live as the narration is recorded. Alternatively, the record cuts can be cued up on a turntable, and played back as needed.

Many productions require a musical introduction which is faded down when the announcer starts talking. These productions usually have a musical "outro" too. An *outro* is music that begins near the end of the narration, fading up and then out to provide a musical conclusion to the program.

Back-Timing a Musical Outro

You'll often want the outro to end simultaneously with the narration. This can be achieved with a technique called *back-timing*. Here's how to do it.

First, find the spot in the script where you want the outro to start fading up. Play the tape starting from there, and time it to the end of the narration. Let's say it's 30 seconds from fade-up to end.

Now, put a tape recording of the outro on a tape deck, but reverse the reels so it plays backwards. Start playing the tape at the end of the musical piece, run it 30 seconds (or whatever), and stop. Then turn the tape over and replace the reels. You now have a musical outro tape cued up 30 seconds from the end.

Here's another way to back-time the outro. First, cue up the end of the outro. Then thread the tape backwards around the capstan (clockwise) and counter-clockwise around the pinch roller. When you hit "play," the tape will play in reverse. Play it for 30 seconds (or however long you need), and then hit "stop." It will be cued up the right distance from the end.

Next, put the narration tape on a 2-track machine. The narration is recorded on track 1. Set up the tape machine to re-record the musical outro tape on track 2.

Start playing the narration tape several seconds before the fade-up point. Then start playing the music tape just before the fade-up point, and fade it up. If your timing is right, the music will end just after the narration ends. This gives a tight, professional touch to the production.

Summary

This chapter covered some basic advice about recording the spoken word with a consistent, clean sound; and it briefly described how to add sound effects and music. This type of studio work should not be neglected, since it is the major source of income for many studios. And it's another skill to add to your resumé.

15 SAMPLING, SEQUENCING, AND MIDI

Two new ways of recording music have been developed: sampling and sequencing. *Sampling* is recording a short segment of a sound and storing that sample in computer memory. *Sequencing* is storing a sequence of synthesizer note parameters in memory chips. These kinds of recording are less common than tape recording, but they are important developments that recording engineers and musicians should be aware of.

First a definition. *Computer memory* is a group of integrated-circuit (IC) chips, each containing thousands of solid-state circuits, which act like switches. Information is stored in binary format (1 = switch ON; 0 = switch OFF). Each 1 and 0 is called a *bit*, which is an abbreviation of *bi*nary dig*it*. These bits of information are stored in memory. Memory space is limited, and is measured in *bytes*, where 1 byte = 8 bits.

Sampling

Suppose you want to sample a live sound, such as a piano note, flute note, tom-tom hit, cymbal crash, or sound effect. You plug your recording microphone into a sampler or sampling keyboard, which records the sample as follows: The analog electrical waveform from the microphone is analyzed or sampled several thousand times a second and converted to digital data by an analog-to-digital converter. This data is then stored in random-access memory (RAM), so that a digital recording can be made using the digital data. This is illustrated in the diagram of Fig. 15-1.

Samples can be recorded from microphones, direct boxes, directly off synthesizers, off records, etc. The recording can be made first on either an analog or digital recorder, and then transferred to a sampling keyboard or external sampler (Fig. 15-2).

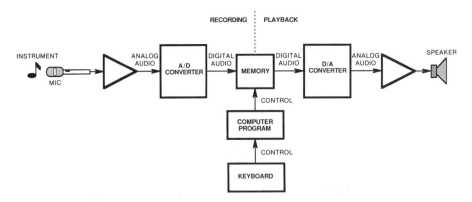

Fig. 15-1. Simplified block diagram showing how a sampling device records and plays back sounds.

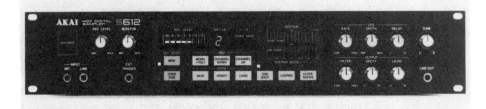

Fig. 15-2. Akai S612 MIDI Digital Sampler *(Courtesy Akai Corp.).*

Later, the sampled sound is played back by pressing keys on the keyboard. The keypress triggers the sample. Which key you press determines which reproduced pitch of the sample you get. That is, different keys on the keyboard cause the digital information to play back at different rates, shifting the pitch of the sample.

However, too much of this pitch shifting can cause an unnatural sound. That's because pitch-shifted notes have a constant relationship among the fundamental and harmonic frequencies, while different notes from a real instrument do not have this constant relationship. Instead of having the entire keyboard control the pitch of one sample, it's best to record several samples at different frequencies—say one octave apart—and control the pitch of each of these samples within a smaller range.

Permanent Samples

Some keyboards and all drum machines have samples stored in permanent memory (ROM, or read-only memory); these are digital recordings of real instruments which are stored in memory chips. The sample chips may be either hard-wired or plugged into IC sockets.

Computer Sampling

Many personal computers can be made to sample and store sounds. The computer software also lets the user edit the sounds and control how they are played back. Sampled sounds can be saved on tape, floppy disk, hard disk, or—in the future—writable optical disks.

Sampling Parameters

Background

When an audio signal is sampled, it passes through an analog-to-digital (A/D) converter. This converter measures, or samples, the voltage of the audio waveform several thousand times a second. Each time the waveform is sampled, a binary number (made up of 1s and 0s) is generated that represents the voltage of the waveform at the instant that it is measured (Fig. 15-3). These binary numbers are stored in memory.

The longer the binary number (the more bits), the greater the accuracy of the measurement. In other words, short binary numbers provide poor resolution of the waveform's amplitude; long binary numbers provide good resolution.

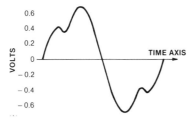

(A) The audio waveform enters the A/D converter.

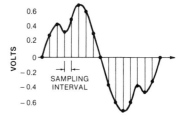

(B) The voltage is measured or sampled at regular intervals.

Fig. 15-3. Sampling an analog waveform.

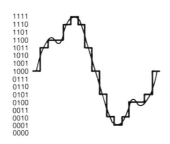

(C) The voltage measurements are quantized.

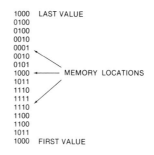

(D) The quantized values are stored in memory.

Quantization Rate

The *quantization rate* of a sampler is its amplitude resolution, measured in bits. The higher the quantization rate, the less the distortion and the greater the dynamic range. Commercial samplers range from 8 to 16 bits of quantization. An 8-bit sampler is good, 12 bits is very good, and a 16-bit unit is excellent.

Sampling Rate

The rate at which the waveform is sampled is called the *sampling rate*, measured in samples/sec. At a sampling rate of 40 kHz, 40,000 samples are generated for each second of sound.

The higher the sampling rate, the wider the frequency response of the recorded sound. The upper frequency limit is slightly less than half the sampling rate. If the sampling rate is, say, 20 kHz, the sound you sampled will be reproduced up to about 9 kHz. High-frequency sounds (cymbals) need a high sampling rate for fidelity; low-frequency sounds (bass, kick drum) can be recorded adequately with a low sampling rate.

Memory Constraints

As the A/D converter generates binary numbers, they are stored in memory. Each number goes to a separate memory location. Unfortunately, memory space is limited. Once it is filled, part of the recorded note is cut off. This puts constraints on the sample time, sampling rate, and quantization rate. The following equation shows how these four factors are related:

$$B = QR \times SR \times ST$$

where
   B is bytes of memory filled by a sample,
   QR is quantization rate in bytes/sample,
   SR is sampling rate in samples/second,
   ST is sample time in seconds.

For example, if you have a sampler with 8-bit (1 byte) quantization, and you set the sampling rate to 40 kHz, and record a 2-second sample, you use up

$$1 \times 40,000 \times 2 = 80 \text{ kilobytes of memory}$$

So, to avoid filling memory and cutting off the ends of notes, either the sample has to be short or the sampling rate has to be low (assuming you have a limited amount of memory).

Stated another way, the higher the sampling rate, the more memory is used up, because a high sampling rate generates more binary numbers than a low rate. To store the full duration of a note in a limited amount of memory, the sample must be relatively short. The higher the sampling rate, the shorter the sample must be. A one-second sample is long enough for the notes of many instruments, but cymbal crashes may require three seconds or more.

Sampling Techniques

When recording a sample, first set the sampler to its highest sampling rate for maximum fidelity. If the end of the sound gets cut off (because memory is used up), try reducing the sampling rate.

Multisampling

If you fill just part of the memory with one sample, you can fill the rest of the memory with other samples, up to the memory limit. In other words, many sounds can be stored in different memory locations. This technique is called *multisampling*.

When you're multisampling, record the high-frequency instruments or long-duration notes first, because they fill the most memory. If you record these sounds last, they may be cut off if memory is used up.

Processing Samples

Samples made for live performances should be already processed by effects boxes, but samples made for recording should be pure so that you can process them during mixdown. In either case, use a high-quality microphone, placed carefully, to get a clean and accurate sample.

Editing Samples

You can edit the sampled waveform by using a computer connected to a port on the sampler. For example, you can remove or truncate silent portions of a sample to save memory. By trimming each sample as you make it, you'll get more samples into a given amount of memory.

Sequencing

With sequencing, you play notes on a synthesizer, and a memory chip stores information about the notes that were played. This information tells which keys were pressed, note duration, pitch bending, patch number, and so on. In other words, the memory digitally stores the note parameters, NOT the audio signal produced by the synthesizer. The sequence of notes you played—chords and melody—can be stored by a sequencer (Fig. 15-4) built into the synthesizer, or by an external computer running a sequencer program.

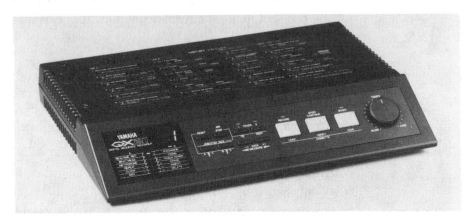

Fig. 15-4. The Yamaha® QX21 Digital Sequence MIDI Recorder *(Courtesy Yamaha Electronic Corporation USA).*

During playback, the sequencer activates the synthesizer. The parameters of each note are set and played according to what is stored in memory (refer to Fig. 15-5B). The synthesizer sounds are generated either from the synthesizer's oscillators, or from samples in memory. In effect, it's a modern-day player piano. The instrument on which the original performance was played also reproduces the performance, with perfect fidelity.

For example, if you play middle-C on a synthesizer (261.63 Hz), the memory does not store a 261.63-Hz audio signal. Instead, it stores an

Fig. 15-5. Simplified block diagram showing memory recording and playback of a sequence of synthesizer notes.

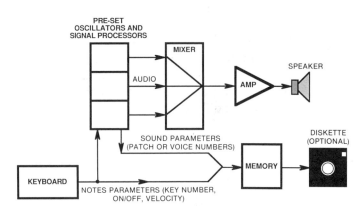

(A) Recording sequence.

indication that the middle-C key was pressed. Similarly, during repro-duction, the memory does not play back a 261.63-Hz signal; rather, it triggers the oscillator that the middle-C key would play. That's how a sequencer records and reproduces music.

Real-Time vs. Step-Time Sequencing

There are two ways of recording note parameters into memory: real time and step time. With *real-time* recording, you perform your music as you would play it on stage. The computer later plays back your music exactly as recorded. If desired, you can edit the piece. *Step-time* recording lets you enter notes one at a time, at your own pace. The music plays back at a normal tempo.

Sequence Storage

Many synthesizers can store sound parameters (*patches*) or rhythm data on cassette tape or magnetic disk. The data can be loaded back into the instrument to recall rhythms or patches. You can even buy pre-recorded patches programmed by professional musicians.

Summary of Sampling and Sequencing

In review, you create sounds by recording them into memory (sampling), by using pre-recorded samples, or by generating sounds with a synthesizer. Once you have these sounds, you play them with the keyboard.

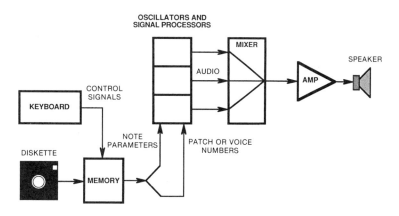

(B) Playback sequence.

A sequencer or external computer can record what you're playing. The memory stores the note parameters (key number, velocity, etc.), not the audio signals. At the touch of a button, the sequencer will automatically reproduce the notes you played by telling the synthesizer what notes to play. The sounds of these notes are generated either from stored samples or from the synthesizer oscillators.

Memory Multitracking

Now, let's say you've sampled many sounds, and have built up a library of these sounds or voices. All of these different voices can be stored and called up at will.

Suppose you play a sequence of notes and record the sequence into computer memory. This sequence might be drum beats, a bass line, chords, or a melody. A sequence of notes of one voice is called a *track*.

After recording a bass line, you can go back to the start of the sequence, play the bass track, and add a flute part in sync with the bass line. The flute melody or sequence is stored separately in memory. Then you can go back to the top and add drums. It's just like overdubbing with a multitrack tape machine, except there's no tape to rewind and no generation loss. You can punch in/out and mix down these tracks just as in multitrack tape recording. You can even change a track's instrument ("voice") without having to re-do the performance on that track!

If you have ever played with a drum machine, you know how synthesizer overdubbing works. You play, for example, a four-bar riff on the hi-hat and kick drum keys. This riff is stored in memory. Then you play it back while adding a tom-tom fill. That combination is also stored. Then you add a cowbell, and so on. The recording can be mixed by adjusting the faders on the drum machine for each instrument.

Synchronizing Synthesizers with MIDI

So far, we've discussed recording with a single synthesizer, but there are more possibilities. Several synthesizers can be synchronized to produce the effect of a band playing. You might have two or three synthesizers and a drum machine synchronized and playing all at once.

Several synthesizers can be linked to a drum machine, which provides the basic pulse that sets the tempo. Or, they can be connected to a click-track machine which generates a timing pulse.

These memory recordings can be played back during live concerts. In this way, a synthesizer musician can play a note-perfect performance every time. Or he can override the sequence and play manually to react to the other musicians' playing.

MIDI

The system used for interconnecting synthesizers is a MIDI interface. Let's explain what MIDI is. MIDI stands for *Musical Instrument Digital Interface*. It is a specification for a computer interface that enables several different brands of MIDI-capable instruments to be connected together. That is, it permits electronic musical instruments and computers to communicate with each other through a standard cable.

With the MIDI connection, several MIDI-equipped synthesizers or drum machines can be controlled from a single keyboard, guitar, microphone, or drum machine. Similarly, a computer program can control several keyboards, drum machines, and effects devices. A program can perform an automated mixdown on certain consoles by remembering and re-setting the console control settings.

With MIDI, you can make an electric guitar sound like a flute, or any other instrument. To do this, you play the guitar, which is patched to a pitch-to-MIDI converter. The MIDI signal controls a synthesizer. The synthesizer follows the fundamental frequencies you're playing on the guitar. If the synthesizer is set to play a flute sound, and you pluck a guitar string, you hear a flute! However, the transformation is imperfect and sounds a little mechanical. In addition, the flute sound lags your playing slightly.

The MIDI cable is standardized with a 5-pin DIN connector. Up to 16 channels of digital data are sent serially through a single MIDI patch cord. The rate of information transfer (baud rate) is 31,250 bits per second. Each channel transmits information that controls a MIDI instrument.

Several instruments can be connected so that one MIDI channel controls all those instruments simultaneously. Musicians can layer several sounds in one pass, as well as recording each instrument separately.

Each manufacturer applies the MIDI specifications in a different way. Not all MIDI instruments are compatible; for example, they may have different functions controlled by the same channel. Fortunately, many instruments can be reliably interfaced with MIDI accessories.

A Tapeless Studio

With sampling keyboards, synthesizers, MIDI, and memory multitracking, you can set up a complete recording studio that operates without tape, and without live musical instruments!

Conventional recording studios have several microphones for picking up instruments and vocals. A tapeless studio might have only one high-quality mic that is used to sample various instruments one-at-a-time into the sampling keyboard.

Conventional studios also have multitrack tape machines to record several instruments, each on its own track. Tapeless studios can do without the multitrack tape machine because the keyboard contains a multitrack memory recorder (sequencer). Or, you can use software that converts a personal computer into a multitrack recorder. (Fig. 15-6 shows several examples of such software, the Passport MIDI software and interface by Passport Designs, Inc. Also noteworthy is the Passport Master Tracks music sequencing program, which allows 16-channel recording.)

Fig. 15-7 shows the diagram of a typical MIDI studio. It includes a personal computer, a drum machine, keyboards, and interfaces. It works as follows: Using sequencing software, the computer acts as a multitrack recorder or sequencer. A MIDI interface lets the computer talk MIDI language to the rest of the system.

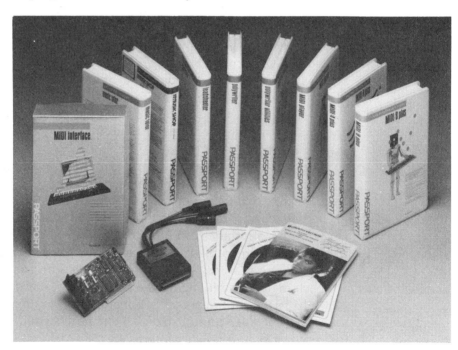

**Fig. 15-6.
Passport MIDI
software and
interface**
*(Courtesy Passport
Designs, Inc.).*

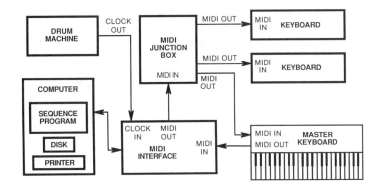

**Fig. 15-7.
Diagram of a
typical MIDI
studio.**

The clock output of the drum machine drives the computer-sequencer, which, in turn, controls the keyboards and a multivoice *sound generator* (Fig. 15-8) through a MIDI junction box. This box feeds MIDI signals to all the keyboards simultaneously. This arrangement is better than a daisy-chain connection, which slows the transfer of MIDI data.

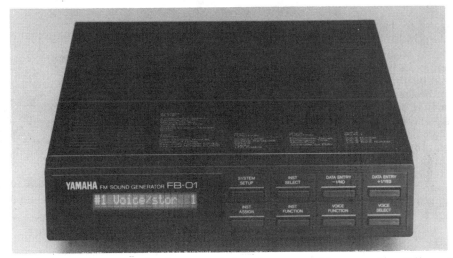

**Fig. 15-8. The
Yamaha® FB-01
FM Sound
Generator**
*(Courtesy Yamaha
Electronic
Corporation USA).*

If the various synthesizers and the drum machine require different synchronizing signals, they can be accommodated by a synchronization adapter, such as the Garfield Electronics Doctor Click 2, shown in Fig. 15-9. It can be driven from steady or varying click tracks, drum-mic signals, MIDI clocks, and other sync sources. The unit provides a variety of synchronization, trigger, and click-track signals.

The master keyboard controls all the others. It is plugged into the MIDI interface and the MIDI junction box.

After all the tracks are recorded, the computer-sequencer plays the multitrack recording, which activates all the keyboards and the sound generator. The outputs of the keyboards, sound generator, and drum

Fig. 15-9. The Garfield Electronics Doctor Click 2 universal musical instrument synchronization adapter *(Courtesy Garfield Electronics).*

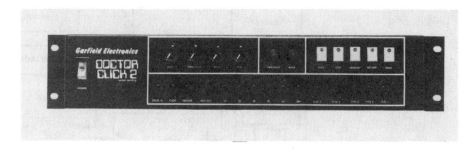

machine are mixed through a console (not shown) onto a 2-track tape deck.

What if you want to add vocals to the mix, but the vocal track is too long to sample? You could record the instrumental mix on a multitrack tape recorder, and then overdub the vocal on another track. Alternatively, some expensive keyboards (such as the Synclavier by New England Digital Corp.) let you digitally record the vocal track onto a magnetic disk (Fig. 15-10).

Fig. 15-10. The Synclavier Digital Music System includes a keyboard, synthesizer, sampler, 32-track sequencer, magnetic disk recording option, and MIDI capability *(Courtesy New England Digital Corp.).*

Summary

We've described two ways of recording music into computer memory: sampling (digitally recording short sounds) and sequencing (storing sequences of note parameters). With memory multitracking, several different instruments can be played, recorded, overdubbed, and mixed with a single keyboard. MIDI connections enable a computer program to play several keyboards, and permit musical instruments to sound like other instruments.

Clearly, the marriage of computers and music is bearing amazing offspring. This is the future of recording.

16 ON-LOCATION RECORDING OF POPULAR MUSIC

Sooner or later you'll want to record a band—maybe your own—playing in a club or concert hall. Many bands want to be recorded live because they feel that's when they play best. Your job is to capture that performance on tape and bring it back alive.

There are many ways to do this. We'll start by explaining simple two-microphone techniques and work our way up to elaborate multiconsole, multitrack setups.

Monitoring

Headphones, rather than loudspeakers, are often used for on-location monitoring because headphones are more portable and provide a consistent sound in different environments. Plus, they partly block out the live sound of the band so you can better hear what's going onto the tape—especially if closed-cup, circumaural headphones are used. However, if you record in the same room that the band is playing in, the live sound of the band will leak through the headphones' ear seal. Then it's hard to hear the monitored signal clearly, especially how much bass you're putting on tape.

The preferred practice is to set up your equipment in a control room separate from the performance room. Then, run some microphone extension cables (or a snake) from your mixer out to the performance area. Close the door, slip on the headphones, and monitor the sound. You'll be able to hear more clearly without the danger of blasting your ears. During intermissions, you can play back the tape to hear what you've just recorded.

The top recording studios park a van or truck outside the recording locale to use as a control room. Inside the van, the recording engineer uses loudspeakers for monitoring. The interior of the van is treated to absorb sound reflections near the monitor speakers. Budget studios can use much smaller vans for on-location recording, and can monitor with headphones or mini-speakers.

Recording with Two Microphones

A beginning recordist might start with just two microphones and a 2-track tape deck. This is the easiest method of recording a group.

Two Crossed Cardioid Microphones

First, mount two high-quality cardioid microphones on a stereo microphone-stand adapter. Angle them 110° apart (55° to the right and left of center) and space their grilles 7 inches apart, horizontally. This is the ORTF (*Office de Radiodiffusion-Television Française*) stereo miking system. Place this arrangement about 3 to 5 feet in front of a folk group or vocal quartet, or 10 to 15 feet in front of a rock group on a stage. Use a microphone stand or hang the mics out of the reach of the audience.

Don't expect this recording to sound like a commercial record! We've become accustomed to the clean, tight, recorded sound of rock groups that is picked up by multiple close-placed microphones. You can't duplicate that sound with a simple two-microphone pickup. However, such a recording is useful for musicians who want to hear how their sound blends in the audience area.

Two Spaced Microphones

Most rock groups use loudspeakers at each end of the stage to reinforce the vocals (and, sometimes, certain instruments). A centrally placed stereo pair of microphones, being far from the sound-reinforcement speakers, may not pick up the vocals adequately. To gain better control over the vocal/instrumental balance, try aiming two cardioid microphones straight ahead toward the group; have them spaced about 5 to 15 feet apart, as in Fig. 16-1.

Place the microphones far apart (that is, close to the sound-reinforcement speakers) to make the vocals louder in the recording. Do the op-

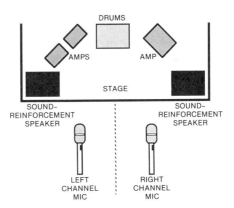

Fig. 16-1.
Recording a rock
group with two
spaced
microphones.

posite to make them quieter. The stereo imaging of this arrangement is poorer than with the ORTF system, but at least you can control the balance between instruments and vocals.

Preventing Mic-Preamp Overload

If the playback sounds distorted even though you did not exceed a normal recording level, the microphones probably overloaded the microphone preamps in the tape deck. With loud sound sources, such as rock groups, a microphone can put out a signal strong enough to clip the tape-deck's microphone input.

Some decks include a pad or input attenuator to reduce the microphone signal level before it reaches the first stage of amplification, thereby preventing distortion. Others have a high-impedance microphone input, which will act as an attenuator if used with a low-impedance microphone. Some condenser microphones have switchable internal pads that reduce distortion within the microphone. You can build a pad (with 20-dB attenuation) as shown in Fig. 16-2, or can buy some plug-in pads from your microphone dealer.

If you have to set your record-level controls very low (less than one third up) to obtain a 0-VU recording level, that's a good indication that you need to use a pad.

Recording from the Sound-Reinforcement Mixer

Sometimes you can get a good recording simply by plugging into the main output of the band's reinforcement mixer. Connect the line output(s)

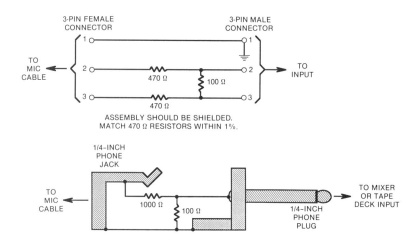

**Fig. 16-2.
Balanced and
unbalanced
microphone
pads.**

of the mixer to the line or aux input(s) of a 2-track recorder. Use the
mixer output that is ahead of any equalization or active crossover used
to correct the speakers' frequency response, as shown in Fig. 16-3. *Note:*
Some mixers can produce a signal that is too high in level for the recorder's auxiliary input, causing distortion. This is probably occurring if
your record-level controls have to be set very low. To reduce the output
level of the mixer, turn it down so that its signal peaks at around −12
VU on the mixer meters, and turn up the power amps to compensate.
Alternatively, you can make a 12-dB pad as shown in Fig. 16-4. The
reason for 12 dB of attenuation is explained in detail in Chapter 20.

Recording from the band's mixer works best when all the instruments
are miked and mixed through that mixer. The recorded mix might be
bad, however. Here's why: The person who operates the band's mixer
hears a combination of the live sound of the band and the reinforced
sound (through the house system), and tries to get a good mix of *both*
these elements. That means the signal is mixed to *augment* the live sound—
not to sound good by itself. A recording made from the band's mixer is
likely to sound too strong in the vocals and too weak in the bass.

**Fig. 16-3.
Recording from
the sound-
reinforcement
mixer.**

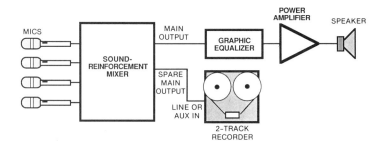

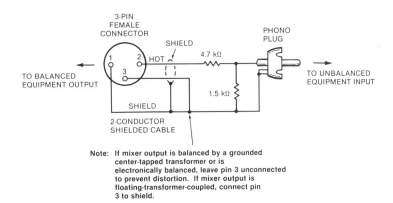

Fig. 16-4. A 12-dB pad for matching a balanced +4-dBm output to an unbalanced −10-dBV input.

However, if the performance is in a large hall or arena, most of the sound heard by the audience comes from the sound-reinforcement system. In this case, a recording made from the reinforcement mixer is likely to have a good mix. That is, it will be as good as the live mix is.

This method works best if the sound-reinforcement speakers were previously equalized to sound "hi-fi" when playing a good recording. If the frequency response of the reinforcement speakers is not wide-range and smooth, the mixer operator may equalize each instrument to compensate for the speakers. If you record this compensated mix and play it back over a good stereo system, the tonal balance will be wrong because of the equalization used on the reinforcement mixer.

In some small systems, only the vocals are reinforced; so you can take a line-level feed from the band's mixer for the vocals, and use your own microphones for the instruments. You'll need a separate mixer for recording. Place your microphones near each instrument and mix their signals with the vocal signal from the band's mixer. Fig. 16-5 shows the

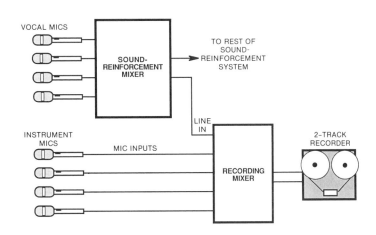

Fig. 16-5. Recording the vocals from the sound-reinforcement mixer, with separate microphones for the instruments.

connections. Check the input-overload LEDs on the band's mixer (if any) to make sure the vocal mics aren't overloading their inputs.

Splitting the Microphones

As we've seen, a good house mix does not guarantee a good recording mix. It's better to make an independent recording mix by using a separate mixer and separate microphones.

The stage will be cluttered if you place a recording microphone next to every reinforcement microphone. It's especially clumsy to double the vocal mics. Instead, you can plug a *"Y" adapter* (Fig. 16-6) onto the end of each vocalist's microphone cable. This adapter splits the microphone signal two ways: to the reinforcement mixer and to the recording mixer. Plug one output connector of the "Y" into a cable going to a reinforcement-mixer mic input. Plug the other output connector of the "Y" into a cable going to a recording-mixer mic input.

This arrangement might cause ground loops and hum unless both mixers are plugged into the same AC outlet strip. Experiment with the AC-plug orientation and with 3-to-2 ground-lift adapters (keeping safety in mind) to obtain the least hum. If you use phantom powering, supply it from one console only.

A better solution is to transformer-isolate the two outputs with a *microphone splitter* (Fig. 16-7), which is available at sound dealers and some music stores. You need one for every microphone you want to share with the sound-reinforcement system.

In some sound-reinforcement systems, every instrument is miked with a high-quality microphone. Then, you can split all the microphones. But, in many other systems, only the vocals are miked for reinforcement. In that case, you split the vocal mics and use your own recording mics on the instruments.

Fig. 16-6. A "Y" adapter for splitting microphone signals.

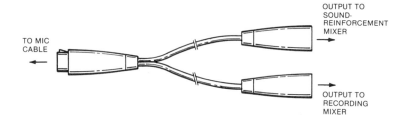

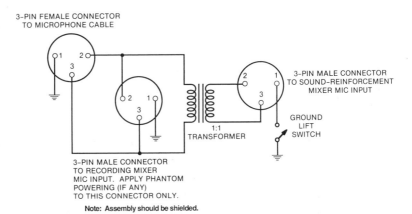

Fig. 16-7. Transformer-isolated microphone splitter.

For on-location work, you have to place each microphone within a few inches of its source to reject feedback, leakage, and room acoustics. Some recommended microphone techniques are covered in Chapter 8.

Ambience Microphones

If you have enough microphone inputs, you can add one or two ambience microphones to pick up the room acoustics and audience sounds. This helps the recording to sound "live." Without ambience microphones, the recording may sound too dry, as if it were done in a studio.

One popular technique is to mount two boundary microphones on the walls or ceiling; they are said to provide a clear, realistic pickup of audience reaction. Alternatively, hang two crossed cardioids or spaced omni's over the audience.

Ambience microphones can muddy the sound if mixed in too loudly. Keep them down in level, just enough to add some "atmosphere." Bring them up gently to emphasize crowd reactions.

Recording Live to 2-Track

A recording that is mixed live to 2-track can sound as good as a commercial LP of a live concert. Although you bypass the noise and distortion added by a multitrack recorder, there is a disadvantage: The mix may not be optimum because you have to mix as the musicians are playing. A multitrack recorder lets you tailor the mix after the concert.

Multitrack Recording

Now we're getting into professional techniques. Each microphone on the stage is split to feed the sound-reinforcement mixer and a separate multichannel recording mixer, as illustrated in the diagram of Fig. 16-8. Some splitters have three outputs to feed a stage-monitor mixer as well. To prevent ground loops between the three systems, the microphone-cable shields are grounded only to the recording console. The cable shields going to the house mixer and the monitor mixer are floated (disconnected) at the splitter with ground-lift switches.

Each microphone, or each instrument's group of microphones, is routed to a separate track of the multitrack recorder. After making the recording, you mix down the tracks back in the studio, spending as much time as needed to perfect the mix. You even can overdub parts that were flubbed during the live performance, taking care to match the overdubbed sound to the original recording.

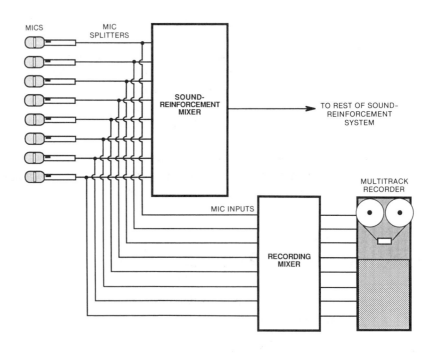

Fig. 16-8. Using microphone splitters to record into a multitrack recorder.

The 4-track format is probably the most difficult to use for live recording. That's because you have to sub-mix several microphones onto each track, and monitor all four tracks. You must set up the 4-track monitor mix very carefully, because you can't change the mix within each track after recording (except slightly with equalization).

Eight tracks are easier to work with because you do most of the mixing after the concert. You might need to mix the drum microphones to one or two tracks at the recording session, but, typically, each microphone feeds its own track. Most of your work during recording is level setting.

Even the 2-track format is easier than the 4-track system. Monitoring is simple—the mix you hear during recording is the mix you'll hear during playback. A situation where 4-track recording is easier might be with a jazz trio. You could put bass on track 1, piano on track 2, drums on track 3, and kick drum on track 4.

24-Track Recording in a Van Studio

Here's the ultimate setup. Each microphone on stage is split three ways to feed the snake boxes for the recording, reinforcement, and monitor consoles. A long multiconductor snake is run to a recording truck or van parked outside the concert hall or club. In the van, the microphone cables connect to a multichannel console, which is used to sub-mix groups of microphones and route the signals to a multitrack tape machine. Sometimes, two tape machines are run in parallel to provide a backup in case one fails. Or, two machines can be synchronized with SMPTE time code to increase the number of tracks available. The SMPTE time code is explained in Appendix B.

This sophisticated setup permits total control over the sound without compromising the house mix, monitor mix, or recording mix. The engineer can set up a quick mixdown, with effects, to play for the musicians after the concert.

During mixdown, the recorded tracks of the ambience microphones can be faded up or down as required—up for liveness and audience reaction, down for cleanest sound.

Summary of Techniques

We've covered a variety of on-location recording techniques. In general, the more sophisticated the setup, the better the sound. Here's a list of the methods we've discussed, from the simple to the complex:

- Place two microphones out front; use with pads into a 2-track tape deck.
- Record from the sound-reinforcement mixer.
- Record vocals from the sound-reinforcement mixer and mike the instruments separately.
- Use microphone splitters. Mix all the microphones live to 2-track with a recording mixer.
- Record onto a multitrack tape machine for later mixdown.
- Do the multitrack recording in a truck or van.

So far we have overviewed various on-location recording methods. The rest of this chapter explores the details of on-location pre-session procedures.

Power Connections

Here are some suggestions for making AC power connections while on location. You may also want to review Chapter 5, on hum prevention, especially the section on connections to electric guitar amps.

- Check that your AC power source is not shared with lighting dimmers or heavy machinery; these devices can cause noises or buzzes in the audio.
- Measure the AC line voltage. Know what your equipment can do under widely varying voltages. You may need to use a Variac™. Use a 3-prong tester to check the AC outlets for reversed polarity or lack of ground.

If possible, get the AC power from the same place the sound-reinforcement company does. Run a long, thick (14 or 16 gauge), extension cord from that point to the control room. Connect AC outlet strips to the extension cord, and then plug all your equipment into the outlet strips.

Interfacing with Telephone Lines

If you're doing a live remote for a broadcast, you'll probably send your signal to the transmitter via rented telephone lines. The Telco (telephone company) noise level of a telephone line is specified in dBrn. A level of

0 dBrn is the "absolutely quiet" reference: 0 dBrn = −90 dBm. Thus, if the noise level is 30 dBrn, the signal-to-noise ratio is 90−30, or 60 dB.

The Telco zero level is +8 dBm. You don't necessarily have to feed +8 dBm from your console into a phone line; +4 dBm will give 4 dB more headroom. The Telco test level is 0 dBm for tones above 400 Hz. You may want to ask for lossless lines (with unity gain). Otherwise, your signal may be down about 20 dB after transmission through the phone lines.

You need a 600-ohm source impedance, which is achieved by putting a 600-ohm resistor in series with the console output connector (300 ohms per leg of the balanced line). Have a terminated transformer on the sending end. To make a receiving line of 600 ohms, put a 600-ohm resistor across pins 2 and 3.

In addition to the program lines, rent a nonequalized private line for communications. Order the program lines 20 or 30 days in advance. Order a standard nonequalized communications line about a week in advance. For stereo programs, specify phase-matched lines.

Cables and Connectors

Let's move now to the subject of cables and cable connectors. In a 3-pin connector, if you tie (connect) pin 1 to the shell grounding lug, you will reduce pickup of electrostatic hum. However, with this wiring method, a ground loop is more likely to occur if the shell contacts a metallic surface on the stage. Furthermore, if pin 1 is grounded to the shell, and you plug the connector into a direct box and push the ground-lift switch, you don't lift ground!

It's probably best NOT to tie pin 1 to the ground lug when you're recording on-location, because a ground loop is a more likely occurrence than electrostatic hum pickup. But in controlled studio situations, it's best to tie pin 1 to the ground lug. In any case, standardize your connector wiring.

- If SCR dimmer noise is a problem, insert an adapter (that ties pin 1 to the shell) between two mic cables.
- To reduce hum pickup and ground-loop problems associated with cable connectors, try to use a single mic cable between each mic and its snake-box connector.

- Number the cables near their connectors and cover the label with clear heat-shrink tubing. Also, label both ends of each cable with the cable length. Put a drop of glue on each connector screw to temporarily lock it in place.

- Avoid bundling microphone cables, line-level cables, and power cables together. If you must cross mic cables and power cables, do so at right angles and space them vertically.

- Don't leave a rat's nest of cables near the stage box. Coil the excess cable at each mic stand. That way, you can move the mics and reduce clutter at the stage box. Don't tape the mic cables down until the musicians are settled.

- Have an extra microphone and cable offstage ready to use, in case a mic fails.

Pre-production Meeting

Have a pre-production meeting with the sound-reinforcement company and the production company putting on the event. Find out the date of the event, the location, the telephone numbers of everyone involved, when the job starts, when you can get into the hall, when the second set starts, etc. Decide who will provide the split, which system will be plugged in first, second, etc. Draw block diagrams for the audio system and communications system, to illustrate their arrangement.

If you're using a mic splitter, note that the mixer getting the direct side of the split provides phantom power for the condenser mics not powered on stage. If the house system has been in use for a long time, give them the direct side of the split.

Overloud stage monitors can ruin a recording, so work with the sound-reinforcement people toward a workable compromise. Ask them to start with the monitors quiet, because the musicians always want them turned up louder.

Make copies of the meeting notes for all participants. Don't leave things unresolved. Know who is responsible for supplying what equipment.

Fig. 16-9 shows a typical equipment layout that was worked out at a pre-production meeting. There are three systems in use: sound-reinforcement, recording, and monitor mixing. The microphone signals are split three ways to feed these systems.

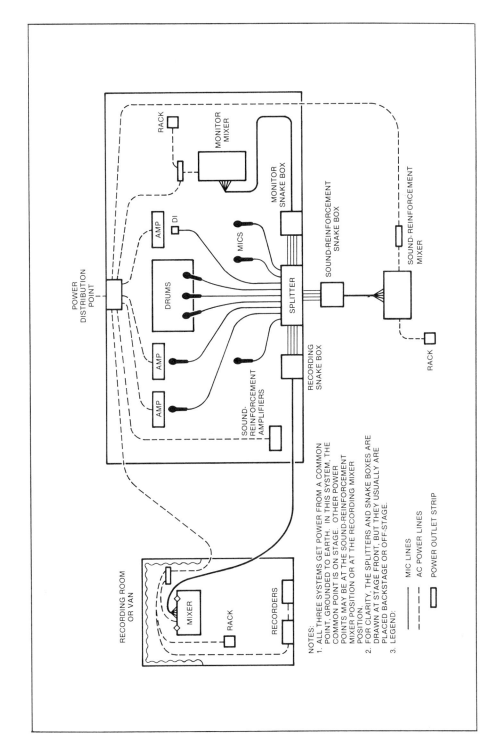

**Fig. 16-9.
Typical layout
for an
on-location
recording of a
live concert.**

Site Survey

Visit the recording site in advance and go through the following checklist:

- Listen for ambient noises—ice machines, coolers, 400-Hz generators, nearby discos, etc. If the room is noisy, you'll need to mike close. If not, you may want to mike at a distance to include the room acoustics.

- Sketch the dimensions of all rooms related to the job. Estimate distances for the cable runs.

- Turn on the sound-reinforcement system to see if it functions all right by itself (no hum, etc.). Turn the lighting on at various levels with the sound system on. Listen for buzzes. Try to correct any problem so that you don't document bad P.A. sound onto your tape.

- Check the AC power on stage with a circuit checker. Are grounded outlets actually grounded? Is there low resistance to ground? Are the outlets of correct polarity? There should be a substantial voltage between hot and ground, and no voltage between neutral and ground.

- Determine locations for any audience/ambience mics. Keep them away from air-conditioning ducts and noisy machinery.

- Plan your cable runs from stage to control room.

- If you plan to hang mic cables, feel the supports for vibration. You may need microphone shock mounts. If there's a breeze in the room, plan on taking along windscreens.

- Find a source of power for the remote truck that can handle the truck's power requirements. Find out whether you'll need a union electrician to make those connections.

- Find the circuit breakers for your power source and label them. Stay away from circuits supplying heavy machinery or old-style cash registers. Use an assistant when checking to see if any devices are on your circuit. Ask the custodian not to lock the circuit breaker box on the day of the recording.

- Make a file on each recording locale including the dimensions and the location of the circuit breakers.

- Determine where the control room will be. Find out what surrounds it—any noisy machinery?

- Visit the site when a crowd is there to see where there may be traffic problems.
- You might want to record the ambient noise with a portable recorder and play it back at home. This will make the ambient noise much more audible.
- If the AC power line is noisy, you might need a power isolation transformer with an electrostatic shield. Use a line voltage regulator if the AC line voltage varies widely.

After doing the site survey, draw a complete system block diagram, including all cables and connectors. Use this to generate an equipment list. Keep a file of system block diagrams for various recording venues.

Setting Up the Monitors

Now let's move into the control room and put together the monitor system. To optimize monitoring, first find a quiet location. Carry speakers and headphones with you. Set up the monitor speakers close to you—a near-field arrangement—to avoid hearing early reflections. Place Sonex acoustic foam on the wall behind the speakers.

While you're setting up the control room, play a familiar tape over the monitor system. This helps your ears adapt to unfamiliar surroundings.

Make a mono-stereo switch that lets you hear mono out of one speaker.

Setting Up the Mixing Console for Live Recording

The following is a suggested procedure for setting up the recording system efficiently:

1. Turn up the monitor system and verify that it is clean.
2. Plug in one mic at a time and monitor it to check for hums and buzzes. Troubleshooting is easier if you listen to each mic as you connect it, rather than plugging them all in and trying to find a hum or buzz.
3. Check and clean up one system at a time: first the sound-reinforcement system, then the stage-monitor system, then the

recording system, etc. Again, this makes troubleshooting easier because you have only one system to troubleshoot.

4. Use as many designation strips as you need for complex consoles. Label the input faders bottom and top. Also, label the monitor-mix pots and the meters.

5. Monitor the reverberation returns. Spring reverberation units often pick up radio-frequency interference or hum, which can be eliminated sometimes by rotating or moving the reverb unit.

6. Make a short test recording and listen to the playback.

7. Verify that left and right channels are correct, and that the pan-pot action is not audibly reversed.

8. If you're recording an orchestra with an overall stereo microphone plus spot microphones, pan the images of the spot mics to coincide with those of the main stereo mic.

9. Do a preliminary pan-pot setup. Panning similar instruments to different locations helps you identify them. While panning instruments, you can create a unique stereo image, or create the performers' point of view, or create the audience's point of view. Typically, rock drums are panned for the player's perspective; jazz drums are panned for the audience perspective.

Doing the Mix

If you're mixing live during the performance, first set the master faders and input faders to design center. Then set the gain trims for a rough mix, and then fine-tune the mix with the faders. If you're recording to multitrack, first set the faders to design center, and then set the gain trims for the desired record level (usually around 0 VU).

Take notes on the gain-trim settings for particular mics and instruments. Then, in future sessions, you can pre-set the trims to these settings.

Before you start mixing, it's very important to have a preconceived notion of what you want to hear. Consider production style, stereo, sense of distance, amount of reverb, spectral balance, and so on. Hear it in your head. Compare what you hear in your head to what you monitor. Determine what the difference is and make an adjustment.

Next, work on equalization, stereo panning, and effects. Do equalization cut as well as boost. Boosting equalization reduces headroom; cutting doesn't.

Here's a suggested mixing process:

1. Take your hands off the console. For some reason, you'll hear a lot better. It helps you relax and listen critically.
2. Listen. If you don't like something, determine specifically what you don't like and what you need to do to change it.
3. Make an intentional adjustment. Move the knob until you can hear a change.
4. Go back to Step 1.

Don't have "twiddle-itis." Usually the mix is untouched—you just make little finesse adjustments. You might bring out a solo, and then pull the fader back down after the solo. If you make a temporary adjustment up, later make a complementary adjustment down.

Avoid drastic changes—make changes slowly and imperceptibly. Live-music mixing requires slow, elegant, fluid movements. By contrast, multi-track mixdowns use quick fader movements, often to pre-marked positions.

In a live recording, never turn off a mic completely unless you know positively that it's not going to be used. Otherwise, you'll invariably miss cues. This is a different procedure from multitrack mixdowns, where you mute silent portions of tracks to reduce noise.

While mixing, monitor frequently in mono to judge the singer/ensemble balance or the soloist/ensemble balance.

If the VU meters are pinned, it indicates you need to monitor more loudly. Just turn the monitors up, and turn all the faders down, until you're peaking around 0 VU. If the VU meters are barely moving, that shows that the monitors are too loud. Turn down the monitor power amp and slowly bring up the faders. Try to establish your own consistent listening level for a 0-VU level.

To test your mix, occasionally play the monitors very quietly, and see if you can hear everything.

Miscellaneous Tips

Here are some helpful hints for successful on-location recordings:

- Connect and use unfamiliar new equipment before going on the road. Don't experiment on the job!
- Arrive several hours ahead of time to allow for setup. Expect failures—there's always something going wrong, something

unexpected. Allow 50% more time for troubleshooting than you think you'll need. Have backup plans if equipment fails. Leave as little to chance as possible. Consider recording with redundant (double) systems so you will have a backup if one fails.

- Don't be caught without the little things, like spare tape reels, spare cables, hub adapters, pencil and paper, and electrical 3-to-2 adapters.

- Bring a tool kit with screwdrivers, pliers, soldering iron, connectors, adapters, cables, 9-volt batteries, guitar cords, guitar strings, AC-outlet checkers, fuses, a pocket radio to listen for interference, ferrite beads of various sizes for RFI suppression, canned air to blow out dirt, Q-tips and pipe cleaners, and Cramoline Red from Cague Labs to remove oxide from the connectors.

- Set recording levels before the concert during the sound check. It's better to set the levels a little too low than too high because during mixdown you can reduce noise but not distortion.

- dbx® noise reduction is a great help in live recording. In addition to reducing tape hiss, it compresses the signal going on tape so that the level variations are less extreme. You're less likely to saturate the tape during loud peaks.

- If a concert will be longer than the running time of a reel of tape, switch reels at intermissions. Another method is to feed the same signal in parallel to two identical tape machines. Record on one machine. As the reel of tape nears the end, start recording on the second machine so that none of the performance is lost. Edit the two tapes together later, back in the studio.

- Walkie-talkies are all right for pre-show use, but don't use them during the performance because they cause RF interference. Assistants can be used to relay messages to and from the stage crew while you're mixing.

- During short set changes, use a closed-circuit TV system and a light table to show what set changes and mic-layout changes are coming up next; transmit this information to the monitor mixer and sound-reinforcement mixer.

- Don't unplug mics that are plugged into phantom power because this will make a popping noise in the sound-reinforcement system.

- After the gig, note equipment failures. Fix broken equipment as soon as possible.

- Don't put tapes through airport x-ray machines because the transformer in these machines is not always well shielded.

- Hand-carry your mics on airplanes. Arrange to load and unload your own freight containers, rather than trusting them to airline freight loaders.

- Get a public-liability insurance policy to protect yourself against lawsuits.

In general, plan everything in advance so you can relax at the gig and have fun! By following these suggestions, you should improve your efficiency—and your recordings—at on-location sessions.

Most of the information in the second half of this chapter (starting with Power Connections) was derived from two workshops presented at the 79th convention of the Audio Engineering Society in October, 1985. These workshops were titled "On the Repeal of Murphy's Law—Interfacing Problem Solving, Planning, and General Efficiency On-Location," and "Popular Music Recording Techniques." The first was given by Paul Blakemore, Neil Muncy, and Skip Pizzi, while the second, "Popular Music Recording Techniques," was given by Paul Blakemore, Dave Moulton, Neil Muncy, Skip Pizzi, and Curt Wittig.

17 ON-LOCATION RECORDING OF CLASSICAL MUSIC

Perhaps your high school band or civic orchestra is giving a concert, and you'd like to make an audiophile-grade recording. Or maybe there's an organist or string quartet playing at the local college, and they want you to record them. This chapter explains how to make professional-quality recordings of these ensembles. It describes the necessary equipment, microphone techniques, and session procedures.

Incidentally, recording classical music ensembles is a great way for the beginning recordist to gain experience. With just two microphones and a 2-track recorder, much can be learned about acoustics, microphone placement, level setting, and editing—all essential skills in the studio.

Equipment

For on-location classical music recording, the necessary equipment is a 2-track tape deck, microphones, cables, mic-stand adapters, mic stands, headphones, and editing hardware. Optional equipment includes a noise-reduction unit and a mixer. Let's look at each of these in detail.

The Tape Deck

A good cassette recorder loaded with metal or chromium tape can be used for live recording, but, for highest-quality performance, a 2-track open-reel tape deck is preferred. Open-reel recorders have more high-frequency *headroom* than cassette decks. That is, open-reel units record high-frequency peaks with flatter response and lower distortion. Also, with open-reel machines, you can edit the tape to remove noises and pauses between musical selections.

A half-track tape machine is preferable to a quarter-track unit because half-track provides a better signal-to-noise ratio and less-severe drop-outs, all else being equal. Furthermore, you can record in only one direction if you plan to edit the tape later on, so half the tape width is wasted using the quarter-track format. (Tape formats were explained in Chapter 9.)

An alternative to an audio tape deck is a videocassette recorder with the Beta Hi-Fi or VHS Hi-Fi system. It can outperform an open-reel recorder.

Highest quality can be had using a *digital audio processor* in combination with a videocassette recorder. The analog signal from your microphones is converted into a digital signal by the processor and is recorded on videotape. The tape playback sounds just like the microphone signal, virtually without added noise, wow and flutter, or distortion. A disadvantage is that the tape cannot be edited except by copying from one machine to another. This is an imprecise procedure unless SMPTE time code is used. (SMPTE time code is explained in Appendix B.)

Microphones

Next on our list of equipment are some quality microphones. You'll need two or three of the same type and model number. Good microphones are essential, for the microphones—and their placement—determine the sound of your recording. You should spend at least $200 to $400 per microphone for professional-quality sound.

For classical music recording, the preferred microphone is the condenser type with a wide, flat, frequency response and very low self-noise (less than 21-dB equivalent SPL, A-weighted). Self-noise was explained in Chapter 6. These microphones are available with an omnidirectional or unidirectional pickup pattern. An omnidirectional microphone is equally sensitive to sounds arriving from any direction, so it helps to add liveness (reverberation) to a recording made in an acoustically dead hall. Most omnidirectional condenser mics have excellent low-frequency response, making them useful for pipe organ or bass drum recordings.

A unidirectional microphone (such as a cardioid) is most sensitive to sounds approaching the front of the microphone, and partly rejects sounds approaching the sides and rear. This helps reduce excessive reverberation in the recording.

Some condenser microphones require an external power supply; others work on internal batteries. Your microphone dealer or product literature can explain what's needed.

Stands vs. Hanging

You can mount the microphones on stands or hang them from the ceiling using nylon fishing line. Stands are much easier to set up, but are more visually distracting at live concerts. Stands are more suitable for recording rehearsals or sessions with no audience present.

The mic stands should have a tripod folding base, and should be able to extend to at least 14 feet high. You can purchase "baby booms" to extend the height of regular mic stands. Many camera stores have telescoping photographic stands which are lightweight and compact.

Stereo Bar

A useful accessory is a *stereo bar* or *stereo microphone adapter*. This device mounts two microphones on a single stand for stereo recording.

Boundary Microphones

In difficult mounting situations, boundary microphones may come in handy. They can lie flat on the stage floor, or can be mounted on the ceiling or on the front edge of a balcony. They also can be attached to clear plexiglass panels that are hung or mounted on mic stands.

Other Equipment

Headphones

For monitoring, you will need some closed-cup, circumaural headphones to block out the sound of the musicians. You want to hear only what's being recorded. Of course, the headphones should be wide-range and smooth for accurate monitoring.

Mic Extension Cables

You'll have to sit far from the musicians to clearly monitor what you're recording. To do that, you'll need a pair of 50-foot microphone extension cables. Longer extensions will be needed if the mics are hung from the ceiling.

Tape

Buy the best high-output low-noise tape you can afford (as recommended by the recorder manufacturer). A tape thickness of 1.5 mil is preferred because it reduces print-through. (Print-through is the transfer of a magnetic signal from one layer of tape to the next, causing an echo or pre-echo.)

A 1200-foot reel of 1.5-mil tape provides 30 minutes of recording time at 7½ ips, recording one direction. An 1800-foot reel of 1-mil tape provides 45 minutes. Avoid using tape under 1-mil thick because the tape can stretch easily and is prone to print-through.

Noise Reduction

You may want to use a noise-reduction system, such as Dolby® or dbx®, to reduce tape hiss by 10 to 30 dB.

Mixer

If you use noise reduction, you'll also need a small stereo microphone mixer to boost the microphones' signal level up to the line level required by the noise-reduction system. A mixer is also necessary when you want to record more than one source—say, an orchestra and a choir, or a band and a soloist. You might put a pair of microphones on the orchestra and another pair on the choir. The mixer blends the signals of all four mics into a composite stereo signal. It also lets you control the balance (relative loudness) among the microphones.

Miscellaneous Hardware

Other miscellaneous equipment includes a power extension cord, multiple outlets, spare mic cables, leader tape, an editing block, splicing tape, a grease pencil, a stopwatch, and duct tape to keep cables in place.

Stereo Microphone Techniques

Many record companies prefer to use multiple microphones and multi-track techniques when recording classical music. Such methods provide extra control of balance and definition, and are necessary in difficult situations. However, the clarity of digital recording is forcing a trend back to simpler techniques. This chapter focuses on some of these simple methods because they seem to be the wave of the future.

Basically, you place two or three mics several feet in front of the group and raised up high, as diagrammed in Fig. 17-1. The microphone placement controls the acoustic perspective or sense of distance to the ensemble, the balance among the instruments, and the stereo imaging.

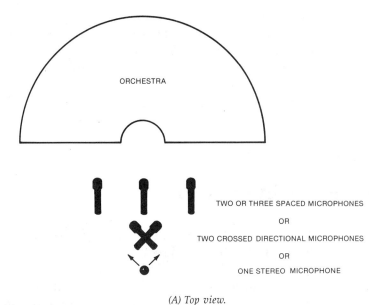

ORCHESTRA

TWO OR THREE SPACED MICROPHONES

OR

TWO CROSSED DIRECTIONAL MICROPHONES

OR

ONE STEREO MICROPHONE

(A) Top view.

**Fig. 17-1.
Typical
microphone
placement for
on-location
recording of a
classical music
ensemble.**

(B) Side view.

There are three microphone techniques commonly used for stereo recording: the coincident pair, the near-coincident pair, and the spaced-pair technique. Their characteristics, advantages, and disadvantages were described in detail in Chapter 7.

To review, the coincident-pair technique uses two directional microphones angled apart with their grilles touching and their diaphragms aligned vertically. The near-coincident technique uses two directional mics angled apart and spaced a few inches apart horizontally. The spaced-pair technique uses two or three matched microphones of any pattern aimed straight ahead toward the ensemble and spaced several feet apart horizontally.

We mentioned earlier that boundary microphones can be mounted on clear plastic panels. These panels can be spaced apart for spaced-pair stereo, or placed with one edge touching to form a "V" for near-coincident stereo, with excellent imaging, as illustrated in Fig. 17-2. Alternatively, two boundary mics can go on opposite sides of a single panel for coincident miking. This last arrangement adds some liveness or ambience to recordings made in an acoustically dead hall.

Preparing for the Session

Armed with the previous information, you're ready to go on-location. First ask the musical director what groups and soloists will be playing, where they will be located, and how long the program will be.

If possible, plan to record in a locale with good acoustics. There should be adequate reverberation time for the music being performed. This is very important, because it can make the difference between an amateur-sounding recording and a commercial-sounding one. Try to record in an auditorium or spacious church rather than in a band room or gymnasium.

Next, get all your equipment ready. Demagnetize the tape heads, tape guides, and capstan. Clean these components as well as the pinch roller. Check all cables and equipment for proper operation.

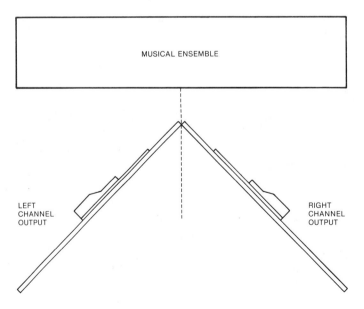

Fig. 17-2. Two boundary microphones mounted on two panels and used for near-coincident stereo recording.

Collect enough tape for the recording. If you can't locate a 10½-inch reel of tape, splice together and wind two 1200-foot reels of tape onto a single, empty, 10½-inch reel. Make two of these. If your machine won't accept a 10½-inch reel, use a 7-inch reel with 1800 feet of tape, which allows 45 minutes of continuous recording time at 7½ ips.

Keep your equipment inside your home or studio until you're ready to leave. Tape decks left outside in a cold car may become sluggish, and batteries may lose some voltage.

Session Setup

Allow an extra hour or so for setup and for fixing broken cables, etc. There's always something unexpected in any new recording situation.

When you first arrive at the recording site, locate some AC power outlets near where you want to set up. Check that these outlets are "live." If not, ask the custodian to turn on the appropriate circuit breaker.

Find a table or some folding chairs on which to set your equipment. Plug into the AC outlets and let your equipment warm up. Leave a few turns of AC cord piled near the outlet, and tape down the cord so it isn't unplugged accidentally.

Now take out your microphones and place them in the desired stereo miking arrangement. As an example, let's say you're recording an orchestra rehearsal with two crossed cardioids on a stereo bar (the near-coincident method). Screw the stereo bar onto a mic stand, and mount two cardioid microphones on the stereo bar. For starters, angle them 110° apart and space them 7 inches apart horizontally. Aim them down so that they'll point at the orchestra when raised. You may want to mount the microphones in shock mounts or put the stands on sponges to isolate the mics from floor vibration.

As a starting position, place the mic stand behind the conductor's podium, about 12 feet in front of the front-row musicians. Connect the mic cables and mic extension cords. Raise the microphones about 14 feet off the floor. This prevents overly loud pickup of the front row relative to the back row of the orchestra. Leave some extra turns of mic cable at the base of each stand so you can reposition the stands. This slack also allows for people accidentally pulling on the cables. Try to route the mic cables where they won't be stepped on, or cover them with mats.

If you're using just two mics, you can plug them directly into your tape deck. If you're using two mics and a noise-reduction unit, plug the mics into a mixer to boost the mic signals up to line level, and then run that line-level signal into the noise-reduction unit connected to the recorder line inputs. If you're using multiple mics and a mixer without noise reduction, plug the mixer outputs into the recorder line inputs.

Now put on your headphones, turn up the recording-level controls, and monitor the signal. When the orchestra starts to play, set the recording levels to peak around 0 VU. The monitored signal indicates the effectiveness of the microphone placement.

Microphone Placement

Nothing has more effect on the production style of a classical music recording than microphone placement. Miking distance, stereo positioning, and spot miking all influence the recorded sound character.

Miking Distance

The microphones must be placed closer to the musicians than to a good live listening position. If you place the mics out in the audience where the live sound is good, the recording will probably sound muddy and distant when played back over speakers. That's because all the recorded reverberation is reproduced up-front along a line between the playback speakers, along with the direct sound of the orchestra. Close miking (5 to 20 feet from the front row) compensates for this effect by increasing the ratio of direct sound to reverberant sound.

The closer the mics are to the orchestra, the closer it sounds in the recording. If the instruments sound too close, too edgy, too detailed, or if the recording lacks hall ambience, the mics are too close to the ensemble. Move the mic stand a foot or two farther from the orchestra and listen again. If the orchestra sounds too distant, muddy, or reverberant, the mics are too far from the ensemble. Move the mic stand a little closer to the musicians and listen again.

Eventually, you'll find a spot where the direct sound of the orchestra is in a pleasing balance with the ambience of the concert hall. Then, the reproduced orchestra will sound neither too close nor too far.

Stereo-Spread Control

Now concentrate on the stereo spread. If the spread heard over the headphones is too narrow, it means that the mics are angled or spaced too close together. Increase the angle or spacing between the mics until localization is accurate. *Note:* Increasing the angle betweeen mics will make the instruments sound farther away; increasing the spacing will not.

If off-center instruments are heard far-left or far-right in your headphones, it indicates that your mics are angled or spaced too far apart. Move them closer together until localization is accurate.

Due to psychoacoustic phenomena, coincident-pair recordings have less stereo spread when heard over headphones than when heard over loudspeakers. Take this into account when monitoring.

Soloist Pickup and Spot Microphones

Sometimes a soloist plays in front of the orchestra. You'll have to capture a tasteful balance between the soloist and the ensemble. That is, your mics should be placed so that the relative loudness of the soloist and the accompaniment is musically appropriate. If the soloist is too loud relative to the orchestra (as heard on headphones), raise the mics. If the soloist is too quiet, lower the mics. You may want to add a *spot* mic about 3 feet from the soloist and mix it in with the other microphones.

If you use spot or accent mics on various instruments or on instrumental sections, mix them at a low level relative to the main pair—just loud enough to add definition, but not loud enough to destroy depth. Operate the spot mic faders subtly or leave them untouched. Otherwise, the close-miked instruments may "jump forward" when the fader is brought up, and then "fall back in" when the fader is brought down.

Recording

Now that the mics are positioned properly, you're ready to record. The recording time at 7½ ips is twice the recording time available at 15 ips. So record at 7½ ips to conserve tape; use 15 ips for cleanest sound and greatest headroom.

If you're recording a live concert, you might want to set your recording levels to read about −10 VU with the opening applause. This procedure should result in approximately correct recording levels when the musicians start playing.

Start recording a few seconds before the music starts. Once the recording is in progress, let the recording-level meters peak at +3 VU on the loudest peaks. Ignore meter pinning on bass drum accents. Leave the recording level alone as much as possible. If you must adjust the level, do so slowly and try to follow the dynamics of the music.

If there is applause at the end of a musical piece, you can fade it out over 3 seconds by carefully turning down the recording-level controls or the mixer master volume control.

At the intermission, fast-forward the tape onto the take-up reel so it is stored tail-out. This reduces print-through. Label the tape reel and its box. Thread on your next reel of tape and record the second half of the concert. After the concert, pack the mics away first; otherwise, they may be stolen or damaged.

Editing

Once you have your tapes home, you may want to edit them to make a tight presentation. Using a splicing block and a single-edge razor blade, cut out the tape between musical selections and replace it with about 4 seconds of leader tape. This is a blank plastic or paper tape without an oxide coating that is used to separate selections on a tape reel. Instead of using leader tape, you may want to insert an interval of recorded "room sound," especially between movements of a symphony.

When editing the tape, mark and cut the tape just before the beginning of each piece, and just after the reverberant "tail" fades out at the end of each piece. A yellow grease pencil or china marker is typically used to mark edit points.

If you plan to send your tapes to a record-mastering company, make up two reels—one for Side 1 of the record; the second for Side 2. Splice on about 30 seconds of leader at the beginning and end of each reel. Try to keep under 18 minutes per side, with 25 minutes maximum, because longer programs will result in the record being cut with reduced level, bass, or stereo separation.

Label each reel and store the tape tail out. Time each reel with a stopwatch from the start of the first song to the end of the last song, including the leader between selections. Put the timing and record-label information in the tape boxes.

Congratulations! You now have your finished product—a realistic, professional recording of a classical music ensemble.

18 JUDGING SOUND QUALITY

Seat an engineer behind a mixing console and ask him or her to do a mix. It sounds great. Then seat another engineer behind the same console and again ask for a mix. It sounds terrible. What happened?

The difference lies mainly in their *ears*—their critical listening ability. The first engineer has a clear idea of what he or she wants to hear and how to get it. The second engineer hasn't acquired the ability to recognize good sound. That ability is essential. By knowing what to listen for, you can improve your artistic judgments during recording and mixdown. You'll be able to hear errors in microphone placement, equalization, etc., and be able to correct them.

To train your hearing, try to to analyze recorded sound into its components—such as frequency response, noise, reverberation—and concentrate on each one in turn. It's easier to hear sonic flaws if you focus on a single aspect of sound reproduction at a time. This chapter is a guide designed to help you do this.

Classical vs. Popular Recording

Classical and popular music have different standards of "good sound." One goal in recording classical music (and, often, folk music or jazz) is to accurately reproduce the live performance. This is a worthy aim because the sound of an orchestra in a good hall can be quite beautiful. The music was composed and the instruments were designed to sound best when heard live in a concert hall. So the recording engineer, out of respect for the music, should always try to translate that sound to tape with as little technical intrusion as possible.

By contrast, the accurate translation of sound to tape is not always the goal when recording popular music. Although the aim may be to reproduce the original sound, the producer or engineer may also want to play with that sound to create a new sonic experience, or to do some of both. In fact, the artistic manipulation of sounds through studio techniques has become an end in itself. Apparently the philosophy is this: Creating an interesting new sound is as valid a goal as recreating the original sound. There are two games to play, each with its own measures of success.

If the aim of a recording is realism or accurate reproduction, the recording is successful when it matches the live performance heard in the best seat in the concert hall. The sound of musical instruments is the standard by which such recordings are judged.

But when the goal is to enhance the sound or to produce special effects (as in most pop music recordings), the aesthetic is less defined. The live sound of a pop group could be a reference, but pop music recordings generally sound better than live performances. Recorded vocals are clearer and less harsh, the bass is cleaner and tighter, and so on. The sound of pop music reproduced over speakers has developed its own standards of quality apart from accurate reproduction.

Good Sound in a Pop Music Recording

Currently, a good-sounding pop recording might be described as follows: well-mixed, wide-range, tonally balanced, clean, and clear. Quality recordings also sound smooth and spacious, with presence, wide and detailed stereo imaging, and sharp transients. Dynamic range is wide but controlled, and special effects are creative and tasteful.

Let's explore each one of these qualities in detail so that we'll know what to listen for. We're assuming the monitor system is accurate, so that any colorations heard are in the recording and not in the monitors.

Well-Mixed

In a good mix, all the instruments and vocals are in a pleasing loudness balance with each other. Everything can be clearly heard, yet nothing is obtrusive. The most important instruments or voices are the loudest; less important parts are in the background.

A successful mix goes unnoticed. When all the tracks are balanced correctly, nothing sticks out and nothing is hidden. Note that there's a wide latitude for musical interpretation and personal taste in making a mix.

Sometimes you don't want everything to be clearly heard. In rare occasions, you may want to mix in certain tracks very subtly for a subconscious effect.

The mix must be appropriate for the style of music. For example, a mix that's right for rock music usually won't work for country music. A rock mix typically has the drums way up front and the vocals only slightly louder than the accompaniment. In contrast, a country mix has the vocals loudest, with the drums used just as "seasoning" in the background. This distinction is lessening as country music is approaching a pop sound.

Level changes during the mix should be subtle, or else instruments will "jump out" for a solo and "fall back in" afterwards. Move faders slowly, or set them to preset positions during pauses in the music. Nothing sounds more amateurish than a solo that starts too quietly and then comes up as it plays. You can hear the engineer working the fader.

Wide-Range

"Wide range" means extended low-frequency and high-frequency response. Cymbals should sound crisp and distinct, but not sizzly or harsh; the kick drum and bass should sound deep, but not overwhelming or muddy. Wide-range sound results from using high-quality microphones and recorders, good tape, a high tape speed, and clean tape heads.

Tonally Balanced

The overall tonal balance of a recording should be neither bassy nor trebly. That is, the perceived spectrum should not emphasize low frequencies or high frequencies. Low bass, mid-bass, midrange, upper midrange, and highs should be heard in equal proportions, as diagrammed in Fig. 18-1. Emphasis of any one frequency band over another eventually causes listening fatigue.

Recorded tonal balance is inversely related to the frequency response of the studio's monitor system. If the monitors have an extreme high-frequency rolloff, the engineer will compensate by boosting highs in the recording to make the monitors sound right. The result is a bright recording.

Before doing a mix, it helps to play over the monitors some records whose sound you admire. This helps you become accustomed to a commercial spectral balance. After your mix is recorded, play it back and

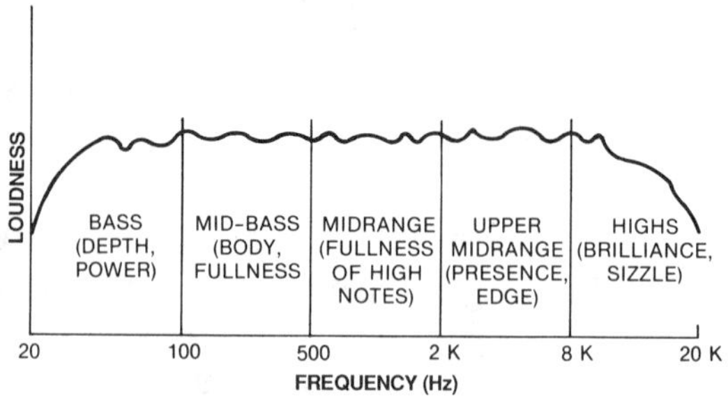

Fig. 18-1. Loudness vs. frequency of a good-sounding pop recording.

Note: The subjective loudness of various frequency bands should be about equal. (The frequency divisions shown here are somewhat arbitrary.)

alternately switch between your mix and a commercial record. This comparison indicates how well you matched a commercial spectral balance. Of course, you may not care to duplicate what others are doing.

In pop music recordings, the tonal balance or timbre of individual instruments does not necessarily have to be natural. Still, many listeners want to hear a realistic timbre from acoustic instruments, such as the guitar, flute, sax, or piano. The reproduced timbre depends on the microphone frequency response, microphone placement, the musical instruments themselves, and equalization.

Clean

"Clean" means free of noise and distortion. Tape hiss, hum, and distortion are inaudible in a good recording. "Distortion" in this case means distortion added by the recording process, not distortion already present in the sound of electric guitar amps or Leslie speakers. "Clean" also means "not muddy"—free of low-frequency overhang and leakage.

A "clean mix" is one that is uncluttered, free of excess instrumentation. This is achieved by arranging the music so that similar parts don't overlap, and not too many instruments play at once. Usually, the fewer the instruments, the clearer the sound. Too many overdubs can muddy the mix.

Clear

In a clear-sounding recording, instruments do not "crowd" or mask each other's sound. They are separate and distinct, and blend well. Clarity arises when instrumentation is sparse, or when instruments occupy different areas of the frequency spectrum. For example, low frequencies are provided by the bass, while mid-bass might be emphasized by the keyboards, and upper midrange may be provided by the lead guitar; the highs are filled in by the cymbals. In addition, a clear recording has an adequate reproduction of each instrument's harmonics. That is, the high-frequency response is not rolled off.

Smooth

Now we get into some subtler aspects of sound. "Smooth" means easy on the ears, not harsh, uncolored. Sibilants or "s" sounds sound clear but not piercing. A smooth, effortless sound allows relaxation; a strained or irritating sound causes muscle tension in the ears or body.

Smoothness is a lack of sharp peaks or dips in the frequency response, as well as a lack of excessive boost in the midrange or upper midrange.

Presence

This is the apparent sense of closeness of the instruments—a feeling that they are present in the listening room. Synonyms are clarity, detail, and punch.

Presence is achieved by close miking, overdubbing, and using microphones with a presence peak or emphasis around 5 kHz. Upper-midrange boost helps too. Most instruments have a frequency range which, if boosted, makes the instrument stand out more clearly or become better defined. Note that presence sometimes conflicts with smoothness. That's because presence often involves an upper-midrange boost, while a smooth sound is free of such emphasis. You'll have to find a tasteful compromise between the two.

Spacious

"Spacious" or "airy" means "having a sense of air around the instruments." Without air or ambience, instruments sound like they're isolated in stuffed closets. Spaciousness is achieved by adding artificial reverberation to the recording.

Sharp Transients

The attack of cymbals and drums generally should be sharp and clear. A bass guitar and piano may or may not require sharp attacks, depending on the song.

Tight Bass and Drums

The kick drum and bass guitar should "lock" together so that they sound like a single instrument—a bass with a percussive attack. The drummer and bassist should work out their parts together so as to hit accents simultaneously.

To further tighten the sound, the kick drum is damped and the bass is recorded direct. They are equalized for presence and clarity.

Good Stereo

Stereo means more than just "left" and "right." Usually, tracks should be panned to many points across the stereo stage between the playback loudspeakers. Some instruments should be hard left or hard right, some should be in the center, and others should be half-left or half-right. Try to achieve a stereo stage that is well balanced between left and right, as shown in Fig. 18-2. Instruments occupying the same frequency range should be panned to opposite sides of center.

You may want some tracks to be unlocalized. Backup choruses and strings should be spread out rather than appearing as point sources. Stereo keyboard sounds can wander between speakers. A lead-guitar solo can have a fat, spacious sound.

There should be some front-to-back depth. Some instruments should sound close or up front, while others should sound farther away.

Fig. 18-2.
Example of
image placement
between
speakers.

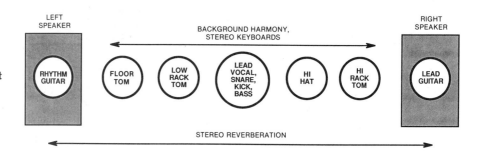

If stereo imaging is intended to be realistic (say, for a jazz combo), then the reproduced ensemble should simulate the spatial layout of the live ensemble. If you're sitting in an audience listening to a jazz quartet, you might hear drums on the left, piano on the right, bass in the middle, and sax slightly right. The drums and piano are not point sources, but are somewhat spread out. If spatial realism is the goal, you should hear the same ensemble layout between your speakers. Often the piano and drums are spread all the way between speakers—an interesting effect, but unrealistic.

Pan-potted mono tracks often sound artificial in that each instrument sounds isolated in its own little space. It helps if there is some stereo reverberation surrounding the instruments to "glue" them together.

Dynamic Range

Dynamic range is the range of volume levels from the softest to the loudest. A recording with a wide dynamic range becomes noticeably louder and softer, adding excitement to the music. This is achieved by avoiding excessive compression (automatic volume control). An overly compressed recording sounds "squashed"—crescendos and quiet interludes lose their impact.

Some compression or gain-riding is needed for vocals because their dynamic range exceeds that of the instrumental backup. A vocalist may sing too loudly and blast the listener, or sing too softly and become buried in the mix. A compressor can even out these extreme level variations, keeping the vocals at a constant loudness. Bass guitar also benefits from compression.

Interesting Sounds

The recorded sound may be too "flat" or neutral—lacking character or color. In contrast, a recording with creative production has unique musical-instrument sounds, and typically uses special effects. Some of these are equalization, echo, reverberation, doubling, chorus, flanging, compression, and stereo effects.

Making sounds interesting or colorful can conflict with accuracy or fidelity, so effects and equalization should be used with discretion.

Suitable Production

A general rule of aesthetics that applies to recording is, "The medium is the message." The way a recording sounds should imply the same message as the musical style or lyrics. In other words, the sound should be appropriate for the particular tune being recorded.

For example, some rock music is rough and raw. The sound should be, too. A clean, polished production doesn't always work for high-energy rock and roll. There might even be a lot of leakage or ambience to suggest a garage studio or nightclub environment. The role of the drums is important, so they should be loud in the mix. The toms should ring.

New Age, Disco, Rhythm and Blues, or Middle-of-the-Road music is slickly produced. The sound is usually tight, smooth, and spacious. Country music is about stories or feelings, so the bass and vocals are emphasized for warmth and emotion. Acoustic guitars and drums are miked at a respectful distance, giving an airy, natural effect.

Actually, each style of music is not locked into a particular style of production. You tailor the sound to complement the music of each individual tune. Doing this may break some of the "rules" of good sound, but that's usually okay as long as the song is enhanced by its sonic presentation.

Good Sound in a Classical Music Recording

Like pop music, classical music should sound clean, wide-range, and tonally balanced. But since classical recordings are meant to sound realistic—like a live performance—they also require good acoustics, balance, tonal accuracy, suitable perspective, and accurate stereo imaging. Let's consider each of these requirements.

Good Acoustics

The acoustics of the concert hall or recital hall should be appropriate for the style of music to be performed. Specifically, the reverberation time should be neither too short (dry) nor too long (cavernous). Too short a reverberation time results in a recording without spaciousness or grandeur. Too long a reverberation time blurs notes together, giving a muddy, washed-out effect. Ideal reverberation times are around 1.2 seconds for chamber music or soloists, 1.5 seconds for symphonic works, and 2 seconds for organ recitals.

Balance

When a recording is well balanced, the relative loudness of instruments is similar to that heard in an ideal seat in the audience area. For example, violins are not too loud or soft compared to the rest of the orchestra; harmonizing or contrapuntal melody lines are in proportion.

Generally, the instruments are balanced acoustically by the conductor, composer, and musicians—rather than being mixed on a mixing console. There are exceptions, as some recording engineers use multiple miking for classical music. Certain instruments or sections may be miked individually for added definition or improved balance. Whether or not this is done, the conductor is consulted for proper balances.

Tonal Accuracy

The reproduced timbre or tone quality should match that of the live instruments. Fundamentals and harmonics should be reproduced in their original proportion.

Suitable Perspective

This is the sense of the distance of the performers from the listener; how far away the stage sounds. Do the performers sound like they're eight rows in front of you, in your lap, or in another room?

The style of music will suggest a suitable perspective. Incisive, rhythmically motivated works, such as Stravinsky's *Rite of Spring*, sound best with closer miking; lush romantic pieces (a Bruckner symphony) are best served by more distant miking. The chosen perspective depends on the taste of the producer.

Closely related to perspective is the amount of recorded ambience or reverberation. A good miking distance yields a pleasing balance of direct sound from the orchestra and ambience from the concert hall.

Accurate Imaging

Reproduced instruments should appear in the same relative locations as they were in the live performance. Instruments in the center of the ensemble should be heard in the center between the speakers; instruments at the left or right side of the ensemble should be heard from the left or right speaker. Instruments halfway to one side should be heard halfway off center, and so on. A large ensemble should spread from speaker to speaker, while a quartet or soloist can have a narrower spread.

Note that you must sit equidistant from the speakers when judging stereo imaging, otherwise the images will shift toward the side on which you're sitting. Sit as far from the speakers as they are spaced apart. Then the speakers will appear to be 60° apart, which is about the same angle an orchestra fills when viewed from the typical ideal seat in the audience (say, tenth row center).

The reproduced size of an instrument or instrumental section should match its size in real life. A guitar should be a point source; a piano or string section should have some stereo spread. Each instrument's location should be as clearly defined as it was in the concert hall, as heard from the ideal seat.

Reproduced reverberation (concert-hall ambience) should either surround the listener, or at least it should spread evenly between the speakers. Extra speakers or add-on ambience enhancers are currently needed to make the recorded ambience surround the listener, although spaced-microphone recordings have some of this effect.

There should be a sense of stage depth, with front-row instruments sounding closer than back-row instruments. Accurate imaging is illustrated in Fig. 18-3.

Training Your Hearing

We've covered a long list of things you should listen for. The critical process is easier if you focus on one aspect of sound reproduction at a

Fig. 18-3. Accurate imaging: sound-source location and size are reproduced during playback, as well as the reverberant field.

REVERBERATION APPROACHES
MICS FROM ALL DIRECTIONS

(A) Recording.

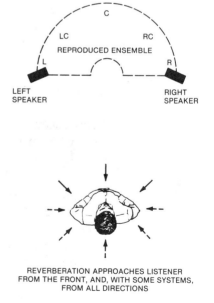

REVERBERATION APPROACHES LISTENER
FROM THE FRONT, AND, WITH SOME SYSTEMS,
FROM ALL DIRECTIONS

(B) Playback.

time. You might concentrate first on the tonal balance; try to pinpoint what frequency ranges are being emphasized or slighted. Next, listen to the mix, the clarity, and so on. Soon you'll have a lengthy description of the sound quality of your recording.

Chart 18-1 is a checklist you can use to evaluate the sound quality of pop music recordings; Chart 18-2 is the same for classical music recordings.

Developing an analytical ear is a continuing learning process. Train your hearing by listening carefully to recordings—both good and bad. Make a checklist of all the qualities mentioned in this chapter. Compare your own recordings to live instruments, and to commercial recordings, to see what you're doing right or wrong.

A pop music record that excels in all the attributes of good sound is "The Sheffield Track Record" (Sheffield Labs, Lab 20), engineered and produced by Bill Schnee. In effect, it's a course in state-of-the-art sound; it should be required listening for any recording engineer or producer.

Chart 18-1.
Pop Music
Recording
Evaluation

Well mixed?	Nothing too loud or too quiet.
Wide range?	Extended lows and highs.
Tonally balanced?	No frequency range too loud or quiet.
Clean?	Free of noise and distortion.
Clean?	Free of low-frequency overhang and leakage.
Clean?	Uncluttered mix.
Clear?	Instruments distinct.
Smooth?	Not harsh—no excessive upper midrange.
Presence?	Clarity, detail, punch, and closeness.
Spacious?	Has reverberation or ambience.
Sharp transients?	Clear percussive attacks.
Tight bass and drums?	Synchronous playing, damped kick.
Good stereo?	Well balanced and various image locations.
Good stereo?	Instruments not too isolated and a sense of depth.
Wide but controlled dynamic range?	Constant-level vocals.
Interesting sounds?	Effects and production tricks.
Suitable production?	Production suits the musical style.

**Chart 18-2.
Classical Music
Recording
Evaluation**

Clean?	Free of noise and distortion.
Wide range?	Extended lows and highs.
Tonally balanced?	No frequency range too loud or quiet.
Good acoustics?	Suitable reverberation time.
Well balanced?	No instruments too loud or too quiet.
Tonally accurate?	High-fidelity timbre reproduction.
Suitable perspective?	Appropriate direct/reverb ratio.
Accurate imaging?	Images correct in size and location.
Depth?	Instruments at various distances.

Another record with brilliant production is "The Nightfly" by Donald Fagen (Warner Brothers 23696-1); it is engineered by Roger Nichols, Daniel Lazerus, and Elliot Scheiner, produced by Gary Katz, and mastered by Bob Ludwig. The sound is razor sharp, elegant, and tasteful, and the music just pops out of the speakers.

The following listings are four more examples of outstanding rock production. They set high standards to work towards.

Song: "I Need Somebody"
Artist: Bryan Adams
Producer: Bob Clearmountain

Song: "The Power of Love"
Artist: Huey Lewis & The News
Producer: Huey Lewis & The News

Album: "Synchronicity"
Artist: The Police
Producer: Hugh Padgham and The Police

Album: "Thriller"
Artist: Michael Jackson
Engineer: Bruce Swedien
Producer: Quincy Jones

Once you're making recordings that are technically competent—clean, natural, and well mixed—the next stage is to produce imaginative sounds. You're in command; you can tailor the mix to sound any way that pleases you or the band you're recording.

Finally, the supreme achievement is to produce recordings that sound beautiful.

Troubleshooting Bad Sound

You now know how to recognize good sound, but can you recognize bad sound? Suppose you're monitoring a recording in progress, or listening to a recording you've already made. Something doesn't sound right. How can you pinpoint what's wrong, and how can you fix it?

The remainder of this chapter includes step-by-step procedures to solve audio-related problems. Read down the list of "bad sound" descriptions until you find one matching what you hear. Then try the solutions until your problem disappears. Only the most common symptoms and cures are mentioned; console maintenance is not covered.

This troubleshooting guide is divided into four main sections:

1. Bad sound on all recordings (including those from other studios).
2. Bad sound on tape playback only (console output sounds all right).
3. Bad sound in a popular music recording.
4. Bad sound in a classical music recording.

Before you start, check for faulty cables and connectors. Also check all control positions; rotate knobs and flip switches to clean the contacts.

Bad Sound on all Recordings

Upgrade your monitor system. Adjust tweeter and midrange controls on the speakers, adjust the relative gains of the tweeter and woofer amplifiers in a bi-amped system, relocate speakers, improve room acoustics, equalize the monitor system, try different speakers, and upgrade the power amp and speaker cables.

Bad Sound Only on Tape Playback

1. Dull sound or dropouts.
   A. Check that the oxide side of the tape is against the heads.
   B. Clean and demagnetize the tape path.
   C. Try another brand of tape.
   D. Align tape heads; calibrate the electronics.
   E. Do maintenance on the tape transport.

F. Check and replace tape heads if necessary.

2. Distortion.

A. Reduce the recording level.

B. Increase the bias level.

3. Tape hiss.

A. Increase the recording level.

B. Use some type of noise reduction, such as Dolby® or dbx®.

C. Use better tape.

D. Align the tape recorder.

Bad Sound in a Pop Music Recording

1. Muddy (excessive leakage).

A. Place the microphones closer to the sound sources.

B. Spread the instruments farther apart to reduce the level of the leakage.

C. Place the instruments closer together to reduce the delay of the leakage.

D. Use directional microphones (such as cardioids).

E. Overdub the instruments.

F. Record the electric instruments direct.

G. Use baffles (goboes) between the instruments.

H. Deaden the room acoustics. Add absorptive material, flexible panels, or slot absorbers.

I. Filter out frequencies above and below the spectral range of each instrument.

J. Turn down the bass amp in the studio.

2. Muddy (excessive reverberation).

A. Reduce the echo-send levels or the echo-return levels.

B. Place the microphones closer to the sound sources.

C. Use directional microphones (such as cardioids).

D. Deaden the room acoustics.

E. Filter out the frequencies below the fundamental frequency of each instrument.

3. Muddy (lacking highs, dull or muffled sound, poor transient response).

A. Use microphones with better high-frequency response, or use condenser mics instead of dynamic mics.

B. Change the microphone placement. Put the microphone in a spot where there are sufficient high frequencies. Keep the high-frequency sources, such as cymbals, on-axis to the microphones.

C. Use small-diameter microphones, which generally have a flatter response off-axis.

D. Boost the high-frequency equalization.

E. Change musical instruments; replace guitar strings; replace drum heads.

F. When bouncing tracks, record bright-sounding instruments last to reduce generation loss.

G. Use a better tape.

H. Avoid excessive recording levels with bright-sounding instruments, because the recorder's high-frequency response gradually rolls off as the recording level is increased. This is especially true of cassette recorders.

I. Use exciter signal processors, such as the Aphex Aural Exciter®.

J. Use a direct box on the electric bass. Have the bassist play percussively or use a pick. When compressing the bass, use a long attack time to allow the note's attack to come through. *Note:* Some songs don't require sharp bass attacks—just do whatever's right for the song.

K. Damp the kick drum with a pillow or blanket, and mike it next to the center of the head near the beater.

4. Muddy (lacking clarity).

A. Use fewer instruments in the musical arrangement.

B. Equalize instruments differently so that their spectra don't overlap.

C. Try less reverberation.

D. Delay the reverberation-send signal by about 30 to 70 milliseconds.

E. Using equalizers, boost the presence range of the instruments that lack clarity.

5. Distortion.

A. Switch in the pad that is built into the microphone (if any).

B. Increase the input attenuation (reduce input gain), or plug in a pad between the microphone and the mic input.

C. Readjust gain-staging: set the faders and pots to their design centers (shaded areas).

6. Bad tonal balance (nasal, rough, boomy, dull, shrill, etc.).

A. Change musical instruments; change guitar strings; change reeds, etc.

B. Change the microphone placement. If the sound is too bassy with a directional microphone, you may be getting proximity effect. Mike farther away or roll off the excess bass.

C. Use the 3:1 rule of microphone placement to avoid phase cancellations. When multiple microphones are mixed to the same channel, the distance between microphones should be at least three times the mic-to-source distance.

D. Try another microphone. If the proximity effect of a cardioid mic is causing a bass boost, try an omnidirectional mic instead.

E. If you must place a microphone near a hard reflective surface, try a boundary microphone on the surface to prevent phase cancellations.

F. Change the equalization. Avoid excessive boost.

G. Use equalizers with a broad bandwidth, rather than a narrow, peaked response.

7. Lifeless sound (unexciting).

A. Work on the live sound of the instruments in the studio to come up with unique effects.

B. Add special effects—reverberation, echo, doubling, equalization, etc.

C. Use and combine recording equipment in unusual ways.

D. Try overdubbing little vocal licks or synthesized sound effects.

8. Lifeless sound (dry or dead acoustics).

A. If leakage is not a problem, put the microphones far enough from the instruments to pick up wall reflections. If you don't like the sound this produces, try the next suggestion.

    B. Add artificial reverberation or echo to dry tracks. *Note:* Not all tracks require reverberation. Also, some songs may need very little reverberation so that they sound intimate.

    C. Use omnidirectional microphones.

    D. Add hard reflective surfaces in the studio, or record in a hard-walled room.

    E. Allow a little leakage between microphones. Put microphones far enough from instruments to pick up off-mic sounds from other instruments. Don't overdo it, though, or the sound will become muddy, and track separation will become poor.

9. Noise (hiss)

    A. Check for noisy guitar amps or keyboards.

    B. Switch out the pad built into the microphone (if any).

    C. Reduce console input attenuation (increase input gain).

    D. Use a more sensitive microphone.

    E. Use a quieter microphone (one with low self-noise).

    F. Increase the sound-pressure level at the microphone by miking closer. If you're using PZMs, mount them on a large surface or in a corner.

    G. Use a noise gate.

    H. Use a low-pass filter (high-cut filter).

10. Noise (low-frequency rumble).

    A. Reduce air-conditioning noise or temporarily shut off the air conditioning.

    B. Use a high-pass filter (low-cut filter) that is set around 40 to 80 Hz.

    C. Use microphones with limited low-frequency response.

11. Noise (thumps).

    A. Change the microphone position.

    B. Change the musical instrument.

    C. Use a high-pass filter that is set around 40 to 80 Hz.

    D. If the cause is mechanical vibration traveling up the microphone stand, put the microphone in a shock-mount stand adapter. Or, use a microphone that is less susceptible to mechanical vibration, such as an omnidirectional microphone, or use a unidirectional microphone with a good internal shock mount.

E. Use a microphone with a limited low-frequency response.

12. Hum.

   This is a subject in itself. See Chapter 5 for causes and cures of hum.

13. Pop (explosive breath sounds in the vocalist's microphone).

   A. Place the microphone above or to the side of the mouth.

   B. Place a foam windscreen (pop filter) on the microphone.

   C. Place the microphone farther from the vocalist.

   D. Use a microphone with a built-in pop filter (ball grille).

   E. Use an omnidirectional microphone, because it is likely to pop less than a directional (cardioid) microphone.

14. Sibilance (over-emphasis of the "s" and "sh" sounds).

   A. Use a de-esser.

   B. Place the microphone farther from the vocalist.

   C. Place the microphone toward one side of the vocalist, rather than directly in front.

   D. Cut equalization in the range from 5 kHz to 10 kHz.

   E. Change to a duller-sounding microphone.

15. Bad mix.

   A. Change the mix.

   B. Compress the vocals or instruments that occasionally get buried.

   C. Change the equalization on certain instruments to help them stand out.

   D. During mixdown, continuously change the mix to highlight certain instruments according to the demands of the music.

16. Unnatural dynamics.

   A. Check the tracking of noise-reduction units. For example, a 10-dB level increase at the input of the encode unit should appear as a 10-dB level increase at the output of the decode unit.

   B. Use less compression or limiting.

   C. Avoid overall compression.

17. Instruments sound too isolated, or sound like they're in different acoustic environments.

    A. In general, allow a little crosstalk between the left and right channels. If tracks are totally isolated, it's hard to achieve the illusion that all the instruments are playing in the same room at the same time. You need some crosstalk or correlation between channels. Some right-channel information should leak into the left channel, and vice versa.

    B. Place the microphones farther from the sound sources to increase leakage.

    C. Use omnidirectional microphones to increase leakage.

    D. Use stereo reverberation or echo.

    E. Pan echo returns or reverberation returns to the channel opposite the channel of the dry sound source.

    F. Pan extreme left-and-right tracks slightly toward center.

    G. Make the echo-send levels more similar for various tracks.

    H. To give a lead guitar solo a fat spacious sound, use a stereo chorus. Or, send its signal through a delay unit, pan the direct sound hard left and pan the delayed sound hard right.

18. The mix lacks depth.

    A. Achieve depth by miking the instruments at different distances.

    B. Use varied amounts of reverberation on each instrument. The higher the ratio of reverberant sound to direct sound, the more distant the track sounds.

    C. Set the "pre/post" switch on the reverb send to "pre" to move the instruments closer and farther as you move the fader.

Bad Sound in a Classical Music Recording

1. Sound is too dead (insufficient ambience, hall reverberation, or room acoustics).

    A. Place the microphones farther from the performers.

    B. Use omnidirectional microphones.

    C. Record in a concert hall with better acoustics (longer reverberation time).

      D. Add artificial reverberation.

  2. Sound is too detailed, too close, too edgy.

      A. Place the microphones farther from the performers.

      B. Place the microphones lower or on the floor (as with a boundary microphone).

      C. Roll off the high frequencies.

      D. Use duller-sounding micophones.

  3. Sound is too distant (too much reverberation).

      A. Place microphones closer to the performers.

      B. Use directional microphones (such as cardioids).

      C. Record in a concert hall that is less live (reverberant).

  4. Narrow stereo spread.

      A. Angle or space the main microphone pair farther apart.

      B. If you're doing mid-side stereo recording, turn up the side output of the stereo microphone.

      C. Place the main microphone pair closer to the ensemble.

  5. Excessive separation or hole-in-the-middle.

      A. Angle or space the main microphone pair closer together.

      B. If you're doing mid-side stereo recording, turn down the side output of the stereo microphone.

      C. In spaced-pair recording, add a microphone midway between the outer pair, and pan its signal to the center.

      D. Place the microphones farther from the performers.

  6. Sound lacks depth (lacks a sense of nearness and farness of various instruments).

      A. Use only a single pair of microphones out front. Avoid multimiking.

      B. If you must use spot mics, keep their level low in the mix.

      C. Add more artificial reverberation to the distant instruments than to the close instruments.

  7. Bad balance.

      A. Place the microphones higher or farther from the performers.

      B. Ask the conductor or performers to change the instruments' written dynamics.

      C. Add spot microphones close to instruments or sections needing reinforcement. Mix them in subtly with the signals from the main microphones.

8. Muddy bass.

      A. Aim the bass-drum head at the microphones.

      B. Put the microphone stands and bass-drum stand on resilient isolation mounts, or place the microphones in shock-mount stand adapters.

      C. Roll off the low frequencies or use a high-pass filter that is set around 40 to 80 Hz.

      D. Record in a concert hall with less low-frequency reverberation.

9. Rumble from air conditioning, trucks, etc.

      A. Temporarily shut off the air conditioning.

      B. Record in a quieter location.

      C. Use a high-pass filter that is set around 40 to 80 Hz.

      D. Use microphones with limited low-frequency response.

10. Distortion.

      A. Switch in the pads that are built into the microphones (if any).

      B. Increase the console input attenuation (reduce the input level).

11. Bad tonal balance (too dull, too bright, colored).

      A. Change the microphones. Generally, use flat-response microphones with minimal off-axis coloration.

      B. Follow the 3:1 rule mentioned in Chapter 7.

      C. If a microphone must be placed near a hard reflective surface, use a boundary microphone to prevent phase cancellations between the direct and reflected sounds.

      D. Adjust equalization.

      E. Place the mics at a reasonable distance from the ensemble (miking that is too close sounds shrill).

      F. Avoid microphone positions that pick up standing waves or room modes. Experiment with small changes in microphone position.

Conclusion

This chapter described a set of standards for good sound quality in both popular music and classical music recordings. These standards are somewhat arbitrary, but the engineer and producer need some guidelines to go by in judging the effectiveness of the recording.

Also mentioned were some causes and cures of various audio ailments. The next time you hear something you don't like in a recording, you'll know better how to define the problem and how to fix it.

19 WHY DO WE RECORD?

In this book, we've focused on techniques for recording music, without paying much attention to the music itself. Occasionally, it's good to remind ourselves that *music* is the main reason why we record!

Music can be exalting, exciting, soothing, sensuous, and fulfilling. It's wonderful that recordings can preserve it. As recording engineers, it's to our advantage to better understand what music is all about.

Music starts as musical ideas or feelings in the mind and heart of its composer. Musical instruments are used to translate these ideas and feelings into sound waves. Somehow, the emotion contained in the music—the message—is coded in the vibrations of air molecules. We convert those sound waves to electricity, and store them magnetically. The composer's message manages to survive the trip through the mixing console and the tape machines. Then we transfer the signal to disk. Finally, the original sound waves are reproduced in the listening room and, miraculously, the original emotion is reproduced in the listener as well.

Of course, not everyone reacts to a piece of music the same way, so the listener may not perceive the composer's intent. Still, it's amazing that anything as intangible as a thought or feeling can be conveyed by a tiny wiggling groove in vinyl, or by pits on a compact disc.

Like life, the meaning of music is itself—its moment-to-moment unfolding or happening—rather than a striving for some distant goal. The point of music lies in what it's doing now, in the present. In other words, the meaning of "Doo wop she bop" is "Doo wop she bop." The meaning of an Am7 chord followed by a Fmaj7 chord is the *experience* of Am7 followed by Fmaj7.

Increasing Your Involvement in Music

Some say that music is best appreciated with an altered state of mind—being in love, high, or simply relaxed and very attentive. Sometimes, to get into music, you have to relax enough to lie back and listen. You have to feel unhurried, to be content to sit between your stereo speakers, or to wear headphones, and listen with undivided attention. Actively analyze or feel what the musicians are playing.

Music affects us much more when we're already feeling the emotion expressed in the song. For example, hearing "Jessie's Girl" when you're envious, hearing "1999" when you want to party, or hearing a piece by Debussy when you're feeling sensuous, is more moving because your feelings resonate with those in the music. And when you're falling in love, any music that is meaningful to you is enhanced.

If you identify strongly with a particular song, that tells you something about yourself and your current mood. And the songs that other people identify with tell you something about them. You can understand individuals better by listening to their favorite music.

Different Ways of Listening

There are so many levels on which to listen to music—so many ways to focus attention. Try this. Play one of your favorite records several times while listening for these different aspects:

1. Overall mood and rhythm
2. Lyrics
3. Vocal technique
4. Bass line
5. Drum fills
6. Sound quality
7. Technical proficiency of musicians
8. Musical arrangement or structure
9. Reaction of one musician to another's playing
10. Surprises vs. predictable patterns

and so on . . .

By carefully listening to a piece of music from several perspectives, you'll get much more out of it than if you just hear it as background music. There's a lot going on in any song that normally goes unnoticed. I recently played an old record and listened to the lyrics for the first time (I usually just listen to the music). The whole meaning of the song changed.

I'd guess that most people react to music on the basic level of mood and rhythmic motivation. But, as recording enthusiasts, we hear much more sonic detail than laymen are aware of, because our occupation demands sustained critical listening. The same is true of trained musicians focusing on the musical aspects of a performance. It's all there for anyone to hear, but you must train yourself to hear selectively, to focus attention on a particular level of the multidimensional musical event. For example, instead of just feeling excited while listening to an impressive lead guitar solo, listen to what the guy is actually playing. You may hear some amazing things.

Here's the secret of really involving yourself in recorded music. Imagine yourself playing it! For example, if you're a bass player, listen to the bass line in a particular record, and imagine that you're playing the bass line. You'll hear the part as never before.

There are other, stranger ways to perceive music. It can be fascinating to respond to music *visually*. A lead guitar playing over a musical background can be a figure cavorting on a landscape.

Follow the melody line and see its shape. Hear where it reaches up, strains, relaxes. Hear how one note leads into the next. How does the musical expression change from moment to moment?

There are times you can almost *touch* music. Some music has a prickly texture (many transients, emphasized high frequencies), while other music is soft and sinuous (sine-wave synthesizer notes, soaring vocal harmonies); still other music is airy and spacious (much reverberation).

All this is meant to show how music is more than just something to dance to, or to make money from, or to fill silence. It's a complex multilevel phenomenon worth exploring. And recordings make such study possible.

Different Ways of Monitoring

Now let's apply different ways of listening to the recording situation. Let's say you're in the control room working on a pop music mix, and you're aiming for a realistic, natural sound. Listen to the reproduced instruments and try to make them sound like they're really playing in front of you. That is, instead of trying to make a pleasant mix or a sonically interesting recording, try to control the sound you hear to simulate real instruments—to make them believable.

This situation is similar to that of an artist trying to draw a still-life as realistically as possible. The artist compares the drawing to the real object and notes the difference between the two. Then, the artist modifies the drawing to reduce the difference. Similarly, when you're striving for a natural sound, compare the recorded instrument with your memory of the real thing. How does it sound different? Turn the appropriate knob on the console that reduces the difference.

Alternatively, when you're mixing, imagine you're creating a *sonic experience* between the monitor speakers, rather than just reproducing the instruments. Sometimes you don't want a recording to sound too realistic. If a recording is very accurate, it sounds like musical instruments, rather than just music itself.

This approach contradicts the basic edict of high fidelity: to reproduce the original performance as it sounded in the original environment. But some songs seem to require unreal sounds. That way, we don't connect the sounds we hear with the physical instruments, but with the music behind the instruments—the composer's dream or vision.

Here's one way to reproduce pure music rather than just reproducing instruments playing in a room: Mike closely or record direct to avoid picking up studio ambience, and then add artificial reverberation. Also add equalization, double-tracking, and special effects to make the instrument or voice slightly unreal. The idea is to make a production, rather than a documentation; a record, rather than a recording.

Try to convey the musician's intentions through the recorded sound quality. If the musician has a loving, soft message, translate that into a warm, smooth, tone quality—add a little mid-bass or slightly reduce the highs. If the musical piece suggests grandeur or space, add reverberation with a long decay time. Ask the musician what he or she is trying to express through the music, and try to express that through the sound production as well.

Why We Record

Recording is a real service. Without it, we'd be exposed to much less music. We'd be limited to the occasional live concert or to our own live music, played once and forever gone.

But, with recordings, we can preserve a performance for thousands of listeners. We can hear an enormous variety of musical expressions whenever we wish. Unlike a live concert, a record can be played over and over for analysis. Records are also a way to achieve a sort of immortality. The Beatles may be gone, but their music lives on.

Records can even reveal our evolving consciousness as we grow and change. A record stays the same physically, but we hear it differently over the years as our perception changes. Records are a constant against which we measure changes in ourselves.

We should be proud that we're contributing to the recording art, for it's done in the service of music.

GLOSSARY

A-B—A listening comparison between two audio programs, or between two components playing the same program, performed by switching immediately from one to the other. The levels of the two signals are matched. *See also* Spaced Pair.

Accent Microphone—*See* Spot Microphone.

Access Jacks—Two jacks in a console input module or output module that allow access to points in the signal path, usually for connecting a compressor. Plugging into the access jacks breaks the signal flow and allows you to insert a signal processor in series with the signal.

Alignment—The adjustment of tape-head azimuth and of tape-recorder circuitry to achieve optimum performance from the particular type of tape being used.

Alignment Tape—A pre-recorded tape with tones for alignment of a tape recorder.

Ambience—Room acoustics, early reflections, and reverberation. Also, the audible sense of a room or environment surrounding a recorded instrument.

Ambience Microphone—A microphone placed relatively far from its sound source to pick up ambience.

Amplitude, Peak—*See* Peak Amplitude.

Analog-to-Digital (A/D) Converter—A circuit that converts an analog audio signal into a digital bit stream.

Assign—To route or send an audio signal to one or more selected channels.

Attack—The beginning of a note. The first portion of a note's envelope in which a note rises from silence to its maximum volume.

Attack Time—In a compressor, the time it takes for gain reduction to occur in response to a musical attack.

Attenuate—To reduce the level of a signal.

Attenuator—In a mixer or mixing-console input module, an adjustable resistive network that reduces the microphone signal level to prevent overloading of the input transformer and mic preamplifier.

Automated Mixing—A system of mixing in which a computer remembers and updates console settings so that a mix can be performed and refined in several stages.

Auxiliary Bus (AUX BUS)—*See* Effects Bus.

Auxiliary Send (AUX SEND)—*See* Echo Send.

A-Weighting—*See* Weighted.

Azimuth—In a tape recorder, the angular relationship between the head gap and the tape path.

Azimuth Alignment—The mechanical adjustment of the record or playback head to bring it into proper alignment (90°) with the tape path.

Back-Timing—A technique of cueing up the musical background to a narration track so that the music ends simultanously with the narration.

Balance—The relative volume levels of various tracks or instruments.

Balanced Line—A cable with two conductors surrounded by a shield, in which each conductor is at equal impedance to ground. With respect to ground, the conductors are at equal potential but opposite polarity.

Bandpass Filter—In a crossover network, a filter that passes a band or range of frequencies but sharply attenuates or rejects frequencies outside the band.

Basic Tracks—Recorded tracks of rhythm instruments (bass, guitar, drums, and, sometimes, the keyboard).

Bass Trap—An assembly that absorbs low-frequency sound waves.

Bi-Amplification (Bi-Amping)—Driving a woofer and tweeter with separate power amplfiers. An active crossover is connected ahead of these power amplifiers.

Bias—In tape-recorder electronics, an ultrasonic signal that drives the erase head, and also is mixed with the audio signal applied to the record head to reduce distortion.

Bidirectional Microphone—A microphone that is most sensitive to sounds arriving from two directions—in front of and behind the microphone. It rejects sounds approaching from either side of the microphone. Also called a cosine or figure-eight microphone because of the shape of its polar pattern.

Binaural Recording—A 2-channel recording made with an omnidirectional microphone in each ear of a human or a dummy head, for playback over headphones. The object is to duplicate the acoustic signal appearing at each ear.

Blumlein Array—A stereo microphone technique in which two coincident bidirectional microphones are angled 90° apart (45° to the left and right of center).

Board—*See* Mixing Console.

Bouncing Tracks—A process in which two or more tracks are mixed, and the mixed tracks are recorded on an unused track. Then, the original tracks can be erased, which frees them up for recording more instruments.

Boundary Microphone—A microphone designed to be used on a boundary (a hard reflective surface). The microphone capsule is mounted very close to the boundary so that direct and reflected sounds arrive at the microphone diaphragm in phase (or nearly so) at all frequencies in the audible band.

Breathing—The unwanted audible rise and fall of background noise that may occur with a compressor. Also called *pumping*.

Bulk Tape Eraser—A large electro-magnet used to erase a whole reel of recording tape at once.

Bus—A common connection of many different signals. An output of a mixer or submixer. A channel that feeds a tape track, signal processor, or power amplifier.

Bus Master—A potentiometer (fader or volume control) in the output section of a mixing console that controls the output level of a bus.

Bus Trim—A control in the output section of a mixing console that provides variable gain control of a bus, and used in addition to the bus master for fine adjustment.

Buzz—An unwanted edgy tone that sometimes accompanies audio, containing high harmonics of 60 Hz.

Calibration—*See* Alignment.

Capacitor Microphone—*See* Condenser Microphone.

Capstan—In a tape-recorder transport, a rotating post that contacts the tape (along with the pinch roller) and pulls the tape past the heads at a constant speed during recording and playback.

Cardioid Microphone—A unidirectional microphone with a side attenuation of 6 dB and a maximum rejection of sound at the rear of the microphone (180° off-axis). A microphone with a heart-shaped directional pattern.

Channel—A single path of an audio signal. Usually, each channel contains a different signal.

Channel Assign—*See* Assign.

Chorus—A special effect in which a signal is delayed by 15 to 35 milliseconds, where the delayed signal is combined with the original signal, and the delay is varied randomly or periodically. This creates a wavy, multiple-voice effect. Sometimes a portion of the output signal is fed back into the input. Also, the main portion of a song that is repeated several times throughout the song with the same lyrics.

Clean—Free of noise, distortion, overhang, and leakage. Not muddy.

Clear—Easy to hear, easy to differentiate. Reproduced with sufficient high frequencies.

Coincident Pair—A stereo microphone, or two separate microphones, placed so that the microphone diaphragms occupy approximately the same point in space. They are angled apart and mounted one directly above the other.

Comb-Filter Effect—The frequency response caused by combining a sound with its delayed replica. The frequency response has a series of peaks and dips caused by phase interference. The peaks and dips resemble the teeth of a comb.

Combining Amplifier—An amplifier in which the outputs of two or more signal paths are mixed together, to feed a single track of a tape recorder.

Combining Network—A resistive network in which the outputs of two or more signal paths are mixed together, to feed a single track of a tape recorder.

Complex Wave—A wave with more than one frequency component.

Compression—The portion of a sound wave in which molecules are pushed together, forming a region with higher-than-normal atmospheric pressure. Also, in signal processing, the reduction in dynamic range caused by a compressor.

Compression Ratio (Slope)—In a compressor, the ratio of the change in input level (in dB) to the change in output level (in dB). For example, a 2:1 ratio means that for every 2-dB change in input level, the output level changes 1 dB.

Compressor—A signal processor that reduces dynamic range by means of automatic volume control. An amplifier whose gain decreases as the input signal level increases above a pre-set point.

Condenser Microphone—A microphone that works on the principle of variable capacitance to generate an electrical signal. The microphone diaphragm and an adjacent metallic disk (called a backplate) are charged to form two plates of a capacitor. Incoming sound waves vibrate the diaphragm, varying its spacing to the backplate, which varies the capacitance, which varies the voltage between the diaphragm and the backplate.

Connector—A device that makes electrical contact between a signal-carrying cable and an electronic device, or between two cables. A device used to connect or hold together a cable and an electronic component so that a signal can flow from one to the other.

Console—*See* Mixing Console.

Contact Pickup—A transducer that contacts a musical instrument and converts its mechanical vibrations

into a corresponding electrical signal.

Control Room—The room in which the engineer controls and monitors the recording.

Crossover—An electronic network that divides an incoming signal into two or more frequency bands.

Crossover, Active (Electronic Crossover)—A crossover network with amplifying components; used ahead of the power amplifiers in a bi-amped or tri-amped speaker system.

Crossover Frequency—The single frequency at which both filters of a crossover network are down 3 dB.

Crossover, Passive—A crossover with passive (non-amplifying) components; used after the power amplifier.

Crosstalk—The unwanted transfer of a signal from one channel to another. Crosstalk often occurs between adjacent tracks within a record or playback head in a tape recorder.

Cue or Cue Send—In a mixing-console input module, a control that adjusts the level of the signal feeding the cue mixer which feeds a signal to headphones in the studio.

Cue Mixer—A submixer in a mixing console that takes signals from cue sends as inputs and mixes them into a composite signal that drives headphones in the studio.

Cue Sheet—Used during mixdown, a chronological list of mixing-console control adjustments required at various points in the recorded song. These points may be indicated by tape-counter or elapsed-time readings.

Cue System—A monitor system that allows musicians to hear themselves and previously recorded tracks through headphones.

dB—Abbreviation for decibel.

dBA—Refers to decibels, A-weighted (*see* Weighted).

dBm—Decibels relative to 1 milliwatt.

dBu—Decibels relative to 0.775 volt.

dBV—Decibels relative to 1 volt.

Dead—Having very little or no reverberation.

Decay—The portion of the envelope of a note in which the envelope goes from maximum to some mid-range level. Also, the decline in level of reverberation over time.

Decay Time—Reverberation time (RT_{60}). The time it takes for reverberation to decay to 60 dB below the original steady-state level.

Decibel—The unit of audio-level measurement. Abbreviated dB.

Decoded Tape—A tape that is expanded after being compressed by a noise-reduction system. Such a tape has normal dynamic range.

De-esser—A signal processor that removes excessive sibilance ("s" and "sh" sounds) by compressing the high frequencies around 5 to 10 kHz.

Degausser—*See* Demagnetizer.

Delay—The time interval between a signal and its repetition. A digital delay or a delay line is a signal processor that delays a signal for a short time.

Demagnetizer—An electromagnet with a probe tip that is touched to elements of the tape path (such as tape heads and tape guides) to remove residual magnetism.

Depth—The audible sense of nearness and farness of various instruments.

Instruments recorded with a high ratio of direct-to-reverberant sound are perceived as being close; instruments recorded with a low ratio of direct-to-reverberant sound are perceived as being distant.

Designation Strip—A strip of paper taped near console faders to designate the instrument that each fader controls.

Design Center—The portion of fader travel (usually shaded), about 10 to 15 dB from the top, in which console gain is distributed for optimum headroom and signal-to-noise ratio. During normal operation, each fader in use should be placed at or near design center.

Desk—British term for mixing console.

Diffusion—An even distribution of sound in a room.

Digital Audio—The encoding of an analog audio signal in the form of binary digits (ones and zeros).

Digital Recording—A recording system in which the audio signal is stored in the form of binary digits.

Digital-to-Analog Converter—A circuit that converts a digital audio signal into an analog audio signal.

Dim—To temporarily reduce the monitor volume by a preset amount (so you can carry on a conversation).

Direct Box—A device used for connecting an amplified instrument directly to a mixer mic input. The direct box converts a high-impedance unbalanced audio signal into a low-impedance balanced audio signal.

Direct Injection (DI)—Recording with a direct box.

Direct Output, Direct Out—An output connector following a mic preamplifier, which is used to feed the signal of one instrument to one track of a tape recorder.

Direct Sound—Sound traveling directly from the sound source to the microphone (or to the listener) without reflections.

Directional Microphone—A microphone that has different sensitivity in different directions. A unidirectional or bidirectional microphone.

Distortion—An unwanted change in the audio waveform, causing a raspy or gritty sound quality. The appearance of frequencies in a device's output signal that were not in the input signal.

Dolby® Tone—A reference tone recorded at the beginning of a Dolby-encoded tape for alignment purposes.

Doubling—A special effect in which a signal is combined with its 15- to 35-millisecond delayed replica. This process mimics the sound of two identical voices or instruments playing in unison.

Drop-Frame—For color video production, a mode of SMPTE time code which causes the time code to match the clock on the wall. Once every minute, except for the tenth minute, frame numbers 00 and 01 are dropped.

Drop-Out—During playback of a tape recording, a momentary loss of high frequencies caused by separation of the tape from the playback head due to dust, tape-oxide irregularity, etc.

Drum Machine—A synthesizer that plays memory-chip recordings of real drums.

Dry—Having no echo or reverberation. Referring to a close-sounding signal that is not yet processed by a reverberation or delay device.

Dynamic Microphone—A microphone that generates electricity when sound waves cause a conductor to vibrate in a stationary magnetic field. The two types of dynamic microphone are the moving-coil and the ribbon. A moving-coil microphone is usually called a dynamic microphone.

Dynamic Range—The range of volume levels in a program—from softest to loudest.

Earth Ground—A connection to moist dirt (the ground we walk on). This connection is usually done via a long copper rod driven into the earth or a connection to a cold-water pipe.

Echo—A delayed repetition of a signal or sound. A sound delayed 50 milliseconds or more that is combined with the original sound.

Echo Chamber—A hard-surfaced room containing a widely separated loudspeaker and microphone that is used for creating reverberation.

Echo Return, Echo Receive—In the output section of a mixing console, a control that adjusts the amount of signal received from a reverberation or echo device. The echo-return signal is mixed with the program bus signal.

Echo Send—In an input module of a mixing console, a control that adjusts the amount of signal sent to a special-effects device, such as a reverberation or delay unit. The echo-send control normally adjusts the amount of reverberation or echo heard on each instrument.

Editing—The cutting and rejoining of magnetic tape to delete unwanted material, to insert leader tape, or to rearrange recorded material into the desired sequence.

Editing Block—A metal block that holds the magnetic tape during the editing/splicing procedure.

Effects—Interesting sound phenomena created by signal processors, such as reverberation, echo, flanging, doubling, or chorus.

Effects Bus—The bus that feeds effects devices (signal processors).

Effects Mixer—A submixer in a mixing console that combines signals from effects sends (echo sends) and feeds the mixed signal to the input of a special-effects device, such as a reverberation unit.

Effects Return—*See* Echo Return.

Effects Send—*See* Echo Send.

Efficiency—In a loudspeaker, the ratio of acoustic power output to electrical power input.

EIA—Abbreviation of Electrical Industries Association.

EIA Rating—A microphone sensitivity specification that states the microphone output level (in dBm) into a matched load for a given sound-pressure level (SPL). SPL + dB (EIA rating) = dBm output into a matched load.

Electret-Condenser Microphone—A condenser microphone in which the electrostatic field of the capacitor is generated by an electret—a material that permanently stores an electrostatic charge.

Electrostatic Field—The force field between two conductors charged with static electricity.

Electrostatic Interference—The unwanted presence of an electrostatic hum field in signal conductors.

Encoded Tape—A tape containing a signal which has been compressed by a noise-reduction unit.

Envelope—The rise and fall in volume of one note. The envelope connects successive peaks of the waves comprising a note. Each harmonic in the note might have a different envelope.

Equalization (EQ)—The adjustment of frequency response in order to alter the tonal balance or to attenuate unwanted frequencies.

Equalizer—A circuit (usually in each input module of a mixing console, or in a separate unit) that alters the frequency spectrum of a signal passed through it.

Erase—To remove an audio signal from magnetic tape by applying an ultrasonic varying magnetic field so as to randomize the magnetization of the magnetic particles on the tape.

Erase Head—A head in a tape recorder that erases the signal on tape.

Expander—A signal processor that increases the dynamic range of a signal passed through it. An amplifer whose gain decreases as its input level decreases. When used as a noise gate, an expander reduces the gain of low-level signals to reduce noise between notes.

Fade-Out—To gradually reduce the volume of the last several seconds of a recorded song, from full level down to silence, by slowly pulling down the master fader.

Fader—A linear or sliding potentiometer (volume control) that is used to adjust signal level.

Feed—To send an audio signal to some device or system. Also, a feed is an output signal sent to some device or system.

Feedback—The return of some portion of an output signal to the system's input.

Feed Reel—The left-side reel on a tape recorder that unwinds during recording or playback.

Filter—A circuit that sharply attenuates frequencies above or below a certain frequency, and used to reduce noise and leakage above or below the frequency range of an instrument or voice.

Flanging—A special effect in which a signal is combined with its delayed replica, and the delay is varied between 0 and 20 milliseconds. A hollow, swishing, ethereal effect—like sound through a variable-length pipe, or like a jet plane passing overhead. A variable comb filter produces the flanging effect.

Fletcher-Munson Effect—Named after the two people who discovered it, this is a psychoacoustical phenomenon in which the subjective frequency response of the ear changes with the program level. Due to this effect, a program played at a lower volume than the original level subjectively loses low- and high-frequency response.

Float—To disconnect from ground.

Flutter—A rapid periodic variation in tape speed.

Flutter Echoes—A rapid series of echoes that occurs between two parallel walls.

Flux—Magnetic lines of force.

Fluxivity—The measure of the flux density of a magnetic recording tape, per unit of track width.

Foldback (FB)—*See* Cue System.

Frequency—The number of cycles per second of a sound wave or an audio signal, measured in hertz (Hz). A low-frequency sound (say, 100 Hz) has a low pitch; a high-frequency sound (say, 10,000 Hz) has a high pitch.

Frequency Response—The range of frequencies that an audio device will reproduce at an equal level (within a tolerance, such as ±3 dB).

Full Track—A single tape track recorded across the full width of the tape.

Fundamental—The lowest frequency in a complex wave.

Gain—Amplification. The ratio, expressed in decibels, between the output voltage and the input voltage, or between the output power and the input power.

Gap—In a tape-recorder head, the thin break in the electromagnet that contacts the tape.

Gate—To turn off a signal when its amplitude falls below a pre-set value. The signal-processing device used for this purpose. *See* Noise Gate.

Generation—A copy of a tape. A copy of the original master recording is a first-generation tape. A copy made from the first-generation tape is a second-generation tape, and so on.

Generation Loss—The degradation of signal quality (the increase in noise and distortion) that occurs with each successive generation of a tape recording.

Gobo—A movable partition used to prevent the sound of an instrument from reaching another instrument's microphone. Short for "go-between."

Graphic Equalizer—An equalizer with a horizontal row of faders; the fader-knob positions graphically indicate the frequency response of the equalizer. Usually used to equalize monitor speakers for the room they are located in.

Ground—The zero-signal reference point for a system of audio components.

Ground Bus—A common connection to which equipment is grounded, usually a heavy copper plate.

Ground Loop—A loop or circuit formed of ground leads. The loop formed when unbalanced components are connected together via two ground paths—the connecting-cable shield and the power ground. Ground loops cause hum and should be avoided.

Grounding—Connecting pieces of electronic equipment to ground. Proper grounding ensures that there is no voltage difference between equipment chassis. An electrostatic shield needs to be grounded to be effective.

Group—*See* Submix.

Guard Band—The spacing between tracks on a multitrack tape or tape head; used to prevent crosstalk.

Half-Track—A tape track recorded across approximately half the width of a tape. A half-track recorder usually records two such tracks simultaneously in the same direction to make a stereo recording.

Harmonic—An overtone whose frequency is a whole-number multiple of the fundamental frequency.

Head—An electromagnet in a tape recorder that either erases the audio signal on a tape, records a signal on tape, or plays back a signal that is already on tape.

Head Gap—*See* Gap.

Headphones—A head-worn transducer that covers the ears and converts electrical audio signals into sound waves.

Headroom—The safety margin, measured in decibels, between the signal level and the maximum undistorted signal level. In a tape recorder, the dB difference between standard operating level (corresponding to a 0-VU reading) and the level causing 3% total harmonic distortion. High-frequency headroom increases with tape speed.

Hertz (Hz)—Cycles per second, the unit of frequency measurement.

High-Pass Filter—A filter that passes frequencies above a certain frequency and attenuates frequencies below that same frequency. A low-cut filter.

Hiss—A noise signal containing all frequencies, but with greater energy at the higher octaves. Hiss sounds like wind blowing through trees. It is usually caused by random signals generated by microphones, electronics, and magnetic tape.

Hot—A high recording level causing slight distortion, and used for special effect. Also, a condition in which a chassis or circuit has a potentially dangerous voltage on it. Also, refers to the conductor in a microphone cable which has a positive voltage on it at the instant that sound pressure moves the diaphragm inward.

Hum—An unwanted low-pitched tone (60 Hz and its harmonics) heard along with the audio signal.

Hypercardioid Microphone—A directional microphone with a polar pattern that has 12-dB attenuation at the sides, 6-dB attenuation at the rear, and two nulls of maximum rejection at 110° off axis.

Idler Wheel—*See* Pinch Roller.

Image—An illusory sound source located between two stereo speakers.

Impedance—The opposition of a circuit to the flow of alternating current. Impedance is the complex sum of resistance and reactance.

Input—The connection going into an audio device. In a mixer or mixing console, a connector for a microphone or other signal source.

Input Attenuator—*See* Attenuator.

Input Module—In a mixing console, the set of controls affecting a single input signal. An input module usually includes an attenuator, a fader, equalizer, echo send, cue send, and the channel-assign controls.

Input Section—The row of input modules in a mixing console.

Input/Output (I/O) Console (In-Line Console)—A mixing console arranged so that the input and output sections are vertically aligned. Each module (other than the monitor section) contains one input channel and one output channel.

Jack—A female or receptacle-type connector for audio signals into which a plug is inserted.

Kilo—A prefix meaning one thousand. Abbreviated K.

Leadering—The process of splicing leader tape between program selections.

Leader Tape—Plastic or paper tape without an oxide coating that is used for a spacer between takes (i.e., for silence between songs).

Leakage—The overlap of an instrument's sound into another instrument's microphone. Also called *bleed* or *spill*.

LEDE—Abbreviation for Live-End, Dead-End; a type of control-room acoustic treatment in which the front half of the control room prevents early reflections to the mixing position, while the back half of the control room reflects diffused sound to the mixing position.

LED Indicator—A recording-level indicator that uses one or more light-emitting diodes.

Level—The degree of intensity of an audio signal—the voltage, power, or sound-pressure level. The original definition of level is the power in watts.

Level Setting—In a tape recorder, the process of adjusting the level of the signal sent to the record head so that maximum tape magnetization occurs without distortion. A VU meter or other indicator shows the recording level.

Limiter—A signal processor whose output is constant above a preset input level. A compressor with a compression ratio of 10:1 or greater, with the threshold set just below the point of distortion of the following device. Used to prevent distortion of attack transients or peaks.

Line Level—In balanced professional recording equipment, a signal whose level is approximately 1.23 volts ($+4$ dBm). In unbalanced equipment (most home hi-fi or semi-pro recording equipment), a signal whose level is approximately 0.316 volt (-10 dBV).

Live—Having audible reverberation. Also, occurring in real time, in person.

Live Recording—A recording made at a concert. Also, a recording made of a musical ensemble playing all at once, rather than overdubbing.

Localization—The ability of the human hearing system to tell the direction of a real or illusionary sound source.

Loudspeaker—A transducer that converts electrical energy (the signal) into acoustical energy (sound waves).

Low-Pass Filter—A filter that passes frequencies below a certain frequency and attenuates frequencies above that same frequency. A high-cut filter.

Magnetic Recording Tape—A recording medium made of magnetic particles (usually ferric oxide), suspended in a binder, and coated on a long strip of thin plastic (usually Mylar®).

Mask—To hide or cover up one sound with another sound. To make a sound inaudible by playing another sound along with it.

Master Fader—A volume control that affects the level of all program buses simultaneously.

Master Tape—A completed tape that is used to generate tape copies or disks.

Memory—A group of integrated-circuit chips, each containing thousands of solid-state components; used to temporarily or permanently store digital data (such as an audio signal in digital format).

Memory Rewind—A tape-recorder function that rewinds the tape to a pre-set tape-counter position.

Meter—A device that indicates voltage, resistance, current, or signal level.

Mic—An abbreviation for microphone.

Mic Level—The level or voltage of a signal produced by a microphone, typically 2 millivolts.

Microphone—A transducer or device that converts an acoustical signal (sound) into a corresponding electrical signal. Abbreviated mic (audio) and mike (radio).

Microphone Techniques—The selection and placement of microphones to pick up sound sources.

MIDI—Abbreviation for Musical Instrument Digital Interface, a specification for a connection between synthesizers, drum machines, and computers that allows them to communicate with and/or control each other.

Mid-Side—A coincident-pair stereo microphone technique that uses a forward-facing unidirectional, omnidirectional, or bidirectional microphone and a side-facing bidirectional microphone. The microphone signals are summed and differenced to produce right- and left-channel signals.

Mike—To pick up with a microphone. Also, abbreviation for microphone (used by older radio operators).

Milli—A prefix meaning one thousandth; abbreviated m.

Mix—To combine two or more different signals into a common signal. Also, a control on a delay unit that varies the ratio between the dry signal and the delayed signal.

Mixdown—The process of playing prerecorded tape tracks through a mixing console and mixing them to two stereo channels for recording on a 2-track tape recorder.

Mixer—A device that mixes or combines audio signals and controls the relative levels of the signals.

Mixing Console—A large mixer with additional functions, such as equalization or tone control, pan pots, monitoring controls, channel assigns, and control of signals being sent to external signal processors.

Monaural—Referring to listening with one ear. Often incorrectly used to mean monophonic.

Monitor—A loudspeaker in a control room, or a set of headphones, which is used for judging sound quality.

Monitoring—Listening to an audio signal with a monitor.

Mono, Monophonic—Refers to a single channel of audio. A monophonic program can be played over one or more loudspeakers, or one or more headphones.

Mono-Compatible—A characteristic of a stereo program, in which the program channels can be combined to form a mono program without altering the frequency response or balance. A mono-compatible stereo program has the same frequency response in either stereo or mono because there is no delay or phase shift between the channels to cause phase interference.

Moving-Coil Microphone—A dynamic microphone in which the conductor is a coil of wire moving in a fixed magnetic field. The coil is attached to a diaphragm which vibrates when struck with sound waves.

M-S Recording—*See* Mid-side.

Muddy—Unclear sounding; having excessive leakage, reverberation, or overhang.

Multiple-D Microphone—A directional microphone which has multiple sound-path lengths between its front and rear sound entries. This type of microphone has minimal proximity effect.

Multiprocessor—A signal processor that can perform several different signal-processing functions.

Multitrack—Having more than two tape tracks, when referring to a tape recorder or tape-recorder head.

Mute—To turn off an input signal on a mixing console by disconnecting the input-module output from channel assign and direct out. The mute function is used to reduce tape noise during silent portions of tracks.

Near-Coincident—A stereo microphone technique in which the two microphones are angled apart symmetrically on either side of center and horizontally spaced a few inches apart.

Near-Field Monitoring—A monitor-speaker arrangement in which the speakers are placed very near the listener (usually on top of the console meter bridge) to reduce the audibility of control-room acoustics.

Noise—Unwanted sound, such as hiss from the electronics or tape. An audio signal with an irregular, nonperiodic waveform.

Noise-Reduction System—A signal processor that is used to reduce tape hiss (and sometimes print-through) caused by the recording process. Some of these systems compress the signal during recording and expand it in a complementary fashion during playback.

Noise Gate—A gate used to reduce or eliminate noise between notes.

Octave—The interval between any two frequencies where the upper frequency is twice the lower frequency.

Off-Axis—Not directly in front of a microphone or loudspeaker.

Off-Axis Coloration—In a microphone, the deviation from the on-axis frequency response that sometimes occurs at angles off the axis of the microphone. The coloration of sound (alteration of tone quality) for sounds arriving off-axis to the microphone.

Omnidirectional Microphone—A microphone that is equally sensitive to sounds arriving from all directions.

On-Location Recording—A recording made outside the studio, in a room or hall where the music is normally performed or practiced.

Open Tracks—On a multitrack tape recorder, the tracks that have not yet been used.

Outboard Equipment—Signal processors that are external to the mixing console.

Output—A connector in an audio device from which the signal comes, and which feeds successive devices.

Out-Take—A take, or section of a take, which is to be removed or not used.

Overdub—To record a new musical part on an unused track in synchronization with previously recorded tracks.

Overhang—The continuation of a signal at the output of a device after the input signal has ceased.

Overload—The distortion that occurs when an applied signal exceeds a system's maximum output level.

Overtone—A frequency component of a complex wave which is higher than the fundamental frequency.

Pad—*See* Attenuator.

Pan Pot—Abbreviation for panoramic potentiometer. In each input module in a mixing console, the control that divides a signal between two channels in an adjustable ratio. By doing so, a pan pot controls the location of a sonic image between a stereo pair of loudspeakers.

Parametric Equalizer—An equalizer having continuously variable parameters, such as frequency, bandwidth, and amount of boost or cut.

Patch—To connect one piece of audio equipment to another with a cable. Also, a setting of synthesizer parameters to achieve a sound with a certain timbre.

Patch Bay (Patch Panel)—An array of connectors, usually in a rack, to which equipment inputs and outputs are wired. A patch bay makes it easy to interconnect various pieces of equipment in a central, accessible location.

Patch Cord—A short length of cable with a coaxial plug on each end that is used for signal routing in a patch bay.

Peak—On a graph of a sound wave or signal, the highest point in the waveform. The point of greatest voltage or sound pressure in a cycle.

Peak Amplitude—On a graph of a sound wave, the sound pressure of the waveform peak. On a graph of an electrical signal, the voltage of the waveform peak. The amplitude of a sound wave or signal, as measured on a meter, is 0.707 times the peak amplitude.

Peak Program Meter (PPM)—A meter that responds fast enough to closely follow the peak levels in a program.

Peaking Equalizer—An equalizer that provides maximum cut or boost at one frequency, so that the resulting frequency response of a boost resembles a mountain peak.

Period—The time between the peak of one wave and the peak of the next. The time between corresponding points on successive waves. Period is the inverse of frequency.

Personal Studio—A minimal group of recording equipment set up for one's personal use, usually using a 4-track cassette recorder/mixer. Also, a simple 4-track cassette recorder/mixer for one's personal use.

Perspective—In the reproduction of a recording, the audible sense of distance to the musical ensemble, the point of view. A close perspective has a high ratio of direct sound to reverberant sound; a distant perspective has a low ratio of direct sound to reverberant sound.

PFL—Abbreviation for Pre-Fader Listen. *See* Solo.

Phantom Power—A DC voltage (usually 12 to 48 volts) that is applied to microphone signal conductors to power condenser microphones.

Phase—The degree of progression in the cycle of a wave, where one complete cycle is 360°.

Phase Cancellation, Phase Interference—The cancellation of certain frequency components of a signal that occurs when the signal is combined with its delayed replica. At certain frequencies, the direct and delayed signals are of equal level and opposite polarity (180° out of phase), and, when combined, they cancel out. The result is a comb-filter frequency response having a periodic series of peaks and dips. Phase interference can occur between the signals of two microphones picking up the same source at different distances, or can occur at a microphone picking up both a direct sound and its reflection from a nearby surface.

Phase Shift—The difference in degrees of phase angle between corresponding points on two waves. If one wave is delayed with respect to another, there is a phase shift between them of $2\pi ft$, where $\pi = 3.14$, f = frequency in Hz, and t = delay in seconds.

Phasing—A special effect in which a signal is combined with its phase-shifted replica to produce a variable comb-filter effect. *See* also Flanging.

Phone Plug—A cylindrical plug used with headphones, microphones, and other audio equipment (usually 1/4-inch in diameter). An unbalanced phone plug has a tip for the hot signal and a sleeve for the shield or ground. A balanced phone plug has a tip for the hot signal, a ring for the return signal, and a sleeve for the shield or ground.

Phono Plug—A coaxial plug having a central pin for the hot signal and a ring of pressure-fit tabs for the shield or ground. Also called an RCA plug.

Pickup—A contact pickup. Also, a transducer in an electric guitar than converts string motion to a corresponding electrical signal.

Pinch Roller—In a tape-recorder transport, the rubber wheel that pinches or traps the tape between itself and the capstan, so that the capstan can move the tape.

Ping-Ponging—*See* Bouncing Tracks.

Pink Noise—A noise signal containing all frequencies (unless band-limited), with equal energy per octave. Pink noise is a test signal used for equalizing a sound system to the desired frequency response, and for testing loudspeakers.

Pitch—The subjective lowness or highness of a tone. The pitch of a tone usually correlates with the fundamental frequency.

Pitch Control—A control on a tape recorder that varies the tape speed, thereby varying the pitch of the signal on the tape. The pitch control is used to match the pitch of pre-recorded instruments with that of an instrument which is to be overdubbed.

Pitch Shifter—A signal processor that changes the pitch of an instrument's sound without changing its duration.

Playback Equalization—In tape-recorder electronics, fixed equalization that is applied to the signal during playback to compensate for certain losses.

Playback Head—The head in a tape recorder that picks up a pre-recorded magnetic signal from the moving tape

and converts it to a corresponding electrical signal.

Plug—A male connector that inserts into a jack (a female connector).

Polar Pattern—The directional pickup pattern of a microphone. A graph of microphone sensitivity plotted vs. angle of sound incidence. Omnidirectional, bidirectional, and unidirectional are some examples of polar patterns. Subsets of the unidirectional pattern are cardioid, supercardioid, and hypercardioid patterns.

Polarity—This refers to the positive or negative direction of an electrical, acoustical, or magnetic force. Two identical signals which are in opposite polarity are 180° out-of-phase with each other at all frequencies.

Pop—A thump or little explosive sound heard in a vocalist's microphone signal. Pop occurs when the user says words having a "p," "t," or "b," so that a turbulent puff of air is forced from the mouth and strikes the microphone diaphragm.

Pop Filter—A screen placed on a microphone grille that attenuates or filters out pop disturbances before they strike the microphone diaphragm. Usually made of open-cell plastic foam or silk, a pop filter reduces pop and wind noise.

Portable Studio—A combination tape recorder and mixer in one portable chassis.

Post-Echo—A repetition of a sound, following the original sound, that is caused by print-through.

Power Amplifier—An electronic device that amplifies or increases the power level fed into it to a level sufficient to drive a loudspeaker.

Power Ground—A connection to the power company's earth ground through the U-shaped hole in a power outlet. In the power cable of an electronic component with a 3-prong plug, the U-shaped prong that is wired (connected) to the component's chassis. This wire conducts electricity to power ground if the chassis becomes electrically hot, preventing shocks. Also called *safety ground*.

Pre-Amplifier—In an audio system, the first stage of amplification that boosts a mic-level signal to line level.

Pre-Delay—Short for pre-reverberation delay. The delay (about 30 to 100 milliseconds) between the arrival of the direct sound and the onset of reverberation. Usually, the longer the pre-delay, the greater the perceived room size.

Pre-Echo—A repetition of a sound that occurs before the sound itself, which is caused by print-through.

Pre-Fader/Post-Fader Switch—A switch that selects a signal either ahead of the fader (pre-fader) or following the fader (post-fader). The level of a pre-fader signal is independent of the fader position; the level of a post-fader signal follows the fader position.

Pre-Production—Planning in advance what you're going to do at a recording session, in terms of track assignments, overdubbing, studio layout, and microphone selection.

Presence—The audible sense that a reproduced instrument is present in the listening room. Some synonyms are closeness, definition, and punch. Presence is often created by an equalization boost in the midrange or upper midrange.

Pressure Zone Microphone—A boundary microphone constructed with the microphone diaphragm parallel with, and facing, a reflective surface.

Preverb—A special effect in which the reverberation of a note precedes it, rather than follows it. Preverb is achieved by playing an instrument's track backwards while adding reverberation to it, and recording the reverberation on an unused track. When the tape is reversed so that the instrument's track plays forward, preverb is heard as the reverberation plays backwards.

Print-Through—The transfer of a magnetic signal from one layer of tape to the next layer on a reel, causing an echo preceding or following the program.

Production—A recording that is enhanced by special effects. Also, the supervision of a recording session to create a satisfactory recording. This involves getting musicians together for the session, making musical suggestions to the musicians to enhance their performance, and making suggestions to the engineer for sound balance and effects.

Program Bus—A bus or output that feeds an audio program to a tape-recorder track.

Program Mixer—In a mixing console, a mixer formed of input-module outputs, combining amplifiers, and program buses.

Proximity Effect—The bass boost that occurs with a single-D directional microphone when it is placed a few inches from a sound source. The closer the microphone, the greater the low-frequency boost due to proximity effect.

Punch In/Out—A feature in a tape recorder that lets you insert a recording of a corrected musical part into a previously recorded track by going into and out of record mode as the tape is rolling.

Pure Waveform—A waveform of a single frequency; a sine wave. A pure tone is the perceived sound of such a wave.

Quarter-Track—A tape track recorded across one-quarter of the width of the tape. A quarter-track recorder usually records two stereo programs (one in each direction).

Rack—A 19-inch-wide wooden or metal cabinet that is used to hold audio equipment.

Radio-Frequency Interference (RFI)—The presence of radio-frequency electromagnetic waves in an audio component, causing various noises in the audio signal.

Rarefaction—The portion of a sound wave in which molecules are spread apart, forming a region with lower-than-normal atmospheric pressure. The opposite of compression.

Real-Time Recording—To record notes into a sequencer in the correct tempo, for later playback at the same tempo as recorded.

Recirculation (Regeneration)—Feeding the output of a delay device back into its input to create multiple echoes. Also, the control on a delay device that affects how much delayed signal is re-cycled to the input.

Record—To store an event in permanent form. Usually, to store an audio signal in magnetic form on magnetic tape.

Record Equalization—In the tape-recorder electronics, equalization that is applied to the signal during recording to compensate for certain losses.

Record Head—The head in a tape recorder that puts the audio signal on tape by magnetizing the tape particles in a pattern corresponding to the audio signal.

Recorder/Mixer—A combination tape recorder and mixer in one chassis.

Recording/Reproduction Chain—The series of events and equipment that are involved in sound recording and playback.

Reflected Sound—Sound waves that reach the listener after being reflected from one or more surfaces.

Release—The final portion of a note's envelope in which the note falls from its sustain level back to silence.

Release Time (Recovery Time)—In a compressor, the time it takes for the gain to return to normal after the end of a loud passage.

Remix—To mix again; to do another mixdown with different console settings or different editing.

Remote Recording—*See* On-location Recording.

Resistance—The opposition of a circuit to the flow of current. Resistance, abbreviated R, is measured in ohms and may be calculated by dividing the voltage by the current.

Resistor—An electronic component that opposes current flow.

Return-to-Zero—See Memory Rewind.

Reverberation—The persistence of sound in a room after the original sound has ceased. It is caused by multiple sound reflections (echoes) that decrease in intensity with time, and are so closely spaced in time as to merge into a single continuous sound, which, eventually, is completely absorbed by the inner surfaces of the room. The timing of the echoes is random, and the echoes increase in number as they decay. An example of reverberation is the sound you hear just after you shout in an empty gymnasium. An *echo* is a discrete repetition of a sound, while *reverberation* is a continuous fade-out of sound. *Artificial reverberation* is reverberation in an audio signal that is created mechanically or electronically rather than acoustically.

Reverberation Time—Abbreviated RT_{60}, the time it takes for reverberation to decay to 60 dB below the original steady-state level. RT_{60} is usually measured at 500 Hz.

Reverse Echo—A multiple echo that precedes the sound that caused it, building up from silence into the original sound. This special effect is created in a manner similar to preverb.

RFI—See Radio-Frequency Interference.

Rhythm Tracks—The recorded tracks of the rhythm instruments (guitar, bass, drums, and, sometimes, keyboards).

Ribbon Microphone—A dynamic microphone in which the conductor is a long metallic diaphragm (ribbon) suspended in a magnetic field.

Ride Gain—To turn down the volume of a microphone when the source gets louder, and turn up the volume when the source gets quieter, in an attempt to reduce dynamic range.

Room Modes—See Standing Wave.

Safety Copy—A copy of the master tape, which is to be used if the master tape is lost or damaged.

Safety Ground—See Power Ground.

Sampling—Recording a short sound event into computer memory. The audio signal is converted into digital data representing the signal waveform, and the data is stored in memory for later playback.

Saturation—Overload of a magnetic tape. The point at which a further increase in magnetizing force does not cause an increase in magnetization of the tape-oxide particles.

Scratch Vocal—A vocal performance that is done simultaneously with the rhythm instruments so that the musicians can keep their place in the song and get a feel for the song. Since it contains leakage, the scratch-vocal recording is usually erased. Then, the singer overdubs the vocal part that is to be used in the final recording.

Sensitivity—The output of a microphone in volts for a given input in sound-pressure level. Also, the sound-pressure level that a loudspeaker produces (at 1 meter) when driven with 1 watt of pink noise.

Sequencer—A device that records a series of synthesizer note parameters into computer memory for later playback. A computer can act as a sequencer when it runs a sequencer program. During playback, the sequencer activates the synthesizer sound generators.

Shelving Equalizer—An equalizer that applies a constant boost or cut above or below a certain frequency, so that the shape of the frequency response resembles a shelf.

Shield—A conductive enclosure (usually metallic) around one or more signal conductors that is used to keep out electrostatic fields that can cause hum or buzz.

Shock Mount—A suspension system which mechanically isolates a microphone from its stand or boom, preventing the transfer of mechanical vibrations.

Sibilance—In a speech recording, excessive frequency components in the 5- to 10-kHz range, which are heard as an over-emphasis the of "s" and "sh" sounds.

Signal—A varying electrical voltage that represents information, such as a sound.

Signal Path—The path that a signal travels from the input to the output in a piece of audio equipment.

Signal Processor—A device that is used to intentionally alter a signal in a controlled way.

Signal-to-Noise Ratio—The ratio in decibels between signal voltage and noise voltage. An audio component with a high signal-to-noise ratio has little background noise accompanying the signal; a component with a low signal-to-noise ratio is noisy.

Sine Wave—A wave following the equation $y = \sin x$, where x is degrees and y is voltage or sound-pressure level. The waveform of a single frequency.

Single-D Microphone—A directional microphone having a single distance between its front and rear sound entries; such a microphone has proximity effect.

Single-Ended—This refers to an unbalanced line.

Slap, Slapback—An echo following the original sound by about 50 to 200 milliseconds, sometimes with multiple repetitions.

Slate—At the beginning of a recording, a recorded announcement of the name of the tune and its take number. The term is derived from the slate used in the motion-picture industry to identify the production and take number being filmed.

SMPTE Time Code—*See also* Time Code. SMPTE is an abbreviation for the *Society of Motion Picture and Television Engineers*, which developed the time code.

Snake—A multipair or multichannel microphone cable. Also, a multipair microphone cable attached to a connector junction box.

Solo—On an input module in a mixing console, the switch that lets you monitor that particular input signal by itself. The switch routes only that input signal to the monitor power amplifier.

Sound—Longitudinal vibrations in a medium that are in the frequency range of 20 Hz to 20,000 Hz.

Sound Generator—A synthesizer without a keyboard, containing several different timbres or voices, which is triggered or played by certain MIDI signals from either a computer sequencer program or by an external keyboard.

Sound-Pressure Level (SPL)—The acoustic pressure of a sound wave, measured in decibels, above the threshold of hearing. dB SPL = 20 log (P/P_{ref}), where P_{ref} = 0.0002 dyne/cm^2.

Sound Wave—The periodic variations in sound pressure radiating from a sound source.

Spaced Pair—A stereo microphone technique that uses two identical microphones horizontally spaced several feet apart, and usually aiming straight ahead toward the sound source.

Speaker—*See* Loudspeaker.

Special Effects—*See* Signal Processor.

Spectrum—The output vs. frequency of a sound source, including the fundamental frequency and overtones.

SPL—*See* Sound-Pressure Level.

Splice—To join the ends of two lengths of magnetic tape or leader tape with an adhesive tape. Also, a splice is the taped joint between two lengths of magnetic tape or leader tape.

Splicing Block—*See* Editing Block.

Splitter—A transformer or circuit used to divide a microphone signal into two or more identical signals to feed different sound systems.

Spot Microphone—A close-placed microphone that is mixed with more distant microphones to add presence or to improve the balance.

Stacking Tracks—The process of recording several performances of a musical part on different tracks, so that the best segments of each performance can be played in sequence during mixdown.

Standing Wave—An apparently stationary waveform that is created by multiple reflections between opposite room surfaces. At certain points along the standing wave, the direct and reflected waves cancel, and, at other points, the waves add together or reinforce each other.

Step-Time Recording—Recording notes into a sequencer, one at a time, without regard to tempo, for later playback at a normal tempo.

Stereo, Stereophonic—An audio recording and reproduction system with correlated information between two (usually) channels, and meant to be heard over two or more loudspeakers to give the illusion of sound-source localization and depth.

Stereo Bar, Stereo Microphone Adapter—A microphone stand adapter that mounts two microphones on a single stand for convenient stereo miking.

Stereo Imaging—The ability of a stereo recording or reproduction system to form clearly defined audio images at various locations between a stereo pair of loudspeakers.

Stereo Microphone—A microphone containing two microphone capsules in a single housing for convenient stereo recording. The capsules usually are coincident.

Studio—A room used or designed for sound recording.

Submaster—A master volume control for an output bus. Also, a recorded tape that is used to form a master tape.

Submix—A small pre-set mix within a larger mix, such as a drum mix, keyboard mix, vocal mix, etc. Also a cue mix, monitor mix, or effects mix.

Submixer—A small mixer within a mixing console that is used to set up a submix, a cue mix, an effects mix, or a monitor mix.

Supercardioid Microphone—A unidirectional microphone that attenuates side-arriving sounds by 8.52 dB, attenuates rear-arriving sounds by 12 dB, and has two nulls of maxiumum sound rejection at 127° off-axis.

Supply Reel—*See* Feed Reel.

Sustain—The portion of the envelope of a note in which the level is constant. Also, the ability of a note to continue without noticeably decaying, often aided by compression.

Sweetening—The addition of strings, brass, chorus, etc. to a previously recorded tape of the basic rhythm tracks.

Sync, Synchronous Recording—Process of using a record head as a playback head during an overdub session to keep the overdubbed parts in synchronization with the pre-recorded tracks.

Synthesizer—A musical instrument (usually with a piano-style keyboard) that creates sounds electronically, and which allows control of the sound parameters to simulate a variety of conventional or unique instruments.

Tail-Out—Refers to a reel of tape that is wound with the end of the recorded program toward the outside of the reel. Tape stored tail-out is less likely to have audible print-through.

Talkback—An intercom in the mixing console that is used by the engineer and producer to talk to the musicians in the studio.

Take—A recorded performance of a song. Usually, several takes are done

of the same song, and the best one—or the best parts of several—become the final product.

Take Sheet—A list of take numbers for each song, plus comments on each take.

Take-Up Reel—The right-side reel on a tape recorder, which winds up the tape as it is playing or recording.

Tape—*See* Magnetic Recording Tape.

Tape Loop—An endless loop formed from a length of recording tape which is spliced end-to-end, and which is used for continuous repetition of several seconds of recorded signal.

Tape Recorder—A device that converts an electrical audio signal into a magnetic audio signal on magnetic tape, and vice versa. A tape recorder includes a transport to move the tape, some electronics, and the heads.

3-Pin Connector—A 3-pin professional audio connector used for balanced signals. Pin 1 is connected to the cable shield, pin 2 is connected to the signal hot lead, and pin 3 connects to the signal return lead. *See also* XLR-Type Connector.

3:1 Rule—A rule in audio applications which states that when multiple microphones are mixed to the same channel, the distance between the microphones should be at least three times the distance that each microphone is from its sound source to prevent audible phase interference.

Threshold—In a compressor or limiter, the input level above which compression or limiting takes place. In an expander, the input level below which expansion takes place.

Tie—To connect electrically; i.e., by soldering a wire between two points in a circuit.

Tight—Having very little leakage or room reflections in the sound pickup. Also, this refers to the well-synchronized playing of musical instruments.

Timbre—The subjective impression of spectrum and envelope. The quality of a sound that allows a person to differentiate it from other sounds. For example, when you hear a trumpet, piano, and a drum, each has a different timbre or tone quality that identifies it as a particular instrument.

Time Code—A modulated 1200-Hz square-wave signal used to synchronize two or more tape transports.

Tonal Balance—The balance or volume relationships among different regions of the frequency spectrum, such as bass, mid-bass, midrange, upper midrange, and highs.

Track—A path on magnetic tape that contains a single channel of audio.

Transducer—A device that converts energy from one form to another, such as a microphone or loudspeaker.

Transformer—An electronic component containing two magnetically coupled coils of wire. The input signal is transferred magnetically to the output, without a direct connection between the input and output.

Transient—A relatively high-amplitude, rapidly decaying, peak-signal level.

Transient Response—The ability of an audio component (usually a microphone or loudspeaker) to accurately follow a transient.

Transport—The mechanical system in a tape recorder that moves tape past the heads. A transport controls tape motion during recording, playback, fast forward, and rewind.

Trim—A control for the fine adjustment of level, as in a Bus Trim control. Also, a control that adjusts the gain of a microphone preamplifier to accommodate various signal levels.

Tweeter—A high-frequency loudspeaker.

Unbalanced Line—An audio cable having one conductor surrounded by a shield that carries the return signal. The shield is at ground potential.

Unidirectional Microphone—A microphone that is most sensitive to sounds arriving from one direction—in front of the microphone. Some examples are the cardioid, supercardioid, and hypercardioid types.

VU Meter—A voltmeter with a specified transient response, and calibrated in VU or volume units, that is used to show the relative volume of various audio signals, and used to set the recording level.

Waveform—A graph of sound pressure (or voltage) vs. time of a signal. The waveform of a pure tone is a sine wave.

Wavelength—The physical length between corresponding points of successive waves. Low frequencies have long wavelengths; high frequencies have short wavelengths.

Weber—A unit of magnetic flux.

Weighted—This refers to a measurement made through a filter with a certain specified frequency response. An A-weighted measurement is taken through a filter that simulates the frequency response of the human ear.

Windscreen—*See* Pop Filter.

Woofer—A low-frequency loud-speaker.

Wow—A slow periodic variation in tape speed.

XLR-Type Connector—The part number of an ITT Cannon device which has become the popular definition for a 3-pin professional audio connector. *See also* Three-Pin Connector.

X-Y—*See* Coincident Pair.

Y-Adapter—A cable that connects two cables in parallel in order to feed one signal to two destinations.

A dB OR NOT dB

Among essential skills in the studio are the setting and measuring of signal levels, matching equipment levels, and understanding microphone output levels. Developing these skills requires an understanding of the *decibel* (dB), the unit of audio level measurement.

Definitions

First let's define the term "level" as used in a recording studio. Originally, "level" meant power, while "amplitude" referred to voltage. Nowadays, many audio people also define "level" in terms of voltage or sound pressure, even though this terminology is not strictly correct. But you have to know both definitions in order to communicate.

Audio level is measured in decibels. One dB is the smallest *change* in level that most people can hear—the just noticeable difference. Actually, the just noticeable difference varies from 0.1 dB to about 5 dB, depending on bandwidth, frequency, program material, and the individual. But 1 dB is generally accepted as the smallest change in level that most people can detect. And, subjectively, a 6- to 10-dB increase in level is considered by most listeners to be "twice as loud."

Sound-pressure level, signal level, and a change in signal level are all measured in dB. Let's look at each of these.

Sound-Pressure Level

Sound-pressure level is the pressure of sound vibration measured at a point. It's usually measured with a sound-level meter in dB SPL (decibels of sound-pressure level).

The higher the sound-pressure level, the louder the sound (Fig. A-1). The quietest sound that we can hear, the threshold of hearing, is 0-dB SPL. Average conversation at one foot is 70-dB SPL. The average home-stereo listening level is around 85-dB SPL. The threshold of pain—so loud that the ears hurt—is 125- to 130-dB SPL.

Sound-pressure level in decibels is 20 times the logarithm of the ratio of two sound pressures:

$$dB\ SPL = 20\ \log \frac{P}{P_{ref}}$$

where

P is the measured sound pressure in dynes/cm^2,

P_{ref} is a reference sound pressure—0.0002 dyne/cm^2 (the threshold of hearing).

Fig. A-1. Chart of sound-pressure levels.

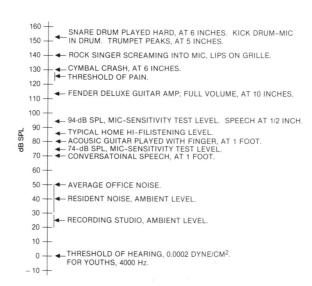

Signal Level

Signal level also is measured in dB. The level in decibels is 10 times the logarithm of the ratio of two power levels:

$$dB = 10\ \log \frac{P}{P_{ref}}$$

where

P is the measured power in watts,
P_{ref} is a reference power in watts.

Recently, it's become common to use the decibel to refer to voltage ratios as well:

$$dB = 20 \log \frac{V}{V_{ref}}$$

where
V is the measured voltage,
V_{ref} is a reference voltage.

This expression is mathematically equivalent to the previous one, because power equals voltage squared divided by the circuit resistance:

$$dB = 10 \log \frac{P_1}{P_2}$$

$$= 10 \log \frac{(V_1^2/R)}{(V_2^2/R)}$$

$$= 10 \log \frac{V_1^2}{V_2^2}$$

$$= 20 \log \frac{V_1}{V_2}$$

Signal level in decibels can be expressed in various ways—dBm, dBu, dBv, and dBV.

dBm: decibels referenced to 1 milliwatt.
dBu or **dBv**: decibels referenced to 0.775 volt. (dBu is preferred.)
dBV: decibels referenced to 1 volt.

Let's explain each one of these.
If you're measuring signal power, the decibel unit to use is *dBm*.

$$dBm = 10 \log \frac{P}{P_{ref}}$$

where
P is the measured power,

P_{ref} is the reference power, 1 milliwatt.

For example, let's convert 0.01 watt to dBm:

$$dBm = 10 \log \frac{P}{P_{ref}} = 10 \log \frac{0.01}{0.001} = 10$$

So, 0.01 watt is 10 dBm (10 decibels above 1 milliwatt).
    Now let's convert 0.001 watt into dBm:

$$dBm = 10 \log \frac{P}{P_{ref}}$$

$$= 10 \log \frac{0.001}{0.001}$$

$$= 0$$

So, 0 dBm = 1 milliwatt.
    Any voltage across any resistance that results in 1 milliwatt is 0 dBm.

$$0 \; dBm = \frac{V^2}{R}$$

$$= 1 \; milliwatt$$

where
    V is the voltage in volts,
    R is the circuit resistance in ohms.

For example, 0.775 volt across 600 ohms is 0 dBm. One volt across 1000 ohms is 0 dBm.
    Some voltmeters are calibrated in dBm. The meter reading in dBm is accurate only when you're measuring across 600 ohms. For an accurate dBm measurement, measure the voltage and circuit resistance, and then calculate:

$$dBm = 10 \log \frac{(V^2/R)}{0.001}$$

Another unit of measurement is called *dBu* or *dBv*. This means decibels referenced to 0.775 volt. The "0.775 volt" figure comes from 0 dBm.

0 dBm = 0.775 volt across 600 ohms, where 600 ohms used to be a standard impedance for audio connections. Thus,

$$dBu = 20 \log \frac{V}{V_{ref}}$$

where V_{ref} = 0.775 volt.

Signal level also is measured in dBV, or decibels referenced to 1 volt. The equation for this is

$$dBV = 20 \log \frac{V}{V_{ref}}$$

where V_{ref} = 1 volt.

For example, let's convert 1 millivolt to dBV:

$$dBV = 20 \log \frac{V}{V_{ref}}$$

$$= 20 \log \frac{0.001}{1}$$

$$= -60$$

So 1 millivolt = −60 dBV (60 decibels below 1 volt). Now let's convert 1 volt to dBV, as follows:

$$dBV = 20 \log \frac{1}{1}$$

$$= 0$$

So, 1 volt = 0 dBV.
To convert dBV to voltage, use the formula

$$Volts = 10^{(dBV/20)}$$

Change in Signal Level

Decibels also are used to measure the *change* in power or voltage across a fixed resistance. The formula for this is:

$$dB = 10 \log \frac{P_1}{P_2}$$

or

$$dB = 20 \log \frac{V_1}{V_2}$$

where
  P_1 is the new power level,
  P_2 is the old power level,
  V_1 is the new voltage level,
  V_2 is the old voltage level.

For example, if the voltage across a resistor is 0.01 volt, and it changes to 1 volt, the change in dB is

$$dB = 20 \log \frac{V_1}{V_2}$$

$$= 20 \log \frac{1}{0.01}$$

$$= 40 \text{ dB}$$

Doubling the power results in a 3-dB increase; doubling the voltage results in a 6-dB increase.

The VU Meter, 0 VU, and Peak Indicators

A VU meter is a voltmeter of specified transient response, calibrated in *volume units* or *VU*. It shows approximately the relative volume or loudness of the measured audio signal.

The VU-meter scale is divided into volume units, which are not necessarily the same as dB. The volume unit corresponds to the decibel only when measuring a steady-state sine-wave tone. In other words, a change of 1 VU is the same as a 1-dB change only when a steady tone is applied.

Most recording engineers use 0 VU to define a convenient "zero reference level" on the VU meter. When the meter on your mixer or recorder reads "0" on a steady tone, your equipment is producing a certain level at its output. Different types of equipment produce different levels when the meter reads "0." This is illustrated in Fig. A-2. Thus, 0 VU corresponds to:

+8 dBm in broadcast and telephone equipment
+4 dBm in balanced recording equipment
−10 dBV in unbalanced recording equipment.

When a tape operator says to a mixing engineer, "Send me a 0-VU tone," he or she means, "Send me a tone that reads zero on your VU meter." The signal level itself isn't too important, because the tape operator receiving the tone just wants to match the tape-deck meters to those on the console.

A *0-VU recording level* (0 on the record level meter) is the normal operating level of a recorder; it produces the desired recorded flux on tape. A "0-VU recording level" does not mean a "0-VU signal level." With a VU meter, 0 VU corresponds to a recording level that is 8 dB below the level that produces 3% third-harmonic distortion on tape at 400 Hz. Distortion at 0 VU is typically below 1%.

The response of a VU meter is not fast enough to track rapid transients accurately. In addition, when a complex waveform is applied to a VU meter, the meter reads less than the peak voltage of the waveform. By contrast, a *peak indicator* quickly responds to peak program levels, making it a more accurate indicator of recording levels. One type of peak indicator is an LED that flashes on peak overloads. Another is the *peak program meter (PPM)*. It is calibrated in dB, rather than VU. Unlike the VU-meter reading, the PPM reading does not correlate with perceived volume.

Fig. A-2. VU meter scale.

EQUIPMENT OUTPUT LEVEL WITH 1000-Hz
STEADY TONE AT 0-VU READING EQUALS

+8 dBm (BROADCAST AND TELEPHONE EQUIPMENT)
+4 dBm (BALANCED RECORDING EQUIPMENT)
−10 dBV (UNBALANCED RECORDING EQUIPMENT)

"VU" MEANS "VOLUME UNITS"
VU = dB ONLY ON STEADY TONES

0-VU RECORDING LEVEL EQUALS
0-VU METER READING, FOR A STEADY TONE.
THIS LEVEL PRODUCES APPROXIMATELY 1%
HARMONIC DISTORTION ON TAPE.

Balanced vs. Unbalanced Equipment Levels

Generally, audio equipment with balanced (3-pin) connectors works at a higher nominal line level than equipment with unbalanced (phono) connectors. There's nothing inherent in balanced or unbalanced connections that makes them operate at different levels; they're just standardized at different levels.

The following are the nominal (normal) input and output levels for the two types of equipment:

Balanced: +4 dBm (1.23 volts)
Unbalanced: −10 dBV (0.316 volt)

In other words, when a balanced-output recorder reads 0 VU on its meter (with a steady tone), it is producing 1.23 volts at its output connector. This voltage is called +4 dBm when referenced to 1 milliwatt. When an unbalanced-output recorder reads 0 on its meter with a steady tone, it is producing 0.316 volt at its output connector. This voltage is called −10 dBV when referenced to 1 volt.

Interfacing Balanced and Unbalanced Equipment

There's an 11.8-dB difference between +4 dBm and −10 dBV. How did we get that? By converting both levels to voltages:

$$dB = 20 \log \frac{1.23}{0.316}$$

$$= 11.8$$

So, +4 dBm is 11.8 dB higher in voltage than −10 dBV (assuming the resistances are the same).

A cable carrying a nominal +4-dBm signal will have a signal-to-noise ratio that is 11.8 dB better than the same cable carrying a −10-dBV signal. This is an advantage in environments with strong radio-frequency or hum fields. But, in most studios using short cables, the difference is negligible.

Connecting a +4-dBm output to a −10-dBV input might cause distortion if the signal peaks of the +4-dBm equipment exceed the headroom of the −10-dBV equipment. If this happens, use a pad as shown in Fig. A-3 to attenuate the level 12 dB. The pad converts from a balanced to unbalanced format as well as reducing the level 12 dB. You may have to substitute a stereo phone plug for the 3-pin connector.

You don't always need that pad. Many pieces of equipment have a $+4/-10$ level switch. You just set the switch to the nominal level of the connected equipment.

Microphone Sensitivity

Here's another area that is concerned with decibels: *microphone sensitivity*. A microphone sensitivity specification tells how much output (in volts) a microphone produces for a certain input (in SPL). A high-sensitivity microphone puts out a stronger signal (higher voltage) than a low-sensitivity microphone when both are exposed to the same sound-pressure level. Microphone sensitivity is specified in several ways:

dBV per microbar
millivolts per pascal
dBm per 10 dynes/cm^2
dBm, EIA rating

We'll explain each of these in detail. First, however, note that

$$10 \text{ dynes/cm}^2 = 10 \text{ microbars} = 1 \text{ pascal} = 94\text{-dB SPL}$$

and

$$1 \text{ dyne/cm}^2 = 1 \text{ microbar} = 74\text{-dB SPL}$$

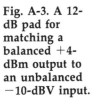

Fig. A-3. A 12-dB pad for matching a balanced +4-dBm output to an unbalanced −10-dBV input.

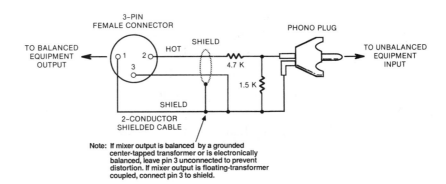

Note: If mixer output is balanced by a grounded center-tapped transformer or is electronically balanced, leave pin 3 unconnected to prevent distortion. If mixer output is floating-transformer coupled, connect pin 3 to shield.

An example of a microphone sensitivity specification is as follows:

Open-circuit voltage: −60 dB re 1 volt per microbar.

That means that when the mic is unloaded (not connected to a load), and the mic is exposed to a sound-pressure level of 1 microbar (74-dB SPL), it produces −60 dBV. You put 74-dB SPL in; you get −60 dBV out.

A typical sensitivity specification is −65 dBV/microbar for a condenser microphone and −75 dBV/microbar for a dynamic microphone.

Another way to express the same sensitivity is:

Open-circuit voltage: 10 millivolts per pascal

That is, the mic produces 10 millivolts, unloaded, when exposed to a sound-pressure level of 1 pascal (94-dB SPL). You put 94-dB SPL in; you get 10 millivolts out.

Still another, less common, way to specify the same sensitivity is:

Power level: −38 dBm per 10 dynes/cm^2

In other words, the mic produces −38 dBm into a matched load, when exposed to an SPL of 10 dynes/cm^2 (94-dB SPL). "Matched load" means that the load impedance equals the microphone impedance. If the mic impedance is 150 ohms, the load impedance of the mic preamp input is also 150 ohms. This is unlikely to occur in practice; usually the load impedance is at least 7 to 10 times the mic impedance so that the microphone is, effectively, unloaded.

The EIA (Electronics Industries Association) rating is useful for calculating a microphone output into a matched load for a given SPL.

SPL + dB (EIA) = dBm output into a matched load

To compare the sensitivities of two microphones specified in different ways, convert them to the same reference using these formulas:

- Millivolts per pascal = $10^{(4 + dBV/20)}$
- dBV/microbar = 20 log (mV per pascal/1000) − 20 dB
- dBm/10 dynes/cm^2 = dBV/microbar + 22.2 dB (if mic impedance = 150 ohms)
- dB (EIA) = dBm/10 dynes/cm^2 − 94 dB.

If you put a microphone in a 20-dB louder sound field, it produces 20 dB more signal voltage. For example, if 74-dB SPL in gives you −75 dBV out, then 94-dB SPL in gives you −55 dBV out. Also, 150-dB SPL in will give you +1 dBV out, which is approximately line level! That's why you need so much input padding when you record a kick drum or other loud source.

B INTRODUCTION TO SMPTE TIME CODE

Have you ever wished you had more tracks? Suppose you've filled up all the tracks of a 16-track recorder, and the band you're recording wants to overdub several more instruments, and you don't have a 24-track machine.

There's an alternative: Synchronize the 16-track machine with an 8-track machine by using SMPTE time code. This is a special signal recorded on tape that can sync together two tape recorders so that they operate as one. The time code can also synchronize an audio recorder with a video recorder.

SMPTE stands for the *Society of Motion Picture and Television Engineers*. The SMPTE standardized the time-code signal for use in video production, and you can use it in audio recording as well. SMPTE time code is something like a digital tape counter, where the counter time is recorded as a signal on tape.

How the Time Code Works

SMPTE time code works as follows. A *time-code generator* creates the time-code signal (a 1200-Hz modulated square wave). You record or "stripe" this signal onto one track of both recorders. A *time-code reader* reads the code off the two tapes. Then, a *time-code synchronizer* compares the codes from the two transports and locks them together in time by varying the motor speed of one of the transports.

Let's explain how the counter time is recorded as a signal on tape. Pictures on a video screen are updated at approximately 30 frames per second, where a frame is a still picture made up of 525 lines on the screen. SMPTE time code assigns a unique number (address) to each video frame—8 digits that specify the hours, minutes, seconds, and frame number. Each video frame is then identified with its own time-code address.

These addresses are recorded sequentially; for each successive video frame, the time-code number increases by one frame count. There are approximately 30 frames per second in the American television system, so the time code counts frames from 0 to 29 each second.

Time-Code Signal Details

The SMPTE time code is a data stream that is divided into *code words*. Each code word includes 80 binary digits, or bits, that identify each video frame (Fig. B-1).

The 80-bit time-code word is synchronized to the start of each video frame. The code uses binary 1s and 0s. During each half-cycle of the square wave, the voltage may be constant (signifying a 0) or changing (signifying a 1). That is, a voltage transition in the middle of a half-cycle of the square wave equals a 1. No transition signifies a 0. This is called

Fig. B-1. An 80-bit time-code word.

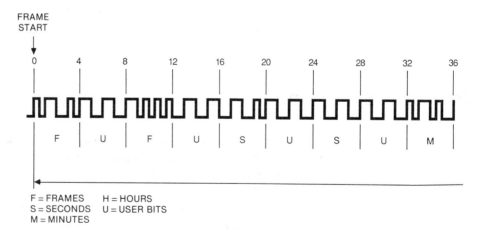

F = FRAMES   H = HOURS
S = SECONDS   U = USER BITS
M = MINUTES

bi-phase modulation (Fig. B-2). It can be read forward or in reverse, at almost any tape speed. A time-code reader detects the binary 1s and 0s, and converts them to decimal numbers to form the time-code addresses.

SMPTE words also can include user information. There are 32 multipurpose bits (8 digits or 4 characters) reserved for the user's data, such as the take number.

The last 16 bits in the word are a fixed number of 1s and 0s called the *sync bits*. These bits indicate the end of the time-code word, so that the time-code reader can tell whether the code is being read forward or in reverse.

Drop-Frame Mode

SMPTE code can run in various modes depending on the application. Let's explain one of these, Drop-Frame mode, and why it's needed.

Black-and-white TV runs at 30 frames/sec. A time-code signal also running at 30 frames/sec will agree with the clock on the wall. Color TV, on the other hand, runs at 29.97 frames/sec. If a color program is clocked at 30 frames/sec for one hour, the actual show length will run 3.6 seconds (108 frames) longer than an hour.

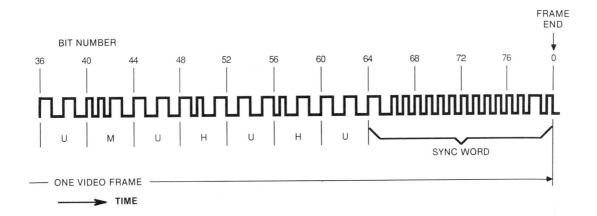

**Fig. B-2.
Bi-phase
modulation used
in the SMPTE
time code.**

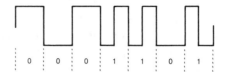

The Drop-Frame mode causes the time code to count at a rate that matches the clock on the wall. Each minute, frame numbers 00 and 01 are dropped, except for the tenth minute. (Instead of seeing frames . . . 27, 28, 29, 00, 01, 02 on the counter; you'll see frames . . . 27, 28, 29, 02.) This speeds up the time-code counter to match the rate of the video frames.

The video frames still progress at 29.97 frames/sec, while the time code progresses at 30 frames/sec, but it drops every few frames, so that, effectively, the time-code frame rate is 29.97 frames/sec.

You can program the time-code generator to operate in *Drop* or *Non-Drop* mode. Non-Drop mode can be used for audio-only synchronizing, but Drop mode should be used if the audio will be synched to a video tape later on.

Setting Up a Time-Code System

To use the SMPTE time code, you need a time-code generator, reader, and synchronizer. These may be either all-in-one or separate units. Fig. B-3 shows a typical system hook-up, in which the generator, reader, and synchronizer are combined in one unit.

**Fig. B-3. Typical
hook-up for
synchronizing
two tape
transports using
SMPTE time
code.**

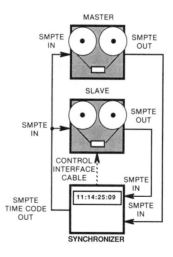

Set the generator to the Time-of-Day code, or any other convenient starting time. If you are synching to video, feed the generator a sync signal from the video source being recorded. This will lock the generator together in time with the video source. For audio-only applications, use the internal crystal sync.

Select either Drop-Frame or Non-Drop-Frame mode, and stay with it for the entire production. Use Drop-Frame mode if you anticipate synchronizing the audio to video in the future.

Next, set the frame rate: 29.97, 30, 24, or 25 frames/sec. Color video productions require 29.97 frames, black-and-white TV or audio-only productions use 30 frames, film usually runs at 24 frames, and European TV—using EBU (European Broadcast Union) time code—requires 25 frames.

The time-code signal appears at the generator output, which is a standard 3-pin audio connector. Signal level is +4 dBm. The signal is fed through a standard 2-conductor shielded audio cable. To avoid crosstalk of the time code into the audio channels, separate the time-code cables from the audio cables. Patch the time-code signal into an outside track of the recorders that you want to lock together. Then, patch the outputs of those time-code tracks to the inputs of the time-code reader. The reader decodes the information recorded on tape and, in some models, displays time-code data in an HOURS:MINUTES:SECONDS:FRAMES format. Some readers have an *error bypass* feature which corrects for missing data.

The time-code synchronizer matches bits between two time-code signals to synchronize them. The synchronizer compares tape direction, address, and phase to synchronize two SMPTE tracks via servo control of the transport motors. (The two tape machines to be synched are called "master" and "slave.") The synchronizer controls the slave by making its tape position and speed follow that of the master.

Connect the shielded multipin interface cable between the synchronizer and the slave machine to control the slave's tape transport and motors. This interface cable has channels for controlling the capstan motor, tape direction, shuttle modes, and tachometer (more on the tach later).

Since the time-code signal becomes very high in frequency when the tape is shuttled rapidly, special playback amplifier cards with extended high-frequency response may be needed to reproduce the SMPTE signal accurately. These cards are available from the recorder manufacturer.

Unfortunately, when the tape is in shuttle mode (fast forward or rewind), the tape usually is lifted from the heads—losing the SMPTE signal. In this case, the recorders are synchronized using tach pulses from the recorders as a replacement for the SMPTE time code. Some synchronizers are fed tach pulses from the slave only.

If *chase* mode is available, the slave follows the shuttle motions of the master. Otherwise, the synchronizer notes the address of the master tape when it is stopped and cues the slave to match that location. Chase mode is useful for repetitive overdubs.

How to Use the SMPTE Time Code

Suppose you want to synchronize two multitrack recorders. First, clean the heads and the tape path. Record the SMPTE time code on an outside track of both recorders at −5 to −10 VU, leaving the adjacent track blank, if possible, to avoid time-code crosstalk. Start recording, or "striping," the code about 20 seconds before the music starts, and continue nonstop with no breaks in the signal. Stripe the two tapes simultaneously. If that is not possible, you'll need a *time-code editor* to correct or insert an offset.

During playback, manually cue the slave to approximately the same point as the master tape, using time-code address information as a reference. Then put both recorders in Play mode. Finally, adjust the slave's tape speed to gradually reduce the error between transports to less than one time-code frame. With some synchronizers, this operation is automatic. You set the slave tape to approximately the same point as the master tape. Then put the master in Play mode. When the synchronizer detects the master time code, it will set the slave machine in Play mode and, in a few seconds, will adjust the slave's speed to synchronize the two recorders.

When you're recording on two synchronized transports, try not to split stereo pairs between two tapes. The slight time differences between machines can degrade stereo imaging. Keep all stereo pairs on the same tape, copying them if necessary onto the other tape.

Re-striping Defective Code

You may encounter degraded or erased sections on a time-code track. This lost code must be replaced with good code in proper sequence. If you need to re-record (re-stripe) a defective SMPTE track, use the *jam sync* mode on the time-code generator. This feature produces new code which matches the original addresses and frame count.

For example, suppose the slave tape needs to be re-striped. Patch the slave's time-code track into a generator set to "jam sync" mode. Patch the generator output into the time-code track input on the slave machine. Play the tape. The time-code reader built into the generator will detect a section of good code and will initialize the generator with that information. At that time, start recording the new regenerated code over the bad data.

Jam sync should also be used when you copy a tape containing time code. With jam sync in operation, the code will be regenerated to create a clean copy. This procedure is preferable to copying the time-code track directly, because each generation can distort the code signal.

Synching to Video

With the advent of MTV and other audio/video combinations, there's a widespread need to sync audio to video. Running audio and video tapes in synchronization for TV audio editing is a typical post-production method.

Synching audio and video machines also eliminates the dubbing step when transferring (*laying back*) the audio sound track to video tape. That is, you can mix the multitrack tape master directly to the video tape (keeping sync), rather than mixing down to 2-track and dubbing that to video tape.

When you sync audio and video, select the *Longitudinal Time Code (LTC)* or the *Vertical Interval Time Code (VITC)* mode. Longitudinal code records along the length of an audio track on the video tape. Vertical Interval code is combined with the video signal and is placed in the vertical blanking interval—the black bar seen over the TV picture when it is rolling vertically. VITC frees up an audio track for other purposes.

If you record the time-code signal on an audio or cue track of the videotape, do not use automatic level control because it may distort the SMPTE waveform. Instead, adjust the time-code signal level manually.

When you play an audio tape that is synched to video, the time-code track on the audio tape will be delayed with respect to the video's code due to the spacing between the record and playback heads in the audio recorder. This delay (about 5 frames) can be corrected by the *offset* function in the synchronizer.

Some time-code systems include a *character inserter* which displays the address on the video monitor. If desired, these addresses can be recorded with (*burned into*) the picture, a feature called *window dub*.

Other Time-Code Applications

SMPTE time code allows video editing under computer control. To edit a video program, you copy program segments from two or more video tapes onto a third recorder. On a computer, you specify the edit points (time-code addresses) where you want to switch from one video source to another. You can rehearse edits as often as required without cutting the tape.

Time code is also used as an index for locating cue points on tape. During a mixdown, you can use these cue points to indicate where to make changes in the mix.

Studios doing sound-track work for film or video can use SMPTE time code to synchronize sound and picture for overdubbing narration, lip-sync, music, or sound effects. Time code also can be used as a reference for console automation and MIDI instruments. With this latter application, MIDI synthesizers can be cued to any point within a sequence, rather than having to start at the beginning.

By using SMPTE time code to lock together multiple audio or video transports, you can greatly expand your operating flexibility.

C FURTHER EDUCATION

The following lists of books and magazines were valuable resources for this book, and are recommended to anyone desiring further education in recording technology.

Books and Magazines

The following books are available from The Mix Bookshelf Catalog, The Recording Industry Resource Center, 2608 9th St., Berkeley, CA 94710:

1. Anderton, Craig. *Home Recording for Musicians*. New York: GPI Publications, Music Sales Corp., 1978.

2. Borwick, John. *Sound Recording Practice*. London: Oxford University Press, 1980.

3. Clifford, Martin. *Microphones*, 2nd Ed. Blue Ridge Summit, PA: Tab Books, 1977.

4. Davis, Don & Carolyn. *Sound System Engineering*, 2nd Ed. Indianapolis: Howard W. Sams & Co., 1986.

5. Eargle, John. *The Microphone Handbook*. Plainview, NY: Elar Publishing, 1981.

6. Eargle, John. *Sound Recording*, 2nd Ed. New York: Van Nostrand Reinhold Co., 1986.

7. Everest, F. Alton. *Acoustic Techniques for Home and Studio*, 2nd Ed. Blue Ridge Summit, PA: Tab Books, 1986.

8. Keene, Sherman. *Practical Techniques for the Recording Engineer*. Hollywood: Sherman Keene Publications, 1981.

9. Nisbett, Alec. *The Use of Microphones*, 2nd Ed. New York: Hastings House, 1977.

10. Pohlmann, Ken. *Principles of Digital Audio*. Indianapolis: Howard W. Sams & Co., 1985.

11. Runstein, Robert, and Huber, David. *Modern Recording Techniques*, 2nd Ed. Indianapolis: Howard W. Sams & Co., 1986.

12. Woram, John. *The Recording Studio Handbook*, 2nd Ed. Plainview, New York: Sagamore Publishing Co., Inc., 1982.

The following books are not in the Mix Bookshelf Catalog, but were useful references:

1. *Are You Ready for Multitrack?* Montebello, CA: Teac Corp.

2. Connelly, Will. *The Musician's Guide to Independent Record Production*. Chicago: Contemporary Books, Inc.

3. Everest, F. Alton. *Handbook of Multichannel Recording*. Blue Ridge Summit, PA: Tab Books, 1975.

4. Halloran, Mark E. *The Musician's Manual*. New York: Elsevier-Dutton Pub. Co., Inc. See Stephen Taylor's chapter on "Cutting Demos."

5. Hickman, Walter A. *Time Code Handbook*. Boston: Cipher Digital, 1984.

6. Martin, George. *All You Need Is Ears*. New York: St. Martin's Press, 1979.

7. Rapaport, Diane Sward. *How to Make and Sell Your Own Record*. Tiburon, CA: Headlands Press, 1984.

8. Rosmini, Dick. *Teac Multitrack Primer*. Montebello, CA: Teac Corp., 1978.

9. Tremaine, Howard M. *The Audio Cyclopedia*, 2nd Ed. Indianapolis: Howard W. Sams & Co.

In addition, much information was gained from the following recording industry magazines:

1. *The Mix*, 2608 9th St., Berkeley, CA 94710.

2. *Music & Sound Output*, 220 Westbury Ave., Carle Place, NY 11514.

3. *Recording Engineer/Producer*, P.O. Box 2449, Hollywood, CA 90078.

4. *db*, 1120 Old Country Rd., Plainview, NY 11803.

5. *Modern Recording & Music* (now part of *db* magazine, Plainview, NY 11803).

Guides, Brochures, and Other Literature

For those who wish other reading material, the *Mix Bookshelf Catalog* mentioned earlier describes many excellent books on recording techniques, audio, studio construction, microphones, MIDI, and the music business. Also available are *Careers in Audio Engineering* and the *Journal of the Audio Engineering Society*, from the Audio Engineering Society, 60 E. 42nd St., New York, NY 10165.

Microphone application guides are available from Crown International, 1718 W. Mishawaka Rd., Elkhart, IN 46517; Shure Brothers Inc., 222 Hartrey Ave., Evanston, IL 60202; Countryman Associates Inc., 417 Stanford Ave., Redwood City, CA 94063; AKG Acoustics Inc., 77 Selleck St., Stamford, CT 06902; Sennheiser Electronic Corp., 10 W. 37th St., New York, NY 10018; and Audio-Technica U.S. Inc., 1221 Commerce Drive, Stow, Ohio 44224.

Much valuable information can be found in the operation manuals and free descriptive literature that is available from manufacturers of recording equipment.

The International MIDI Association has MIDI technical information for sale, such as the MIDI 1.0 specification and a 50-page detailed explanation of MIDI. Write to International MIDI Association, 11857 Hartsook St., North Hollywood, CA 91607.

Recording Schools

The July, 1986, issue of *Mix* magazine had a comprehensive directory of recording schools, seminars, and programs. Universities and colleges in most major cities also have recording-engineering courses. Listed here are some of the better-known schools. Investigate them thoroughly, however, before making a decision.

1. Aspen Audio Recording Institute, Box AA, Aspen, CO 81612. (303) 925-3254.
2. Berklee College of Music, 1140 Boylston, St., Boston, MA 02215. (617) 266-1400.
3. California State University Domninguez Hills, 1000 E. Victoria St., Carson, CA 90747. (213) 516-3543.
4. Center for the Media Arts, Conservatory of Music for the Media, 226 W. 26th St., New York, NY 10001. (212) 807-6670.

5. College for Recording Arts, 665 Harrison St., San Francisco, CA 94107. (415) 781-6306.

6. Fullerton College, Music Dept., 321 E. Chapman Avenue, Fullerton, CA 92634. (714) 871-8000, Ext. 336.

7. Full Sail Center for the Recording Arts, 660 Douglas Ave., Altamonte Springs, FL 32714. (800) 221-2747, in Florida: (305) 788-2450.

8. Georgia State University, Dept. of Commercial Music/ Recording of the College of Public and Urban Affairs, University Plaza, Atlanta, GA 30303. (404) 658-3513.

9. Golden West Community College, 15744 Golden West St., Huntington Beach, CA 92647. (714) 895-8780.

10. Grove School of Music, Dick. 12754 Ventura Blvd., Studio City, CA 91604. (818) 985-0904.

11. Houston Community College System, 901 Yorkchester, Houston, TX 77079. (713) 468-6891.

12. Indiana University School of Music, Bloomington, IN 47405. (812) 335-1613, 335-1900.

13. Institute of Audio Research, 64 University Place, New York, NY 10003. (212) 677-7580.

14. Institute of Audio/Video Engineering, 1831 Hyperion Ave., Dept. E, Hollywood, CA 90027. (213) 666-3003, Ext. 6.

15. ITM Workshop of Recording Arts, Box 686, Knox, PA 16232. (814) 797-5883.

16. Los Angeles Recording Workshop, 5287 Sunset Blvd., Hollywood, CA 90027. (213) 465-4254.

17. Lowell, University of. College of Music, Lowell, MA 01854. (617) 452-5000.

18. Loyola Marymount University, Dept. of Communication Arts, Loyola Blvd. at W. 80th St., Los Angeles, CA 90045. (213) 642-3033.

19. Memphis State University, Music Dept., Memphis, TN 38152. (901) 454-2559.

20. McGill University, Faculty of Music, 555 Sherbrooks St. W., Strathcona Music Bldg., Montreal, Quebec, Canada H3A 1E3. (514) 392-5776.

21. McLennan Community College, Commercial Music Dept., 1400 College Dr., Waco, TX 76708. (817) 756-6551.

22. Miami, University of. School of Music, Coral Gables, FL 33124. (305) 284-2439.

23. Music Business Institute, 3376 Peachtree Rd., Atlanta, GA 30326. (404) 231-3303; 1-800-554-3346.

24. Northeast Technical Community College, 801 E. Benjamin Ave., P.O. Box 469, Norfolk, NE 68701. (402) 371-2020.

25. Omega Studio's School of Applied Recording Arts and Sciences, Omega Recording Studios, 5609 Fishers Ln., Rockville, MD 20852. (301) 946-4686.

26. Peabody Institute of the John Hopkins University, 1 E. Mt. Vernon Pl., Baltimore, MD 21202. (301) 659-8136.

27. Recording Workshop, 455 Massieville Rd., Chillicothe, OH 45601. (614) 663-2544; 1-800-848-9900.

28. SKE Publishing, P.O. Box 2519-M, Sedona, AZ 86336. (602) 282-1258.

29. Sound Master Recording Engineer Schools, Audio/Video Institute, 10747 Magnolia Blvd., North Hollywood, CA 91601. (213) 650-8000.

30. South Plains College, 1401 College Ave., Levelland, TX 79336. (806) 894-9611, Ext. 271.

31. State University of New York at Fredonia, Mason Hall, Fredonia, NY 14063. (716) 673-3221.

32. Studio Production Techniques, P.O. Box 741444, Dallas, TX 75374. (214) 426-3766.

33. Texarkana College Recording Studios, 2500 N. Robinson Rd., Texarkana, TX 75501. (214) 838-4541, Ext. 257 or 360.

34. Trebas Institute of Recording Arts, 6602 Sunset Blvd., Los Angeles, CA 90028. (213) 467-6800.

INDEX

A

A/B stereo microphone technique, 113-116
Absorption methods, 35-36
AC outlets, 67
  with floating grounds, 69
  and safety, 76
Access jacks, in input modules, 215
ACN (active combining networks), 207
Acoustic baffles, and leakage, 40-41
Acoustic bass, 144-145
Acoustic guitars, 136-139
Acoustics
  and absorption, 35-36
  judging quality of, 318
  and monitor systems, 47-48
  and sonic effects, 247-248
  studio, 2-3, 23, 25, 27-43
Active combining networks, 207
Active crossover networks, 50
A/D converters. *See* Analog-to-digital converters
ADT (automatic double tracking), 191-192
Alignment, tape recorder, 157, 163-165
Ambience microphones
  and distant miking, 104
  for drum overdubbing, 131-132
  and on-location recording, 287
Amplitude, of sound waves, 29
Analog-to-digital converters, 176
  and sampling, 269, 271
Attack, 31-32, 185-186
Attenuators. *See* Input attenuators
Audio, synching of, to video, 379-380
Audio cables, and hum, 71-75
Audio Engineering Society, workshops by, 299

Audio-frequency generators, for alignment, 164
Automated mixing controls, in input modules, 218
Automatic double tracking, 191-192
Automatic level controls
  and compressors, 184
  and SMPTE, 379
Azimuth alignment, 157, 163-164

B

Background vocals, 153
Back-timing, and outros, 268
Backwards tracks, for sonic effects, 256
Balance. *See* Stereo balance
Balanced audio lines, and hum, 72-73
Balanced circuits, 11
Balanced equipment, 71, 369-371
Bandpass filters, and crossover networks, 49
Banjos, 140
Bass, 316
  controls for, 178-179
  and Fletcher-Munson effect, 60
  traps for, 35, 38
Beatles, and sonic effects, 256
Bi-amped systems, 50-51, 57-58
Bias, tape, 158, 164-165
Bidirectional microphones, 84-85
Binary code, and digital recorders, 176
Binary numbers, and sampling, 271
Binaural recording, and sonic effects, 248
Bi-phase modulation, and SMPTE, 374
Bits, 176, 269
Blakemore, Paul, 299
Bleed. *See* Leakage

Bluegrass bands, 146
Blumein array coincident pair method, 112
Bongos, 136
Booms, microphone, 97, 303
Bouncing tracks, 16, 166, 224-228
Boundary microphones, 93-94
  and drums, 132
  and on-location recording, 287, 303
  for on-surface mounting, 107
  for pianos, 142, 144
Brass, 146-147
Break down, session, 235-236
Buses and bus controls, 15, 206, 209, 212, 219-220
Buzz. *See* Hum
Bytes, 269

C

Cables, 11-12, 58
  audio, and hum, 71-75
  microphone, 97-98
  for on-location recording, 291-292
  wrapping of, 235-236
Calibration
  tape recorder, 157, 163-165
  tones, for mixdowns, 239
Capstan, 158
Cardioid microphones, 85, 282
Center-channel buildup, 60
Channel assignment switches, 15, 210, 217-218
Chase mode, for SMPTE, 378
Chorus effect, 192
Circumaural headphones, for on-location monitoring, 281
Classical music recordings
  guitar solos, 139
  judging sound quality of, 311-312, 318-322
  on-location, 301-310
  reverberation time for, 34
  troubleshooting bad sound in, 329-331
  vocal solos, 153
Claves, 135
Cleaning, tape path, 162
Clipping. *See* Distortion
Close miking, 34-35, 102-103, 141-144, 149-150
Code words, and SMPTE, 374-375
Coincident pair, stereo microphone technique, 110-113, 116, 142

Cold-water pipes, and earth grounding, 67-69
Color TV standards, and SMPTE, 374, 376
Comb-filter effect. *See* Phase-cancellation
Combining amplifiers, 207
"Come Together" (Beatles), sonic effects in, 256
Compression, 27, 167-168, 185
Compressors, 23, 184-187
  and dynamic range, 151
  for electric bass, 123
  and sonic effects, 256
Computers
  editing by, and SMPTE, 380
  and MIDI, 277-278
  and sampling, 269-273
Condenser microphones, 81, 91
Congas, 136
Consistency, and narration, 259-260
Construction, studio, for noise reduction, 42
Control layouts, for mixing consoles, 213-214
Control rooms
  overdubbing in, 121, 238
  setting up of, for sessions, 230-231
Country music, mixdowns for, 241
Creative leakage, 41
Crossover frequencies, 49-50
Crosstalk, 159, 166, 226
Cue headphones, 12-13
Cue mixer, 6
  in multichannel consoles, 211-212
  for recorder/mixers, 15-16
  setting of, 234, 237
Cue pots, 212, 217, 231
Cue sheets, for mixdowns, 241
Cue systems, 6, 62-63
Cymbals, 127, 130-131

D

D/A (digital-to-analog) converters, 176
Davis, Chips, 54-55, 59
Davis, Don, 54-55
DB (decibels), 363-372
DB SPL, 363
DBm, 365-366
DBu, 365-367
DBV, 365, 367
Dbx noise-reduction system, 168-169

and calibration tones, 239
and generation loss, 226
and meter matching, 170-171
Decay, in sound envelope, 31-32
Decibels (dB), 363-372
Decoded tapes, and expansion, 168
De-essers, and silibance, 151, 264
Delay units, 23, 122, 188-191
Demagnetizing, tape path, 163
Design center, of faders, 232
DI (direct injection), 121-122
Diffusion, sound, 33, 43
Digital audio processors, 176, 302
Digital recorders, 175-176, 304
Digital reverberation, 195
Digital-to-analog converters, 176
Dimmers, SCR. *See* SCR dimmers
Direct box, 10-12, 121-122
Direct injection, 121-122
Direct output, 15, 215, 232
Direct recording, 40, 123
Directional microphones, 35, 40, 99-100
Directional patterns, 84-87
Dispersion, speaker, 52
Distant miking, 103-104, 141, 143
Distortion
  and 0-VU levels, 369
  and bi-amped systems, 51
  and digital recorders, 176
  engineering terms for, 201
  and limiters, 187
  and monitor speakers, 52
  overload indicators for, 14-15, 209
  and power amplifiers, 58
  and tape saturation, 162
  troubleshooting, 324-326, 331
Dobros, 140
Documentation, 236, 246, 259-260
Dolby noise-reduction systems, 168-169
  and calibration tones, 169, 239
  and generation loss, 226
Doubling, 152, 191-192
Drop-frame mode, for SMPTE, 374, 376
Drop-outs, 158
  and edge tracks, 166
  and half-track tape decks, 302
  and overbiasing, 165
  from oxide deposits, 162
  troubleshooting, 323-324
Drum machines, 134
Drums, 125-135, 238
Dynamic microphones, 81, 83-84
Dynamic range, 317
  and compressors, 184
  troubleshooting, 328

of vocals, controlling, 150-151

E

Earth ground, 66-69
EBU (European Broadcast Union), 377
Echo mixers, 209
Echo return, 209, 219, 221, 241
Echo send, 209, 216-217, 241
Echoes, 32-33
  compared to reverberation, 34, 196
  and delay units, 189-191
  from print-through, 165
  and sonic effects, 250-253
  and vocals, 152
Editing, 172-175, 265-267, 310
Effects panning, 219
Effects return, 209, 219, 221, 241
Effects send, 209, 216-217, 241
EIA (Electronics Industries Association)
    microphone ratings, 372
Eight-in four-out mixers, 19
Eight-track systems, 17-18, 289
Electric bass, 123-124
Electric guitars, 78-79, 119-123
Electric keyboards, 124-125
Electronic dividing networks, 50
Electronic drums, direct recording of, 134
Electronics, tape recorder, 157-158
Electronics Industries Association
    microphone ratings, 372
Electrostatic interference, and hum, 72
Encoded tapes, and compression, 168
Engineering terms for audio
    characteristics, 199-202
Envelope, sound, 31-32
Equalization, 15
  and drums, 134
  and equalizers, 177-184
  in mixing consoles, 209
  recorder, 15, 157-158, 164-165
  room, 58-60
  setting of, 181-182, 233
  and sonic effects, 182-183, 256
  of vocals, 153
Erase heads, 156
European Broadcast Union, and SMPTE, 377
Expansion, and noise, 167-168, 188

F

Fade-outs, 235, 242
Faders, 15, 207, 209, 219, 232
Fagen, Donald, 322
Fiddles, 140
Filters
    and equalization, 181
    frequency, and speaker crossover
        networks, 49
    line and noise, 66
    RFI, 79
Flanging, 192-194
Fletcher-Munson effect, 60, 184
Floating-ground AC outlets, 69
Fluorescent lights, and hum, 66
Flutes, 148
Flutter echoes, 32-33, 43, 48
Fluxivity, 164
Foldback connectors, in output modules,
    219
Footswitch, for punch in/out, 16, 237
Four-track recorders, compared to 8-track,
    18
Four-way speaker systems, 49
French Broadcasting Network, 115
Frequencies
    of room modes, 37-38
    of sound waves, 29-30
    speaker, and crossover networks, 49-50
    See also High frequencies; Low
        frequencies
Frequency response
    curve of, 89
    and equalizers, 177-181
    and LEDE rooms, 55
    of microphones, 89-90, 99-100, 117
    for monitor speakers, 52
    and playback equalization, 158
    and pop filters, 150
    and reverberation, 35
    and room equalization, 58-60
    and sampling rates, 272
Full-track systems, track widths for, 159
Fundamental frequencies, 30

G

Gain
    microphone, and noise, 90
    reduction, and compressors, 185
    riding of, on vocals, 151

Gain-trim pots, in mixer consoles, 209
Gap, head, 157
Gated reverberation, 133, 195
Generation loss, 161, 226
Gobos, and leakage, 40-41
Grand pianos, 140-143
Graphic equalizers, 58-59, 180, 256
Ground bus, 68
Ground loops, 67, 69, 71-77
    and cable connections, 291
    and microphone splitters, 286, 288
Grounding procedures and wiring, 66-71
Ground-lift adapters, and hum, 76-77
Group, 210, 233
Group modules, 210, 219-220
Guard bands, and crosstalk, 159
Guiros, 135
Guitar amps, connections to, 75-76
Guitar solos, miking of, 139

H

Half-track systems, 159, 302
Harmonicas, 149
Harmonics, of sound waves, 30, 197
Harps, 146
Hash. *See* Radio-frequency interference
Headphones, 6
    compared to speakers, 61-62
    cue, 12-13, 62
    for on-location monitoring, 281, 303
Headroom
    and dbx, 168
    of open-reel decks, 301
    and tape speed, 309
Heads, tape recorder, 155-157, 159-160
Hearing
    damage, prevention of, 60
    threshold of, 364
    training of, 320-322
Hertz, and frequency, 29
Hi hat, miking of, 128-129
High frequencies
    and bouncing tracks, 166
    engineering terms describing, 200
    response of, and open-reel decks, 301
    and reverberation, 35
    and speaker placement, 54
    and track assignments, 224
High-pass filters, 49, 181
Hiss, tape, 16, 162, 324
Hot chassis, 68

Hum, 65-80, 91, 286
Hypercardioid directional microphones,
    85

I

Impedance
    of microphones, and cables, 91, 97-98
    of telephone lines, 291
Incoherent signals, 114
Indicators. *See* Level indicators; Peak
    indicators
In-line console construction, 214
Input attenuators
    adjusting of, for sessions, 232, 234
    for equipment interfacing, 370-371
    in input modules, 216
    and on-location recording, 283
    for recorder/mixers, 14-15
Input modules, of mixing consoles, 211,
    213-218
Inputs, mixer, 206
Inserts, 259, 264, 267
Instrument layout charts, and session
    planning, 228
Instrumentation microphones, and room
    equalization, 58-59
Instruments, musical
    modification of, for sonic effects, 247-
    248
    transformation of, by MIDI, 277
    views of, 2
Insurance, liability, 299
Interference
    and hum, 72
    radio-frequency. *See* Radio-frequency
        interference
Intermodulation distortion, and bi-amped
    systems, 51
Isolation transformers, and hum
    AC, 66, 295
    audio, 73, 76

J

Jam sync mode, and SMPTE, 378-379
Judging sound quality, 311-332
Junction boxes, microphone, 98

K

Katz, Gary, 322
Kick drums, 126, 131

L

Lavalier condenser microphones, 260
Lazerus, Daniel, 322
Leader tape, 172-174, 244
Leakage, 38-41, 43
    and distant miking, 104
    and drums, 125, 135
    engineering terms for, 201
    and equalization, 183
    and noise gates, 188
    and overdubbing, 161
LED indicators
    level, 17
    overload, 14, 209
    peak, 17, 162
LEDE (live end-dead end) room
    treatment, 54-55
Leslie organ speakers, 124
Level indicators, 17, 211, 220
Light-emitting diodes. *See* LED indicators
Limiters, 187
Line filters, and hum, 66
Line voltage regulators, 295
Line-level inputs, mixer, 206
Listening, ways of, 334-335
Live end-dead end (LEDE) room
    treatment, 54-55
Live remotes, telephone lines for, 290-291
Localization, stereo, 109
Long, Ed, and near-field monitoring, 54
Longitudinal Time Code, and audio/
    video synching, 379
Lossless lines, for live remotes, 291
Loudspeakers. *See* Speakers
Low frequencies
    engineering terms describing, 199
    and reverberation, 35
    and speaker placement, 54
Low-pass filters, 49, 181
LTC (Longitudinal Time Code), and
    audio/video synching, 379
Ludwig, Bob, 322

M

Magnetic interference, and hum, 72
Mandolins, 140

Maracas, 135
Master faders, in recorder/mixers, 15
Master reels, assembling of, 243-246
Matched loads, and microphones, 372
Memory, computer, 269-270, 272-273
Memory multitracking, 275-276
Memory rewind, 16-17, 158, 242
Meters, 161-162
    matching of mixer and recorder, 170-
        171
    sound-level. *See* VU-meters
    switches for, in output modules, 220
Mic extension cables, 303
Mic-preamp overload, 283
Microphone placement 102-108
    and equalization, 183
    for narration, 260-263
    for on-location classical recording, 308-
        309
Microphone techniques, 4
    for on-location classical recording, 304-
        306
    for sonic effects, 248-250
    for specific musical instruments, 119-
        153
    stereo, 109-117
Microphones, 3-4, 81-83, 93-94
    accessories for, 96-98
    assignments of, 232
    cables for, shielding, 73-75
    characteristics of, 84-92
    hum from, 77-78
    input lists for, 227-228
    instrumentation, 58-59
    and leakage, 39-41
    for narration, 260
    for on-location recording, 282-283,
        302-303
    for personal studios, 10
    placement of. *See* Microphone
        placement
    quantity needed, 100-102
    and reverberation, 34-35
    selection of, 95-96, 99-100
    sensitivity of, 90-91, 371-372
    snakes for, 19-20, 98
    splitters for, 76, 98, 286-287
    stands for, 97, 261, 303
    techniques for. *See* Microphone
        techniques
    transporting, 299
MIDI (Musical Instrument Digital
    Interface), 276-280, 380
Mid-Side recording coincident pair
    method, 112

Miniature condenser microphones, 94,
    137-138
Mix
    judging quality of, 312-313
    and leakage, 39
    for on-location recording, 296-297
    setting of, for mixdowns, 240
    troubleshooting, 328-329
Mixdowns, 213, 238-242
    automated, and MIDI, 277
Mixers and mixing consoles, 5, 205, 236,
    253
    input section, 213-218
    meter matching, 170-171
    monitor. *See* Monitor mixers and
        systems
    output section, 219-220
    setting up of, for on-location recording,
        295-296, 304
    signal flow in, 206-213
Modes, 36-38, 43, 48
Monitor mixers and systems, 6-7, 45-63
    eight-in four-out, 19
    in monitor modules, 220
    in multichannel consoles, 211-212
    for on-location recording, 281-282
    for personal studios, 12
    for recorder/mixers, 15-16
    select switches, in monitor modules,
        221
    setting of, 237, 295
Monitor section modules, in mixing
        consoles, 213, 220-221
Monitoring, ways of, 335-336
Mono mixers, signal flow in, 206-207
Mono-compatible stereo microphones,
    112-113
Motors, tape recorder, 158
    synchronization of, and SMPTE, 373
Moulton, Dave, 299
Moving-coil dynamic microphones, 81,
    83-84, 91
MS (Mid-Side) recording coincident pair
    method, 112
Multichannel consoles, 210-212
Multiple echoes, and delay units, 191
Multiple sound systems, interconnecting,
    76-77
Multiple-D dynamic microphones, 87,
    260
Multiple-frequency equalizers, 179
Multiprocessors, and special effects, 202-
    203
Multisampling, 273
Multitrack systems, 6, 160-161, 288-289

Muncy, Neil, 299
Music
  emotional effects of, 334
  for narrations, 267-268
Musical Instrument Digital Interface, 276-
      280, 380
Musical instruments. *See* Instruments,
      musical
Mute, in input modules, 218

N

NAB (National Association of
      Broadcasters) curve, 158
Narration, recording, 259-268
Near-coincident pair, stereo microphone
      technique, 115-116
Nichols, Roger, 322
"Nightfly, The" 322
Noise, 31, 41-42
  and digital recorders, 176
  and drums, 126-127
  engineering terms for, 201
  and equalization, 183
  filters, for fluorescent lights, 66
  gates, 188
  and microphones, 90, 92
  pink, 52-53
  reduction, 16, 168-171, 304
  tape, 157
  and tape recording, 166-171
  troubleshooting, 327-328
Nonparallel walls, and room modes, 38
Normal modes, 36-38, 43, 48
Note parameters, and sequencing, 273-
      274

O

Octaves, and sound frequency, 29
Off-axis coloration, microphone, 108
Omnidirectional microphones, 84, 87
"On the Repeal of Murphy's Law",
      workshop, 299
One-way speaker systems, 49
On-location recording
  of classical music, 301-310
  of popular music, 281-299
On-surface microphone techniques, 106-
      108

Open-reel tape decks, 17-18, 301-302
ORTF, and near-coincident pair method,
      115, 282
Oscillators
  in mixing consoles, 221
  ultrasonic, 158
Outlets, AC, 67, 69, 76
Output levels, and compressors, 186
Output modules, in mixing consoles, 213,
      219-220
Outputs
  mixer, 206
  recorder/mixer, 15
Outro, for narration, 268
Overdubbing, 236-238
  in control room, 121, 238
  and cue systems, 62
  and leakage, 41
  with multitracks, 160-161
  in recorder/mixers, 16
  signal path for, 212
Overload
  indicators, LED, 14, 209
  mic-preamp, 283
Overtone frequencies, 30
Oxide deposits, and drop-outs, 162

P

Pads. *See* Input attenuators
Pan pots, 15, 207-209, 239-240
Parameters, sampling, 271-272
Parametric equalizers, 179, 256
Passive crossover networks, 50
Patch panels, 23-24
Payment, for master reels, 245
PCM (pulse code modulation), 176
Peak indicators, 17, 162, 369
Peak power output, and bi-amped
      systems, 51
Peak program meters, 369
Peaking equalizers, 179-180
Percussion, 135-136
Periods, of sound waves, 28-29
Personal studios
  acoustical treatment of, 23-25
  equipment for, 9-23
Phantom images, 109
Phantom power supplies, 82-83, 206, 298
Phase
  of AC mains, and hum, 65-66
  cancellation, 30, 54, 107, 192-193

differences, and spaced microphones, 114
interference, 93
shift, of sound waves, 29-30
speaker, 55-56
switch, in input modules, 218
Phasing, 194
Pianos, 140-144
Pinch rollers, 158
Ping pong effect, 114
Ping-ponging, 16, 166, 224-228
Pink noise, 52-53
generators of, 58-59
Pitch, 17, 29, 197
Pizzi, Skip, 299
Plate reverberation, 194
Playback equalization, 157, 164
Playback heads, 156
Polar patterns, 84-87
Polarity, speaker, and stereo balance, 55-56
Polarity-reversing adapters, 256-257
Pop
filters for, 96-97, 149, 261
troubleshooting, 328
Popular music
judging sound quality of, 311-318, 321-322
mixdowns for, 240-242
on-location recording of, 281-299
reverberation time for, 34
troubleshooting bad sound in, 324-329
"Popular Music Recording Techniques" workshop, 299
Post-echoes, and print-through, 165
Potentiometers. *See* Faders
Power
amplifiers, 6, 53
connections, for on-location recording, 290
cords, and hum, 67-68
distribution systems, for touring companies, 70-71
ground, 67
levels, 364-365, 367-368, 372
line radiation, and hum, 66, 71-75
for monitor system speakers, 57-58
wiring, and hum, 65-66
PPM (peak program meters), 369
Preamplifiers, mono mixer, 206-207
Pre-delay, and reverberation, 196
Pre-echoes, and print-through, 165
Pre-production planning, 223-228, 292-293, 306-307
Pre-reverberation delay, 196

Presence, 89-90, 102, 315
Preverb, for sonic effects, 254
Print-through, 165-166
and digital recorders, 176
and narration, 264-265
and tape thickness, 303-304
Production schedules, planning, 224
Program buses, in mixing consoles, 209
Proximity effect, 87-88, 145, 149, 260
Psychoacoustic processor, 197
Pulse code modulation, and digital audio processors, 176
Punch in/out feature, 16, 237-238

Q

Quantization rate, and sampling, 272
Quarter-track systems, 160, 302

R

Racks, 23, 70-71
Radio-frequency interference, 79-80
and audio cables, 71-75
and earth grounding, 68
isolation transformers for, 66
and walkie-talkies, 298
RAM (random-access memory), 269
Rarefaction, and sound waves, 27
Read-only memory, 270
Real-time analyzers, 58-59
Real-time sequencing, 275
Recirculation, and multiple echoes, 191
Record equalization, 157, 165
Record heads, 156
Recorder/mixers, 9-12
mixer section, 13-16
recorder section, 16-17
Recording
levels, 161, 233-234
mix, 242
of narration, 259-268
on-location, 281-310
overdub, 237-238
room, choosing, 42-43
of sessions, 231-235, 265
Recording and reproduction chain, 1-8
Record-mastering companies, preparing tapes for, 310
Reed, Lou, and sonic effects, 250

Reference monitors, 61
Reflection Phase Gratings (RPG)
    diffusers, 55
Reflections, 32-33, 43, 107, 262-263
Release
    in sound envelope, 32
    time of, and compressors, 186
Return-to-zero function, 16-17, 158, 242
Reverberation, 33-36
    and close miking, 102
    compared to echo, 34, 196
    and distant miking, 104
    engineering terms for, 201
    for sonic effects, 250-253
    and strings, 144
    and vocals, 152
Reverberation time, 34, 43, 48
Reverberation units, 21, 23, 194-196, 209
Reverse echo, for sonic effects, 254
RFI. *See* Radio-frequency interference
Ribbon dynamic microphones, 81, 84, 88
    for narration, 260
    sensitivity of, 91
ROM (read-only memory), 270
Room equalization, 58-60
Room modes, 36-38, 43, 48
Room simulators, and digital
    reverberation, 195
RPG (Reflection Phase Gratings)
    diffusers, 55
RTA (real-time analyzer), and room
    equalization, 58-59
Running time, computing, 245

S

Safety, 67, 69, 75-76, 78
Sampling, 269-273
Saxophones, miking of, 147-148
Scheiner, Elliot, 322
Schnee, Bill, 322
Schwann catalog, for sonic effects, 267-
    268
SCR dimmers, and RFI, 66, 79, 290-291
Self-noise, microphone, 92
Sequencing, 244, 269, 273-275
Servo motor control, and SMPTE, 377
Session procedures, 223-246
"Sheffield Track Record", 321-322
Shelving equalizers, 179-180
Shield connections, and hum, 72-75, 77
Shock mounts, microphone, 97, 261

Shuttle mode, and SMPTE, 377-378
Signal
    flow, mixer, 206-213
    level, and decibels, 364-368
    power, and dBm, 365-366
    processors, 5, 122-123, 177-203
Signal-to-noise ratio
    and compressors, 185
    and dbx, 168
    of delay units, 189
    and Dolby, 169
    and half-track tape decks, 302
    and microphone sensitivity, 90
    and recorder equalization, 157
    and track width, 159
Silibance, 151, 264, 328
Simplex phantom power supplies, 82-83,
    206
Sine waves, and harmonics, 30
Single-D directional microphones, 87
Site surveys, 294-295
Slap echoes, and delay units, 190
Slate function, in mixing consoles, 221,
    234
Slope, 185
SMPTE time code, 289, 302, 373-380
Snare drums, 126-128
Society of Motion Picture and Television
    Engineers time code, 289, 302,
    373-380
Solo button, in input modules, 218
Solos, 139, 153, 309
Sonic effects, 247-258, 267-268
    and delay units, 188-191
    and equalization, 182-183
    and multiprocessors, 202-203
Sound accuracy, meaning of, 59-60
Sound characteristics
    engineering terms describing, 199-202
    judging, 311-332
Sound-hole miking, 137, 142
Sound-level meters. *See* VU-meters
Sound-pressure level, 91, 363-364
Sound-reinforcement mixers, 283-286
Sound-wave basics, 27-32
Spaced pair, stereo microphone
    technique, 113-116
    for grand pianos, 141-142
    for on-location recording, 282-283
Speakers
    compared to headphones, 61-62
    for monitor systems, 48-53
    parallel, 53
    placement of, for monitor systems, 53-
    55

ratings of, and amplifier power, 57-58
Special effects. See Sonic effects
Spectral Recording System, Dolby, 169
Spectrum, of frequencies, 177
Speech, recording, 259-268
Spill. See Leakage
SPL (sound-pressure level), 91, 363-364
Splicing, tape, 174-175
Splitters, microphone, 76, 98, 286-287
Spot microphones, for soloists, 309
Spring reverberation, 195
Stacking tracks, in overdubbing, 238
Standing waves, 36-38, 58
Step-time sequencing, 275
Stereo
    balance
        judging quality of, 318-319
        in mixdowns, 239-240
        and speaker polarity, 55-56
        troubleshooting, 330-331
    bars, 116, 303
    echo, for sonic effects, 251
    imaging, 55, 113, 202, 319-320
    judging quality of, 316-317
    microphones, 94-95, 112-113
        adapters for, 116, 303
        techniques for, 109-117, 304-306
    reverberation, 196
    and SMPTE, 378
    spread, 109-110
        control of, 308-309
        of string ensembles, 145
        troubleshooting, 330
Storage, sequence, 275
Strings, 144-146
Striping, of SMPTE time code, 378-379
Studio effects, 122-123
Studios
    construction of, and noise reduction, 42
    MIDI, 277-280
    personal. See Personal studios
    setting up, for session, 228-229
Submaster modules, 213, 219-220
Submix modules, 213, 219-220
Submixes, 210, 233
Summing networks, 207
Supercardioid directional microphones, 85
Sustain, in sound envelope, 32
Sweepable equalizers, 179
Synchronization, of motor speed, and
    SMPTE, 373
Synchronous recording, 16, 160-161
Synthesizers, interconnecting, and MIDI,
    276-277

T

Tail out storage, 165-166, 245
Tailored response, in microphones, 90
Take sheets, for sessions, 234
Talkback function, in mixing consoles, 221
Tambourines, 135
Tape
    erasing, 156, 240
    handling of, 171-172
    hiss, 16, 162, 324
    logs, 236
    loops, for sonic effects, 254
    noise, 157
    saturation of, 157, 162, 187
    speed, 16-17, 158, 309
    splicing of, 174-175
    storage of, 165-166, 171-172
    thickness, and print-through, 165, 303-304
    width, 160
    and x-ray machines, 299
Tape counters, 16-17, 158
Tape path cleaning, 162
Tape recorders, 5-6, 155-176, 253-256, 301-302, 307. See also Recording
Tape speed, 16-17, 158, 309
Telephone lines, interfacing with, 290-291
Television, and SMPTE, 374, 376-377
3:1 microphone rule, 108
Three-way speaker systems, 49
Threshold levels, and compressors, 184, 186
Timbales, 136
Timbre, 2, 30-31, 177, 182
Time-code equipment, and SMPTE, 373, 376-379
Tom-toms, 125-126, 129-130
Tonal balance, 313-314, 326, 331
Tone control, 15, 105-106, 196
Tone quality, 2, 30-31, 177, 182
Track assignment switches, 15, 210, 217-218
Track assignments, 224-227
Track sheets, 224-225, 236
Tracks
    in memory multitracking, 276
    number of, and noise, 167
    stacking of, in overdubbing, 238
    tape, 5-6, 158-160
Transducer types, microphone, 81-84
Transformers, isolation. See Isolation transformers

Transient response, 136
  and bi-amped systems, 51
  engineering terms for, 201
  judging sharpness of, 316
  and monitor speakers, 52
Transport, tape, 158
Treble controls, 178
Tri-amped systems, 51
Triangles, 135
Trim controls, 14, 215-216
Troubleshooting of bad sound, 323
  in classical music, 329-332
  in popular music, 324-329
Tweeters, 48-50
24-track systems, 289
Twisted-pair cables, and magnetically
    induced hum, 73, 77
Two-channel mixing consoles, 208-209
Two-channel stereo mixers, 207-208
2-track
  cassette decks, 12
  stereo heads, track widths for, 160
  tape recorders, 6, 18, 287-288
Two-way speaker systems, 49

U

Unbalanced audio lines, and hum, 72-73
Unbalanced circuits, 11
Unbalanced equipment
  and decibels and normal levels, 369-
    370
  grounding of, 70-71
  interfacing of, with balanced, 370-371
Unidirectional microphones, 84-85
Upright pianos, 143-144

V

Variable-D directional microphones, 87
Vertical Interval Time Code, and audio/
    video synching, 379
Vibraphones, 136
Video, and SMPTE, 374, 376-377, 380

Videocassette recorders, recording audio
    with, 302
VITC (Vertical Interval Time Code), 379
Vocals, 149-153, 224, 227
Voltage ratios, and decibels, 365
VU-meters, 60
  and decibels, 368-369
  for tape recording, 161-162

W

"Walk on the Wild Side" (Reed), sonic
    effects in, 250
Walkie-talkies, and RFI, 298
Wave reflections, and on-surface
    microphone techniques, 107
Wavelength, of sound waves, 29
Windscreens, 96-97, 149, 261
Wittig, Curt, 299
Woodwinds, 147
Woofers, 48-50
Words, recording, 259-268
Work-print tapes, 227, 234
Workshops, audio engineering, 299
Wow and flutter, 158, 162, 176

X

X-ray machines, and tapes, 299
X-Y method, 110-113, 116, 142
Xylophones, 136

Y

Y adapters, and microphone splitting, 286

Z

0-VU recording level, 161, 368-369